NEW YORK UNIVERSITY SERIES IN
EDUCATION AND SOCIALIZATION IN AMERICAN HISTORY

General Editor: Paul H. Mattingly

THE CLASSLESS PROFESSION
American Schoolmen in the Nineteenth Century
Paul H. Mattingly

THE REVOLUTIONARY COLLEGE
American Presbyterian Higher Education, 1707–1837
Howard Miller

COLLEGIATE WOMEN
Domesticity and Carreer in Turn-of-the-Century America
Roberta Frankfort

SCHOOLED LAWYERS
A Study in the Clash of Professional Cultures
William R. Johnson

THE ORGANIZATION OF AMERICAN CULTURE, 1700–1900:
Private Institutions, Elites, and the Origins of American Nationality
Peter Dobkin Hall

AMERICAN COLLEGIATE POPULATIONS
A Test of the Traditional View
Colin B. Burke

OLD DARTMOUTH ON TRIAL
The Transformation of the Academic Community in
Nineteenth-Century America
Marilyn Tobias

American Collegiate Populations:

A Test of the Traditional View

Colin B. Burke

New York *and* London NEW YORK UNIVERSITY PRESS 1982

Library of Congress Cataloging in Publication Data
Burke, Colin B., 1936–
American collegiate populations.

(New York University series in education and socialization in American history)
Bibliography: p.
Includes index.
1. Education, Higher—United States—History.
2. College attendance—United States—History.
I. Title. II. Series
LA226.B85 378.73 81-16846
ISBN 0-8147-1038-7 AACR2

Manufactured in the United States of America

Clothbound editions of New York University Press Books
are Smyth-sewn and printed on permanent and durable acid-free paper.

To my wife Rose, who gave me Andy, my son and
very special gift in life.
And,
to Carl and Marie
who do so much for us.

I am a farmers's boy, and have been one since August 25, 1837. I am credited with having some Pilgrim blood in my veins; indeed, further claims are now being made carrying my pedigree historically back to time not far from the Norman conquest.

I was brought up to look forward to some humble success in four things: work, school, the ideal embodied in the New England townmeeting, and the democracy of the Congregational churches. Hence growing life took me along through the Public school to Williston Seminary, to Amherst College, and to Andover Theological Seminary, teaching school both from a liking for it and the money it brought me. In the church in my native town I was ordained to the ministry for home missionary service on September 14, 1865.

For nearly 50 years I have been credited with standing for the best in this age, ten years as a pioneer at the foot of the Rocky Mountains in Boulder, Colorado, as pastor and church builder, on the school and university boards, establishing the present system of schools and the state university. For five years I was pastor in Boxborough, Massachusetts, starting a town library; for five years principal of Lawrence Academy at Groton, Massachusetts, and also four years in Elgin Academy, Elgin, Illionis. Since 1890 I have been in Maryland doing preparatory and college work introductory to the Women's College of Baltimore, then in charge of Latin and Greek in Morgan College, of Baltimore, superintendent of the Enoch Reformatory for negro boys, for years the only institution of the kind for them in the world. Then, in the main, to private life in Laurel, Maryland, still continuing my interest in the churches and the schools.

While in Boulder, Colorado, I was married to Mary E. Dart, January 1, 1870. Our two daughters were born there, January 3, 1873 and March 9, 1875.

Nathan Thompson
Amherst College
Class of 1861

The following note is all that we have been able to draw from Mr. Wharton:

Boston, 127 Beacon St.,

Dec. 17, 1878.

Dear Sir—I did receive your letter of Nov. 27th ult., but cannot persuade myself to answer its requirements....

I have done otherwise: busy without usefulness, occupied without progress, I remember no lifework suitable for such a record as you propose, for use and the information of others interested. Therefore, the less the future of this world shall know of me the better.....

I remain, dear sir, very cordially yours,

William Craig Wharton.

Class of 1832

Yale College.

Contents

Introduction

The Traditional View

The early nineteenth–century American colleges have been the target of as much criticism as has any segment of American education and, to a significant degree, "good" educational practice and policy for modern times has been defined as the opposite of the supposed characteristics of the antebellum higher educational system. Almost every aspect of the early colleges has been used to show what not to do to achieve a democratic, equitable and efficient base for American life and, from at least the 1830s, reformers have denounced the early institutions as examples of elitist and dysfunctional education.

Richard Hofstadter, representing the viewpoints of professional intellectuals and research oriented educators, drew a relatively temperate summary of the traditional interpretation of antebellum higher education in his book, *Academic Freedom in the Age of the College,* an interpretation that remains dominant despite the emergence of a new literature on the early colleges.[1] Hofstadter called the period between 1800 and 1860 the "Great Retrogression" because he thought that the colleges retreated from the promise of the American enlightenment to become bastions of educational, political, and ideological conservatism. The colleges, he felt, suppressed freedom of thought and prevented both faculty and students from pursuing their true function of producing new knowledge. Even worse, the established college leaders blocked educational reforms that would have brought education in America to an intellectual level equal to that of the leading systems of Europe. To Hofstadter, the colleges of the period, especially in the Jacksonian era, were irrationally planned, unattractive, illiberal, and self–defeating. Because college foundings and policies were determined by local and denominational leaders rather than by a professional educational elite, the country was filled with small, inefficient, and inflexible institutions which reflected the premodern attitudes and values of their sponsors. The only thing that distinguished one of these colleges from another was the particular religious dogma that was the focus of its educational efforts. There was no support for scholarly activity and little recognition that colleges should engage in more than the teaching of classical languages and a smattering of basic science and mathematics through recitation and memorization. The colleges lacked both the type of leaders and the institutional resources to keep pace with the changes in Western thought and with the new developments in the sciences and arts. And, by design, the colleges were the defenders of a village mentality rather than the advance agents of intellectual and artistic change.

To Hofstadter and Whig historians, other consequences of the oversupply of such intellectually retrogressive institutions were predictable. A system controlled by anti–intellectuals and a laissez–faire philosophy and motivated by denominational competition and local boosterism could only lead to institutional inadequacy and instability, a lowering of educational standards, and to the slowing of the natural evolution of the scholarly professions in America.

Hofstadter stated that colleges failed at an alarming rate, especially in the South and West, as they competed with each other for the diminishing number of students who were willing to subject themselves to unnecessary discipline and simplistic moral teachings. The colleges admitted and retained young and ill–prepared boys who had little interest in academic excellence and whose attitudes and behavior frustrated the few faculty members who maintained any scholarly goals; the type of students attracted to the colleges meant that the faculty had to act as surrogate parents rather than as researchers and teachers of specialized knowledge. The oppressive role that was forced upon the faculty, combined with institutional instability and a demand for religious conformity, discouraged the development of professional scholars. The brightest young men of America were not attracted to academia because of the low salaries provided by institutions which survived on the whims of sponsors who had little interest in the development of a new liberal and cosmopolitan culture in America. And even if a young man did desire to enter the insecure world of an academic career, the presence of so many small colleges which wasted educational resources meant that he faced the difficulty that there were no adequate programs for advanced academic or professional study in America.

The dozens of other interpretive works on the early colleges tell the same sort of story, but with more vehemence and self–assurance. While Hofstadter focused upon the intellectual qualities of the colleges and stressed the role of the attitudes of educators and sponsors, Earle D. Ross, a leading historian of the state colleges, emphasized democracy and the interrelation of education and the social and economic systems. With a firm commitment to equality, he underscored the class biases and elitist nature of antebellum higher education and he explained the stability and enrollment problems of the colleges in the context of economic determinism.[2]

To Ross, the classical curricula of the colleges had little functional relationship to the needs of the common man or to the new economic order of the country. Educators could have easily replaced the old curricula with new subjects that would have made the colleges and their students compatible with the new age of industry and technology. If educators' attitudes had been different, students from all classes and ethnic backgrounds would have flocked to the colleges because all the social and economic conditions for a new educational order were established.

> Enrollments were kept low, not by financial or social restrictions but instead by a narrow subject matter–usually presented in a highly formal manner–that wholly failed to connect with the dynamic passing scene. The old classicism seemed to have nothing to contribute to an era of transformation in production, distribution and communication with all the attending social change.[3]

Ross's and Hofstadter's criticisms do not exhaust the complaints about the early system. Walter P. Rogers asserted that the colleges, because of their sponsors' ideologies, were producing conservative men who blocked all social, religious and economic progress. And educators' attitudes prevented the colleges from performing their natural function of providing technical services to government and the private sector of the economy.[4] Freemen Butts and Lawrence Cremin elaborated on this theme in their influential text on the history of American education by citing the conservative force of the faculty–psychology used by the colleges.[5] And Frederick Rudolph claimed that the antebellum colleges were exploiting their instructors. The colleges attracted so few students that they could not pay adequate salaries to their professors. In his view, the colleges were underpricing education because low tuitions were their only attractive feature.[6] And critic after critic complained about the lack of vocational and technical training in the inflexible colleges.[7]

All of the criticism of the early colleges makes some contribution to an understanding of the development of education in the United States, but because they are based upon sets of questionable assumptions about the state of American society and its economy before the Civil War and because they rely upon interpretive and evaluative frameworks derived from implicit and often muddled theories of the nature and role of higher education in modernization, the criticisms distort the historical picture of the possibilities and contributions of higher education in the antebellum period. For example, determinists such as Ross not only assumed that the American social and economic order before the Civil War was ready to support a highly differentiated and specialized educational system, but that technical education was the one type that could make a significant contribution to both democracy and modernization.

Hofstadter assumed that the allocations of educational resources and the types of educational structures and values necessary to support specialized intellectuals were compatible with other democratic goals. And the critics of training for the professions assumed that highly intensive education with an emphasis upon the production of a few specialists would not impinge upon the goals of the widespread distribution of basic services at low cost to the society.

Because almost all of the critics assumed that social and economic conditions of the early nineteenth century matched those of the twentieth century, little attention was given to the very significant constraints imposed upon educators. As a result, the history of higher education was abstracted from its historical context. Rarely was the college movement tied to the even broader educational revolution of the antebellum era. The levels and distributions of wealth during the period and their importance to the accessibility of higher education were ignored. The comparative rates of return on investment in formal versus informal training were not integrated with the study of the development of professional and technical training. And all the critics assumed that there was an intellectually and financially rewarding body of specialized knowledge in the humanities and sciences ready to be assimilated by the colleges that would make them inherently attractive.

Add to these assumptions the idea that technical training was the major source of modernization and it is easy to understand why the critics developed an image of higher education as free from restraining outside forces and why they all condemned the early colleges. The supposed problems of the system were seen as the outcome of the attitudes and values of denominational and local elites, not of social and economic factors.

And when the common historical image of the ease and pace of educational change after the Civil War is integrated with the other assumptions of the historical writers, a negative evaluation of the antebellum colleges and their leaders seems inescapable.

The critics failed to see that they were condemning the lack of consensus in and the actual character of the American economy and society. They assumed as already established the type of social and economic order that could develop only after economic modernization had taken place, after significant social and political problems had been solved and after an accepted and useful modern science and technology had emerged. They failed to see that their ahistorical treatment of the colleges had led them to assume that higher education was the primary and autonomous cause of social and economic change, when, at most, it had a reciprocal relationship to modernization.

Furthermore, the bias of the critics prevented them from recognizing the contributions that the early system made and the underlying reasons why it developed as it did. Few of the critics saw that the colleges were distributors of basic knowledge, skills and values, were servicing students from cultural, economic and social backgrounds who might not have attended the "better" schools, and that the small rural colleges had arisen partly because of the exclusive nature and the high costs of the more acceptable institutions. Even the extreme flexibility of many of the early schools was overlooked because of the bias of the critics. The term "low–quality" was used to interpret the fact that the small colleges were multi–level, multi–purpose institutions that compensated for the absence of a democratic and efficient primary and secondary educational system in the rural and less econcomically affluent areas of the country.

The critics' focus upon what they did not want higher education to be in their own time also led them away from recognizing the social and economic contributions of the alumni of the colleges. The traditional histories emphasized the great number of ministers and teachers produced by the small colleges, but treated this simply as an indication of the irrelevance of early higher education. The critics could not recognize that ministers performed many positive social functions in an era before social services became the domain of the bureaucrats. And despite the great value they placed upon education, the critics could not see the contributions the college–bred men made to the development of the educational system.

The impact of the models of higher education used by the critics was so great that, although they demanded efficiency and social relevance on the part of the colleges, they dismissed any but the professional and technical contributions of education as aberrations. They assumed that the paternalistic regimen of many of the colleges was a breed of premodern illiberalism and could not treat it as a perhaps necessary means to develop and encourage modern discipline and behavior among their students. The orientation of faculties to their institutions and localities rather than to the abstraction, their profession, was never interpreted as a factor leading to student centered, flexible and highly personal education. And the involvement of many of the colleges in the struggle for two of the most important steps in the history of the modernization of the United States, abolition and women's rights, was pictured as an example of how the antebellum colleges deviated from the new modern norms for education by being concerned with politics, rather than with the development of objective knowledge.

The consideration of the colleges out of their historical context and the bias caused by the use of the various interpretive frameworks are the result of a more fundamental deficiency. Historians have been explaining and interpreting many "facts" about the antebellum system that are not true or that are so incomplete that they are misleading. And, even the historical image of the educational system after the Civil War, vital to the arguments of the traditional critics, has been so simplistic that it serves no useful historical purpose.

The history of the early liberal arts colleges and professional education rests upon a set of unverified generalizations about the number and stability of the colleges, the enrollment levels, the geographic distribution of colleges and professional schools, and the backgrounds and occupational destinations of the students of the colleges. In fact, most of the general histories of liberal education rest upon three empirical sources: Donald Tewksbury's work on the number and stability of liberal arts colleges; Henry Barnard's series on enrollment levels; and Bailey Burritt's study of the occupational distribution of the alumni of the major colleges of the antebellum period.[8] The picture of the extent and the nature of change after the Civil War seems to have a similarly weak empirical if not conceptual foundation.

The purpose of this monograph is to present the results of a ten–year search for statistics concerning the early educational system. This work focuses upon the presentation of the new facts in comparison to the series used in the established historiography and does not attempt to construct a typical historical narrative. Because of the nature of the evidence, the controversial character of the findings, and the desire to present as many facts as possible in order that other scholars will not have to repeat the time–consuming and expensive data search, much detail is included. The last section of the work attempts to place the antebellum experience and its interpretation in perspective by reexamining post–Civil War American higher education.

The results of the analysis of the more detailed and comprehensive data on the early system and its students are quite different from the conclusions and evaluations given in the traditional literature. The differences range from the finding that the construct, "the antebellum college," is of very limited value to the more mundane conclusion that the founding and instability rates of the colleges were much lower than thought. And by abandoning the strategy of studying the antebellum colleges as an ideal type, the opposite of what higher education should be, the early colleges appear as far more dynamic than they were described to be.

Viewing the colleges in the context of a longer time span and in the social and economic conditions of the antebellum period leads to an understanding of the constraints on educational change and the evolutionary rather than revolutionary character of education after the Civil War. The early colleges, despite the constraints imposed upon them by the social and economic systems of the country, were much more flexible and dynamic than would seem to be the case from the inherited histories. Curricula was expanding, the colleges attempted to keep abreast of the developments in science and they adjusted to new types of students. The colleges were not only developing new approaches to higher education but were becoming differentiated from each other, in part due to changes in the American socioeconomic order. Moving from relative similarity in the first decade of the century, the colleges began to serve different types of students, with the student characteristics rather than curricula differentiating the colleges. And, as the system adjusted to demands for higher education by students from new social and class backgrounds, it became more democratic. The new colleges of the period were oriented to educating students who were much less likely to have come from an elite background and who had different occupational goals than those who entered the established colleges. The character of the institutions was shaped by the backgrounds and objectives of their students.

The colleges were not removed from the course of modernization of the country. The careers of their students indicate that the colleges were enrolling young men who were aggressive, mobile and involved in the development of the American society and economy. The students, if they did form an elite, formed a working elite. They entered science, business, and the professions and made significant contributions in all of those fields. They were involved in politics and government at levels far above expectation and they contributed leadership and expertise to the growth of American industry.

The colleges were shaped by forces beyond the control of even the most progressive educators, however. The structure of the professions, the availability of different occupations to young men from lower social and economic origins, and even social norms for the timing of life progressions influenced the colleges and their students. The impact of the cultures and economies of the various regions was extremely important; regional and socioeconomic rather than denominational influences were the deciding factors in shaping both the colleges and the lives of their students.

As the underlying determinants of education changed, the colleges altered and differentiated. The university did not develop simply because of the emergence of a few new leaders who made sudden changes in college curricula and organization. The emergence of the university depended upon alterations in the nature and orientation of students, a restructuring of the professions, and changes in the American economy. Many of the underlying supports for the university model and the technical school did begin to emerge before the Civil War in several areas of the country, but the development of the social and economic prerequisites for the university ideal did not mean an increase in either democracy or equality. The institutions which took the lead in the development and implementation of the research–technical university models were, even before the Civil War, the most socially elite institutions and they serviced a unique student population. And the examination of the post–Civil War era indicates that neither of these educational models fulfilled the roles in educational "progress" implied in the traditional historiography—both older educational forms and new institutions besides the university and technical school, such as the normal school and the store–front trade school, dominated the era. And the old problems and contributions of the antebellum colleges continued because of the intransigence of the socioeconomic orders which, even in the age of industry, would not conform to the ideals of the traditional historians.

Because this investigation was premised upon the logic of hypothesis generation and testing (as far as can be employed in historical research) it does not contain a full and positive reinterpretation of the history of the nineteenth–century colleges and the collegiate populations. It will take many more years of research before an interpretation which meets the criteria of "scientific" history can be built. But the destructive nature of this book does have its peculiar positive aspect. Hopefully, the data and conclusions it contains will put to rest some of the most primary ways of "seeing" American educational history and, perhaps, the contemporary educational scene. Future scholars may thus find it easier to make a fresh start at the history of higher education because they will not have to face the torment of throwing out very cherished ways of organizing information about our educational past.

What future scholars will have to explore and test is the hypothesis that the pattern of change in the nineteenth century was almost the opposite of what we have imagined and that the causes of change were much more complex than those put forward in the literature generated by scholars committed to public higher education and the research ideal. And the pattern of change was not a simple progression, as Whiggish historians have pictured, of the expansion of opportunities and alternatives for America's youth. Not only do ideas such as, the rise of the normal school was a direct threat to established institutions, have little empirical basis, but they are conceptually naive. Such institutions were the partners of new social and institutional parameters which "forced" many students into them because of the changes of rules for entry and renumeration in the professions. As well, the history of other types of state–sponsored institutions has to be examined and a new political economy of public higher education has to be built asking why the state institutions failed to respond to so many needs and why, even within a state, resources were so unevenly distributed. The role of the "shadow" institutions of the era, the proprietary trade and business colleges, has to be examined and the reasons for their popularity, despite the rise of the public college, have to be identified. The continued attractiveness and health of the liberal arts college after the Civil War also has to be confronted, not just dismissed. The small college can not be viewed as a retreat for those fearful of the new social world which was emerging or as a haven for the rich. The romantic treatment of the university will have to be replaced with a more realistic examination of its internal workings and its social role. The relatively weak record of the technical schools during the late nineteenth century will have to be explained, as well.

All of these questions will have to be answered within a more sophisticated and unbiased framework than an implicit advocacy model or the assumption that higher education has always had an unlimited if not effective demand to maximize. None of these questions can be resolved if we continue to assume that the changes in American higher education after the Civil War established timeless institutional and attitudinal models, an assumption that has led historians and the public into a complacency concerning the nature and condition of higher education in our own time.

Chapter 1

The Institutions

In 1923, Donald G. Tewksbury published what has become a classic in the history of American higher education and the major source for those interested in the rationality and stability of antebellum American colleges. *The Founding of American Colleges and Universities in the United States* was completed at Teachers College, Columbia University, an institution devoted to the application of science to every level and aspect of education.[1] Teachers College was committed to the modernization of education through the use of the tools of research and rational planning and it was a leader in the establishment of efficiency, centralization and a value–free scientific curricula as goals for America's schools. Its professors, no matter what particular version of Progressivism they advocated, searched for a science–based metaculture that would provide the country with professional educators who could remove the educational system from the troublesome realms of local and cultural politics. To investigators with such views and goals, the decentralized, denominational, ethnically divided antebellum college system seemed to be the antithesis of sound educational policy.[2]

Although Tewksbury's work was written in a highly objective tone, it reflected the Teachers College perspective. Rejecting previous estimates by Cubberley, West, and Dexter of the number of colleges that were founded, he went to session laws of various states to identify both foundings and failures. The result of his study was a story of educational chaos, chaos caused by an excess of democracy on the frontier and the irrationality of denominational competition. Instead of discovering some two hundred foundings before the Civil War, as estimated by Cubberley and Dexter, he found five hundred sixteen in just sixteen states, and hinted that similar founding rates occurred throughout the remainder of the country. He never specified the total number of foundings before the Civil War, but if his average for the sixteen (mostly Southern) states are projected to the remaining non–New England states, the result is over nine hundred colleges, or one for every one thousand white males age fifteen to twenty in the United States in 1850.[3] Tewksbury concluded that 81 percent or over seven hundred of these colleges failed, and he explained the failures as the outcome of legislatures, without any thought to the needs for stability, allowing poorly funded, unattractive, and low–quality institutions to obtain charters. The results of political control of higher education were an overabundance of pretentious and unstable schools which prevented the rise of efficient, large–scale institutions. (Table 1.1)

Only in New England, Tewksbury stated, was such chaos and irrationality avoided. He did not mention the problems of elitism and religious

Table 1.1

Tewksbury's Table of
Mortality of Colleges Founded Before the Civil War
in Sixteen States of the Union

Name of State	Total Colleges	Living Colleges	Dead Colleges	Mortality Rate
Pennsylvania	31	16	15	48%
New York	36	15	21	58
Ohio	43	17	26	60
Virginia	32	10	22	69
North Carolina	26	7	19	73
Maryland	23	5	18	78
Alabama	23	4	19	83
Tennessee	46	7	39	84
Georgia	51	7	44	86
Louisiana	26	3	23	88
Missouri	85	8	77	90
Mississippi	29	2	27	93
Texas	40	2	38	95
Kansas	20	1	19	95
Florida	2	n0	2	100
Arkansas	3	0	3	100
Total for 16 states	516	104	412	81%*

*Average mortality rate for 16 states.

prejudice in the region, and he did not point out that New England's colleges had benefited from the type of state economic support withheld from the colleges in the new states.[4]

Tewksbury's work is still valuable, but it has several significant faults which call for the rejection of his estimates of foundings and failures and for a modification of his interpretation of the causes underlying the development of antebellum higher education. For at least three states, Ohio, Missouri, and Texas, official lists of college charterings do not match his findings.[5] But more importantly, his choice of the issuance of college charters as the indicator of foundings is very questionable. The issuance of a charter did not mean that a college was established. And even if an institution was founded under the legislative grant, it may not have operated as a college or competed for college students. It may have confined itself to what are now called primary and secondary education.[6]

Tewksbury made several very strong assumptions to arrive at his interpretation of the causes of the supposed college explosion. He assumed that colleges were founded to compete with other demoninations rather than to serve intra–denominational needs, and he assumed that any degree of denominational affiliation reflected domination of a college by the religious body. He implied that any ideological differences among the colleges were insignificant, irrational, and premodern, and he overlooked the possibility that denominational lines coincided with very significant class, ethnic, and political differences.

Tewksbury's use of survival into the twentieth century as the criteria for success of the colleges was ahistorical in concept, masked the timing of failures and left his readers with little indication as to when and why particular colleges failed. Furthermore, he deemphasized the number of foundings and failures before the late 1830s and the instability of state institutions.[7]

Only two pages of the *Founding of American Colleges* were concerned with the presentation of evidence on foundings and failures. The remainder of the book was devoted to details on the institutions that survived into the 1920s and with interpretative comments on the instability and irrationality of the early system. Tewksbury included only one short table listing the numbers of foundings and failures by state and this was for sixteen states only. Twelve of the states in the table were in the South, although much of his discussion of the reasons for failures seemed to be directed to the Midwest.[8] (Table 1.1)

Tewksbury referred readers seeking more detail to a file he had placed in the Teachers College library. But this file cannot be located and it has not been cited in a published work since the appearance of his book. The loss of the file has left investigators with little specific information —the detail needed to verify Tewksbury's estimates, to check his assumptions, and to use his original efforts in other investigations.[9] Because Tewksbury's work is questionable and because the estimates by investigators such as Cubberley were not accompanied by detailed analyses, a new search for both foundings and failures was conducted for this study. Instead of using charters as an unambiguous indicator of foundings, contemporary and historical sources likely to mention operating colleges were searched to identify colleges active in the period between 1800 and the outbreak of the Civil War. Post Office directories, atlases, national, state and local almanacs and registers, denominational publications, collections of college catalogs, and histories of the states and education within them were surveyed for any mention of a college in operation. Once a mention was noted, attempts were made to verify that the male or coeducational institution actually taught students in an educational track leading to a college degree and that contemporaries regarded the institution as a college.[10]

The result of the search, which included the hundreds of sources examined in a tracing of the lives of twenty–four thousand college and professional school students of the period, gives a different picture of the stability of antebellum higher education from that put forward in *The Founding of American Colleges and Universities.* Two hundred and forty–one institutions, including some seventy suspected of academy or preparatory operation only, were identified as operating during the period. (Tables 1.2, 1.3)

Seventy percent of the total survived into the twentieth century and 80 percent survived until the Civil War. If Catholic colleges are removed from consideration, the failure rate before the Civil War was 14 percent and if nondenominational colleges are also deleted, the sixty–year failure percentage was 10 percent. If state institutions are also excluded, the estimate drops to less than 8 percent.

The timing of the founding of colleges did not follow the pattern Tewksbury implied. Although he never attempted to construct a decade–by–decade series for all college foundings, he pointed to the 1830s, the Jacksonian years, as the beginnings of the irrational growth of the number of colleges in the country. But the increase in the number of schools began much earlier than he thought and the expansion was not in isolation from other changes in the American educational system.

Approximately twenty colleges were in operation in the United States in 1800. By the 1850s, two hundred seventeen were open. This tenfold increase began in the first decade of the century when twelve additional institutions either first began or resumed operation—a 60 percent increase over the first year of the century. Perhaps due to the turmoil of the years of conflict with England, the 1810s added only eight colleges. The 1820s began the accelerated growth of institutions with a 50 percent

Table 1.2

Distribution of Liberal Arts Colleges In Operation by State and Number of Failures By Decade.

	1800's		1810's		1820's		1830's		1840's		1850's		Total		% Failure 1800-1860
	O	F	O	F	O	F	O	F	O	F	O	F*			
Alabama	0	0	0	0	0	0	2	0	4	0	6	1	6	1	17
California	0	0	0	0	0	0	0	0	0	0	3	0	3	0	0
Connecticut	1	0	1	0	2	0	3	0	3	0	3	0	3	0	0
Delaware	0	0	0	0	0	0	1	0	1	0	2	0	2	0	0
District of Columbia	1	0	1	0	2	0	2	0	2	0	3	0	3	0	0
Georgia	1	0	1	0	1	0	4	0	5	1	4	0	5	1	20
Illinois	0	0	0	0	0	0	4	0	6	1	13	0	14	1	7
Indiana	0	0	1	0	3	1	5	0	7	1	10	0	12	2	17
Iowa	0	0	0	0	0	0	0	0	1	0	9	1	9	1	11
Kentucky	3	1	3	1	5	1	8	0	9	3	8	1	14	7	50
Louisiana	1	0	1	0	2	1	2	0	4	1	9	2	11	4	36
Maine	1	0	1	0	2	0	2	0	2	0	2	0	2	0	0
Maryland	2	0	2	0	2	0	4	1	5	0	8	2	9	3	33
Massachusetts	2	0	2	0	3	0	3	0	4	0	5	0	5	0	0

Table 1.2 - Continued

	1800's		1810's		1820's		1830's		1840's		1850's		Total		% Failure 1800-1860
	O	F	O	F	O	F	O	F	O	F	O	F*			
Michigan	0	0	0	0	0	0	1	1	3	1	4	0	6	2	33
Minnesota	0	0	0	0	0	0	0	0	0	0	1	0	1	0	0
Mississippi	0	0	1	0	1	0	4	0	5	0	7	1	7	1	14
Missouri	0	0	0	0	0	0	6	0	8	2	11	1	13	3	23
New Hampshire	1	0	1	0	1	0	1	0	1	0	1	0	1	0	0
New Jersey	2	0	2	0	2	0	2	0	3	0	3	0	3	0	0
New York	2	0	3	0	4	0	6	0	9	1	13	0	14	1	7
North Carolina	1	0	1	0	1	0	3	0	3	0	4	0	4	0	0
Ohio	0	0	1	0	6	0	11	1	17	1	25	2	27	4	15
Oregon	0	0	0	0	0	0	0	0	0	0	2	0	2	0	0
Pennsylvania	4	0	5	0	7	0	13	3	13	1	16	1	19	5	26
Rhode Island	1	0	1	0	1	0	1	0	1	0	1	0	1	0	0
South Carolina	3	0	3	0	3	1	3	0	3	0	5	0	6	1	17
Tennessee	1	0	1	0	3	0	5	0	9	0	15	1	15	1	7

Table 1.2 - Continued

	1800's		1810's		1820's		1830's		1840's		1850's		Total		% Failure 1800-1860
	O	F	O	F	O	F	O	F	O	F	O	F*			
Texas	0	0	0	0	0	0	0	0	1	0	5	1	5	1	20
Vermont	2	0	2	0	2	0	3	0	3	0	3	0	3	0	0
Virginia	3	0	3	0	4	0	7	0	9	0	11	1	11	1	9
Wisconsin	0	0	0	0	0	0	0	0	1	0	5	0	5	0	0
	32	1	37	1	57	4	106	6	142	13	217	15	241	40	17

*O: in operation

F: Failures

Table 1.3

Liberal Arts Colleges In Operation and Founded, 1800-1860

	1800's	1810	1820	1830	1840	1850's
In Operation	32	37	67	106	142	217
Founded	12	8	23	56	42	88

increase in the number of colleges in operation. The 1830s had a near doubling of the number of institutions in operation, but the economic pressures of the 1840s resulted in a slowdown of the growth rate. The 1850s experienced a 50 percent expansion with eighty–eight new colleges being founded. (Tables 1.2, 1.3)

The growth in the number of colleges coincided with a shift in their geographic distribution. The colleges followed the movement of the American population to the West. New England's share of the colleges dropped from 25 percent to 7 percent in the sixty years, while the combined share of the Southwest and Midwest increased from 16 to 60 percent. The new areas of the country acquired colleges early in their development, and even the three states without colleges by the 1850s, Arkansas, Florida, and Kansas, had made attempts to found some. Arkansas chartered over thirty colleges and universities, Florida attempted to found a state system, and Kansas chartered eighteen universities and ten colleges in just the five years between 1855 and 1860.[11] (Tables 1.4, 1.5, 1.6, 1.7)

Table 1.4

Number of States With Liberal Arts Colleges And Average and Standard Deviation of Number of Colleges by State

	1800's	1810's	1820's	1830's	1840's	1850's
Number of States	18	21	21	26	29	32
$\overline{X}$	2	2	3	4	5	7
Q	1	1	2	3	4	5

Table 1.5

Colleges in Operation by Region and Decade as a Percent of All Colleges in Operation

	1800	1810	1820	1830	1840	1850
New England	25	22	20	13	10	7
Middle Atlantic	25	27	20	20	17	15
South Atlantic	34	32	23	23	10	17
Southwest	16	16	20	26	28	28
Midwest	0	5	16	20	24	31
West	0	0	0	0	0	2

But the growth of colleges was not a simple matter of the addition of new states. Over the six decades a much more complex process was at work leading to increasingly diverse educational profiles among the various states and regions. Colleges spread from eighteen to thirty-two states in the six decades, with the average number of colleges per state increasing from two to seven. At the same time, the states and regions became differentiated in respect to the number of colleges they maintained, reflecting state policies, denominational differences, and the degree of elitism in the states.

The relative shift of college location and the differentiation of the states and regions came in uneven steps. New England's share of the in-

Table 1.6

Colleges in Operation by Region and Decade

	1800	1810	1820	1830	1840	1850
New England	8	8	11	13	14	15
Middle Atlantic	8	10	13	21	25	32
South Atlantic	11	11	13	24	28	37
Southwest	5	6	11	27	40	61
Midwest	0	2	9	21	35	67

Table 1.7

Average Number of Colleges in Operation Per State in the Regions and Coefficient of Variation

	1850's	
	Average	Coefficient of Variation
New England	2.5	.55
Middle Atlantic	8.8	.67
South Atlantic	3.5	.55
Southwest	8.7	.36
Midwest	9.6	.76

stitutions showed only a slight decline until the 1830s because of the relatively slow growth of colleges across the country and because three new colleges were opened in New England in the 1820s. After the 1820s, New England would add only four colleges, despite its population growth and its ethnic diversification; and one of the four had to wait until after the Civil War to receive an official charter because of the bias in New England against Catholicism.[12] By the 1850s, the small number of college foundings in New England led to its average number of colleges per state being less than one–half the national average; the frontier state of Oregon had more operating "colleges" than three of the New England states.

The older Southern states and the Middle Atlantic region did not face such drastic declines in the percentage of colleges in operation. The South Atlantic share dropped from the country's largest in 1800 to the third largest in the 1850s, although the number of colleges in the region increased threefold. The experience of the South Atlantic states illustrates that the expansion of the 1830s was not confined to the West. In that decade the number of colleges in the old South nearly doubled, and only the District of Columbia maintained the same number of colleges that it had in the 1820s. In the Middle Atlantic states there was a greater increase in the number of colleges in the sixty years. Although their share dropped by 40 percent, two of the region's three states, New York and Pennsylvania, each had as many or more colleges than any other state except Ohio, Tennessee, and Illinois in the 1850s. Pennsylvania had more colleges than any state except Ohio.

The changes in the relative standing of the regions was accompanied by an increase in diversity among them, reflecting differences in chartering policies, denominational interest, and the ability to muster economic support for education. The Midwestern states had the highest variance, primarily due to policy decisions by the state governments. Ohio, for example, had twenty-five operating colleges in the 1850s while Michigan had four. One of the reasons for this difference was that Michigan pursued a very restrictive chartering policy until the Republicans took power in the 1850s. Ohio had always maintained a liberal policy, although it offered almost no economic support to its colleges.[13] But across the country, political preference in national politics did not determine the chartering policies of the states. There was no statistically significant relationship between percent Democratic or percent Republican vote for president and the number of colleges per state from the 1830s to the Civil War.[14] The support of colleges by the new denominations of the country somewhat conforms to the picture drawn by Tewksbury, but few colleges were controlled by a single denomination, and it was extremely difficult to classify colleges by denominational affiliation because of the mixture of local and denominational support.[15] New and lower-status denominations and denominational subgroups began to sponsor colleges in the 1830s, with the Baptists and Methodists increasing the number of colleges they aided fourfold. The smaller denominations did not begin to enter the college market until the 1840s and 1850s, however. (Tables 1.8, 1.9, 1.10, 1.11)

The result of the entry of the new denominations, including the concerted effort of the Catholics to found institutions above the primary level, was a significant change in the sources of support and control of higher education. In the 1800s and 1810s, the three older denominations were connected with almost 70 percent of all colleges, but in the 1830s

Table 1.8

Liberal Arts Colleges by Denominational Affiliation as Percentage of Colleges in Operation, Each Decade

	1800	1810	1820	1830	1840	1850
Denominational	84	82	83	85	85	86
State and Non-Denominational	16	18	17	15	15	14

Table 1.9

Denominational Colleges
as Percentage of all Liberal Arts Colleges
in Operation by Decade

	1800's	1810's	1820's	1830's	1840's	1850's
Congregational	21	20	17	10	9	8
Presbyterian	33	37	33	28	22	21
Methodist	3	3	6	11	10	16
Baptist	3	3	6	13	13	14
Episcopal	12	11	13	8	10	7
Catholic	9	6	4	9	13	10
Lutheran	0	0	2	3	3	3
Disciples	0	0	0	1	1	3
United Brethren	0	0	0	0	1	1
Quaker	0	0	0	1	1	1
Universalist	0	0	0	0	0	1
Dutch Reformed	3	2	2	1	1	1
German Reformed	0	0	0	1	1	1
Totals	84	82	83	86*	85	87*

*Percentage differences due to rounding.

the share supported by Congregationalists, Episcopalians, and Presbyterians declined to 50 percent. By the Civil War, the older denominations (including the many ethnic and theological variants of Presbyterianism) were associated with one–third of the schools. The Methodists and Baptists were allied with another third of the colleges, and the smaller denominations, such as the Disciples, Lutherans, United Bretherans, and Universalists, accounted for no more than 10 percent.

The denominations followed the geographic migration of the American population, but the denominational colleges were not evenly distributed across the country. New England remained dominated by Congregational and Unitarian colleges. Congregational, Lutheran, Quaker, and Disciples colleges were concentrated in a few regions, but the other denominations tended to locate their institutions rather evenly across the areas outside of New England.

Table 1.10

Percent of a Denomination's Colleges in Each Region

	New England	Middle Atlantic	South Atlantic	South-West	Mid-West	West
Congregational	47	0	0	0	47	6
Presbyterian	0	26	15	40	22	0
Baptist	3	18	15	39	12	0
Methodist	3	13	15	28	38	5
Episcopalian	18	22	33	18	22	0
Catholic	3	10	28	38	14	7
Disciples	0	0	17	33	50	0
Lutheran	0	0	20	0	80	0
Universalist	33	33	0	0	33	0
Quaker	0	67	0	0	33	0

The timing of failures followed the general trends stated by Tewksbury, but the absolute number was much smaller than he asserted and the distribution and causes of the failures were more complex. The highest percentage of failures came in the 1840s, but the highest absolute number was in the 1850s.

Eighteen states had at least one failure in the sixty years, but 40 percent of the failures occurred in three states and 50 percent in four. Close to 60 percent of all the failures were in the Southern states, with another

Table 1.11

Liberal Arts College Failures
By Percent of Colleges in Operation
and Absolute Number of Failures
By Decade

	1800's	1810's	1820's	1830's	1840's	1850's
Percent	3	3	7	6	9	7
Absolute Number	1	1	4	6	13	15

25 percent in the Midwest. Older states in the East and South did have some failures. There was a loss of one–third of Maryland's schools and Pennsylvania saw 26 percent of its colleges disappear. Only New England had no failures. (Table 1.12)

The antebellum colleges, especially the denominational institutions, were more stable than indicated by either Tewksbury's estimates or the evidence presented above. Baptists, for example, did have two failures in the sixty years, but one of these was a Pennsylvania school that probably did not operate as a college and the other was a Virginia institution destroyed by a fire. The five Methodist failures were concentrated in the Southwest. The one Methodist failure in the North was a Pennsylvania institution, founded in the 1830s, that is suspected of having operated on the academy level. The six Presbyterian failures were more widespread, with one each in Pennsylvania, Michigan and Iowa. Although Presbyterian failures did occur outside of the South, the three Northern failures, again, were institutions that disappeared within a few years of their founding. There was only one failure among the schools of the minor denominations, a Disciples closing in Kentucky, and this had the character of a merger rather than a clear–cut failure.[16] (Tables 1.13, 1.14, 1.15)

There was no certain failure of a Protestant denominational college in the Midwest, and the highest failure rates occurred among the colleges associated with supposedly more secure sources of support and rational control. The pattern of failures does not fully agree with the denomina-

Table 1.12

Failures of Liberal Arts Colleges
as Percent of Total Failures
by Decade and Region

	1800	1810	1820	1830	1840	1850	1800–1860
New England	0	0	0	0	0	0	0
Middle Atlantic	0	0	0	50	15	7	15
South Atlantic	0	0	25	17	8	20	15
Southwest	100	100	50	0	46	53	45
Midwest	0	0	25	33	31	20	25
West	0	0	0	0	0	0	0
Totals	1	1	4	6	13	15	40

Table 1.13

Foundings and Failures by Denomination or Other Affiliation of Liberal Arts Colleges

	Foundings	Failures	% Failures
Baptist	35	2	6
Congregational	17	0	0
Disciples	7	1	17
Episcopalian	18	3	17
Catholic	27	8	30
Methodist	40	5	13
Presbyterian	46	6	13
United Brethren-Disciples	2	0	0
Lutheran	5	0	0
Dutch Reformed	1	0	0
German Reformed	3	0	0
State	19	5	26
Non-Denominational	16	10	63
Universalist	3	0	0
Swedenborgian	1	0	0
	241	40	

tional–competition thesis. Nondenominational, state and Catholic colleges had more failures than the schools supported by the denominations that have been considered the aggressive leaders in the evangelical movement. Episcopal colleges, for example, had a greater percentage of failures than the colleges associated with the lower–status denominations. And the policies of states such as Maryland, Louisiana, and Indiana led to great instability among their colleges.[17]

But the failure of colleges is only one indicator of instability. Many institutions had to suspend operations because of economic difficulties, internal squabbles, political problems, or natural disasters such as fires or epidemics. Thirty temporary closures were identified in the antebellum period. These suspensions occurred in sixteen states and involved seven

Table 1.14

Active Colleges by Denominational Association Membership In Denomination and Membership per College

Denomination	Colleges	Membership	Membership/ Colleges
Baptist	35	982,693	28,077
Congregational	17	227,196	13,364
Episcopalian	18	67,550	3,753
Catholic	27	586,580*	21,735
Methodist	40	1,179,526	29,488
Presbyterian	46	485,386	10,552
United Brethren	2	136,000	68,000
Lutheran	5	163,000	32,600
Dutch Reformed	1	32,849	32,849
German Reformed	3	69,750	23,250
Universalist	3	60,000	20,000
Unitarian*	1		30,000
Disciples		400,000	57,000

*One-half reported Catholic membership.

denominations and both state and nondenominational colleges. The suspensions happened in every area of the country; the South had the highest frequency, but even New England had them in the 1810s and 1850s. And state institutions and the comparatively wealthy Congregational colleges had some suspensions. At least seven state colleges were temporarily closed.

However, the pattern of suspensions does not parallel the pattern of failures. Baptist and Methodist colleges had more suspensions and fewer failures than did nondenominational institutions. In comparison to the Baptist and Methodist ability to rescue their institutions, Catholic, Episcopal, and nondenominational colleges either had a smooth history or faced complete failure. It is also significant that, except for the Quakers with their one known suspension, the minor denominations were free of temporary closures as well as failures.

Table 1.15

Actual and Expected Number of Colleges by Denominational Membership

Denomination	% Membership	1 Actual Colleges	2 Expected Colleges
Baptist	29	35	52
Methodist	35	40	62
Presbyterian	14	46	25
Episcopal	2	18	4
Congregational	7	17	13
Dutch Reformed	5	5	9
Totals	92	178	165

The revised estimates of failures and suspensions indicate that the system was more stable than Tewksbury stated, and a consideration of college foundings suggests that the system was more rational than he concluded. First, consider the distribution of institutions compared to the number of colleges in the state Tewksbury held to be the most rational, Massachusetts.[18]

There was a great difference in the concentration of population among regions and states; the new states naturally had fewer persons per square mile. If Massachusetts, because of the stability of its colleges, is taken as the norm for the number of colleges, both by young male population and by the degree of population concentration, then the high number of colleges in the other areas of the country seem much less irrational. (Tables 1.16, 1.17, 1.18, 1.19) The results for 1860 by this rough projection of the expected number of colleges indicate that only the District of Columbia, Maryland, and Delaware had more than the number of predicted colleges (approximately one too many each) and that even Ohio, with a college at "everyone's doorstep", had many too few institutions. By the Massachusetts model of numbers and geographic concentration, the Midwest needed close to 250 more colleges; the Middle Atlantic states, 50; the Southwest, 300; and the South Atlantic, 75.[19]

The college foundings also matched the distributions of denominational resources and memberships, and the denominations aided the establishment and maintenance of colleges in areas where their members

Table 1.16

Distribution of Colleges
by Church Accommodations and Property

	1860–% of $ Value of Church Property	1850's % of Colleges	% of Church Accommo-dations	$ per Accommo-dations	% Col-leges all Decades
Adventist	0.06	0	0.09	5.91	0
Baptist, all	12.34	17	21.14	5.21	.75
Christian	1.41	33	3.56	3.70	0.46
Congregational and Unitarian	10.29	8	5.72		
Unitarian				31.39	.46
Dutch Reformed	2.60	1	1.10	21.10	.46
Episcopalian	12.53	9	4.38	25.64	7.87
Friends	1.48	1	1.41	9.43	1.39
German Reformed	1.41	1	1.43	8.85	1.39
Jewish	0.66	0	0.18	33.09	0
Methodist	19.31	19	32.72	5.20	14.35
Moravian	0.13	1	0.11	11.19	0
Presbyterian, all	15.31	22	13.41	10.47	17,59
Catholic	15.20	13	7.34	19.81	10.18
Universalist	1.67	1	1.23	12.14	1.39
other	2.46				0.93
Lutheran	3.14	2	3.96	7.08	2.78

Table 1.17

White Males Age 15–20
per Colleges in Operation
By Base Year and Decades

1800	1800's	1810's	1820's	1830's	1840's	1850's	1860
11,000	9,000	10,000	10,000	7,000	7,600	6,500	7,000

Table 1.18

Thousands of White Males Age 15-20 Per College
By Region and Decade and Base Years
(By States with Colleges)

Region	1800	1810	1820's	1830's	1840's	1850's	1860
New England	5.8	6.8	9.8	8.6	10	11	11
Middle Atlantic	6.7	9.7	12	7.7	13	11	11
South Atlantic	5.2	5.9	8	4.4	4.4	5	4.6
Southwest	2.7	4	6	5.7	4.6	4.9	4
Midwest	-	-	-	4.2	7.8	9	6.7
West	-	-	-	-	-	-	7

had located. The denominations supported colleges in proportion to their memberships, and the ones that founded colleges beyond the numbers expected on the basis of their membership were not the new and lower–status denominations, but the established ones. (Tables 1.14, 1.15, 1.16)

If the Unitarians, the sponsors of the very successful Harvard University, are taken as the norm for the number of members needed for the support of a college, the majority of the denominations made fairly rational choices as to the number of institutions to aid. Table 1.15 indicates that the worst offenders in respect to the founding of colleges on the basis of insufficient numbers of potential supporters and students were, in order, the Episcopalians, the Presbyterians, and the Congregationalists. Baptists, Methodists and the other lower–status denominations had a college–to–membership ratio by the 1850s that approached or exceeded the Unitarians. Only the Universalists, among the newer denominations, seem to have founded too many colleges according to this criteria. And this denomination, which was not noted for its evangelical efforts, had fewer members per college than the expansive Catholics whose members–per–college figure is based upon a half of its reported members.[20]

The relationship between membership and the number of colleges is highlighted by the reallocation of colleges to the various denominations based upon a denomination's percent of total Protestant membership. If the colleges were redistributed among the denominations according to membership, the Methodists, Baptists, and Lutherans would receive more institutions while the older denominations would have significant numbers taken from them.

Despite the non–centralized nature of both the denominations and the educational system, college locations fit a rational pattern. In the 1850s the percent of all operating colleges correlated, by state, in the mid–eighties with the percentage of all church accommodations. And among the denominations, the share of their colleges in each state matched the geographic distribution of their church accommodations.[21] (Table 1.16)

Although the relationship between a denomination's share of total church property was highly correlated with its share of the colleges, another economic relationship indicates that the lower–status denominations acted irrationally. Because the economic resources available to the newer denominations were much less than those of the established ones, they took greater risks of failure when they decided to support a college.

Table 1.19

Ratio of Colleges in Operation During a Decade to the Population of White Males Age 15–20 in Succeeding Census Decade. For States with Colleges. In Thousands.

		1800	1810's	1820's	1830's	1840's	1850's	1860's
New England:								
Connecticut		9	10	13	9	6	6	7
Massachusetts		8	9	11	11	12	12	11
Maine		5	8	14	12	14	17	18
New Hampshire		7	7	11	16	16	17	17
Rhode Island		3	3	4	5	6	7	8
Vermont		3	4	6	8	6	6	6
	$\overline{X}$	5.8	6.8	9.8	10.2	10	11	11.2
	Q	2.4	2.5	3.6	3.4	4.2	4.8	4.8
Middle Atlantic:								
New Jersey		4	4	6	9	10	8	11
New York		10	17	20	27	22	17	12
Pennsylvania		6	8	10	11	7	8	9
	$\overline{X}$	6.7	9.7	12.7	16	13	11	10.7
	Q	2.5	5.4	5.9	8.1	6.5	4.2	1.2

For example, Methodists and Baptists faced a greater organizational task to muster economic support for their colleges than did the Unitarians. The average church accommodation of the Unitarians was worth thirty dollars compared to the five dollar value of the Baptist's and Methodist's facilities. As Table 1.16 shows, the denominations had very different levels of resources available to them. However, the average value of church accommodations does not seem to explain failure rates.[22]

Table 1.19 - Continued

	1800	1810's	1820's	1830's	1840's	1850's	1860's
South Atlantic:							
District of Columbia	.2	.6	1	.7	1	1	1
Delaware	-	-	-	-	3	4	3
Georgia	4	6	8	17	5	6	8
Maryland	5	5	7	8	4	4	3
North Carolina	13	14	19	28	8	10	9
South Carolina	2	3	4	5	5	5	3
Virginia	7	7	9	10	5	5	5
$\overline{X}$	5.2	5.9	8	11.5	4.4	5	4.6
Q	4.1	4.16	5.6	8.9	2.0	2.5	2.7
Southwest:							
Kentucky	2	4	3	6	4	5	6
Louisiana	3	4	4	2	3	3	2
Alabama	-	-	-	-	8	6	5
Mississippi	-	-	2	4	3	3	3
Missouri	-	-	-	-	3	4	5
Tennessee	3	4	15	11	7	5	3
Texas	-	-	-	-	-	8	4
$\overline{X}$	2.7	4	6	5.8	4.6	4.9	4
Q	.5	0	5.2	1.3	2.1	1.6	1.3

Table 1.19 - Continued

		1800	1810's	1820's	1830's	1840's	1850's	1860's
Midwest:								
Indiana		-	-	7	7	7	8	8
Illinois		-	-	-	-	6	8	8
Iowa		-	-	-	-	-	9	4
Michigan		-	-	-	-	2	7	10
Minnesota		-	-	-	-	-	-	6
Ohio		-	-	28	9	7	6	6
Wisconsin		-	-	-	-	-	15	7
	$\overline{X}$	-	-	17.5	8.0	5.5	8.8	7.0
	Q	-	-	14.8	1.4	2.4	3.2	1.9
West:								
California		-	-	-	-	-	-	5
Oregon		-	-	-	-	-	-	1
	$\overline{X}$	-	-	-	-	-	-	3
	Q	-	-	-	-	-	-	2.8

As well as the relationship between college foundings and the indicator of disposable wealth available to the denominations, the relationship between the founding of colleges and the number of potential students might indicate that the early system was irrational and inefficient. Tewksbury and many others stressed the point that the explosion in the number of colleges led to too many institutions competing for too few students. But the emphasis upon student–to–college ratios in the historiography and the interpretation of their causes and consequences flowed from a particular model of what a college should be. The use of the normative concept distorted the motivations and contributions of the college–founding movement.

No matter what population base is used, it is clear that the rate of college foundings did exceed the growth rate of the American population. Using white males age fifteen to twenty as the base, the number of potential students per college dropped by four thousand in the sixty years.

The ratio of colleges in operation to the white males, by decade, decreased from one to eleven thousand to one to seven thousand in the six decades. The decrease was not steady. The 1810s and 1820s had an increase over the first decade of the century, then, the 1830s had a sharp drop in the number of young males per college. But the ratio remained relatively constant from the early Jacksonian years to the Civil War.[23] (Table 1.19)

The national figures, however, do not reflect the great differences in college–to–youth ratios which developed among the areas of the country. The major regions had important differences in respect to the demographic context in which their colleges operated. This was compounded by the state of development of their educational and social systems. The majority of the new colleges of the period were founded in the Southwest and Midwest, leading to the lowest college–to–youth ratios being in areas where both the lower educational systems and the levels and distributions of income and wealth were unlikely to support higher education. In contrast, the fewest foundings occurred in the areas most able to support higher education. (Tables 1.18, 1.19)

The inverse relationship between numbers of colleges and the number of potential students and the social and educational resources to support colleges is much more than an indicator of the irrationality of the early college system. When the normative models of higher education used by the traditional historians are replaced with a more empirical approach, these relationships become one of the most important keys needed to understand the antebellum college movement.[24]

New England followed a policy of increasing the population ratios by restricting the founding of colleges. The result was that the number of its available young men per college increased by almost 100 percent in the six decades. In the Middle Atlantic region, more liberal policies and subsequent growth in the number of colleges were offset by a population boom; consequently the Middle Atlantic ratios remained very close to New England's throughout the period. But because so many new colleges were founded in the South Atlantic and South Western states, the Southern ratios became less than half those of the North. Although the Southern seaboard area had two states with ratios close to New England's, the Southwest was uniformly low in its support potential. The Midwest and West ended the period with college–to–youth ratios which approximated the East's levels of fifty years before the outbreak of the Civil War.

The number of young men per college does provide some indication of the differences among the regions, but it overstates the numbers of possible students available to the colleges and underestimates the differences among the regions. Basic education was not universal and a large percentage of the college–age population had not received adequate preparatory or even primary education. Thus, significant percentages of the young were incapable of doing college level work. This reduced the numbers from which the colleges could draw and greatly magnified the regional differences.

In the 1840s, New England was sending more than three–quarters of its children to primary schools and 20 percent to academies and grammar schools. In contrast, the Midwest sent less than 4 percent to academies and 20 percent to its primary institutions. The Southern states pursued more explicitly elitist policies with 20 percent of their young enrolled in academies and grammar schools and less than 20 percent in primary institutions. Support of public education in the South was so skewed that Virginia and South Carolina were spending more public money on their state universities than on the entire public school system in the 1850s.[25]

By 1860, the educational profile of the Midwest had changed so that its primary school attendance was about that of New England and its academy and grammar school atendance rate had increased to 60 percent of New England's. The Middle Atlantic region maintained its academy enrollment level mid–way between New England and the West, but increased its primary attendance by 1860. The South, however, did not devote more attention to widespread basic education.[26]

Taking the status of primary and secondary education into account inflates the collegiate population regional differences. Based upon academy and grammar school enrollment levels in the 1850s, the estimates of regional support indicate that New England had more than twice the available students per college than the Midwest; the New England advantage was probably four to one. A similar reduction in the estimate of the number of possible students relative to New England is applicable to the Middle Atlantic region, and the enrollment levels in the South suggest that it had an even less favorable ratio.

The differences in the numbers of potential students were compounded by the distributions and levels of wealth and property within the regions. New England, for example, had the highest wealth and property level and a relatively equal distribution, while the Western and Southern states had either low levels or highly skewed distributions, both of which made higher education inaccessible to much of the population.[27]

Although differences in the numbers of possible students and economic conditions created different educational environments in the regions, they do not seem to explain failure rates. The linear correlation between young white males per college for the states and the percentages of failures of colleges within the states was never greater than –.20, a 4 percent explanatory factor. The correlation between male academy and high school students per state for the 1870s (the first decade with census reports on high schools) and failure rates in the 1850s also explained less than 5 percent of the variance. Nor do per capita property values by state explain either foundings or failures.[28]

Colleges may have survived in unlikely settings, but the regional differences and founding patterns meant that after the 1820s American colleges were located in areas which, according to the theories of historians such as Tewksbury and Hofstadter, should not have had institutions for higher education. From the perspective of the Progressive era, with its devotion to large–scale and stable institutions which could support a professionalized faculty and research, the location pattern was inefficient and could only be explained by irrational and antimodern forces. The distribution of colleges had to be explained and implicitly evaluated through such factors as denominational competition and town boosterism, neither of which could possibly have made a positive contribution to the development of education. But it is exactly this supposed irrationality of location which makes sense of the antebellum college movement and which points to the positive contributions of the early system, especially when the colleges are considered within the context of their own time period.

The increase in the number of colleges in the country occurred within the context of a widespread expansion and upgrading of all levels of American education. The development of the antebellum colleges cannot be understood unless it is viewed as an integral part of the struggles and successes of the general expansion and alteration of American education. And the college movement cannot be explained or evaluated if it is assumed that the other educational institutions of the antebellum period had achieved a twentieth century level of sophistication and security.

The number of primary schools in America doubled between 1840 and 1860 and both the resources devoted to them and the number of days students attended increased. Although the cities took the lead in developing primary education, the small towns and rural areas of the country, despite their economic handicaps, joined in the movement to bring more and better basic education to their young.[29]

The expansion of education was not confined to the teaching of basic reading skills. In the Jacksonian years more attention began to be paid to the education of older students. The number of academies and grammar schools, the early nineteenth century version of "secondary" education, jumped from thirty–two hundred in 1840 to over sixty–seven hundred in 1860, an increase only slightly below that for the primary schools.[30] (Table 1.20)

The changes in post–primary education did not mean, however, that a fully articulated and hierarchical system developed or that the economic

Table 1.20

Number of Academies and Other Schools
by Region and Census Year

Region	Census Year 1840	1850	1860
New England	630	985	988
Middle Atlantic	861	1,626	1,648
South Atlantic	969	1,366	1,515
Southwest	560	1,371	1,361
Midwest	184	550	903

and administrative problems of secondary education had been resolved. Nor had a new and meaningful set of names for various types of institutions evolved. There were few concepts and resources to guide the definition and rationalization of this new and expanded higher education. And, especially in the small towns and rural areas of the country, the relationship between government and secondary education remained undefined.

The modern concept of a high school was unknown at the time and would be evolved slowly. The term college had been used traditionally to indicate an institution teaching a formalized curricula to students with preparation above the primary level in the classical languages and mathematics, and very few knew what the term university meant aside from referring to a collection of liberal arts and professional schools. (Professional schools were vocational and did not demand college preparation.) Even age groupings did not conform to modern notions. Colleges, academies and, in some cases, primary schools, taught students whose ages nearly spanned a generation. As late as the 1850s, and in the most developed regions of the country, reputable sponsors founded institutions with the name high school that granted degrees and admitted students below fifteen years of age.[31]

The difficulty of defining and financing the new education in America is illustrated by the popular and ubiquitous academies of the period. These all-purpose institutions (about which relatively little is known) were being spread across the country, but their organization and orientations were so varied that their existence is more of an indication of educational difficulties than a solution. Teachers may have been turning academies into formalized preparatory schools in some areas,[32] but in most cases they remained as ill–funded, private, and general–purpose schools that taught a variety of subjects and diverse age groups. By the 1850s, however, the term began to connotate an institution with less–formalized curricula than a college and one that did provide some preparation for those who aspired to a higher education.[33]

The private and semi–public academies were not the result of any centrally directed plan, nor were the emerging high schools. And neither the national or the state governments took the lead in the expansion of education beyond the primary level. The expansion of what we might now call the secondary system as well as higher education, especially in the small towns and rural areas, was the product of the usual sources of social change in nineteenth–century America: the voluntary association and local government. Perhaps receiving minimal aid from state governments, and an average of $120 a year from all governmental sources in 1860, the academies and grammar schools relied upon local support and direction.[34] The academies were the dominant form of higher education in the period, outnumbering high schools (which were concentrated in a few states and were usually located in urban areas) by a factor of seventeen to one in 1860.[35] Thus, although there was a great increase in government support for "secondary" education in the 1850s, the system remained underfunded and dependent upon local sources. The development of this version of secondary education was uneven across the country. The results of the increased governmental interest were concentrated in New England and a few Midwestern states. New England, which had virtually halted the growth of academies during the 1850s, was spending five times the amount of public funds per student as were the states in the Midwest and Middle Atlantic regions and twice what was being spent per student by governments in the South. But even in New England the level of support was so low that it took the expenditures for two hundred pupils just to match the salary of an adequately paid principal.[36] (Table 1.20)

The proliferation of colleges was part of the growth of private and semi–public education that swept across the country. Like academies and grammar schools, colleges were founded in the areas with the least public support and most poorly developed secondary systems. In a very real sense, the antebellum colleges were leaders in bringing education to areas with the greatest need for educational upgrading. Almost every antebellum college in the West and South began as one of those ill–defined institutions, an academy. An academy was turned into a college when there were signs that a demand for more formal and regular education had arisen in the area and when local sponsors could muster enough economic support to raise endowments above the average two thousand six hundred dollars of the academies and grammar schools.[37]

The denominations and local boosterism were, in the most direct way, helping to bring education to areas and groups that had not been well served by the public sector. They were bringing upgraded education to the small towns and rural areas of the country and to groups of people who had not benefited from the old state college and university systems. The denominations were subsidizing the education of a new segment of the American population, the emergent middle classes of rural and small–town America whose economic position had improved enough to enable them to envision "higher" education for their sons and daughters.

The new colleges, especially in the West and new South, were not the simple result of a denomination's desire to create a ministerial factory. In almost every case, the new colleges were the product of an interaction between a local denominational organization's willingness to help subsidize a college and a town's desire for education for its sons and daughters. Although the denominations were badly in need of trained ministers in the West, production of ministers was only one motivation for founding and supporting colleges. Denominational leaders also desired to support education in general, as evidenced by their aid to academies, and knew that only a few institutions could survive or prosper without enrolling those who would enter the secular world.

Because of their base–of–support and by philosophy, the new colleges, especially those in the small towns, were extremely flexible (given the resources available to them) and responded to their environments. Almost all were multi–level, multi–purpose institutions which maintained preparatory (academic) departments to compensate for the few adequately trained students for the college courses. And they supported primary departments which were advances on the haphazard older schools. Oberlin College, for example, was a huge educational complex with hundreds of students being taught in departments ranging from the primary through a normal school to the regular college and a theological department. Most other institutions were a scaled–down version of Oberlin, and many associated themselves with law and medical schools.[38]

The varied nature of the institutions not only met the needs of the local areas, but also economic necessity. The income from the primary schools and academies helped to support the college operations until endowments and other sources of funds could be found to sustain a more specialized institution.[39]

The antebellum colleges were also responsive to changing demands by their students. Within the college program many adjustments were made to relate to the economic and social conditions of the times. Teacher–training programs were developed and curricula were initiated for those who did not desire to learn the classical languages. "Partial" and "English" courses emphasized practice in the vernacular instead of the study of the old languages. Classes in modern foreign languages were started (usually at some extra cost) if student demand was high and a trained teacher was available, and even classes in business and clerical skills were offered in some schools. Agricultural training was attempted in many of the colleges, and a majority seemed to have offered civil engineering classes. Especially in the newer areas of the country, this flexibility was assumed by all denominations. Catholics taught business courses in St. Louis and Washington, D.C.; Disciples first called their Kentucky college an agricultural and civil engineering institute; and Methodists and Baptists frequently began their schools as early versions of work–study institutes in which the students earned part of their tuition through manual labor, to lower costs and because of an ideological commitment to maintain ties with rural life. Physical education perhaps began in a Disciples' institution, elective programs were tried in the West, and most schools, after they had adequate enrollments, allowed and even supported the existence of debating clubs and fraternities which engaged students in important contemporary questions.[40] And interest in the sciences was not confined to the more affluent institutions of the East nor to the state universities. Most schools taught some sort of general course in science and many, by the 1850s, were teaching chemistry and some geology and astronomy. Howard College in Alabama, a Southern Baptist Institution, hired a professor of chemistry and agriculture before the Civil War and constructed a separate building for chemistry demonstrations and laboratory work. Baptist, Methodist and even the Disciples' institutions in all the regions taught some type of chemistry and the colleges representing ethnic groups, such as German–Wallace in Ohio, paid as much attention to science as their budgets would allow. In fact, the evidence gathered from a reading of the histories of all the colleges indicates that all of the denominations were receptive to the existing sciences.[41] They would have offered more science in their schools, but the high costs of teaching the subject, the lack of student demand, and the scarcity of adequately trained instructors hindered many of the institutions. Advanced scientific training was more frequently offered in the East and in some of the state institutions because they had the necessary economic surplus. Student demand was sufficient because of employment opportunities in the economies of the developed areas, and the young American teachers who had received specialized training in Europe desired salaries that only the Eastern and state institutions could pay.[42]

The new colleges were not only flexible and receptive to science, but were oriented to a broader spectrum of the population than many of the established and prestigious institutions. They were the only institutions many of the young men of their regions could afford to attend, especially in the South and West. Many of the older and affluent institutions, including state universities in the South and West, were creatures of the regional elites and did not make themselves attractive to many possible students from the emerging middle class. The Southern state universities, including the University of Virginia, were very expensive, and many of the schools were perceived to be hostile to members of the new and lower–status denominations. Throughout the South the state institutions charged tuition and fees that were as high or higher than those at the denominational colleges. In Virginia, Jefferson's university asked ninety–five dollars for tuition during the 1850s while a Lutheran institution charged thirty–five and a Baptist school fifty–five dollars. In South Carolina, its university was more expensive than the denominational colleges, a pattern followed in all the other Southern states.[43]

High charges and reputations of bias also marked the North's prestigious institutions. In the Midwest the University of Michigan was the only well–established state institution which pursued a low–tuition policy, but it was considered by many to be an urban, Presbyterian college and a hotbed of elitism and antiabolitionism. The larger colleges in the East asked students to pay up to three times the tuition required by the new denominational colleges, and there is no evidence that the scholarship programs of these institutions were used for purposes of compensatory social mobility.[44]

The newer colleges actively pursued a policy of subsidizing students. They priced their education so that it was economically accessible to more of the population than that of the larger schools. Not only did they provide free tuition for future ministers, and in some cases the sons of ministers, but they consciously kept their stated tuition and fees at low levels compared to the prestigious institutions. For example, in the 1850s, Harvard University, which was paying very high salaries to its professors, received a yearly return from its endowments that was greater than the total value of many of the Western and Southern colleges. However, Harvard set its tuition so that each student paid 4 percent of an average professor's salary. Most of the small colleges, in contrast, expected each of their students to pay no more than 2.5 percent of the salary of their average professor, or 1 percent of the salary of a Harvard faculty member.[45] And, compared to modern times, the burdens placed upon the students of the early small colleges were slight. In the mid–1970s, the tuitions from twenty–seven students were needed to pay the salary of one professor, but in the antebellum period's small colleges forty full–tuition students were needed to support one faculty member.[46]

While the smaller institutions were using available resources to lower student costs, the renowned colleges made investments in facilities—but not necessarily ones related to research. The large institutions used their relatively large endowments to construct monumental buildings and to maintain high faculty salaries rather than to make higher education more economically accessible. Harvard and Columbia are the most outstanding example of this pattern, but even some small denominational institutions began to devote their funds to the construction of attractive campuses. And Tappan of Michigan decided to shift funds to facilities rather than to maintain the auxiliary campuses (high schools) of his university or to provide more subsidies to his students.[47] While certain institutional leaders pursued the policy of devoting resources to upgrading facilities, the majority of the small colleges attempted to attract students through low tuition and charges. But, especially in the Midwest, the student subsidization policies were followed without government aid. In the Colonial and post–Revolutionary periods it was common for "denominational" institutions to receive substantial economic aid from state funds. And even during the nineteenth century, several Eastern colleges received government support. Harvard University, for example, had been granted over a half million dollars from the state of Massachusetts during the Colonial period (plus another half million from private sources) and was given approximately three times the total endowment of a typical Western college for a scientific collection in the 1850s. The University of Pennsylvania, Bowdoin, Amherst, Dartmouth, Yale, Colby, and Columbia, to mention only a few of the other denominational institutions, received significant state aid during the early nineteenth century, and Williams College continued to receive state support throughout the period, totaling over one hundred thousand dollars by 1860.[48]

But such governmental aid was becoming rare in the nineteenth century. Pennsylvania, until the 1830s, and New York, for a longer time, did provide small grants for the initiation of programs at many institutions but the amounts were small compared to those of the Colonial period. In the West and Southwest it was very unusual if a school received adequate land grants. Most of the new colleges of the country, especially those of the minor and lower–status denominations, arose when a tradition of support was dying, forcing them to turn to other sources of badly needed funds.[49]

The absence of uniform state or national support for the new colleges made them dependent upon unpredictable, insecure and inadequate sources of economic aid. College administrators had to turn to local and denominational sponsors, and only the most fortunate institutions found a wealthy benefactor who would provide a large endowment and who would guide its investment into safe and profitable channels. The types of available sponsors for higher education and the levels of economic support shaped the policies and potentials of the colleges as much as did philosophies of education because educators had to conform to the wishes of contributors and they had to work within the constraints imposed by the funds available to them.

Most colleges were dependent upon local support in their first years of operation. Location of a college was decided on the basis of which town in a general area would offer the most economic support, and some colleges relocated when another town seemed willing to provide more funds. The University of Michigan, for example, moved from Detroit to Ann Arbor because of the attractive offer made by the town's representatives, rather than because the new site was geographically ideal.[50]

For prospective institutions without state support the offers from towns of free land and pledges of financial aid were more important than was the consideration of a theoretically optimal location. Once established in an area, the college or the academy seeking to improve its financial condition and its image by renaming itself a college, scoured the area for additional funds. College presidents and the financial agents of the colleges canvassed the surrounding areas in search of donations and conducted pledge drives which yielded promises of contributions ranging from hand–made blankets, homemade furniture, and building supplies to cash and credit at local banks. Many times the pledges could not be redeemed, especially when economic recessions hit the country, as in the late 1830s and the 1850s. When pledge drives proved inadequate, the colleges appealed to private organizations, such as Masonic lodges, for funds or sold perpetual scholarships. The holders of these scholarships were allowed to send a designated student to the college free of tuition. Unfortunately, there were no time limits on their use and several institutions became financially embarrassed when large numbers of students appeared claiming rights under the instruments which had originally been seen as one of the most expedient ways to save an institution.[51]

Just as in the Colonial period, when colleges turned to England for contributions, most institutions in the nineteenth century had to seek support outside their immediate area. College representatives traveled through their states and regions giving lectures and sermons in every possible church and meeting. Usually stressing the ungodly nature of their area and the need for more ministers because of the nature of the audience they addressed, they pleaded for funds for their institutions. Some were successful and were able to raise significant amounts through donations that at times averaged less than one dollar each. But most colleges found that such appeals did not yield enough to cover the expenses of their agents. Several institutions applied to state governments and received permission to hold a lottery in order to raise money. The University of Delaware and Union College in New York were rescued by this form of legalized gambling, but most other attempts were failures.[52]

The inadequacies of local and state support sent the colleges in search of other sources of funds. If an institution was fortunate, it received more regular aid from the controlling state or regional body of its denomination, but even these contributions were relatively small. All of the institutions searched for a wealthy benefactor or for the recognition necessary to receive aid from organizations that were capable of redistributing wealth from the richer to the poorer regions of the country.

Midwestern colleges, especially, sent representatives to the areas that had both the wealth and organizations capable of providing significant support. The older Protestant denominations went in search of funds from their national organizations and those wealthy New Englanders who were associated with the evangelical and reform movements of the period. A few institutions found rich benefactors such as Amos Lawrence, and others received aid from the Protestant denominational organizations most concerned with colleges and the education of ministers.[53] But most colleges came away with very little other than the realization that there was not an efficient or equitable means to transfer educational funds from one region to another. As late as 1860, Massachusetts had a per capita value of personal property that was three times that of Iowa's and twice that of Michigan's, but relatively little of this wealth was transferred to the West for education. Prior to the Civil War the SPCTW, the interdenominational organization for the support of colleges in the West, raised less than one–third of Harvard's 1860 endowment and dispensed what it did collect in small amounts to a few selected colleges. The American Education Society, designed to support ministerial students, was not only moribund after the 1840s, but had used most of its funds for the support of candidates in colleges in the East.[54]

The sources and levels of funding for the colleges had many significant consequences for the system. Because there were few if any nondenominational organizations willing and able to fill the old role of the states in the financing of colleges the leaders of the new colleges had to orient their rhetoric to the religious aspects of their institutions. The economic dependency on local areas led to the unique American system of colleges being at least formally controlled by bodies of laymen, rather than by faculties. The decentralized nature of financial support had the consequence of great inequalities among the institutions, including state colleges and universities. These inequalities, as might be expected, were always in favor of the older denominations and regions.

Other than tuition, endowments were the major source of income for all but a few favored state institutions. The income of the state colleges and universities was not always secure because no college before the Civil War was tied to a fixed and adequate tax base. State subsidies meant involvement in ongoing political battles to maintain funding in

Table 1.21

Known Endowments, 1850's.
Range in Thousand Dollars.
By Denomination and State
(? = poor data recovery)

By Denomination:	
Baptist	0-300
Methodist	0-150
Presbyterian	0-700
Episcopal	0-700
Catholic	0-120
Lutheran	0- 53
State	?-900
Disciples	0- 50
Non-Denominational	0-100
Congregational	17
Quaker	?- 35
By State:	
Alabama	0-343
California	0-?
Connecticut	10-380
Delaware	50
District of Columbia	0?-75
Georgia	25-120
Illinois	0?-100
Indiana	0?-149

Table 1.21 - Continued

Iowa	0-173
Kentucky	0?-80
Louisiana	?
Maine	0-100
Maryland	0-20?
Massachusetts	0-1,000
Michigan	0?-600
Minnesota	0?-?
Mississippi	0?-900
Missouri	0?-100
New Hampshire	182
New Jersey	90
New York	0?-700
North Carolina	0?-148
Ohio	0-200
Pennsylvania	0-200
Rhode Island	193
South Carolina	800
Tennessee	0?-200
Texas	10
Vermont	?
Virginia	250
Wisconsin	0?-100

every state. Endowments were the only economic support that allowed colleges to pursue policies free from outside organizations or very unpredictable state legislatures. (Table 1.21)

Although the average endowment income per student increased to at least three times its 1800s size by the mid–1850s, endowments remained at inadequate levels and were unequally distributed. On the average, the colleges of the 1850s received less than twenty–five dollars per student from endowment funds. Few institutions had endowments large enough to provide for faculty salaries or even for adequate libraries, equipment, or buildings. Many institutions had to use their endowment incomes to pay the interest on the debts remaining from the construction of their original buildings; some had to sell the lands donated to them before their value was great enough to build a cash endowment. Others had almost all their funds disappear when the economic recessions of the period led corporations and banks into insolvency.[55]

The funds that had been accumulated were unequally distributed. In the 1850s, endowments ranged from nothing to over a million dollars and yearly endowment income from one hundred dollars per student to, of course, nothing. New England had the greatest endowments for "denominational" colleges, but even in that wealthy region the funds ranged from ten thousand dollars to over a million dollars. In contrast, the Midwest had only one institution with an outside income equivalent to five hundred thousand dollars, the University of Michigan, and that fund was subject to manipulation by the state legislature. The next highest endowment in the region was two hundred thousand dollars, and most colleges in the Midwest felt extremely secure if they had a fifty thousand dollar endowment which, when well managed, might pay their president's salary.[56]

The Southern states had the greatest inequalities in endowments, or their equivalents, in the form of state guarantees, ranging from the University of Mississippi's state managed nine hundred thousand dollars (frequently mishandled) to the more usual endowments of the denominational colleges of less than twenty–five thousand dollars. The Middle Atlantic region also had great inequalities. Columbia and Union had endowments of close to seven hundred fifty thousand dollars, while other colleges with known endowment funds had to be satisfied with less than those in the Midwest.[57]

As with other indicators of institutional resources and policies, the variations in endowments within the denominations undermines concepts such as "Presbyterian" or "Methodist" colleges; within each major denominational category the range of endowments was too great. Although the new and minor denominations did not acquire the great endowments of some of the older denominational colleges, a study of the intereaction between denominational resources in general and the regional location of a college is necessary to understand the variations in endowment funds and other resources of the colleges.

The value of buildings and grounds, libraries, and even faculty salaries, were also unequally distributed. The value of buildings and grounds per student increased over four and one–half times in the six decades, the average value in the late 1850s in constant–dollars becoming almost twelve hundred dollars per student. Most institutions seemed to have had buildings and grounds worth at least twenty–five thousand dollars after the first few years of their existence, but some of the new Western colleges in the 1850s were able to erect buildings only because they relied on student labor and cheap local lumber supplies. But even with this minimal average investment, the disparities in facilities remained. As with endowments, the older denominations and their Eastern colleges had the most amenities to offer their students and with which to impress their communities. Harvard and Columbia led the way with values of over one million dollars, followed by the larger state institutions, such as Michigan and the University of Virginia. The number of library books had a similar distribution, ranging from Harvard's one hundred thousand volumes to the few hundred in the Southern and Western colleges. Scientific equipment was probably more unequally distributed because of the high costs of such collections and instruments. The cost of scientific equipment was so great that minimal "cabinets" and surveying tools cost more than the entire libraries of many institutions, and observatories were beyond the financial reach of the majority of the colleges.[58]

Faculty salaries and benefits and the size of faculties were also conditioned by the distribution of economic resources. Salaries in the 1850s ranged from three thousand dollars a year plus firewood and housing to five hundred dollars a year without free housing. The prestigious urban colleges in the East and a few of the state institutions in the elitist South paid their average professors close to three times what was paid to professors in the best–paying colleges in the Midwest, such as the University of Michigan. These income differences were compounded by the fact that the lowest paying institutions were those most likely to have to suspend payments to their instructors or to substitute shares in the institution for cash salaries.[59] (Table 1.22)

Stated average faculty salaries were significantly different among the regions, but there also was an important difference between the colleges supported by the various denominations. New England colleges paid relatively high salaries and the known minimum faculty income in the region was as great as the highest salary in the Midwest. The South was marked by great inequalities. The instructors at the elite state institutions received salaries close to those paid in New England, but professors in denominational colleges were promised less than one–fifth of their government–supported colleagues. The poorer denominations tended to provide much lower incomes to their faculties than did the established denominations.

The average size of faculties in American colleges remained small during the 1850s. The few large faculties in the liberal arts colleges contained about twenty members and even the University of Michigan and the University of Virginia, schools dedicated to the idea of specialization,

Table 1.22

Known Salaries 1850's,
By Denomination and Region
(? = Poor data recovery)

	Salaries	
	High	Low
By Denomination:		
Baptist	$1,500	$ 800
Methodist	1,600	800
Presbyterian	2,200	500
Congregational	3,000	1,000
State	2,500	1,000
Lutheran	750	500
Episcopalian	3,000	?
Non-Denominational	850	750
German Reformed	500	?
By Region:		
New England	3,000	1,200
Middle Atlantic	3,000	750
South Atlantic	2,500	500
Southwest	2,000	500
Midwest	1,200	500

did not exceed this limit. Most institutions in the West and South had between four and six members, a faculty that could not pretend to teach more than the essentials. And most of the faculty members were ministers, the usual exception being the individual who was hired to teach a foreign language if it was offered by the college. The ministerial background of faculties was a natural outcome of two conditions in the country. First, they were the largest group of men with high investments in formal education and, second, their careers as ministers were compatible with college teaching. Ministers could transfer from teaching to ministerial work without jeopardizing their futures. College teaching was, in fact, a means of advancement to better-paying ministerial posts. And ministers, especially in the new areas of the country, were the only men with the economic support and the time schedules allowing participation in the rather risky profession of teaching. Few colleges in the country could offer enough money to induce qualified professionals in other fields to forego their incomes while indulging in full–time teaching in a rural area.[60]

There was not only a small number of faculty, but there were few students, as well. The largest institutions in the country had no more than four hundred students and these colleges were concentrated in the East. Colleges in the Midwest and South were considered large if they had one hundred students, and most had between twenty–five and eighty. In their early years, institutions in the newer regions enrolled less than twenty students in their regular college program. These small student bodies could not support large faculties and could not, therefore, support specialized instruction.[61]

Despite the problems of support and the resulting crude and unstable conditions of the colleges in the 1850s, there had been improvements in the liberal arts colleges over the sixty years. The value of facilities per student had increased fourfold; the value of endowments per student had increased three times over what it had been in 1800; and the established colleges had maintained and even increased faculty salaries over the years. The constant–dollar expenditures per student had more than doubled, as had the instructional costs per student. The student to faculty ratios stabilized at approximately one faculty member to twenty students in the institutions with any longevity. In fact, a greater percentage of the national expenditures on education were committed to higher education before the Civil War than after it.[62]

The colleges had become more varied and flexible. The classical curricula was modified significantly and some colleges began to devote attention to training and research in the advanced sciences. The supposedly conservative schools, such as Harvard, Yale, Dartmouth, and Columbia, made investments in schools of science and chemistry by the 1850s. However, even these colleges demanded separate funding for the new departments because of the possible demands such costly programs might make on the budgets of the schools.[63]

But these advances, in the context of the educational economics of the period, led educational leaders into a dilemma. The increased costs of modernized education were making the colleges less accessible to many segments of the American population. Advocates of more changes in the system, especially those who were so impressed by the educational systems of Europe, were demanding alterations that would be even more costly. The colleges were already subsidizing students at a level equal to that of the very liberal California state system in the late 1950s and

1960s, and the traditional sources of support for the colleges, primarily the denominations, were finding it more and more difficult to provide support equal to rising expectations. Average tuition and fees in the liberal arts colleges during the 1850s were three times what they had been in 1800, and this constant–dollar rise was pricing education above the level of what many of the poor–but–respectable students could bear. Not only tuition, but the costs of room and board were rising faster than the incomes of most Americans, making it much more difficult for self–supporting students to attend college. The only institution in the country that had both a modernized education and low tuition was the University of Michigan. The other leading modernizing colleges and their departments were charging as much as three to four times the average tuition of the 1850s.[64]

The average direct cost of going to college, tuition, fees and room and board, rose from one–third of a skilled manual laborer's income in 1800 to approximately 60 percent in 1860. Attendance at one of the better modern schools in the East was precluded because the costs of education exceeded the total income of such a worker by the 1850s. The son of a farm laborer faced similar trends. Because of the rise in living expenses and the level of wages of rural teachers, it was becoming more difficult for a hard–working young man to save enough from a combination of several years of full–time work plus part–time teaching between semesters to finance himself through the inexpensive institutions of the 1850s.[65]

Income from some occupations was increasing at a faster rate than were the costs of higher education. But as the level of wealth increased with the commercialization of agriculture and the spread of commerce and trade, the distributions of income and wealth in America became more and more unequal. The new economy did begin to create a rather broadly based middle class, but it also left many with few chances to participate in the new lifestyles and in the modernizing educational system. The wave of protest concerning higher education may have been caused by the escalating costs of modern higher schooling, and the emergence of new institutions, such as the normal school, may well have been motivated by the new economic burdens of modern education, rather than by objections to classical learning or other internal aspects of the existing colleges.[66]

The increasing costs of higher education posed a serious problem. Because of the lack of secure, equitable, and liberal subsidies for the colleges, there was little higher education and its leaders could do to stop the trend towards elitism among the colleges. And despite the advances of the period, many colleges, especially those in the poorer areas of the country, remained unstable and unable to fulfill many of the demands by various groups for even more modernized and therefore expensive higher education. The country remained without a single school able to offer a doctoral degree: only a handful of the colleges could support professional scholarship; and technical and modern agricultural education remained both to be defined and adequately financed.[67]

The traditional historians of higher education, however, assumed that these problems of definition and financing had ready–made solutions available well before the onset of the Civil War. But their assumption that twentieth–century conditions, structures, and ideas were in operation in the antebellum period was wrong and its continued use only serves to make the history of early higher education an ahistorical and normative exercise. The use of the assumptions concerning the availability and applicability of modern ideas and institutions was one of the reasons why scholars such as Tewksbury dichotomized the history of higher education. The assumptions about social and educational conditions before and after the Civil War led to insensitivity to the motives, contributions, and nature of the antebellum college movement.

Although much more detailed historical work must be done to document the history of education after the Civil War, there is now every reason to believe that it was post–Civil War America that witnessed the great explosion in the number and instability of small liberal arts colleges and the spread of elitism among them. Enough studies have been accumulated to show that the alternatives to liberal arts colleges took much longer to develop than the old historiography intimated. The spread of high schools, the development of viable technical and agricultural colleges, and the institutionalization of the university ideal came much later in the nineteenth century than the dichotomization of higher education suggested.[68]

The use of the construct, the antebellum college, with its in–built assumptions about the condition and possibilities of American education before and after the Civil War, made many historians insensitive to the goals, needs, and contributions of the antebellum colleges and their sponsors, especially those in the smaller towns of America. By assuming that every educational institution with the term "college" in its title was designed to compete with what the historians viewed as the legitimate higher educational institutions, they misinterpreted the reasons why the institutions were founded. And the assumption that the educational profile of antebellum America could have matched the reform ideals if only the antebellum colleges had not been founded led to invalid historical evaluations of the colleges.

There were examples of pretentious institutional foundings. Paper–colleges were established with grandiose titles and few resources in areas with so little population that the institutions could not have supported themselves. But projected institutions such as Matagorda University in

Texas, Newton University in Baltimore, or the Protestant University of America in Ohio, were examples of attempts to plan for the future and to establish the type of modernized institution demanded by the critics of early higher education. There was little difference between these schools and others that were applauded by historians except success. The University of Michigan was begun based on one of the most fantastic educational plans and philosophies ever known to America; the University of Virginia might well have gone the way of Matagorda University; and the University of California was envisioned when California was still a rugged frontier area. But most of the antebellum colleges were begun with more humble goals.[69]

The founders of the most frequently condemned colleges were filling an educational void in America. The expansion of the colleges, especially in the rural areas, came at a time when government was not providing the type of education desired by many segments of the population. Local and voluntary sources sponsored the development of higher education, education above the primary level, during an historical period when few organizations besides those of the denominations could organize and distribute the necessary support. By the time America had an educational elite and enough consensus and wealth to allow the spread of high schools and more specialized "higher" education, the sponsors of the small colleges had developed a vested interest in the preservation of their institutions. But the educational biases of many historians, especially those concerning efficiency, professionalism, and objectivity, determined that they treat these vested interests as illegitimate. Such judgments were defended as purely objective by the argument that the threatened position of the colleges was the result solely of natural and determinant forces, rather than of policy decisions which were based upon the concept that the university model was the only one which fit the needs of all types of students and institutions.

Much of the traditional history of antebellum higher education seems to be a justification of conscious decisions such as those to withhold governmental support from "denominational" colleges, to concentrate funds for higher education in a few institutions, and to centralize the administration of the colleges. Tewksbury's tendency to define the early nineteenth–century "college" in twentieth–century terms was not only an indication of his ahistorical approach, but a means through which the deficiencies of a decentralized system could be demonstrated. By assuming that a charter indicated the intention to found what we now define as a college and to classify failures on the basis of non–recognition as a full–fledged college in the twentieth century, his work could only show a determined outcome of educational chaos.[70]

Chapter 2

Enrollments

The thesis that enrollments were declining is critical to the traditional interpretations of the antebellum colleges. Both the intellectual–meritocratic historians such as Hofstadter and egalitarian critics cited studies by Henry Barnard and Francis Wayland to show that the colleges were not keeping pace with population growth and that many states and colleges within them were facing a decline of the absolute number of students.[1] Although the estimates of enrollments in the early and midnineteenth century were based upon the experience of New England and although the critics of higher education complained about the growth of colleges in the country (which implies enrollment increases) Barnard's and Wayland's estimates and conclusions were accepted as accurate and as representative of the entire nation.[2]

With the acceptance of the thesis of declining enrollments, historians focused upon trying to explain the failure of higher education. Following the logic of Francis Wayland, they blamed the supposed decline on the rigidity of curricula and assumed that the American society and economy were ready to generate large numbers of students if and when the colleges turned to the teaching of practical and professionally linked subjects, subjects that would increase the employment potential of students in business and industry.[3] Thus critics and historians, although conceding the importance of the increased numbers of foreign-born young men to the decline of the percentage of the population enrolled, focused upon factors internal to the colleges.

Wayland's logic dominated the historical approach to the colleges. His reports coincided with a populistic desire for pure vocational education, and his assumptions about the society, the economy, and higher education were accepted by other reformers and later historians. He assumed a great unfulfilled and effective demand for higher education; he assumed that the colleges could easily throw off the outdated components of the traditional curricula and replace them with more practical but intellectually legitimate courses; and he assumed that New England's situation was typical of the country as a whole or that its advanced stage of development predicted the future of enrollments in the rest of the nation. But more important was his assumption that enrollments in the liberal arts colleges had actually declined during the antebellum period.[4]

A very careful and conservative recount of the numbers of students in the male or coeducational liberal arts colleges yields a very different conclusion about enrollments. The new estimates, which included only male students in the regular programs that led to a bachelor's degree and which excluded some thirty of the two hundred forty–one colleges because they were suspected to be academies, indicates that enrollments were increasing both absolutely and relatively. Although some New England colleges were experiencing declines in enrollment, the reasons for both gains and losses in the numbers of students were much more complex than those put forward by critics such as Wayland. The new estimates do not support the thesis that the major determinants of enrollment levels in the antebellum period were curricula or entrance requirements. (Tables 2.1, 2.2)

The liberal arts colleges, although narrowing the range of ages of their students, experienced a fourteenfold increase of enrollments in the six decades. And, between 1800 and 1860, the percentage of the young white males of the country who entered the colleges more than doubled. Using the number of white males between fifteen and twenty years old as the population base (because the census directly tabulated that group in many years) leads to the estimate that enrollments rose from 0.6 percent to 1.18 percent over the sixty years. The use of the age group between fifteen and twenty–five as the population base decreases the percentage estimates but does not change the trends of enrollment.

TABLE 2.1

Enrollments in Regular Programs of American Liberal Arts Colleges for Beginning Years of Each Decade, 1800-1860, Enrollments as Percent of White Males Age 15-20 and Percent Change of Absolute Number of Enrollments

	1800	1809-1810	1819-1820	1829-1830	1839-1840	1849-1850	1859-1860
n	1156	1939	2566	4647	8328	9931	16600
%	0.59	0.69	0.65	0.78	1.05	0.91	1.18
% Change		68	32	81	79	19	67

If the students of the partial, English, scientific, and other irregular programs are added to the numbers who chose the regular academic programs in the colleges, the population percentage for 1860 rises to 1.33 percent. And if a crude control for the foreign–born is used to eliminate those who were unlikely to enroll in any type of higher education because of language, education, and economic difficulties, the ratio of college students to young males is increased to 1.6 students for every one hundred young men. Thus, the percentage of America's young males who chose to enter liberal arts colleges increased at least 200 percent and perhaps as much as 250 percent between 1800 and 1860.

The new estimates, based upon a search through the records and histories of all the institutions, are lower than those previously published. Other estimates of the number of students in the 1850s have ranged from twenty to thirty thousand. The higher estimates are perhaps the result of the inclusion of irregular students, those in military schools, or all the students enrolled in a collegiate institution. Students who were in the primary, female, or preparatory departments of the colleges were rigorously excluded in this study.[5]

To twentieth–century Americans, enrollment levels of less than two persons per one hundred may seem extremely low and might be interpreted as proof of the failure of the liberal arts colleges. But the enrollment percentages were high in the context of the midnineteenth century. For example, ministers, professors, editors, physicians, and lawyers accounted for 1.58 percent of the American work force in 1860. If this percentage is used to predict enrollments, although few professionals had to attend college, over 80 percent of the expected number of students were enrolled in the regular programs of the liberal arts colleges.[6] In 1900, after what has been described as a major and progressive revolution in American higher education, the record was not any better; and, perhaps, it was worse. Enrollment in all institutions of higher education, including female, normal, professional, and technical colleges, was between 3.6 and 4.0 percent of the relevant age group. Professionals comprised 4.5 percent of the work force.[7] And high school graduates comprised approximately 6 percent of the age group.[8]

The antebellum enrollment levels also seem high when the distribution of wealth is considered. The American economic order had not yet generated the abundance that would make comparative luxuries such as higher education commonplace. In 1860, 4 percent of the adult males in the United States had a total estate large enough so that if all of it were invested at 5 percent, the returns could support one student through college with no economic difficulty. But total estate was comprised of all assets, mainly personal property and real estate. Most men's estates were their homes and they had little liquid wealth. Therefore, far less than 4 percent of American families could have gained a return on their holdings that was large enough to provide for higher education for even one of their children. A reasoned guess is that 2 percent of American families could have called upon savings to provide significant support for their children's higher education. This, however, may be a high estimate because it is now felt that the midnineteenth century was the highpoint of the concentration of wealth in America.[9] And from what is known about the salaries of professionals during the period, there were few heads of households who could have easily supported their children through college from their immediate incomes.[10]

The economics of the early nineteenth century did impose severe constraints on the growth of enrollments, but other forces outside the control of educators conditioned the history of increase in the number of students. The growth of total enrollment and the percentage of the young males in college did not progress evenly over the period. Demographic trends, the pattern and timing of population migration and college location, and the social, political, and economic conditions of the country led to uneven growth.

Between 1800 and 1810, the number of students increased 68 percent. But the percentage of young men enrolled grew by only 17 percent because of the increase in the age group. The next decade, the 1810s, was critical for higher education. Perhaps because of the turmoil of the conflict with England and then the westward migration and the economic boom followed by collapse, there was only a 32 percent increase in enrollments. The continued growth of the number of young men in the society combined with the social and economic problems of the decade to lower the student–to–population ratio, and, in many areas, altered the nature and goals of the students.

Despite the panic of 1819 and the first rumblings of Jacksonian democracy, the 1820s were encouraging years for the American colleges. But the near doubling of the number of students did not mean that all colleges ended the decade with optimism about the future. The expansion of colleges into new areas of the country accounted for much of the growth, and, although New England's newer colleges had adjusted to increased enrollments in the early 1820s, the region faced what appeared to many to be a permanent decline beginning in the middle of the decade. (Table 2.2)

Fears for the colleges of New England and perhaps for the colleges of the rest of the country were short lived. A near doubling of the nation's students and a 35 percent increase in the percent of the age group that was enrolled in the schools occurred in the 1830s. And, despite the economic debacle of the late 1830s, growth continued into the 1840s.

But something happened in the last years of that decade. Enrollments sharply dropped, so much so that the last year of the decade saw only

TABLE 2.2

Absolute Number of Students Enrolled in Each Region, Enrollments in Each Region as a Percentage of White Males Age 15-20 in the Region and Percentage Increase of Absolute Numbers of Students for Beginning Academic Year of Each Decade, 1800-1860

		1800	1810	1820	1830	1840	1850	1860
New England	n	549	967	1150	1451	2035	1926	2606
	%	1.22	1.79	1.51	1.29	1.68	1.28	1.67
	% Change		76	19	26	40	-05	35
Middle Atlantic	n	347	460	691	1171	1881	2316	3446
	%	0.72	0.64	0.59	0.58	0.79	0.78	0.93
	% Change		32	50	69	61	23	49
South Atlantic	n	205	406	520	870	1326	1895	3324
	%	0.38	0.71	0.64	0.63	1.11	1.28	1.90
	% Change		98	29	67	52	42	75
South-west	n	50	81	205	762	1840	2272	3184
	%				0.91	1.52	1.20	1.21
	% Change	.				141	23	40
Midwest	n	-	-	-	293	946	1522	3961
	%	-	-	-	0.38	0.60	0.59	0.94
	% Change					222	61	160

one thousand more students enrolled than in the last year of the 1830s. Again, New England was the hardest hit. And as in the 1820s, it would take the lead in bemoaning the condition and nature of American higher education.[11] The decrease in enrollments during the middle and late 1840s was so great that the percentage of young males in the colleges actually declined, and the 19 percent growth in the absolute number of students in the 1840s, compared to the 80 percent increases of the 1820s and 1830s, seemed to foreshadow the end of liberal education.

There was another outburst of pessimism and protest by educators, especially those in New England. But in the 1850s people became optimistic over the future of the liberal arts colleges. The growth of the number of students returned to the levels of the 1820s and 1830s and the percent of the age group enrolled reached the period's highest level. The growth rate of the 1850s was so high that if its 67 percent increase had continued, the early twentieth–century liberal arts colleges of the country would have had more male students than were actually enrolled in all of the institutions devoted to higher education in 1900.[12]

Enrollments increased in all regions of the country during the antebellum years, but the rates of growth and the resulting enrollment levels in the regions varied. Inequalities in enrollments remained despite the growth of both higher and lower education in the various regions. Some of the inequality, however, may be explained by student migration patterns. Midwestern and Middle Atlantic students, for example, tended to migrate to New England for their education, lowering the enrollment ratios for their regions. And a significant number of the remaining disparities in enrollment ratios are explained when controls for wealth, age distributions, and the foreign–born are used. (Table 2.2)

New England deserves special attention because the history of its colleges was the basis for most generalizations concerning enrollment trends during the antebellum period and because the previous analyses of its enrollment history were used for both the explanation and evaluation of early liberal education. The new estimates of enrollments and the examination of the old explanations do not support the accepted idea that curricula and entrance requirements were the keys to the success or failure of the various New England colleges. The analysis of the enrollment trends in the region, in fact, raises more questions as to the reasons for college selection than may be answered by any available information. Much more research will have to be conducted before the enrollment histories of the various colleges can be explained.

New England had been the center of American higher education and in 1810 it had an enrollment ratio higher than the national average of 1860. It remained as the region with the greatest gross enrollment ratios, but it had the lowest growth rates for both absolute and relative enrollments over the sixty years. And, considering the stage of social and economic development of the region, it had the greatest inequalities of enrollments among its states.

New England began the nineteenth century with both the greatest number of students and the highest enrollment ratios. It retained its foremost position until the 1830s when the appearance of large numbers of colleges in the other regions threatened its numeric dominance and, perhaps, the security of its educators. And although it had enrollments of close to 2 percent in 1860, it experienced several crisis which caused alarm and an outpouring of rhetoric aimed at politicians, educators, and the general public. (Tables 2.2, 2.3)

The 1800s were the years of the most rapid expansion of New England's student population; in ten years the number of students increased by 70 percent. New England was unable to match that expansion in the remainder of the antebellum period. The 1810s and 1820s were decades of less than moderate growth and of severe crises within many of the colleges. Apparently, the region was hurt by Jeffersonian policies and the War of 1812, and the economic boom of the post–war period did not stimulate a recovery of enrollments. The growth rate dropped to 20 percent in the 1810s, one–half of what it had been, and the region's colleges were saved only by an influx of new types of students whose attendance may have been caused by the loss of opportunities for young men as a result of the war and the rise of Western economic competition.[13] But the new students could not fully compensate for the decline, and in 1820 New England's enrollment ratio dropped below the national average of 1860.

In one respect the 1820s were years of astounding recovery for New England. During the early years of the decade enrollments increased. But by the last years of the 1820s a sharp decline of attendance at many of the established colleges in the area resulted in a ratio that was close to what had been achieved in 1800, 1.3 percent. The furor that led to the Yale Report and the many attempts to make the colleges more attractive during the late 1820s were the product of a very real threat.[14]

TABLE 2.3

Enrollments in New England, Enrollments as a Percentage of White Males Age 15-20 and Percent Change of Absolute Number of Enrollments, for Beginning Years of Each Decade, 1800-1860

	1800	1810	1820	1830	1840	1850	1860
n	549	967	1150	1451	2035	1926	2606
%	1.22	1.79	1.51	1.29	1.68	1.28	1.67
% Change		76	19	26	40	-05	35

But before any radical changes were implemented by the colleges, New England's enrollments rebounded. In spite of the growing competition from colleges in other regions and the flow of the foreign–born into New England, the number of students increased by 40 percent and the enrollments jumped to 1.68 percent during the 1830s. They continued to climb in the early 1840s, but then an inexplicable decline hit most the colleges in the later years of the decade. The enrollment ratio plummeted, and the region experienced a decrease in the absolute number of students.

As in the crisis of the late 1820s, demands for reform, especially for a reorientation of the colleges to the needs of future businessmen, spread throughout the academic establishment. But, as in the 1820s, before many such reforms could be defined and implemented, enrollments grew. Total numbers increased by over one–third, and, controlling for the foreign–born, New England's enrollment ratio exceeded that of the 1810s. In 1860, total liberal arts enrollments in New England reached almost 2 percent.

The threats to the New England colleges in the late 1820s and late 1840s led many of its educational leaders to turn to an early version of a socioeconomic explanation of their enrollment problems. Leaders such as Francis Wayland explained what he perceived as permanent decreases in enrollment as the product of the irrelevance of higher education to the emerging economic order of New England and demanded, among other reforms, that colleges become tied to the business world.[15] But his and similar theses give inadequate explanations of New England's enrollment history. Much more than a thesis of simple economic change is needed to account for New England's enrollment trends. Institutions directly connected to the occupational world, such as technical, medical, and law schools, faced similar enrollment problems, indicating that more complex socioeconomic factors were at work.

The region was facing more limits on the growth of enrollments than a simple economic or deterministic argument would suggest. It was much more difficult than the reformers thought to achieve a direct functional relationship to business and industry. The history of the attempts to implement the demands for an increased tie to capitalism in New England indicate that other social and economic conditions were as or more immediately important than reformed curricula or the lowering of entrance requirements.

A list of the immediate limits on the increase of enrollments in New England should begin with the realization that the region's native population was not growing fast enough to provide its colleges with young men to increase an already high enrollment level. New England's young white male population grew 20 percent between 1840 and 1860, compared to a 77 percent increase across the nation. And over 14 percent of its young men were of foreign birth in 1850. The high percentage of usually poor and ill–educated youth combined with the famous New England out–migration to reduce the absolute number of potential students in the region.[16]

The number of young men enrolled in schools of higher education in New England, furthermore, was close to the limits imposed by the level and distribution of income and wealth. Its approximately 2 percent figure for liberal arts enrollments matches the reasoned guess as to the percent of families who could support college students. And New England was the leading region in the nation in the development of alternative forms of "higher" education. Its high schools, professional, and normal schools, as well as its rapidly changing preparatory schools, not only prepared students for college but satisfied educational demands which, in earlier years, could only have been fulfilled by the colleges. As well as these influences, the increasing admission standards of the New England colleges led them to narrow the range of ages of admittance, reducing even further the numbers of possible students.[17]

Another factor influenced the enrollment history of the region, and it was extremely important to the determination of curricula and orientation of the New England institutions. Its colleges had been rescued by a sudden, at least relative, rise in the demand for ministerial training in the 1810s. But the social and demographic conditions of New England and the appearance of competing colleges in other regions led to a decline in the demand for ministerial candidates after the 1830s. While the education of men who would enter the ministry remained as both an opportunity and pressure for the colleges, their expansion was limited by the declining regional market for ministers.

Between 1850 and 1860, New England added fewer than six hundred men to its number of ministers and this 12 percent increase (including Catholic priests) was far below the national average of 40 percent. One reason for the decline in demand was that New England had become saturated with ministers. The national ratio for ministers to young white males age fifteen to twenty in 1860 was one to thirty–eight, but New England had one minister for every twenty–four young men.[18]

Many of the New England colleges had been dependent upon ministerial candidates and the outside economic support they generated, and the schools had accommodated themselves to their training. But the high–point of future ministers as a percentage of all students was reached in the 1820s and 1830s, as illustrated by Table 2.4.[19] By the 1850s only Wesleyan and Amherst produced 40 percent or more ministers, and five of the twelve established New England colleges produced less than 20 percent. However, the early decline in the demand for ministers is also

TABLE 2.4

Mean Percentage of Alumni Entering the Ministry and Standard Deviation. New England Colleges. Calculated Across Colleges By Decade

	1800's	1810's	1820's	1830's	1840's	1850's
$\overline{X}$	24	37	42	34	26	23
Q	6	13	13	11	11	11

an indication that many of the colleges had adjusted to train students destined for other occupations. The enrollment increases of the 1850s were accomplished in spite of the decline in the need for ministerial candidates.

Although general forces such as slowed population growth, out–migration, and shifts in occupational goals by students help explain the limits on enrollments in New England, they do not explain other aspects of the region's enrollment history. Other factors must be considered in order to understand the different growth patterns among the New England states, the timing of enrollment crises and recoveries, and the migration of students within the region.

The New England states and their colleges had very different enrollment histories. All increased the number of students they serviced over the sixty years, but the growth in some states was negligible. The enrollment ratios, even if the number enrolled who came from within each state is considered, were very unequal. Some of the states, in fact, experienced declines in ratios over the period. (Tables 2.5, 2.6, 2.7, 2.8, 2.9, 2.10, 2.11, 2.12)

Most of New England's states had enrollment ratios above the national average, but the range within the region was always great. In the late 1810s, the ratios ranged from 0.10 to 3.75 percent and in the 1850s from 0.39 to 3.3 percent, a relatively constant spread, but some of the states had important reductions in the percent of possible students they enrolled. Rhode Island, Wayland's state, never regained its high ratios of the 1810s; Vermont hit its peak in the same decade; and New Hampshire never again achieved its late 1800s enrollment level. Maine, despite valiant attempts, barely exceeded its 1839–1840 ratio in the 1850s. Only Massachusetts and Connecticut were able to maintain or surpass earlier

TABLE 2.5

Students Enrolled in Various New England States as Percent of White Males Age 15-20 in State for Beginning Year of Each Decade, 1800-1860

State	PERCENT 1800	1810	1820	1830	1840	1850	1860
Connecticut	1.7	2.0	2.7	2.8	3.7	3.1	3.3
Maine	0	0.2	0.1	0.2	0.4	0.3	0.4
Massachusetts	1.4	1.7	1.4	1.6	1.5	1.4	1.8
New Hampshire	1.2	2.8	1.3	0.9	1.8	1.1	1.8
Rhode Island	1.0	3.3	3.8	2.0	3.2	2.1	2.3
Vermont	1.1	1.6	1.7	0.8	1.7	1.2	1.5

TABLE 2.6

Estimate of Mean Percent of All Students Enrolled in New England Colleges Coming From Within New England and Standard Deviation Across Colleges By Decade

	1800's	1810's	1820's	1830's	1840's	1850's
$\overline{X}$	91	90	79	86	76	70
Q	8	10	17	13	13	17

ratios, and Connecticut, even with the great influx of students, may well have had a higher enrollment ratio in the 1830s than in the 1850s. (Table 2.5)

Much of the inequality among New England's states is accounted for by out–of–region and out–of–state enrollments and the numbers of foreign–born in the states. New England's colleges, especially the larger

TABLE 2.7

All Students Enrolled in New England Colleges And Students Enrolled in New England Colleges from Within New England as Percent of Native White Males in Respective States For Academic Year 1859-60

	% All Students/ Native White Males Age 15-20	% In-Region Students/ Native White Males Age 15-20
Connecticut	3.3	1.6
Maine	0.4	0.4
Massachusetts	1.8	1.0
New Hampshire	1.8	1.5
Rhode Island	2.3	1.7
Vermont	1.5	0.8

TABLE 2.8

Estimates of Percent of Students Enrolled Within Various New England States from Outside of the Respective State Calculated Across Colleges By Decades

	P E R C E N T					
State	1800's	1810's	1820's	1830's	1840's	1850's
Connecticut	18	29	38	47	37	53
Maine	0	1	3	8	13	6
Massachusetts	12	10	25	27	25	33
New Hampshire	1	0	1	8	7	18
Rhode Island	4	8	6	16	13	26
Vermont	11	16	30	15	25	21

ones, became dependent upon out–of–region students and the success of colleges, as well as their size, hinged upon attracting students from beyond their immediate geographic area. Compensating for out–of–region students reduces the range of enrollment ratios and highlights the dependency of some of the states on inter–regional migration.[20] (Tables 2.6, 2.7, 2.8)

At midcentury, New England was a significant importer of students and the particular states that the students chose affected the enrollment ratios. Geography seems to have played a significant role in the determination of the selection patterns of the in–migrants. Vermont became heavily dependent upon students from up–state New York; Connecticut drew from New York city; Massachusetts drew from the Middle Atlantic states; and Rhode Island attracted men from the border South and the Middle Atlantic. But migration to the New England colleges was not confined to inter–regional movements. There was a very important intra–regional flow that also affected the enrollment ratios of the states. Table 2.11 reflects the relative attractiveness of the various New England states to their own potential students. (Tables 2.9, 2.10, 2.11) Because few New England students migrated from their home region for liberal arts educa-

TABLE 2.9

Estimates of Enrollments in Various New England States as Percent of White Males Age 15-20 in the Respective State 1860 For All Students Enrolled in the State and For Students Enrolled in the State Who Were from New England

	% All Enrollments	% Within New England Students
Connecticut	3.30	1.62
Maine	0.39	0.36
Massachusetts	1.80	1.02
New Hampshire	1.81	1.48
Rhode Island	2.28	1.67
Vermont	1.50	0.79

TABLE 2.10

Enrollments of Within-State Students for Various New England States as a Percentage of White Males Age 15-20 in the Respective States, 1859-60

Connecticut	0.79
Maine	0.28
Massachusetts	0.98
New Hampshire	0.83
Rhode Island	0.76
Vermont	0.75

tion, Table 2.11 suggests that over 30 percent of all the region's students chose education in another state in New England. And Table 2.11 indicates that the geographically isolated states were less able to retain their own students. The samples of students also suggest that the colleges of the states that were unattractive to students from outside New England were unattractive to potential students within their own borders.

The migration patterns of the New England students cannot be easily explained. The linear correlation between per capita property value by state and the percent of young white males enrolled in the various New England states was 0.93, but the lower correlations for students from the region, 0.80, and for enrollments from within the same state, 0.54, indicate that while students from outside of New England were attracted by the general wealth of a state, potential students from within the region and its various states based their selection of a particular college upon more subtle and complex factors. Distance from home to college, the denominational affiliation of a college, and its public image must have played a significant role in the decision making process of the local students.[21]

The profile of New England's states provides some insight into the nature and causes of enrollment trends within the region, but it is an analysis of the individual colleges in the context of the major enrollment crises that has to serve as the basis for challenging the simple functionalist thesis. The explanation of enrollment levels by differences in curricula, entrance requirements, or even college behavioral rules is unacceptable. And other factors expected to explain growth and decline in New England because of their compatibility with both functionalist and populistic theories proved to have little explanatory power. For example, tuition and fees, and the political and social orientation of the colleges do not account for New England's enrollment history in the antebellum period.[22]

A negative conclusion is all that emerges from the examination of the old economic–functionalist thesis and its implications. Beyond a general state level relationship between indicators of wealth and enrollments, the selection of colleges by students cannot be explained by available quantified data or by simplistic models of college selection.

New England faced three crises because of enrollment declines in the antebellum period. Each had different characteristics, but two of the three generated serious attempts to change the colleges. In the two later crises, those of the 1820s and the 1840s, several colleges instituted famous reforms (including some aspects unnoticed by historians) which fit with the demands of the functionalists. Because of this, the two later responses provide test cases for the old explanatory thesis.

TABLE 2.11

Enrollments of Students from a New England State Enrolled in Any United States College and Enrolled In A College Within Their Home State as: A) Percent of White Males in the Home State and; B) Percent of Native White Males in the Home State - 1859-60

	% In Any U.S. College		% From State Enrolled in State	
	A	B	A	B
Connecticut	1.11	1.96	0.79	1.59
Maine	0.59	0.62	0.28	0.30
Massachusetts	1.46	1.77	0.98	1.19
New Hampshire	1.15	1.22	0.83	0.88
Rhode Island	1.03	1.25	0.76	0.93
Vermont	1.34	1.48	0.75	0.82

The first crisis came in the second half of the 1810s and seems to have been the product of the dislocations caused by the policies leading to the war of 1812, the war, and its aftermath. This decline would have been catastrophic for New England's enrollments but the newer and rural colleges of the region, such as Williams, increased their enrollments, compensating for the declines at the established colleges. But this dislocation did not generate immediate cries for reform. It was the second, in the late 1820s, that led to demand for change and to the famous counter–argument to pleas for the teaching of practical subjects and liberalization of the colleges, the Yale Report.[23]

The 1820s crisis is difficult to explain by either political or economic events, but the Panic of 1819 may have had some delayed impact on decisions to invest in higher education. Beginning in the mid–1820s, the larger institutions faced serious declines in enrollments. Again, it was the continued growth of the "ministerial" colleges that saved New England from disaster. If the rural institutions had not prospered, there would have been an absolute decline in enrollments because Brown, Yale, Dartmouth, and Vermont and, later, Harvard, suffered.

In this crisis educators began to respond and demanded that the colleges liberalize. Some colleges did revise their programs. Harvard, for example, attempted to encourage enrollments by instituting an early and restricted, but still revolutionary, elective system.[24]

But the changes in the colleges do not account for the recovery of enrollments in the 1830s. Harvard had only slight increases in its number of students through the 1830s, while more conservative institutions had experienced appreciable growth. Yale and Dartmouth, for example, had important increases without instituting major reforms. Brown, under its aggressive and energetic president, Francis Wayland, did institute some changes, such as expanding the role of partial courses, but increased entrance requirements slowed its growth. Amherst, with its even broader reforms, had to adjust to significant decreases in the 1830s. At the same time, the colleges which continued their older curricula and programs grew or maintained their enrollments.[25] (Table 2.12)

The crisis of the 1840s provides a better test for the functionalist thesis because it led to or coincided with some of the most radical and well–publicized reforms of the antebellum period. The decline of the late 1840s was not peculiar to New England or to liberal arts colleges. Unlike the earlier crises, colleges everywhere were affected, as well as many of the medical and law schools. Perhaps the enrollment declines were caused by another delayed impact upon educational plans. The economic downturn of the late 1830s and early 1840s may have caused families to forego plans to send their young to higher schools. And the turmoil of the Mexican War may have had more of a direct influence. But whatever

TABLE 2.12

Percent Change in Size of Student Populations
of the Various New England Colleges
For the Period 1830-1860

College	P E R C E N T 1830-1840	1840-1850	1850-1860
Amherst	-20	-17	42
Bowdoin	227	11	25
Brown	84	-16	24
Colby	40	9	13
Dartmouth	130	-24	59
Harvard	-08	29	38
Middlebury	-16	-20	42
Trinity	-27	-13	-15
Vermont	206	-21	8
Wesleyan	168	-07	20
Williams	47	19	50
Yale	28	-07	30

the proximate causes, the decline was severe. It left New England with a 5 percent decrease in absolute enrollments, compared to 1839. The damage, however, was not confined to New England's liberal arts colleges; it affected the region's version of a technical school, Norwich, and it slowed the growth of its professional schools.[26]

The decline of the late 1840s was shared by all the states in New England. Four of the six states in the region had decreases in the number of students and all had declines in their enrollment ratios. Of the twelve established liberal arts colleges, eight had absolute reductions and the other four barely maintained their enrollments. In this crisis all types of liberal arts institutions experienced declines. Unlike the 1810s and 1820s, both old and new, urban and rural, and ministerial and secularly oriented colleges were affected. Only Williams, Amherst, and Harvard did not suffer significant decreases.

Even those institutions joined in a widespread reaction to what were considered long-term and universal trends endangering higher education. Harvard, Yale, Amherst, and Dartmouth opened some version of a scientific school and in varying degrees modified their undergraduate programs. All of the New England colleges continued to expand undergraduate training in pure and practical science, and even little Trinity College in Connecticut expanded the courses and programs open to its students.[27]

The most radical and historically noteworthy reforms were made by Francis Wayland at Brown University. Located at Providence, Rhode Island, an affluent urban center which was involved with the expansion of commerce and industry, Brown's environment made it a logical choice, it seemed, to prove the need for liberalization and modernization of the colleges.

Wayland instituted reforms more revolutionary than those that had been made at Harvard and Yale. The costs of the new science programs at Brown were supported by its regular budget, allowing charges for the new abstract and applied courses to be as low as those for the traditional program. Two of the country's most dynamic and innovative academic scientists, John A. Porter and William Norton, were hired to found the new departments of civil engineering and agriculture, and local experts were recruited to lecture on subjects such as metallurgy. An intense program was begun to advertise the college and to gather students from around the nation.[28] And Wayland did even more to open Brown to the new world of industry and to the new types of students envisioned by the reformers. Partial courses were expanded and entrance requirements were changed, allowing those without thorough training in the classical languages to enter the school. Traditional courses were modified to fit the needs of the ideal new student, as well. Thus Brown, under Wayland, seems to have fulfilled all the demands of the reformers, reforms that had been called for since at least the 1820s. Its low tuitions and attractive campus were the finishing touches and Brown stood ready to be the example that would save liberal education in New England.[29]

But the reforms failed. After a short burst of enrollment increases, Brown's student population returned to the size it had been in the late 1840s. And of those who entered during the short period when enrollments were increasing, a high percentage withdrew from the college within a few months. With the decline in enrollments, Brown's faculty, irked by what they claimed was a drop in student abilities, demanded that the reforms be reversed. The high costs of the new programs, faculty dissatisfaction, and decreasing enrollments convinced Brown's leaders to dismantle Wayland's new liberal arts college and to return to older, proved ways. Even Norton's and Porter's practical programs did not attract enough students, and they soon left the college.[30]

That Brown's experience was not an isolated example or that the failure of the reforms was due to faculty attitudes or administrative ineptitude is shown by the history of the reform college of the early postbellum period. Cornell University was founded in a state that had a long history of agitation for scientific and agricultural colleges. Several attempts at founding such institutions had failed before the Civil War because, many claimed, of inadequate financing. But Cornell began as one of the richest institutions in the United States and hired a renowned and enthusiastic faculty that was large enough to offer programs and specialized courses in all the pure and applied sciences.[31]

Cornell offered students an extremely expensive education at a very low cost. It did not demand preparation in the classical languages for many of its programs, and it prided itself on its orientation towards the common man. It awarded one hundred twenty–eight full scholarships in its first year, promised employment to all students who needed extra income, and proposed to lower the necessary economic investment in higher education by reducing the number of years needed for graduation. The college launched an intense recruitment campaign and even advertised in Europe and Australia. All the school districts of New York participated in a competitive scholarship program and Cornell's professors contacted the academics of America in order to entice qualified students to the new campus in upstate New York.

In its first year, before all of its buildings were completed, Cornell enrolled over four hundred students, making it one of the largest colleges in the country. And it had respectable growth after that. However, even with the highly liberalized policy that allowed students to structure their own programs, they did not select the expected subjects, did not stay the expected number of years, and did not enter the expected occupations after they left the college. Only a fraction of the students decided to complete even the short programs. Approximately 10 percent of the school's first freshman class graduated in either the three–or four–year programs and, it appears, many of the members of the first classes of the late 1860s and early 1870s left the school before completing a full year. Such behavior seemed to continue; 1873 had the school's largest graduating class until 1888.[32]

Cornell's early history also indicates that the reformers' prediction of a large and effective demand for practical and scientific training in the non–trade–school context was in error. Up through 1873–74 there were only two graduates in agriculture. Of the two hundred thirty–five graduates through 1874, forty took degrees in civil engineering, three in mechanical engineering, two in veterinary science, and one in architecture.[33]

A sample of the students of the first entering class, 1868, also suggests that students used the Cornell programs for very short stops in college and that they entered the traditional occupations and professions, with the exception of the ministry, in proportions similar to those of the antebellum period.[34]

As at Brown and Cornell, the changes at other colleges did not prove as successful as was hoped. Reform attempts do not explain the enrollments at the various colleges in New England. The advanced scientific programs begun at Harvard, Yale, and Dartmouth in the early 1850s did attract students, but not as many as envisioned, and Amherst abandoned its attempt at more advanced training. There is no indication that these advanced programs increased undergraduate enrollments.[35] The history of the reforms made in the 1850s in undergraduate programs also points to the inadequacy of the functionalist interpretation. Harvard, for example, had an appreciable increase in undergraduate enrollments in the 1850s. But this followed a tightening of its entrance requirements and the abandonment of many of the elective options it had allowed students since the 1830s. Its modern foreign language courses, one of the innovations demanded by those who thought such training would appeal to future international businessmen, cannot account for its greater attractiveness to students because such instruction had been offered by the college for decades.[36]

In contrast to Harvard's growth, was the serious decline at Trinity College. Its very important liberalizing reforms did not lead to success, but to a negative growth rate in the 1850s. And in contrast to both Harvard and Trinity, Williams, Bowdoin, and Colby, which instituted only moderate reforms at most, had significant growth throughout the later decades of the antebellum period. Perhaps the most puzzling case was the increase in enrollments at Dartmouth. Without great reforms, with an increase in tuition, and with no change in its geographic accessibility, Dartmouth had the greatest enrollment growth of all the New England colleges except Amherst, Williams, and Middlebury.[37] (Table 2.12)

Along with curricular change, little else seems to account for the recovery of enrollments in New England during the 1850s. No significant relationship was found between changes in the percent of students with homes outside the region and growth. There were no important changes in the age distributions of students in the various colleges, and recovery rates cannot be explained by changes in the percentages of rural or urban students in the institutions. From what little informatijon is available on the political and denominational preferences of students, growth and decline cannot be accounted for through such variables. The only indication of denominational influence is the lower recovery rates for the non–Congregational colleges of the region. The Baptist, Methodist, and Episcopalian institutions had lower growth during the 1850s, perhaps because of the competition from denominational colleges in the Middle Atlantic region.[38]

The history of future occupations of New England students had little relation to either curricular change or the recovery of the 1850s. Colleges such as Brown, Yale, and Harvard had a long history of increases in the percentage of students entering business, and curricular changes in the 1850s seem to have followed, rather than led, alterations in occupational destinations. All the colleges of New England had been moving towards the production of students who would enter the secular occupations since the 1820s and 1830s, including those which did not radically alter the traditional curricula. If Bailey Burritt's study of the occupations of New England's graduates is accepted, the history of the most technical occupation of the period, engineering, indicates that curricular change did not have a significant effect. Brown's students chose engineering as a major occupation more frequently both before and after the curricular reforms, and tiny Bowdoin College had a greater percentage of its students entering the profession than did Harvard.[39]

Even the relationship between the growth of enrollments and the costs of going to college in New England does not explain the recovery that was made in the 1850s. The correlations between the increase in percent enrolled and changes in tuition and absolute costs of college–going were in the correct direction, but they explain less than 2 percent of the variance in growth.[40]

One trend did appear in New England in the 1850s which may be related to curricular change. The sample of the students yielded estimates which indicate that New England students began to remain in their home states for education. But this is an ambiguous indicator. It may support the thesis that curricular change within the colleges led to greater student satisfaction with local schools, or it may be interpreted as a signal that the radical curricular reforms at schools such as Brown were unattractive to students within the region.[41]

The history of enrollments in the other regions of the country reinforces the conclusion that simple functionalist premises and assumptions about the results of curricular change are inadequate to explain differences in enrollments. The comparison of New England with the other regions indicates that there were forces outside of the control of educators which helped to determine enrollment levels and trends. Each of the regions had unique social and economic configurations which created important enrollment differences. Especially significant were the differences between North and South. While the Northern regions, for example, shared common relationships between levels of wealth and attendance, the Southern states remained a separate educational region.

An analysis of the apparent differences in enrollments among the regions suggest that the expansion of the numbers of colleges in the country had a positive effect. The rise of the antebellum colleges compensated, in many cases, for the low attraction of the older institutions of the various regions. The Middle Atlantic states, New York, New Jersey, and Pennsylvania, increased the number of regular liberal arts students tenfold, in the sixty years, but their gross enrollment ratios remained surprisingly low. Despite the increased number of colleges in the region, the Civil War approached with the Middle Atlantic region's enrollment ratio approximately a half that of New England's. Its growth rate for numbers of students, although the region's population was expanding, remained below New England's in the 1850s. However, the near 50 percent increase of that decade was appreciable. (Tables 2.13, 2.14, 2.15, 2.16, 2.17)

Unlike New England, the 1800s were not years of great expansion for the Middle Atlantic states. The region had to wait until the 1820s for the type of increase that was typical of New England. But while New England was suffering from the decline of the 1820s, the Middle Atlantic states increased their number of students by 70 percent. However, the increase in the number of young men in the region meant that its ratio continued to drop below the level of 1800 despite the availability of prestigious and developed institutions such as Princeton and Columbia.

Combined with a slowing of the growth of the age group, the expansion of the number of colleges in the region during the 1830s had a significant impact. Between 1830 and 1840, the region's enrollment ratio increased by over 35 percent and finally exceeded its 1800 level. The Middle Atlantic states were hurt in the late 1840s, but the drop in the growth of the numbers of students was not as severe as in New England. Total enrollments grew, the ratio stayed relatively constant, and the region's total enrollments exceeded those of New England for the first time. As in New England, the 1850s were years of renewed growth, but the region continued with what appeared to be an inability to support or attract a significant proportion of its population into formal higher education. (Table 2.13)

As in New England, there were enrollment differences among the Middle Atlantic states but the inequalities are, to an important degree, explained by student migrations, the percentages of foreign–born in each state, and variance in property values. The apparent differences among the states are reduced when out–of–state and out–of–region enrollments are controlled. The major cause of the spread of ratios was the attraction of Princeton University to students from other areas of the country. Applying estimates of the percentages of in–state students in the various colleges to the gross enrollment percentages reduces New Jersey's advantage, compresses the range of enrollment scores, and turns Pennsylvania into the region's leading provider of higher education.[42] (Tables 2.14, 2.15)

The importance of student migrations was almost matched by the influence of the foreign–born on enrollment in the three states. Compen-

TABLE 2.13

Absolute Number of Students Enrolled in Middle Atlantic Colleges, Enrollments as Percent of White Males Age 15-20, and Percentage Change in Absolute Enrollments. By Beginning Year of Each Decade, 1800-1860

	1800	1810	1820	1830	1840	1850	1860
n	347	460	691	1171	1881	2316	3446
%	0.72	0.64	0.59	0.58	0.79	0.78	0.93
% Change	0.32	0.50	0.69	0.61	0.23	0.49	

TABLE 2.14

Enrollments in Various Middle Atlantic States in 1860 As Percent of White Males Age 15-20 in the Respective State

New Jersey	1.67
New York	0.82
Pennsylvania	0.90

sating for the percent of the foreign–born in the age group in each state highlights the different limits on enrollment levels for each of them. For example, controlling for the foreign–born in New York raises its percentage enrolled by 40 percent while Pennsylvania's is adjusted by 17 percent. (Table 2.16) Perhaps as important for the history of higher education is that the differences among the Middle Atlantic states and the

Within-State Enrollments for Middle Atlantic States For 1860 as Percent of White Males Age 15-20 in the Respective State

New Jersey	0.67
New York	0.56
Pennsylvania	0.72

TABLE 2.16

Enrollments in Middle Atlantic States as Percent of Native White Males Age 15-20 in Respective States, 1860

New Jersey	2.04
New York	1.15
Pennsylvania	1.05

differences between New England and its neighboring region were the product of economic forces. Establishing controls for economic and nativity differences not only reduces the variation within the region but reveals the underlying similarity of the two areas. Controls for wealth levels suggest that the increase in the number of colleges in the Middle Atlantic states had a positive effect upon enrollments.

If, as in the historical literature, New England is taken as the norm, and its relationship between per capita property value and enrollment percentages is projected to the Middle Atlantic states, one of the major reasons for the enrollment differences between the two regions is revealed. Controlling for the foreign–born and out–of–state students, as well as for property values, significantly reduces the disparities of enrollment percentages. Instead of the approximately 100 percent enrollment ratio advantage of New England, the adjusted expectations indicate that the Middle Atlantic region had a much better attendance record and that its colleges were attractive and accessible to its population.[43] (Table 2.17)

The redefined expectations for enrollments in the Middle Atlantic states suggest that much of the criticism aimed at its colleges was misplaced. As in New England, liberal education was dependent upon social and economic conditions and limitations. Furthermore, its enrollments cannot be accounted for by the curricular–reform thesis. Too many of the colleges in the Middle Atlantic states had practical courses and liberal requirements, including "ministerial" colleges such as Hamilton in New York, to allow the increases of enrollments to be treated as the result of modernization by a particular set of institutions. Union College, often noted for its secular orientation, did have high growth during the decade, but its enrollments have been explained by highly respected scholars through reference to the college's toleration of students rejected by other institutions rather than its scientific programs.[44]

There were other differences among the Middle Atlantic states that indicate students were dissatisfied with available colleges in New York

TABLE 2.17

Actual and Expected Enrollments in Middle Atlantic States, 1860
Expected Enrollments Based Upon Application of Regression of New England Attendance By State to New England Per Capita Property Values By State for Categories of Enrollments to Middle Atlantic States

	All Students Enrolled/ Native White Males in State Age 15-20		In-State Students Enrolled/Native White Males in State Age 15-20	
	% Actual	% Expected	% Actual	% Expected
New Jersey	2.04	2.65	0.67	0.78
New York	1.15	1.64	0.56	0.67
Pennsylvania	1.05	1.69	0.72	0.68

and New Jersey. Based upon the estimates from the biographical sample, New York, with its relatively planned and centralized university system, was sending one student to New England for every three it enrolled within the state. In contrast, Pennsylvania, with its rather open chartering policy and high enrollment, was sending one to thirteen. New Jersey, offering Princeton and Rutgers to its young, sent students to New England in the same proportion as Pennsylvania, but had a low adjusted enrollment ratio.[45]

New England benefited from the discontent with Middle Atlantic institutions, especially in New York. New England sent only a few of its students to the Middle Atlantic states, and almost all of its migrants went to Union College—but it received sizable numbers. The flow of students from the Middle Atlantic states does not indicate that modernized curricula was the major attraction. Rather, geographic proximity and tuitions seemed to have been the significant influences. Conservative Yale was the most popular New England college and the smaller colleges of the region remained, in the 1850s, more attractive to students from the Middle Atlantic states than sophisticated Harvard College.[46]

Although educational profiles in the New England and Middle Atlantic regions become more similar than thought when some of the economic and social conditions in the regions are controlled, the American South continues to appear to be a separate educational region. For example, the regressions and correlations between per capita property values and enrollment ratios were very similar for New England and the Middle Atlantic, with the correlations in the low nineties, but the correlations for the South and its subregional groups of states hovered close to zero.[47] (Tables 2.18, 2.19, 2.20)

But even more startling, given the common image and fact of the deficient lower educational system of the South, are the high enrollment levels in the region. When the enrollments of students within the region are combined with the estimates of the numbers of Southern students who migrated to the North for liberal education, the results are enrollment levels higher than in the North.

Despite Hofstadter's image of the American Enlightenment and its consequences for higher education, the South Atlantic region began the nineteenth century with in–region enrollment ratios that were well below those of the North. They were at a level that matched those of the frontier years in the Midwest.[48] The established institutions of the region were unable to attract a large proportion of the young men of the South. (Table 2.18) But there was an increase in the number of students in the 1800s which doubled the enrollments as well as its 1800 enrollment percentage which had been one–third that of New England's. As in New England, the 1810s were years of much lower growth and there was a

TABLE 2.18

Enrollments in the South Atlantic and Southwestern Regions For Beginning Years of Each Decade, 1800-1860, Absolute Numbers, as Percent of White Males Age 15-20, and Percent Change of Absolute Number of Enrollments for Beginning Year of Each Decade

REGION	1800	1810	1820	1830	1840	1850	1860
South Atlantic							
n	205	406	520	870	1326	1895	3324
%	0.38	0.71	0.64	0.63	1.11	1.28	1.90
% Change		98	29	67	52	42	75
Southwest							
n	50	81	205	762	1840	2272	3184
%				0.91	1.52	1.20	1.21
% Change		-	-	-	141	23	40

decrease in the enrollment percentage. The South Atlantic rebounded in the 1820s, but the 1830s were years of only moderate growth. However, because of only a slight increase in the numbers of young men in the region, the percentage of population enrolled nearly doubled. The impact of the 1840s was not as great as in New England and increases of the number of colleges led to a small but significant growth of enrollments and enrollment percentages. The 1850s, with its continued addition of colleges in the region, led to a 75 percent increase in the number of students in the regular liberal arts programs. By 1860, the South Atlantic states had enrollments higher than the gross percentages in the Northern regions.

The Southwest was a frontier area for much of the antebellum period, but its enrollments were those of a developed region. The 1830s expansion led the area to an enrollment ratio in 1840 that was one of the highest in the nation. This may have been inflated by the lower age of admittance in the region, but the unadjusted percentage is well above those of the Middle Atlantic and South Atlantic areas. The closure of colleges in the region during the 1840s and the general decline of enrollments during the decade harmed education in the Southwest. Its enrollment growth slowed and the percentage of its young in the higher schools decreased. As in the other regions, however, the 1850s brought recovery. Despite the turmoil among its colleges, the Southwest ended the antebellum era with gross enrollment percentages that were larger than those in the Middle Atlantic and Midwestern states and with an absolute number of students greater than New England. Even when controls for foreign–born are applied to Northern enrollments, the Southern enrollment percentages remain higher than all other regions except New England. One result of the expansion of higher education in the South was a decline in the migration of Southern students to the North for their education. Estimates from the biographical sample suggest that students began to remain in the South well before the sectional crisis of the 1850s. However, a major decline in the percentage of students who went to Northern schools occurred in the decade of the Missouri Compromise and its political ramifications.[49] The estimated decline meant that approximately four hundred fifty Southern students were enrolled in Middle Atlantic and New England colleges in 1860. More Southern students went to the Middle Atlantic than to the New England colleges. And, as with the migration of Middle Atlantic students to New England, the flow was not in conformity with the thesis that modernized curricula improved enrollments. Princeton was dependent upon Southern students throughout the period and was the largest recipient of Southern young men; and Dickinson, Gettysburg, and Washington–Jefferson in Pennsylvania accepted relatively high proportions of Southern students. The migrants to New England were, it appears, more likely to select Yale rather than Harvard or the modernized Brown. The regional contact was in one direction. Even the rich and secular University of Virginia could not attract Northern students. (Table 2.19)

The migration patterns of Southern students provide weak support for the curricular thesis. Students from many areas of the South were attracted to the University of Virginia and its specialized programs, but the effect of reforms in the other states of the region indicate that the selection of a college by Southern students was the product of more than a college's program.

The history of students from Maryland and Delaware illustrate the problem of explaining college selection. These two states seem to have accounted for as much as one–third of all the students who migrated to New England and Middle Atlantic colleges in the 1850s. Their high migration rates did follow the general pattern of border states sending more students than interior states to the North, but their rates were exceptionally high. Following a trend seemingly set well before the Civil

TABLE 2.19

Estimates of Percent of All Southern Students Enrolled in New England and Middle Atlantic Colleges by Beginning Year of Each Decade

	1810	1820	1830	1840	1850	1860
%	16	20	11	8	9	7

War and which continued into the twentieth–century, Maryland and Delaware perhaps sent one student to the North for every three they educated within their own borders at the same time that most other Southern states, it appears, sent as few as one for every twenty native students.[50]

Maryland and Delaware were states with very different higher educational systems by the 1850s, despite the similarities in their migration percentages. Delaware had its version of a state university, one which had liberal curricula and which had hired some of the outstanding young scientific scholars to establish engineering and agricultural programs. Maryland, despite many attempts to found comprehensive colleges, such as the ambitious Newton University, had many colleges but none was noted for its modernized programs. And Delaware had a respectable total enrollment percentage compared to Maryland's estimated enrollment ratio of .79 percent. But both had a great number of young men dissatisfied with their states' educational offerings, and, it seems, those who left these states followed a similar logic in the selection of colleges. Both flowed to colleges in adjacent states with many from Maryland migrating to Delaware and the District of Columbia, but very few chose the institution which should have been their logical choice under the modernization thesis, the University of Virginia.[51]

As well as significant numbers of students who left from several of the Southern states, the South was marked by great enrollment ratio differences. In 1860, it contained states with the highest and the lowest enrollment percentages in the nation. And, there seem to be few ready explanations for many of the differences. In some cases, such as Texas, Florida, and Arkansas, frontier conditions and the competition of established colleges in developed states account for their low enrollments and their lack of colleges. Migration into states such as Virginia, North

Carolina, and the District of Columbia help explain their relatively high ratios. But many of the differences must remain unexplained and some raise questions about the applicability of the functionalist thesis to the South in the antebellum period.

For example, why were the ratios for Virginia and North Carolina, states with modernized universities and with significant numbers of out-of-state students, so close to those of Tennessee, one of the states famous for its number of small liberal arts colleges? And why was the ratio for South Carolina so high?

But even more important to an understanding of Southern higher education are the adjusted enrollment ratios in the region. The reported levels of property values in the South were among the highest in the nation, but its unequal distribution of wealth and the nature of its professional and occupational structures worked against the region matching the New England based expectations.[52] Unlike the case of the Northern regions, the prediction of enrollment ratios through the New England regression for 1860, using per capita personal property and controlling for the percent blacks in the Southern states, leads to a prediction that the Southern states should have had many more students than they did. Thus, while the South had an unexpectedly high number of college students, the unique character of its society and economy meant that it had fewer students than expected on the basis of the wealth indicator. In fact, the New England model fit the South closely when the percentage of blacks remained uncontrolled. (Table 2.20)

The Midwest had states with colleges that were still in frontier areas in 1860, but it ended the period with high enrollments and, unlike the South, controls for the foreign-born and indicators of economic well-being make the region more like New England and the Middle Atlantic. But, social and political influences and the varied stages of development of its states led to significant differences in enrollment levels. (Tables 2.21, 2.22, 2.23)

Although commentators pictured the Midwest as an area of educational chaos, the region was very successful in attracting students to its liberal arts colleges. In the thirty years before the Civil War, which witnessed Indian wars and a decade of disruptive conflict over slavery, the region increased the numbers of student tenfold and its enrollment ratio grew 300 percent. The Midwest was challenged by the national downturn in enrollments in the 1840s, and its growth was reduced to one-third of what it had been in the 1830s. But, typically, it rebounded in the 1850s and doubled the percentage of all young males in its colleges despite the addition of frontier states such as Wisconsin and Minnesota. And, by 1860, the Midwest had the greatest number of liberal arts students of the five major regions of the nation. However, even

TABLE 2.20

Expected and Actual Enrollment Percentages (Enrollments to White Males Age 15-20 in the State) for Various Southern States, 1859-60.

State	% Actual	% Expected Black Controlled	% Expected Black Not Controlled
Alabama	1.38	2.44	1.55
Arkansas	0	2.38	1.51
Delaware	1.44	1.69	1.19
District of Columbia	5.86	2.62	1.67
Florida	0	2.20	1.58
Georgia	1.53	2.95	1.89
Kentucky	1.15	2.47	0.93
Louisiana	0.80	4.20	2.72
Maryland	0.79	2.15	1.67
Mississippi	1.80	3.76	2.43
Missouri	1.09	1.24	1.61
North Carolina	2.02	1.33	1.02
South Carolina	3.11	3.80	2.47
Tennessee	1.98	2.04	1.31
Texas	0.27	2.91	1.86
Virginia	2.03	2.81	2.03

with corrections for the foreign–born, its enrollment percentages remained below those of the other regions and few of its states achieved the ratios of other areas even though it had a 50 percent increase in the number of students during the 1850s. (Table 2.21)

Although the enrollment ratios in the Midwest were not as diverse as in New England, there were important differences within the region. Ohio and Wisconsin had gross enrollment percentages higher than New York, but their 1.3 students per 100 young males were only slightly

TABLE 2.21

Enrollments in Midwest Colleges,
Enrollments as Percent of White Males
Age 15-20 and Percent Change of Enrollments
For Beginning Year of Each Decade, 1830-1860

	1830		1840		1850		1860
n	293		946		1522		3961
%	0.38		0.60		0.59		0.94
% Change		222		61		160	

greater than the national average. In contrast to these two states, Illinois, though relatively developed, had one of the lowest enrollment ratios in the nation. And many of the differences among the Midwestern states were in directions opposite to those implied by the functionalist thesis and interpretations by scholars such as Tewksbury. Ohio, one of the most condemned states because of its liberal chartering policy, had a higher enrollment ratio than Michigan with its specialized, free tuition, and apparently successful state university. Students in Ohio were, it seems, taking advantage of a "college at everyone's doorstep." In contrast, Illinois and Indiana, though attracting many Southern students, remained with enrollment ratios lower than the frontier states of Iowa and Minnesota, possibly because political problems over slavery hindered the founding and support of both private and state institutions.[53] (Table 2.22)

Despite the very poor records of Illinois and Indiana, the Midwestern achievements were significant. And the region's enrollment history is more impressive when controls for wealth and migrating students are established. In 1860, the New England enrollment ratio was twice that of the unadjusted ratio of the Midwest. But applying an adjustment for per capita property value reduces the difference by two–thirds. When the out–of–region students in New England are eliminated, the Midwestern states' gross enrollment ratios exceed the expectations based upon the projection of the New England relation between per capita property value and enrollments.[54] (Table 2.23)

TABLE 2.22

Enrollments in Midwestern States, 1860, as Percent of White Males Age 15-20 and as Percent Native White Males Age 15-20 in Respective States

	Enrollments/ White Males Age 15-20	Enrollments/ Native White Males Age 15-20
Illinois	0.54	0.67
Indiana	0.75	0.82
Iowa	0.69	0.82
Michigan	0.87	1.09
Minnesota	0.56	0.84
Ohio	1.12	1.30
Wisconsin	0.81	1.26

Knowledge of the economic and demographic conditions in the Midwest reinforce the conclusions from the use of the New England model. Soltow pointed out that Midwestern personal estates were from one–third to one–half the dollar value of those in New England just before the Civil War and that the average age of males in the Midwest was ten years younger than in New England. The lower value of estates suggests that few in the Midwest were able to support their children through college with ease. And the lower average age of males also suggests that there were fewer men in the Midwest who had reached the stage in life where the accumulation of funds allowed the support of students through the increased number of years of education—even in cities where the wealth potential might have been as great as in the East.[55]

But as in the South and the Middle Atlantic states, Midwestern students showed some dissatisfaction with the region's schools. Although Midwestern students were offered an increasing range of options in their region, there appears to have been a growing migration to the East for higher education. New England attracted many, the estimate for 1860 being slightly over one hundred, but the smaller colleges of the Middle Atlantic states may have been more popular. Perhaps 8 percent of the Midwest's students chose colleges in the two other regions and there

TABLE 2.23

Actual and Expected Enrollments in Midwestern States, 1860, Expected Enrollments Based Upon Projection of Regression of New England Attendance By State to New England Per Capita Property Values By State for Categories of Enrollments to Midwestern States

Midwestern States	Enrollments/ White Males Age 15-20		Enrollments/ Native White Males Age 15-20		Within-State (New England) Enrollments/ Native White Males Age 15-20	
	% Actual	% Expected	% Actual	% Expected	% Actual	% Expected
Illinois	0.54	1.54	0.67	1.79	0.67	0.92
Indiana	0.75	1.28	0.82	1.26	0.82	0.84
Iowa	0.69	0.48	0.82	0.42	0.82	0.79
Michigan	0.87	0.96	1.09	1.03	1.09	0.81
Minnesota	0.56	0.82	0.84	0.85	0.84	0.78
Ohio	1.12	1.54	1.30	1.79	1.30	0.92
Wisconsin	0.81	0.99	1.26	1.08	1.26	0.81

may have been a tendency for them to enroll in the larger colleges in greater numbers in the 1850s, with Yale the most popular institution and Harvard beginning to be attractive in the last decade of the period. (Table 2.24)

The successes of the regions usually pictured as backwards educational areas, such as the Midwest and South, were matched by the record of the new denominations in America. An important result of the expansion of colleges in the country was the displacement of the older and established denominations as the dominant forces in American higher education. In 1800, Congregational and Presbyterian colleges, with some help from Episcopalians, attracted almost all of the country's students. By 1860 the Congregational–Presbyterian share of students was reduced to 35 percent. (Table 2.25) State institutions barely kept pace with the changes in enrollments. They accounted for 11 percent in 1830 but were only able to increase their share to 13 percent in 1860. This was just twice the percentage of students enrolled in the schools supported by or associated with Episcopalians.

TABLE 2.24

Estimate of Percent of All Midwestern Students Enrolled in New England and the Middle Atlantic By Representative Yearly Figure for Decades

Year	Percent to New England	Percent to Middle Atlantic
1830	1	2
1840	3	8
1850	3	4

Table 2,25

Percent of Total Enrollment in Colleges of Major Denominations and State Colleges, 1810-1860

	1810	1820	1830	1840	1850	1860
Baptist	6	7	4	7	11	14
Methodist	0	0	4	14	11	12
Presbyterian	29	22	29	23	23	20
Congregational	46	37	31	19	16	15
Episcopalian	11	7	10	7	9	6
Catholic	1	2	2	8	11	6
Lutheran	0	0	1	1	2	2
State	6	14	11	14	10	13
Non-Denominational and Other Denominations	1	11	8	7	7	13
Total Enrollment	1939	2566	4647	8328	9931	16600

The shares of enrollments held by the various denominations disguise the growth in absolute numbers and thus one important aspect of the challenges facing the denominations. Between 1810 and 1860, Baptists increased the number of students their associated colleges were servicing twenty–twofold; Methodists by ten times; Presbyterians by six times; and, Congregationalists by less than threefold. Episcopalians managed, despite the problems of their associated colleges, to increase their enrollments 500 percent but the Catholics had the most amazing record, with a 520 percent increase between 1810 and 1850.

The 1830s must have been a decade of challenge to the security of the educators who represented the interests and viewpoints of the older denominations. In the Jacksonian years, the Methodists had a 500 percent increase in enrollments and the Catholic's student population jumped by close to 800 percent. But the Presbyterians and especially the Congregationalists had increases far below those of the other denominations. The Congregationalists had less than a 10 percent increase and all the various Presbyterian denominations were able to increase their student population by less than 50 percent.

The older and established denominations were the ones most threatened by the various enrollment crises of the antebellum era. Their experiences may have conditioned the history of higher education because the educational leaders of the period were likely to have been members of these denominations as well as being associated with New England. The newer denominations had continued growth in their small enrollments in the 1810s but the three major denominations faced, at best, stagnation. The Presbyterians and Congregationalists did have significant growth in the 1820s but experienced, as did state institutions, serious problems in the late 1840s. The recovery of the 1850s was shared by all the denominations, but somewhat unequally. The Presbyterians and Congregationalists had appreciable growth, about a 50 percent increase, but while this was close to that of the Methodist's, it was less than one–half the growth of Baptist enrollments.

Enrollments by denomination were highly correlated with the distribution of the denominational church accommodations. In the 1850s, the correlations between percent of students by state and percent of all church accommodations ranged from 0.67 for the Baptists to 0.99 for Congregationalists. And there are some indications that the migration patterns of students followed denominational lines because of the match between church centers and the distriibution of their higher educational facilities. Students from the Middle Atlantic states, where 12 percent of the Congregational accommodations were located, had to go to New England because there were no Congregational colleges in the middle states and many students may have migrated from New England to Union

College because of the absence of a Presbyterian college in New England.[56]

As with the denominational distribution of colleges, there seems to have been a bond between denominational wealth and enrollments. The statistical relationship between average dollar value of denominational accommodations and the ratio of the percent of enrollments to the percent of all accommodations in 1860 for the four leading Protestant denominations was .944.

Although the denominations varied as to how they calculated their membership (some included very young children) the number of reported denominational members to each student in a denomination's associated colleges does indicate that the newer and lower–status denominations were acting rationally. For example, in 1860 the Congregationalist–Unitarians had one student for every ninety–two members while the Methodists had one for every five hundred eighty–two. The Baptists had four hundred eighteen reported members for each student, but Episcopalians had sixty–three members for each student in their colleges.[57]

The history of the denominational support of students as well as the general history of enrollments indicates a more rational pattern than suggested in the traditional interpretations of antebellum higher education. Enrollment was growing, not stagnating, and the growth meant that more, not less, of America's young men were going to college in all regions of the country. If enrollments are indicators of the success of the educational efforts in the various regions, the Middle Atlantic states and the Midwest were, when social and economic conditions are controlled, doing well. Further, the differential growth of enrollments in the liberal arts college cannot be explained by the simple economic–functionalist argument because some of the colleges with the modern curricula and orientations were unable to keep pace with the growth of other institutions which, though not educationally backwards, did not institute such radical reforms. Broader social and economic forces were at work in determining levels of enrollments and the selection of particular colleges.

But enrollment history is only one part of the traditional argument concerning antebellum higher education. The older interpretation was also based upon an image of who students were and what they did. And essential to the simple functionalist argument was the idea that the antebellum colleges were unable to attract or produce the new aggressive man of business and industry needed by the evolving economic order or the men who would be capable of modernizing the intellectual and cultural life of America.

Chapter 3

Student Backgrounds

The critics of the early colleges applied the same sets of values, concepts, and assumptions to the study of the students of the antebellum period that they used to interpret the institutions and the enrollment patterns. The result was a picture of a uniform antebellum student who was the antithesis of what the historians desired for their own time. Just as the colleges were turned into an ideal and polar type, the thousands of students of the hundreds of colleges in different regions and times were frozen into an image of the "antebellum student".[1] The backgrounds and careers of the students were pushed into a stereotype that paralleled the image of the colleges and their effect on American society. The colleges were viewed as conservative and irrelevant, so the students were seen as timid and ineffective. Because the colleges supposedly did not adopt science and technical training, the students could have made few contributions to the modernization and democratization of America. And because the colleges were so backward, the students who were attracted to them were either from old elite families with outmoded views of the world or were from rural backgrounds that made their best possible contribution to America to be reactionary village leaders.

Combined with a lack of systematic information on the backgrounds and careers of the antebellum students, the assumptions used by the traditional historians could only lead to that type of description and to the pervasive negative evaluation of students' achievements. The assumption that social and economic conditions were the same before and after the Civil War led historians to believe that the country was filled with potential students who possessed all the characteristics of the ideal modern student. Therefore, the actual antebellum students and their backgrounds and lives appeared to be unnecessarily premodern. The assumption that only scientific, vocational, and specialized courses could attract the desired type of students and allow them to make later contributions also led traditional historians to assume that the antebellum students were removed from business, the development of science, and the industrialization of America.

The combination of the use of an ideal type and the assumption that higher education could have easily changed itself led to both the students and the colleges being abstracted from their social and economic contexts. Students' ages, their behavior, and their backgrounds and careers were treated in an ahistorical manner. This was compounded by the assumption that higher education could determine the careers of students. Just as the colleges were essentially treated as autonomous, the future of their students was not seen as the product of regional economies, the structure of their professions and occupations, or the influence of students' social backgrounds. The image of the antebellum student, usually arrived at through deduction from the premises concerning the state of higher education and the social and economic orders, conditioned the historical view of the colleges. The ideal antebellum student came to be used as more evidence to show the backwardness of the old colleges and the revolutionary nature of the changes in higher education after the Civil War. One of the major reasons why the traditional history of the antebellum colleges has continued to be accepted is the persuasiveness of the stereotype of the antebellum student.

The image of the ineffectual antebellum alumnus has been accepted because, until very recently, there have been few systematic and comprehensive studies of the backgrounds and careers of the students of the early colleges and because there has been little empirical and objective work on the nature of the occupational and social worlds of the antebellum period. The one major investigation of the careers of the students that was available to historians is not only marked by flaws of design and sampling but has rarely been carefully analyzed and interpreted. Bailey Burritt's early study, published in 1912, was concerned with only the single major occupation of the alumni of the colleges, was focused on the large institutions of the Northeast, and has been the source of conflicting interpretations because of the occupational categories he used. Other studies, such as *The Vital Statistics of College Graduates* had even more pronounced problems of design and data recovery.[2]

Until the last decade there has been little scholarly work on the nature of the social and occupational world of the early nineteenth century. Only with the emergence of the recent histories of the professions, youth, families, and social mobility has it become clear that many of the assumptions of the critics of the colleges about American life were normative judgments rather than correct descriptions of the socioeconomic context of early higher education. Works ranging from Thernstrom's studies of economic and geographic mobility, through the new investigations of the nature and role of family and kin, to Kett's work on youth have highlighted the differences between the nineteenth-century's socioeconomic system and the idealistic image imposed upon it by Progressive historians. The new investigations of the professions and work in America have outlined the great differences between twentieth–century patterns and the more fluid and unstructured nineteenth century which was characterized by the absence of formalized certification procedures, imprecise definitions of professional boundaries, and a great deal of career instability.[3]

Because the histories of higher education were based upon a biased view of American social life, even correct "facts" about the antebellum students were fundamentally misinterpreted. The wide age distribution of students was treated as a fault of the colleges instead of something imposed upon them by the economic and educational systems of the period. The occupations of the alumni were seen simply as the result of college policies and curricula instead of being the product of the interaction of the early socialization of the students, the social structure, and the nature of the professions. Student rebellions were not only overemphasized by historians but consistently interpreted as if they were the result of irrational college policies rather than of child–rearing patterns, general social antagonisms, a societal bent towards such protests, or specific political problems of the country. And when historians did mention the lower socioeconomic backgrounds of some students, the social origin of these men was interpreted as an indication that the colleges could not attract qualified students, rather than as a sign that many of the colleges were providing an opportunity for social mobility.[4]

But few correct facts about the students are found in the traditional histories of the colleges. And the consequences of the scarcity of information on the students and the use of the assumptions concerning the social and economic orders go far beyond a distorted picture of antebellum higher education. The interpretation of the colleges and their students has been important to the historical view of higher education since the Civil War, especially the treatment of the rise of the university and technical training. Partially because the antebellum liberal arts colleges were assumed to be incapable of attracting or producing aggressive young men, the concentration of Morrill Act funds, the first large–scale Federal aid to education for all sections of the nation, in a few institutions was interpreted as the only possible rational decision. But if the colleges and their students were more flexible and modernized than thought, an effective policy to achieve the goal of widespread knowledge of science and related skills would have been to subsidize such training in all the colleges. The static nature of the image of the antebellum student led historians to treat the rise of the university after the Civil War as a sudden and revolutionary change caused by the actions of a few educational reformers, rather than as a gradual evolution that came in response to alterations in American society and to the demands of an already changed student population. And because the antebellum student was the antithesis of what a modern student should be, the achievements of the later colleges and their students, by comparison, seemed beyond criticism.[5]

Such views were based upon little systematic evidence about the students of either the ante–or postbellum periods. To correct this basic problem and to test many of the assertions about the colleges, a search for information on the students in all colleges and in all regions of the country between 1800 and 1860 was conducted. The first step in this ten–year project was to locate complete lists of the students of the various institutions and then to take a 10 percent random sample from them. A complete list of students, whether it was for a single year or the full period, was insisted upon in order to avoid the biases that would be created through using lists of eminent alumni or only those who managed to stay in direct contact with their colleges.[6]

All the materials held by the Library of Congress and all the works listed in the various catalogs it sponsored as well as the holdings of the old Bureau of Education, the National Library of Medicine, the libraries of almost all colleges and universities, and many state, local, and professional historical society libraries were surveyed to find the lists of students. When it was decided that these sources were exhausted, the alumni registers (usually all editions including those contained in annual catalogs of the colleges down to the twentieth century), class books, and alumni and archival files of the colleges were used to trace the lives of the students. At the same time, the sample was followed through all national, regional, state, and large city biographical registers and through professional rolls, local histories, and biographical volumes. Governmental registers and fraternity materials were also surveyed.[7]

The goal of the search was to find and code for computer usage a complete life history of the students of the colleges. The profile for each student included the following items:

1. the code number and geographic location of the colleges and professional schools attended;
2. the place of birth and the place where the student was located at the time he first entered college;
3. the birth date, death date, and date of completion of higher education;
4. the total number of years of higher education;
5. four occupations of the student and his/her father's occupation;
6. four places where the student resided during his postcollege career and the decades when the student was in each location;
7. the student's denominational affiliations (two) and his political affiliations (two);
8. the student's recognition by editors of biographical volumes such as

national, state, or regional biographical registers or fraternity and professional biographies;

9. the types of political offices held by the student during his postcollege career;

10. the student's membership in scientific organizations and fraternities;

11. the type of professional practice pursued by the student if he was a physician such as botanic, eclectic, etc.;

12. the participation by the student in the military during the Civil War.

It was found very early in the history of the project that certain information was so irregularly reported that an attempt to include it directly in the study would be fruitless. Therefore, such important information as how and where a student prepared for college was not coded on the computer biographical files. Cause of death, whether or not the student married, and his number of children and their histories were also found to be so irregularly cited in both college and biographical reports that they were not coded.

The result of the search for lists of students and their histories was a sample of some twelve thousand students of the liberal arts colleges (with a sample of similar size for students of professional and scientific schools which will be analyzed in a future study). The sample appears to be as close as we can come to a random selection of early college students unless lists for more of the early schools in the South and small colleges in frontier areas are located. The profiles for the students are as complete as possible until funds are obtained to search county, town, and census records.[8] Complete information on all students was not recovered. Biographical volumes, professional registers, and the archival materials were biased towards the large institutions of the North and there was a higher recovery rate for the larger and famous institutions. However, more information was obtained for more students than in any other study, and a careful consideration of the biases in both the original samples and the supplemental information allows many inferences to be made concerning the areas and colleges with relatively weak coverage.[9]

Besides the biases in data recovery, inferences from even perfect samples impose restraints upon an investigator. Sample sizes must be large enough to ensure that the results of the sampling are representative of the population under study. The estimation of exact percentages, for example, demands, in traditional statistical theory, a pure random sample of over one thousand cases when a high degree of statistical confidence is to be placed on the estimate. Tests of statistical difference between estimates demand fewer cases, but an investigator still faces the problem of not being absolutely sure that statistically significant differences are substantively important.[10]

In situations where sample sizes were too small or known to be biased, generalizations in this and the following chapter are qualified by such terms as, "the data suggests" or "the data gives us reason to believe." The most frequent use of such qualified generalizations is in situations where sample sizes, relative to the range of scores, are so small that the results of tests of significance or estimation seem to be in conflict with historical patterns in the data or with findings for colleges with similarities on predictor variables. In a few cases, estimates that are not statistically valid are included with qualifications when the obtained scores appear to be a relatively precise estimate of the true score because of data patterns over time. However, in such cases the character of the inference is made clear.[11]

But the inferential problem is not as bleak as pictured above. The major generalizations contained in these chapters are based upon enough evidence to fulfill the mandates of statistical tests.[12] Furthermore, when several estimates from this study were checked against complete series, such as Burritt's study of occupations and Allmendinger's survey of ages in New England, both series proved quite compatible.[13] As with many of the findings on the institutions and enrollment levels, the statistical profiles of the students raise as many questions as they provide explanations for both old and new facts about ante–and postbellum higher education. And, as with the findings concerning institutions and enrollments, a conscious attempt has been made to avoid the use of merely plausible explanations for many of the surprising facts about the students. In many instances there is not enough information or acceptable generalizations and theoretical frameworks to provide well–grounded explanations. Hopefully, the unexplained facts will generate further research.

The substantive results of the search for information on the antebellum liberal arts students lead to a much more complex and dynamic picture of early higher education than can be found in the traditional literature. The profiles of the students suggest few simple generalizations, but they dictate an interpretation marked by a very complex evolution of an increasingly differentiated college system, the character of which was determined to a great degree, by forces outside the control of educators. The evolution of the colleges was guided by influences ranging from regionalism, changes in the professions and the emergence of institutionalized religion in America, to the new wealth and economic conditions of the Jacksonian era and a more sophisticated and regularized lower educational system.

Several major trends emerged from the biographical profiles. And these trends challenge many firmly held views concerning antebellum higher education. The colleges were moving from attracting students from an urban elite with relatively homogeneous backgrounds and careers, to providing education for a much broader segment of the American population. The liberal arts colleges, because of changes in the occupational and economic structures, were acting to provide social mobility to a degree as great as in any period of American history before the post–World War II era. And the colleges were much more open to students from non–elite backgrounds than the supposedly meritocratic institutions of Europe.[14]

As colleges became more democractic, they faced problems of adjusting to new types of students. But they were responsive, and they altered curricula, schedules, and even rules of behavior to satisfy at least some of the growing number of demands by their increasingly diverse students. Perhaps it was these adjustments to the needs and pressures of the new students that caused historians such as Hofstatdter to judge the antebellum period so harshly. His reaction may well have been to the democratization of the colleges and the changes that the democratization made necessary.[15]

Because the relative democratization was uneven across regions and colleges, a second trend emerged in the early nineteenth century, the differentiation of the colleges. Student backgrounds and careers began to differ among regions and among individual schools in the regions. One of the surest ways to classify the colleges of the period is by their student profiles. Distinctions grew between old and new colleges, colleges of the various regions, and rural and urban institutions. The reasons for the diversity among the colleges were complex, too complex to allow the continued reliance upon the concept of the "denominational college". There was a continuous reciprocal interaction between college and student that shaped the "personality" of institutions. Rural or urban location and the characteristics of regional economies were important to the types of students attracted to a college, as were tuition policies, economic support for students, and the availability of preparatory training. A student's family background and the social and occupational connections of the faculty and alumni were important to the careers of students, which, in turn, reflected on their college. But more important than these influences on the lives of the students was the interaction among their pre–college educational goals and aspirations, conditioned by their early experiences, the professions they entered, the levels and areas in which the students began their careers, and the regions in which they worked.

The unique patterns of these causal factors led the early colleges to have student populations which were significantly different from each other. Stronger than denomination and curricula, regional and historical conditions led to the differentiation of the antebellum colleges. And this process created an anomaly. The colleges which seem to have been the most parochial and least involved in the democratization of antebellum higher education became the leaders of the university movement in America. Harvard, Columbia, and Pennsylvania had the least experience in dealing with diversity, with inadequately prepared students who had to spend many of their college years working, and with students who came from family backgrounds not fully congruent with either academic or elite cultures. But these colleges became the models for much of American higher education in later years when the system supposedly adjusted to the comman man.

The later success of the elite institutions of the antebellum era may be partially explained by trends in the occupations of students. The emphasis on the numbers of ministers produced by the early colleges has masked the long–term trend towards the secular occupations. Only a few colleges remained ministerial factories at the coming of the Civil War because the sudden upsurge in the selection of the ministry in the 1810s was countered by increasing numbers of students of all the colleges entering business, law, education, and even science. The 1830s were a turning point for many colleges in the country but institutions such as Harvard and Columbia had long before been accustomed to students who entered the worlds of finance and commerce. These colleges had a long history of enrolling students from the large cities of the country who would build their careers in the centers of economic power. Although other colleges had a bias towards urban students and sent increasing numbers of them to the cities, institutions such as Harvard had always attracted unexpectedly high percentages of urban men who were able to return to their homes to pursue successful careers.[16]

At the same time that the colleges which became the university models focused upon America's urban world, other colleges became the centers for another set of functions. Depending upon the region, the other institutions provided education for rural students. Combined with the influence of the occupations chosen by students, these colleges pushed them into the cities across the nation. It was the small institutions that, in conjunction with contemporary professional forces, moved students from old to new cultures and environments.

The small colleges, with few resources, fulfilled other functions besides aiding the transfer of young men from rural to urban life. These colleges provided leaders for the small towns and rural areas of America. They helped bridge a gap between two cultures, the rural and the urban. They did train local leaders, but not necessarily reactionary ones, for they educated, at least in the North, a mobile elite for America's small towns and agricultural communities. Because of the nature of professions during the period, especially the ministry, the students moved to and from urban and rural areas throughout their careers.[17]

The geographic mobility of the students was high, and they acted as agents of cultural transfer. Only the South and the elite institutions produced students who were less than many times more mobile than the general population. This mobility was not just the result of higher education or regional influence. The ministry was especially important to the dispersion of the students across the country and to the migration of ideas and knowledge. Interacting with the higher probability that a young man who entered the ministry had come from an area that was unable to support all of its young in high–status positions and with the greater likelihood that a minister came from a lower–status family, the new demands of the profession pushed the ministers away from their home areas. Ironically, it was not the students who became businessmen who stood out as the examples of geographic or social mobility during the period, but those who entered the profession which led many critics to condemn the colleges and their students as elitist and dysfunctional, the clergy.[18]

Not only did the bias of the traditional historians prevent them from seeing the importance of the ministry, and thus the colleges, to American society, but from discovering direct indicators of the influence of the antebellum students on the nation. Although the colleges were educating more young men without the elite family profiles that would have contributed to successful and influential careers, the colleges continued to produce a high percentage of alumni who received national attention. The students were important to national and local government, industry, and finance, and even science and invention in America. The alumni had a higher participation rate in government, including Congress, than the non–college population, and they were much more likely than others to be remembered in biographical volumes and to be members of the scientific societies of their time.

Although the detailed evidence on the success of the antebellum students was not readily available to the critics of the colleges, there was enough evidence on the nature of the early student population to show that the most highly condemned "denominational" colleges were achieving many of the goals demanded by egalitarian–minded historians and functionalists. Perhaps some historians' involvement with educational questions in their own time prevented them from perceiving the contributions, as well as the limits, of the antebellum colleges.

In 1800, the American liberal arts colleges were relatively similar and primarily were serving the urban elite of the nation and the sons of the agricultural leaders of the South. But changes in the nature of the American socioeconomic order, the influence of the institutionalization of denominationalism, the opening of various professions, and the fluidity of the American institutional structure led to the development of an increasingly diverse and stratified higher educational system. By 1860 the schools clearly reflected the increase in the economic well–being of the country, the new opportunities for youth, and the forced dislocations caused by rapid social and economic change. But the pace of change and its incidence did not affect the regions or social and economic groups evenly. Significant regional and subregional differences, interacting with the original status of colleges, led to important regional variations in higher education, and to differences among colleges in the same general areas.

The impact of social and economic forces upon the development of the increasingly diverse system is most evident in New England because of the more complete history that is available concerning its students and colleges. Although similar trends are discernable in all the other areas of the country, they seem to have first appeared in New England and in the most obvious ways. But caution must be exercised when we consider the history of New England's students. New England was different from other regions of the country, even those which had been populated by its alumni.[19] New England had unique patterns of student backgrounds, shifts in occupational opportunities and choice, and the achievements of students.

David Allmendinger's sensitive and detailed study of the students of the New England colleges focused upon the changes forced upon those schools by an influx of new types of students in the first two decades of the nineteenth century. Through a compilation and analysis of the ages of students at graduation and the tracing of the backgrounds of some of those who he came to call "paupers," he concluded that significant changes occurred in many of the colleges because of the needs and demands of the new students.[20] (Table 3.1) Allmendinger found that the interaction of economic, demographic, and denominational forces caused a change in the student bodies of many of the New England colleges. The rural and recently founded colleges in New England began to cater to a group of men from relatively humble rural backgrounds who entered college at or well after the age of majority. The inability of their fathers to pass along farms or businesses to their sons caused young men to seek entry into the professions. Of special importance to them and the colleges was the ministry.[21]

The ministry was the one profession of the period which allowed status mobility and maintenance, was open to those from relatively humble backgrounds, was directly linked to liberal education, and which provided economic support for students on an institutionalized basis. And the

Table 3.1

David Allmendinger's Results from a Study of the Age at Graduation of Students at New England Colleges, 1801-1810 and 1851-1860 - Percent of Students Graduating at or Above Age 25

	Harvard	Yale	New Colleges	Ten Colleges
1801-1810	12.5	9.9	26.2	18.4
1851-1860	5.6	17.1	33.3	24.6

ministry was the profession with a widely distributed recruitment system. The established local ministry had contact with potential entrants and with the educational and benevolent institutions that could provide economic support to worthy young men. For many men feeling the pressures which led to New England's famous out–migration, the ministry was a readily available solution to the frustrations caused by spending so many years providing support for their families, only to face, in their early and mid–twenties, either the inheritance of an unprofitable small farm or the prospects of no inheritance at all and little or no training in a respectable occupation or profession.

Thus, while many young men from similar socioeconomic backgrounds entered other professions, the ministry was of special importance to the colleges. Law and medicine had more fragile links with liberal education than did the ministry and did not have institutionalized subsidization systems. The other professions could not provide the guarantees of employment which resulted from the rise in demand for trained ministers in the first decades of the century. The two other traditional professions may also have become closed to those of lower social status because of relative overcrowding in New England resulting, perhaps, from the rush into the legal profession by young men after the Revolution.[22]

But the impact of the forces dislocating the rural New England population were unevenly spread over the colleges. The new institutions located outside of the major cities, such as Middlebury and Amherst, felt the influence of the new students. The established colleges, especially Harvard and Yale, remained relatively aloof from the dominant trends in New England.[23] The data from the survey of students for this study reinforces Allmendinger's conclusions. But it also embelllishes them and indicates ramifications of the changes in the nature of the backgrounds and careers of students not given emphasis in Allmendinger's study. For example, although finding age distributions similar to those in Allmendinger's complete survey of graduates, the spread of ages rather than their concentration at or above the age of maturity is stressed in order to highlight the complex demands and conditions imposed upon the colleges. (Table 3.2)

Because the ministry was especially attractive to New England's displaced young men, many of the region's colleges had to accommodate themselves to a student body very different from that of the established colleges. The new students appear to have come from socioeconomic backgrounds lower than the older students of the eighteenth century. They had less standardized preparation and brought new perspectives and demands to the colleges. According to Allmendinger, the result was a significant change in the conduct and content of higher education. And

Table 3.2

Mean Age At Entry, Percent Entering College Below Age Seventeen and Above Age 21 for New England Colleges by Decade of Entry, 1800-1860

	1800's				1810's				1820's				1830's				1840's				1850's			
	$\bar{x}$	% <17	% >21	n cases	$\bar{x}$	% <17	% >21	n cases	$\bar{x}$	% <17	% >21	n cases	$\bar{x}$	% <17	% >21	n cases	$\bar{x}$	% <17	% >21	n cases	$\bar{x}$	% <17	% >21	n cases
Harvard	17.22	46	7	59	19.05	36	11	56	-	-	-	6	17.53	48	8	148	18.76	33	16	150	18.34	21	9	238
Yale	17.47	38	5	78	17.65	39	9	23	-	-	-	3	19.14	31	19	142	18.51	19	24	146	19.46	16	16	188
Other Colleges	17.98	42	9	117	19.38	18	22	103	-	-	-	23	19.68	22	23	443	19.90	18	27	482	19.99	13	21	610

there was a significant change in the careers of students, which, over later years, exerted special pressures on the institutions and created unique images and channels of recruitment and influence for each of the colleges. The impact of changes in the economy and professions of New England thus had both immediate and long term influences which conditioned the nature and possibilities of its colleges.

New England's colleges always had a large proportion of their students entering at an older age and there had been differences between the age distributions at Harvard and Yale and the other institutions since the eighteenth century. From the settlement of the French and Indian Wars to the beginning of the nineteenth century, Harvard and Yale had 15 percent of their students graduating at or above twenty–five years of age. The smaller institutions had even higher percentages during the period. The Revolutionary era saw nearly 40 percent of the students entering at or above the age of majority.[24] (Table 3.2) In fact, what Allmendinger calls the "new" institutions of the region, as a group, never quite equalled the percentage of older students enrolled during the 1770s. Their nineteenth–century high–point for the proportion of older students came in the 1810s and 1820s when approximately 37 percent entered at or above age twenty–one, a somewhat higher percentage than in the 1790s and 1800s. After the 1820s, the small institutions of the region experienced a slight and gradual drop in the percentage of older students. And although the Civil War marked the beginnings of a more accelerated decline in the percentage of mature students, the new colleges still had 22 percent of their students entering over the age of twenty in 1900. In contrast to the record of the rural institutions were the experiences of Harvard and Yale. Both Harvard's secularly oriented matriculants and Yale's ministerially bound students had significantly different age profiles during the nineteenth century. These two colleges experienced trends in the percentage of older students similar to those for the smaller colleges, but despite their greater affluence and reputations, they remained with less than one–half the percentage of mature students served by the other institutions.[25]

Emphasis upon the mature students does indicate that the early colleges were fulfilling social functions much like the community and junior colleges of today. In contrast to claims in much of the previous historiography, they were not educating a youthful and irresponsible elite. The percentage of older students in the smaller institutions was perhaps greater than in any other period of American history (after the Revolutionary era) until the surge of older students generated by the aftermath of World War II.

Recognition of the maturity of the New England students does counteract the image of the colleges as havens for juveniles, but it draws attention away from one of the important conditions imposed upon the early liberal arts colleges—the wide range of ages they were asked to serve because of the socioeconomic conditions of the country and the state of the lower educational system. The American social, economic, and educational orders were generating older students with established career goals who demanded autonomy. At the same time these forces were supplying the colleges with, according to modern standards, extremely young men whose parents demanded the supervision and training commensurate with their youth.

The New England institutions had always had student populations with great variations in age of entry, and even with the developments in the lower educational system of the area during the nineteenth century, approximately 50 percent of the students of the smaller colleges were above or below modern age norms for entry into college at the time of the Civil War. Institutions such as Harvard, which seemed to be serving the sons of the most highly modernized segment of American's population, had even higher percentages. New England's colleges served students whose ages at entry ranged from twelve or thirteen to the mid–thirties.[26] But there were trends in the entry of younger as well as mature students that created differences among colleges. In the first decade of the nineteenth century, New England colleges had 19 percent of their students graduating at or above the age of twenty–five and 38 percent who entered college at or below the age of sixteen. By the 1820s, older students comprised 30 percent of the population, while the younger students' percentage remained stable. But the constancy of the percentage of immature students was a product of changes among the colleges. The percentage of younger students in the smaller institutions dropped sharply. By the 1820s, the average percent of students entering at or below age sixteen in those colleges declined by a half and remained close to 20 percent until the Civil War.[27]

In contrast to the age distributions of the smaller institutions (colleges with the greatest need of the economic support generated by attendance) were those of Yale and Harvard. Yale, despite its production of ministers, remained a "younger" institution than the new colleges until the 1830s. Harvard's advantageous location in one of the most prosperous and modern areas of the United States and its secular curricula made it distinct from the other colleges well beyond the Civil War. But Harvard had a significantly younger, not older, student population than the smaller institutions and was an even "younger" college than Yale. It appears that the average age of Harvard students was two years below that of the other colleges until the 1840s. A significant change in its student population then resulted in an increase of one year in its average age, but Harvard maintained a higher percentage of students who entered below the age of seventeen and a significantly lower percentage who entered at or above the age of majority.[28]

Harvard's age distribution, furthermore, was more homogeneous than that of the other institutions. Its average age not only began to approach, by the 1850s, the modern norm for entry into college, but the age range it served was more constricted than in the smaller schools. Perhaps the economic and urban backgrounds of Harvard students, which allowed a life progression marked by great continuity, presaged the future of the rising middle classes of the later nineteenth century. But the elite model of life may have become an independent influential norm shaping the criteria and expectations for higher education later in the era.[29]

Whatever the exact causes of the rise of the modern age distribution, the critics assumed that the age of antebellum students was the fault of the schools. The colleges' disregard for quality education was seen as the cause. But the age distribution was not the fault of the liberal arts colleges; it was the product of the social, economic, and educational orders of the period. Age groupings similar to those in the rural colleges have been found in other educational institutions of the era, especially the ubiquitous academy.[30] In the nineteenth century the norms, economy, and institutions had not been developed to support the regularized life progressions needed to create and sustain the age structuring of life so familiar to twentieth-century America. These age groupings, now believed by many modern Americans to be natural and fixed, were the product of the later nineteenth and early twentieth century when changes in the society and the occupations and the rise of concepts such as adolescence led to the familiar age segregation in education.[31]

Additional evidence is available to support the idea that social and economic factors rather than disregard for "quality" education were the major forces determining the age of antebellum college students. The age of students in the secular and modern colleges suggest that the content of the curriculum, even when a program was intended for the mature student, did not have much effect. The samples for Norwich and Rensselaer, schools noted for the training of engineers, suggest that their students were even younger than those in the typical liberal arts college of New England. No students above the age of twenty were found in either sample and the mean age was lower than in the liberal arts colleges. Furthermore, the mean age at Harvard's scientific school was only slightly higher than for its liberal arts program during the 1850s, and the percentage entering the scientific program below seventeen years of age was only 3 percent less than in the regular college. However, Harvard's scientific school's sample did suggest that it enrolled three times the percentage of students over twenty years of age. But these older students do not seem to have been from the same background as the mature students in the smaller colleges. Almost all were men already established in the professions. Medicine, the ministry, and manufacturing were the usual professions of the older students in Harvard's scientific program.

The small samples for the students of the scientific programs at Yale, Dartmouth, and Union College yielded estimates of ages similar to those at Harvard. As at Harvard's scientific school, the older students tended to be ministers or physicians returning to school for training. Thus, if age is accepted as an indicator of social status, the history of the scientific schools does not support the concept that "scientific" education was necessarily more democratic or more likely to play a compensatory role in social mobility than was liberal education.[32]

The age distributions in the liberal arts colleges, whether or not related to social status, had much influence on college policies and the tone of institutions. Regulations, orientations, and teaching methods were conditioned by the age of students. The presence of even a small number of students below the legal age of responsibility created special burdens for the faculties. The supervisory role, so detested by the emerging professional college teachers, was a legal and ethical consequence of the presence of young men. A school's reputation depended upon its ability to ensure that students did not lose their money gambling or spend essential funds on drinking and parties. The concept of in–loco–parentis not only was a logical outcome of the liberal arts philosophy in which character training was a major goal, but a product of the presence of younger students. The paternal concept did not disappear with the emergence of the modern schools; it has been a constant in American education, although called by different names depending upon the fashionable paradigm of educators and the public. Dewey's mandates to teach the "whole–child," emphasis upon socialization, and even behavior–modification, are all similar in goals and methods to the parental tone of the early liberal arts colleges. And in modern colleges, with their older age of entry and with students who have been the product of an educational system designed to produce students already prepared for college life and responsibilities, formal rules and regulations, much like those of the early colleges, appear in catalogs and other institutional documents.[33]

Nevertheless, the wide range of ages did create strains in the early colleges. Older students not only disliked supervision but had financial needs that called for modifications of college policies, schedules, and attitudes. Most institutions responded to the needs of the poorer students by altering their semester schedules to allow students to acquire funds by teaching; many allowed the formation of cooperative boarding houses by the poorer students (which in some cases developed into fraternities). The institutions had to search for funds to aid students in financial difficulties, and the colleges found themselves financially pressured because they could not serve such students and charge high tuitions.[34]

The age distributions in the colleges also conditioned teaching methods. The pedagogy of the period was due to much more than faculty conservatism or nonprofessionalism. The recitation methods, which were not as pervasive as some historians have claimed, were a product of the age and financial conditions imposed upon the colleges. Lectures to audiences with disparate backgrounds and ages were and are difficult. In contemporary America teaching methods with euphemisms such as "individuated instruction" are used to label techniques designed to serve classes with students of diverse backgrounds and achievements. Mechanized aids, such as computerized instruction, are widely used and are sophisticated substitutes for recitation. Such techniques fulfill the same functions as the rules to enforce study hours used by the early colleges and have the same goal of reducing the time the faculty spends with students.[35]

But the colleges put some limits upon the strains and pressures through their recruitment, admittance, and certification policies. Depending upon the financial status of a college, students were asked to meet as many as three criteria. The first required a student to present statements from relatively prominent individuals certifying his good moral character. These were usually supplied by local ministers, officials, and other community leaders. If the student had attended a respected preparatory school, its recommendation was sufficient. The second criteria that students were expected to meet, usually by examination, was academic. Basic knowledge of mathematics and science and sometimes history, philosophy, and English were tested, and the student was expected to have some skills in the classical languages. The third demand was that, except for "pauper" students who received outside support, the prospective student guarantee the payment of college bills and expenses. In some institutions with high tuitions and fees, the financial criteria was assumed to filter out all those who might not fit the subculture of the college.[36] But the recommendation concerning the moral character of the student was probably the most important limit to the diversity of the student body. Obtaining the necessary testimonial of good character, especially for those from lower socioeconomic status, forced the prospective student to pass through a test of cultural homogeneity. For the men who anticipated entering the ministry and who were from lower–status backgrounds, the demands were extremely high. Not only did these men pass through the typical process of recruitment and training by the local minister or schoolmaster, but they had to provide sponsoring agencies with statements from many community leaders.[37]

Students, then, had to show evidence of conformity to local social norms and some ability in and tolerance for college culture. However, because it was local norms and standards that were applied to the evaluation of character and attitudes, the degree of homogeneity in the colleges was limited. In respect to academic preparation, class backgrounds, attitudes and culture there was diversity within, as well as among, the college student bodies. But for whatever the reasons, ranging from economics to previous levels of preparation, few of the "new" and probably poor ethnics of the Jacksonian era were enrolled in the major Protestant colleges. The new migrants to the Midwest, such as the German Lutherans, did found their own schools, but few Irish, or Scandinavian, or new–German students seem to have attended the higher schools. Even in Catholic institutions in the North, where Irish names abounded, the students seems to have come from families which were established in business and the professions.[38]

Despite the lack of diversity among the students, the New England colleges were changing and were marked by increased differences between institutions' student populations. Indicators other than age point to the important changes within and among the colleges and to their timing. There were important shifts in the migration patterns of students, their occupational choices, their origins, and their participation levels in national government, as well as their socioeconomic backgrounds. Most of these factors began to change in the first and second decades of the nineteenth century, two decades that set many of the trends of the antebellum period. But during the 1840s there may have been another turning point in the history of the colleges. The trends from the 1810s through the Jacksonian decade began to change, and many of the forces that had made the colleges more egalitarian weakened. Most institutions continued to attract and educate a broader segment of the population but in some regions, especially New England, the social and economic conditions were beginning to turn colleges inward upon themselves and their alumni. (Tables 3.2, 3.3, 3.4)

The 1810s, a decade of lowered attendance, was a crucial period that saw a significant change in the patterns of student characteristics in the New England colleges. They were years in which trends were set which created increasing differences among various schools in the region. Between 1800 and the 1810s, the average age of students in the smaller colleges of the region significantly increased. The sample suggests a two–year upward jump of the average age at entry, a significant decline in the percentage of students below seventeen and a signficant increase in the percentage entering at or above the age of majority. The age at entry for the smaller institutions remained relatively constant throughout the remainder of the period.

Table 3.3

Geographic Background Characteristics of Students at New England Colleges by Decade of Entry, 1800-1860.
A) Percent of Students from Large Cities
B) Percent of Students From Within the State of Each College C) Percent of Students From Within New England D) Percent of Students From Within 100 Zip Codes of Each Colleges

	1800's				1810's				1820's				1830's				1840's				1850's			
	A	B	C	D	A	B	C	D	A	B	C	D	A	B	C	D	A	B	C	D	A	B	C	D
Harvard %	20	82	94	37	33	76	83	48	41	77	87	46	36	86	92	59	43	77	86	48	39	47	81	51
n cases	60	60	60	60	143	144	144	146	119	115	119	115	177	172	177	172	187	187	187	184	227	222	227	222
Yale %	19	68	81	22	31	49	71	17	34	41	66	13	36	38	68	19	37	24	57	12	37	29	52	51
n cases	90	91	91	91	35	35	35	35	99	93	99	93	189	189	189	188	187	183	188	183	259	252	261	253
Other Colleges %	10	47	94	27	10	44	90	19	14	50	83	26	15	50	80	20	14	47	76	24	17	28	72	21
n cases	177	175	177	176	217	215	216	215	330	331	333	332	521	527	529	527	556	556	557	558	713	723	696	698

Table 3.4

Regional Locations of Home Areas of Liberal Arts Students For Various Colleges and Groups of Colleges, By Decade of Entry Into College, 1800-1860 - In Percents

	1800's						1810's						1830's						1850's					
	NE	MA	SA	SW	MW	n cases	NE	MA	SA	SW	MW	n cases	NE	MA	SA	SW	MW	n cases	NE	MA	SA	SW	MW	n cases
Harvard	94	2	2	0	0	67	83	1	9	6	0	144	86	3	10	1	1	177	80	10	4	1	4	261
Yale	81	10	8	0	0	90	71	20	9	0	0	35	57	25	10	5	3	98	51	30	6	5	7	228
Other New England Colleges	94	4	2	0	0	187	90	6	2	1	1	217	80	13	3	1	1	532	72	17	2	2	3	713
Princeton	2	61	33	4	0	46	7	66	25	2	0	44	2	63	26	9	1	108	2	72	12	12	1	99
Union	11	85	0	2	0	46	16	75	6	4	0	80	14	80	5	1	1	141	12	74	1	3	8	121
Columbia	-	-	-	-	-		5	89	5	0	0	19	0	93	0	7	0	15	0	93	6	2	0	44
University of Pennsylvania	0	86	7	0	0	14	16	76	4	0	0	25	0	91	6	3	0	106	0	97	2	2	0	136
Other Middle Atlantic Colleges	5	65	26	0	4	38	8	68	17	3	3	78	7	77	10	1	5	371	4	73	9	3	8	764
University of Virginia													1	1	77	21	0	124	0	1	74	24	0	332
University of North Carolina	0	0	100	0	0	27	0	0	95	5	0	40	0	2	92	6	0	66	0	1	76	21	1	210
Other South Atlantic Colleges	0	3	96	0	0	32	2	0	97	2	0	42	0	6	85	8	1	241	1	3	86	10	1	585
University of Alabama													0	0	0	100	0	48	0	0	3	96	0	101
Other Southwestern Colleges													0	2	14	86	0	56	1	1	3	91	5	446
Oberlin													19	48	0	0	33	27	9	23	0	0	66	44
University of Michigan																			3	11	0	2	83	44
Other Midwestern Colleges													7	10	8	15	61	215	4	12	3	8	70	676

In contrast, Harvard and Yale had age profiles that slowly changed. Both institutions did not undergo significant shifts until the 1830s and 1840s. As a result of the changes in the other colleges during the 1810s, Harvard and Yale remained with comparatively younger student populations in the 1850s, despite their increases in the fourth and fifth decades of the period.

Accompanying the abrupt increase in student ages in the 1810s and 1820s came other changes which added to the growing differences among the colleges. The smaller institutions, considered as a group and separately, showed a sudden and important increase in the percent of students entering the ministry in the 1810s. After that, the colleges experienced only a slight increase in the percent becoming clergymen through the 1830s when the period's highpoint was reached. Then they faced a moderate downward trend. The 1810s were also witness to a sharp decline in the estimates of the percentage of students ever to enter the United States Congress. This indicator of influence and popularity remained stable throughout the rest of the antebellum period for the small institutions, but Harvard, after decades of variation, ended the era with a significantly higher representation in Congress than the other New England colleges.[39]

One of the most significant changes among the New England colleges was a shift in the enrollment of students from the large cities of the country. The data on the home areas of New England students suggest the colleges were beginning to represent two different cultures—the rural and the urban. In the first decade of the century approximately 10 percent of the students in the smaller colleges came from large cities while Harvard and Yale had 20 percent "urban" students. (In the United States as a whole, 6 percent of the population lived in places of 1500 or more, and only a tiny fraction of the population lived in the large urban centers.) (Table 3.3)

Although all of New England's colleges continued to be attractive to students from large cities, they began to differ in their enrollment of students from urban areas. The sample for the smaller institutions (treated as a group and including some highly "urban" schools such as Trinity and Brown) indicated that the small colleges slightly increased their percentage of urban students in later decades. The estimates reached 15 percent in the 1830s and hovered there until at least the Civil War. In contrast, Harvard and Yale more than kept pace with the increased population of America's large cities. Between 1800 and the late 1810s, urban students at those two institutions increased to 30 percent and continued to climb until the Civil War when the estimataes reached 40 percent. Although some of the smaller colleges such as Brown, located in a seaport, and Trinity, which drew heavily from New York City, had estimates at the levels of Harvard and Yale, the majority of the small institutions catered to rural and small–town youth.

As the colleges of New England differentiated on the basis of the urban backgrounds of students, their ages, and their political achievements, the geographic origins of students began to distinguish the institutions. The smaller colleges became more cosmopolitan over the period while Harvard became a creature of the Boston area. The samples suggest that, when the century began, the smaller colleges drew only one–half of their students from within their own states, had accepted 95 percent from within New England, and 30 percent from within their immediate area. And the average distance from a student's home to his college was eighty–eight miles. (Table 3.4) Through very gradual changes, significant alterations in the geographic backgrounds of students emerged by the 1850s. Although the percentage of students coming from within a small college's own state remained relatively constant, there was a decrease of the percentage of those coming from within its immediate area (to about 20 percent). There was an important increase in the percentage of students from other regions and a doubling of the average number of miles from a student's home to his college.

Yale and Harvard developed distinct patterns of attraction. They became increasingly different from each other and from the smaller schools. It was not Harvard, with its supposedly advanced and liberal curricula, that became the most cosmopolitan institution, but the conservative Yale. The samples strongly suggest that Yale experienced radical changes, with the 1810s being a turning point in its history. Yale began the century with 68 percent of its students coming from within Connecticut and 81 percent from within New England. In the 1800s, 22 percent came from within the immediate area of New Haven. In the 1810s, despite the decline of attendance, the scope of Yale's attraction expanded. There was a significant increase in the numbers and percentages of students from urban centers besides New Haven and from other states, and a regional reorientation of the college. The changes continued until the Civil War, and the estimates for the 1850s indicate that 28 percent of Yale's students came from Connecticut, 15 percent from New Haven and its vicinity and only 52 percent from New England. As Yale developed into an urban but cosmopolitan institution, Harvard moved towards a configuration distinct from both Yale and the newer colleges. Harvard's geographic attraction did change during the antebellum era, but it remained a college for New England's, especially Massachusetts', urban population. For the 1800s, the estimates point to 97 percent from the region, 82 percent from the state, and 37 percent from the Boston area. After inconsistent changes in the succeeding decades, Harvard ended the period with an astounding profile of geographic attraction. While

Yale attracted 52 percent of its students from within New England, Harvard continued to have 80 percent. And in contrast to Yale's approximately 30 percent and the small colleges 47 percent of their students from within their states, Harvard had 75 percent of its students coming from within Massachusetts. Even more significant for the history of American higher education was that over 50 percent of Harvard's students of the 1850s were from within the immediate area of Cambridge and Boston. Along with its extremely high percentage of urban students, Harvard's geographic parochialism made it a unique American college.

The differences among the student populations of the colleges extended to specific home regions. Yale's proximity to New York had always made it attractive to students from the Middle Atlantic states. By the 1850s almost 30 percent of its students came from that region, a percentage close to that for the Episcopalian Trinity College with its extremely high percentage of New Yorkers. Yale always drew approximately 10 percent of its students from the South Atlantic states and greater proportions from the Southwest and Midwest than either Harvard or the smaller colleges.

Harvard's slight dependency on students from outside of its region was biased towards the South until the 1850s. Drawing fewer outside students than the other New England institutions, Harvard looked to the upper strata of Southern society, perhaps due to Boston's connections with the cotton trade. Until the 1850s, the samples, as well as complete surveys of home areas of Harvard graduates, indicate that there was a better than two–to–one chance that a Harvard student from outside the region came from the South. And until the significant drop in the percentage of Southerners in the 1850s, Harvard remained separated from both the Middle Atlantic and Midwestern states. However, the samples indicate that there were significant changes in the distribution of Harvard students in the 1850s. Well before the reforms of Eliot and his successors, the percentage of those from the Middle Atlantic states doubled, while the percentage (not the absolute number) of Southern students declined by by one–half.

Because of the small number of cases in the samples for the smaller institutions, precise estimates of the geographic locations of the home areas of their students are impossible. But the recovered data and the few complete lists of home areas do suggest there were significant differences among the colleges. For example, Brown and Trinity probably were institutions with a great appeal for students from urban centers in the Middle Atlantic and Southern border states while the other colleges in New England attracted more rural Middle Atlantic and Midwestern students. Considered as a group, however, the smaller institutions had profiles quite different from Harvard and even Yale, especially when urbanity is controlled. By the mid–1850s, approximately 20 percent of the students of the small colleges came from the three other Northern regions. Although they did attract some Southernors, the proportion never exceeded 4 percent of the student bodies. Many of the Southern migrants were from Maryland, Delaware, and the District of Columbia rather than the deep South. As with Yale's experience, there was no significant drop in the percentage of Southern students in the smaller New England colleges in the 1850s.

Unfortunately, one of the most important series for a comparative analysis of the New England colleges remains incomplete. The occupations of the fathers of the students, a direct indicator of social status, were underreported and reported in a biased manner. The percent of reported father's occupations varied from school to school, and the reports tended to overstate the status of the families. The patterns suggest that if a student came from a lower–status family, his father's occupation was rarely stated. Further, the categories used for occupations were extremely crude and vague. The terms "educator" and "farmer" were very popular categories but ones which have little specific meaning.[40] Despite these limitations it is clear that professional families were overrepresented in New England's colleges. Doctors, lawyers, government officials, and especially ministers relied upon the colleges to train their sons in ways compatible with the demands of their positions. Parents from these occupations must have been a significant influence on the colleges, shaping the curricula and the social tone of the institutions.[41]

But the presence of so many young men from professional backgrounds, despite the influx of the "pauper" scholars, did not mean that each college had the same constituents. A lawyer from a small village exerted different pressures on his sons and the colleges than one who practiced in a major urban center. And the significance of the fathers who were ministers probably shaped much of the public rhetoric, if not the actual conduct of a college. Predominant in the smaller colleges of the region because of the tuition reductions given to ministers' sons, 10 percent of New England's students may have come from clerical families.

But an even more significant difference among the colleges than the number of minister's offspring, was the developing imbalance in the percentages of businessmen among the parents. The samples for the early decade of the century suggest a rather uniform distribution, but that changed by the time of the Civil War. In the 1850s, the estimates for Harvard, Brown, Yale, and Trinity, the urban colleges of the region, indicate problems of devising a new higher education that was compatible with the views of both the urban businessmen and the desires of more traditional types of parents. Perhaps as many as one–third of the students of these colleges came from business backgrounds, compared to the perhaps 10 to 15 percent in the other colleges of the region.

The other regions faced similar changes in the demands and pressures on their colleges, but shifts in parents' occupations and in the social and economic systems did not mean that the liberal arts colleges of the various regions served similar student populations. Although all the regions shared in the trends toward democratization and differentiation, and perhaps a slowing of such trends later in the period, each of them had distinctive characteristics. Some of the differences among the regions were caused by their economies, but others remain unexplained. For example, the age distributions in the small Middle Atlantic colleges, despite the relatively developed economy of the region, is difficult to understand. Students in New York, New Jersey, and Pennsylvania were always younger than those in the rural colleges of New England. Even the Middle Atlantic versions of the "pauper" schools enrolled students with an average age one year younger than New England's. And despite the increase in ages in the 1810s, the distribution in the Middle Atlantic states continued to be different from the other areas. (Tables 3.5, 3.6) The smaller Middle Atlantic colleges taught a higher percentage of students who enrolled before reaching seventeen and a significantly smaller proportion of mature students. And the age distributions in the established colleges of the region were more diverse than in New England.

Because the Middle Atlantic sample sizes, compared to New England's, were inadequate, some caution is necessary, but patterns over the decades support the conclusion that, except for Columbia and Pennsylvania, the mean age in the famous colleges of the region were similar to those at the small colleges. However, the age distributions were dissimilar. And the distribution differences are not explained by students who were enrolled from other areas or by occupations of the alumni. Only the national pattern of established institutions serving young students seems to account for the age distributions of students in the Middle Atlantic states.

Princeton, with its great attraction for Southern students and future ministers, matched the small colleges of the region on the percent of young men, but had significantly fewer mature entrants. Union College had a more homogeneous age distribution with extremely low percentages of students who entered below seventeen or over twenty years old. While the ages of students attending Princeton and Union are difficult to explain, those at Columbia and the University of Pennsylvania were related to their institutional histories and urban locations. Even more than Harvard, these two prestigious colleges were schools for very young men. The sample for the University of Pennsylvania yielded an

Table 3.5

Mean Age At Entry, Percent Entering College Below Age Seventeen and Above Age 21 for Middle Atlantic Colleges By Decade of Entry, 1800-1860

	1800's				1810's				1820's				1830's				1840's				1850's			
	$\bar{x}$	% <17	% >21	n cases	$\bar{x}$	% <17	% >21	n cases	$\bar{x}$	% <17	% >21	n cases	$\bar{x}$	% <17	% >21	n cases	$\bar{x}$	% <17	% >21	n cases	$\bar{x}$	% <17	% >21	n cases
Princeton	16.09	63	3	32	17.00	43	6	16	-	-	-	1	18.36	32	20	65	18.69	21	15	59	18.20	30	5	74
Union	16.20	80	6	5	19.18	25	25	16	-	-	-	0	19.73	22	28	80	19.82	20	29	84	18.91	7	6	49
University of Pennsylvania	14.77	88	0	9	14.66	67	0	3	-	-	-	0	16.84	61	1	98	16.57	59	6	166	16.05	66	0	123
Columbia	14.00	88	0	8	19.28	43	29	7	-	-	-	1	15.33	67	0	18	18.81	36	21	11	16.05	66	0	14
Other Colleges	16.54	54	0	11	18.25	50	12	8	-	-	-	5	18.62	38	20	204	19.41	30	24	280	18.90	27	15	238

Table 3.6

Geographic Background Characteristics of Students at Middle Atlantic Colleges by Decade of Entry, 1800-1860
A) Percent of Students from Large Cities
B) Percent of Students from Within the State of Each College C) Percent of Students from Within the Middle Atlantic D) Percent of Students from Within 100 Zip Codes of Each College

	1800's				1810's				1820's				1830's				1840's				1850's			
	A	B	C	D	A	B	C	D	A	B	C	D	A	B	C	D	A	B	C	D	A	B	C	D
Princeton %	33	41	61	17	41	36	66	14	40	58	73	8	42	32	63	9	31	28	57	7	28	40	72	16
n cases	46	46	46	46	44	44	44	44	40	40	40	40	108	108	108	108	93	94	94	94	99	99	99	99
Union %	42	83	85	24	33	70	75	13	24	61	71	13	26	74	80	13	25	75	77	11	24	67	74	5
n cases	45	46	46	46	80	80	80	80	112	111	112	111	141	141	141	141	136	138	138	138	120	121	121	121
Columbia %	-	-	-	-	58	84	89	83	-	-	-	-	53	87	93	87	63	91	100	78	89	89	93	80
n cases	-	-	-	-	19	18	19	18	-	-	-	-	15	15	15	15	24	23	24	23	43	44	45	44
University of Pennsylvania %	69	79	86	57	67	63	76	52	88	97	94	85	90	86	91	72	89	90	90	85	93	93	95	91
n cases	13	14	14	14	24	24	25	25	34	33	34	34	105	102	106	102	181	181	183	181	134	133	136	133
Other Colleges %	28	57	65	16	22	65	68	21	17	54	66	14	27	65	77	24	20	57	20	18	24	63	73	24
n cases	29	30	31	31	74	75	75	75	153	153	153	152	322	325	326	324	421	428	426	428	691	712	716	714

estimate of much more than a majority of its students entering at sixteen or below during the 1850s and none enrolling above the age twenty. The weak samples for Columbia suggest a similar profile but with a few mature students.

The differences between New England and the Middle Atlantic were not confined to ages of students. Although the general population of the Middle Atlantic states was more rural than New England's, its students were always more likely to have come from a large city than those who entered New England's smaller institutions. The percentage differences between the smaller institutions of the two regions decreased over time, but the larger colleges of the Middle Atlantic, especially Columbia and the University of Pennsylvania, became institutions for students from major cities. Like Harvard, these two schools followed a trend of attracting students from within their immediate, urban, areas. The samples for Columbia and Pennsylvania suggest that 90 percent of their students came from large urban centers. However, Union and Princeton had student populations that led them away from the geographic localism of Columbia and Pennsylvania at the same time that they became "urban" institutions. Pennsylvania and Columbia became more parochical over the period and by the 1850s had almost all of their students from within Philadelphia and New York City respectively. The other colleges had significantly fewer students from within their states, immediate areas, or the region. And Princeton's sample indicates that it had a greater range of geographic attraction than the smaller colleges or even Union College which was so popular among New Englanders.

Just as in New England, the origins of students from outside of the region differed among the colleges in the Middle Atlantic states. Possibily because of the proximity of Pennsylvania to the South and New York to the West, their new colleges were more attractive to students from those regions than New England's small colleges. The estimates for the 1850s suggest that the Middle Atlantic colleges probably had a greater draw than Harvard or Yale. Although the percentages varied, it seems that the estimates from the grouped samples apply to many Middle Atlantic colleges, but schools such as Dickinson and Gettysburg were colleges for those from the border South. The region was, however, isolated from New England. Middle Atlantic students enrolled in New England's colleges, but only Union attracted important percentages from the Eastern area. Union was the single college in the Middle Atlantic states to accept as much as 4 or 5 percent of its students from New England. Despite the absence of a Presbyterian college in the older region, Princeton attracted few New England students.

Princeton and Columbia, as well as Pennsylvania, were also different from the region's small colleges because of the occupations of the parents of their students. As in New England, reported parental occupations revealed high percentages of professionals in all the schools with a predominance of ministers in the smaller colleges. And the increase in fathers involved in business paralleled New England with the Middle Atlantic's older urban institutions enrolling increasingly high numbers of students from commercial backgrounds. But in the Middle Atlantic states, the Southern migrants did not seem to come exclusively from the planter class. The smaller colleges enrolled a broader sample of Southern society than New England's schools or the large colleges in their region, possibly because of their border locations.

The older and richer institutions of the South followed the patterns of the large Northern colleges. They served a student population different from that of the South's smaller colleges because they catered to the region's elites. But even in its large colleges, the peculiar society of the South created student bodies very different from those of the North. And its experience of moving towards democracy and differentiation was more complex and diverse than that of New England.[42] (Tables 3.7, 3.8, 3.9, 3.10)

As in the other regions, the broadening of Southern liberal arts colleges was due to the actions of the small denominational colleges, rather than to its large and supposedly secular institutions. The crucial role in the relative democratization of the system was not performed by the famous state universities; even the University of Virginia, the great reform institution of the South, attracted a different type of student than did the small denominational colleges. The developing differentiation of Southern colleges was more complex than that of the North. And although the student populations in the region shared many characteristics among themselves and with the North, the special nature of Southern society and its economy, the variations in its subregions, and its lower educational system made Southern higher education unique even before the devastating impact of the Civil War and Reconstruction.

The most apparent difference between North and South (but note the relatively poor samples for the region) was that Southern students were always younger than New England's. In its rural colleges, the average age at entry was more like that at the large urban schools of the North, such as Pennsylvania and Harvard, than the small colleges of New England. As in the Northern urban institutions, few mature students were pushed or attracted to the Southern colleges. But after the 1830s, the small colleges of the region did begin to enroll some older men. And the older colleges of the South were "younger" than the denominational schools. The mean age of the students of the large state universities was not only lower, but the secular colleges had a more homogeneous population. Thus, if age is accepted as an indicator of social status, the state universities of the South have to be seen as enclaves for the elites of the region.

Table 3.7

Mean Age at Entry and Percent of Sample Entering College Below Age Seventeen and Above Age 21 for South Atlantic Colleges by Decade of Entry, 1830-1860

	1830's				1840's				1850's			
	$\bar{x}$	% <17	% >21	n cases	$\bar{x}$	% <17	% >21	n cases	$\bar{x}$	% <17	% >21	n cases
University of Virginia	17.16	44	5	101	19.25	11	25	81	18.67	19	12	284
University of North Carolina	16.89	55	6	29	17.17	41	2	41	17.98	29	9	84
University of South Carolina	18.00	71	28	7	--	--	--	1	16.40	80	20	5
University of Georgia	17.05	42	5	19	16.75	45	0	20	17.88	26	0	27
Other South Atlantic Colleges	17.51	48	14	29	18.06	47	14	43	18.82	39	10	76

Table 3.8

Geographic Background Characteristics of Students at South Atlantic Colleges by Decade of Entry, 1800–1860
A) Percent of Students from Large Cities
B) Percent of Students from Within the State of Each College C) Percent of Students from Within the South Atlantic D) Percent of Students from Within 100 Zip Codes of Each College

	1800's				1810's				1820's				1830's				1840's				1850's			
	A	B	C	D	A	B	C	D	A	B	C	D	A	B	C	D	A	B	C	D	A	B	C	D
University of Virginia %	–	–	–	–	–	–	–	–	15	84	95	9	20	64	77	14	16	69	90	9	18	52	74	7
n cases	–	–	–	–	–	–	–	–	55	55	55	55	124	124	124	124	105	104	104	104	332	329	329	329
University of North Carolina %	0	78	100	22	13	75	95	25	11	84	90	16	12	73	92	9	16	65	84	19	10	64	76	10
n cases	27	27	27	27	40	40	40	40	63	63	63	63	66	66	66	66	105	103	104	103	210	209	210	209
University of Georgia %	–	–	–	–	–	–	–	–	34	62	83	14	9	61	87	20	18	76	85	25	15	85	89	28
n cases	–	–	–	–	–	–	–	–	29	29	29	29	46	46	46	48	55	55	55	55	54	54	54	54
Other Colleges %	7	93	96	38	8	81	97	16	23	65	88	35	25	58	85	26	23	56	81	17	18	70	86	51
n cases	29	29	29	28	38	38	38	36	56	57	58	56	229	233	230	233	293	297	293	291	548	544	548	542

Table 3.9

Mean Age at Entry, Percent Entering College Below Age Seventeen and Above Age 21 for Southwestern Colleges, By Decade of Entry, 1830-1860

	1830's				1840's				1850's			
	$\bar{x}$	% <17	% >21	n cases	$\bar{x}$	% <17	% >21	n cases	$\bar{x}$	% <17	% >21	n cases
University of Alabama	16.02	57	0	38	16.46	46	0	32	17.02	48	3	94
Other Colleges	18.55	29	11	85	18.66	32	13	18	17.84	34	14	71

Table 3.10

Geographic Background Characteristics of Students at Southwestern Colleges by Decade of Entry, 1830-1860.
A) Percent of Students from Large Cities
B) Percent of Students from Within the State of Each College C) Percent of Students from Within the Southwest D) Percent of Students from Within 100 Zip Codes of Each College

	1830's				1840's				1850's			
	A	B	C	D	A	B	C	D	A	B	C	D
University of Alabama %	15	90	100	25	11	97	100	46	20	77	96	23
n cases	48	48	48	48	35	35	35	35	99	99	101	99
Other Colleges %	26	57	85	26	18	53	86	24	17	70	91	34
n cases	53	53	53	53	163	167	168	165	416	413	417	414

It does appear that there were some exceptions to the general patterns in the South. Among the smaller institutions, such colleges as Cumberland, Tusculum, and William–Jewell, which represented new denominations and segments of the Southern social order, may well have had age structures very similar to those of the small New England colleges. This was perhaps due to the production of ministers by these institutions and because they were the creations of social groups just emerging into respectability. And of the larger institutions of the South, the University of Virginia may have been unique. "Mr. Jefferson's college" had a mean age of entry close to that for the grouped smaller institutions, making Virginia the only large college in the South with students whose ages were close to the Northern norms. Virginia also had approximately the same proportion of mature students as the denominational colleges and a smaller percentage of students who had entered at or below the age of sixteen. However, caution should be used in interpreting the estimates for the University of Viriginia. Its older mean age at entry might be accounted for by what is suggested by the samples for other Virginia institutions. Virginia may have had an educational system which generated the somewhat older students.[43]

Perhaps reflecting the distributions of wealth and education in the region, Southern colleges were very "urban" relative to the distribution of the population. And they tended to become more so over the period. The samples for the grouped smaller colleges indicate that they accepted a greater percentage of students from the large cities of the area than did the established colleges. The state universities of the South, because of their link with the plantation culture, had significantly lower percentages and even the University of Virginia and the University of South Carolina, which served the Charleston elite, did not have samples with appreciably higher percentages of students from large cities. Although there was a decided urban bias, the Southern institutions were "local" colleges. The small colleges of the South approached the Civil War with percentages of students from within the state and region similar to those of the small New England colleges in 1800 and the prestigious urban colleges of the North in the 1850s. The state institutions of the South were also very local and, like the small colleges, were isolated from the other regions of the country. Even the University of Virginia, with its radically liberal curricula, could not attract young men from the North and West. The state institutions, which had many amenities to offer their students, were more isolated from the rest of the nation than the denominational colleges of the South. The estimates of a 7 percent attraction of Northern students for the smaller institutions and the zero percent estimate for the large colleges reflect the cultural and social gaps between the two major regions of early nineteenth–century America.

Furthermore, the estimate for the smaller colleges overstates the attraction of those institutions. The migration between regions was probably confined to border–state students and colleges.

The migration of Southern students within their region was important to the history of the South and its colleges. Students from the new Southern states often migrated to the older South and there was a reverse movement. Perhaps 25 percent of the students of the large colleges in the South Atlantic states, such as the University of North Carolina and Virginia, came from the Southwest by the 1850s, and 10 percent of the other students in the older South may have been from the new states.

Despite the internal migrations within the South, the Southern colleges were more community based than most of the colleges in the North. With a very dispersed population, the percentage of students of the small Southern colleges coming from within the immediate area of the respective college was close to the percentage for the small New England schools, as was the average distance between a student's home and his college. And except for the University of Virginia, the large colleges of the South had significant proportions of their students from within their immediate areas.

Recovery of information on the family backgrounds of Southern students was disappointing, and the biographers of Southerners probably had a greater tendency to overreport high social status than those in the other regions. But with the help of information on the homes of the students, such as descriptions of birthplaces as manors or plantations, some limited generalizations are possible about the socioeconomic backgrounds of Southern students. The older institutions of the South, especially the state universities, served the planter elite and the professionals of the larger urban centers. The new schools appear to have attracted a somewhat different strata of Southern society. The information on the families of students of the smaller colleges consistently showed a higher percentage of ministers, businessmen, and professionals than did the state institutions, and the descriptions of those in agriculture suggested that they did not come from the elite. But the larger institutions of the South did have representations of professionals and businessmen. The universities of Virigina and North Carolina had 30 percent of their reported parental occupations within the professions and business in the 1850s.

A special effort, with small results, was made to identify and trace students who had received scholarships from the state institutions of the South. It was not only difficult to identify these students because of the nature of the record keeping of the colleges, but little information was gained on their backgrounds. There is no positive proof or disproof that the large state institutions used their mandated scholarships to broaden the socioeconomic backgrounds of their student population.[44] However, it is likely that Southern colleges were providing the opportunity for social mobility. It was offered by the newer denominational colleges of the region, but it was unlike that offered by the "pauper" institutions of New England. Both the statistical evidence and the impressionistic knowledge gained from reading the histories of the Southern institutions and the biographies of their students suggest that a middle class was arising in the South, and it was legitimatizing and serving itself through the new denominational colleges. The new colleges reflected the religious and social differences in the region and the emergence of professionals and respectable farmers in and near the growing number of new towns. These groups used the colleges as avenues to the professions and as a means to assume local leadership roles. But although the ministry was an important source of status for young men, it did not play the predominant role that it did in New England because the small colleges of the South remained distinct even in respect to the occupational destinations of their students.[45]

Although the South was not producing large numbers of ministers through its colleges, the Midwest became a haven for ministerial students. Furthermore, the students in the Midwest were different from those in the South and even those in other Northern regions. Despite the great social, ethnic, and economic variations in the Midwest, the information on the backgrounds of its students indicate that it was a distinguishable educational region at the beginning of the Civil War. However, in some ways the Midwestern students were similar to those of New England. Although its economy and stage of social development were unlike those of the East, many of the students of the region behaved as if they were New Englanders.[46] (Tables 3.11, 3.12)

The Midwest was distinct because of the high percentages of both younger and mature students, the great numbers of urban students and the unexpected distribution of ages in its more famous colleges. The recovery of information of the entry ages of Midwestern students was not as satisfactory as that for New England, but enough information exists to provide a basis for more than guarded generalizations. Student ages in the Midwest indicate that it was a distinctive educational region. In its smaller colleges there was less age homogeneity than in other areas and, in contrast to the typical relation between large and small institutions, the large colleges tended to be "older". Within the small colleges, the average ages were similar to those in New England in the 1850s, although statistical tests did show significant differences. There was a significantly greater percentage of both older and younger students than in the other regions where one or the other age groups predominated. The samples indicate that the schools of the 1850s had age distributions

Table 3.11

Mean Age at Entry, Percent Entering College Below Age Seventeen and Above Age 21 for Midwestern Colleges by Decade by Entry, 1830-1860

	1830's				1840's				1850's			
	$\bar{x}$	% <17	% >21	n cases	$\bar{x}$	% <17	% >21	n cases	$\bar{x}$	% <17	% >21	n cases
Oberlin	–	–	–	–	20.94	5	44	18	22.04	4	54	24
University of Michigan	–	–	–	–	19.83	22	27	18	20.15	11	32	58
Other Colleges	18.55	29	11	85	19.65	26	27	129	19.10	28	17	237

Table 3.12

Geographic Background Characteristics of Students at Midwestern Colleges by Decade of Entry, 1830-1860.
A) Percent of Students from Large Cities
B) Percent of Students from Within the State of Each College C) Percent of Students from Within the Midwest
D) Percent of Students from Within 100 Zip Codes of Each College

	1830's				1840's				1850's			
	A	B	C	D	A	B	C	D	A	B	C	D
Oberlin %	15	28	33	12	7	39	57	18	16	43	66	23
n cases	27	25	27	25	44	44	44	44	44	44	44	44
University of Michigan %	-	-	-	-	14	72	79	52	19	60	83	32
n cases	-	-	-	-	28	29	29	27	94	94	98	94
Other Colleges %	14	44	50	16	13	47	61	19	13	57	70	23
n cases	143	142	143	138	277	286	288	280	588	597	597	594

much like those of the small New England colleges of 1800, with the Midwestern schools having double the New England percentage of students who entered below seventeen years of age in the 1850s.

The two most famous colleges of the Midwest, Oberlin and the University of Michigan, did not have age distributions like the region's small colleges. Although the curricula and general orientations of these institutions were very different, they both had greater percentages of mature students and fewer young students. The secular University of Michigan and the radical denominational Oberlin had students whose ages were distibuted like those of the small New England colleges of the 1850s. One result of the age distributions of the Midwestern colleges was a special teaching environment. Perhaps because of a poorly developed lower educational system and its family and economic structures, the colleges faced the problems of dealing with extreme age diversity and probably great differences in preparation levels and orientations. Except for the two larger colleges, the region was far from achieving conformity with modern age norms, and the schools accepted the task of teaching students with ages ranging from twelve or thirteen to the middle thirties. However, most Western colleges continued to maintain preparatory departments in order to ensure some homogeneity.

The Midwest also differed from New England in respect to the urban and rural backgrounds of its students. And the difference was in a direction opposite of what might be expected from the image of the egalitarian Midwest and the geographic distribution of its population. The small colleges had estimates of the percentage of students from large urban centers which ranged from 13 to 15 percent, a much greater than expected score for an essentially agricultural region. In comparison to the area's general population, the colleges were probably more "urban" than New England's, and the University of Michigan and Oberlin had the same urban bias as the small colleges. Despite the unexpected numbers of students from large cities, the region had the highest percentages of small–town and rural students. However, there may have been several institutions among the small colleges that serviced an exclusively rural population. As in the South, Midwestern schools such as Iowa Wesleyan, rather than the state colleges, were the ones oriented to the majority of the region's population.

The Midwestern colleges were community oriented and accepted a greater proportion of their students from local areas than did the small colleges of New England. In the 1850s, perhaps 60 percent of the students went to college in their home state, and the percentage that came from the immediate area of a college was equal to that in New England —despite the greater dispersion of the general population in the Midwest. Approximately 25 percent of the students of the small colleges lived in the immediate area of the college during the 1850s. The University of Michigan and Oberlin were not significantly different from the small colleges but the samples do hint that some of the denominational collges, such as Kenyon, did not depend upon local students but, very early in their histories, were able to draw from a much wider geographic area.

One difficulty in attempting to understand the nature of Midwestern collegiate populations is the seeming tendency of many of its institutions to report birth places as the home areas of their students. This makes it difficult for an investigator to determine whether the colleges were truly attracting students from other regions. Accepting home areas as reported in the pooled sample for the small colleges does, however, make the Midwest appear to have been well–connected with the other regions. Perhaps 20 percent of its students were from other regions, with the Middle Atlantic states being the source of the majority of students coming from outside the region. The South contributed almost as many students but less than 5 percent came from New England. The regional migrations were not, it appears, evenly spread over the Midwest. Illinois and Indiana played host to more Southern students than the other states, and migrants from the Northeast tended to select colleges in Ohio and Michigan. Despite Oberlin's connections with New England and Michigan's reformed curricula and low tuitions, both colleges may have been more local than many of the smaller colleges. Oberlin had a somewhat greater attraction for students from the East than did Michigan, and both colleges, despite their different political orientations, had almost no Southern students.

Although the estimates of geographic origins were based upon relatively large samples, the recovery of information on the occupations of the fathers of the Midwestern students was very discouraging. Typically, professionals seem to have been overrepresented, but there was an unexpectedly high percentage of businessmen. The poor recovery rate, however, may be an indication that despite the bias toward students from large cities, the Midwestern schools enrolled the sons, and, in the case of Oberlin, the daughters, of farm families.

The social backgrounds of Midwestern students and their ages and urbanity raise questions about Allmendinger's explanation of change in the American colleges. He explained the alterations in the backgrounds of students and the diversification of New England's colleges through specific economic and demographic factors. The number of "pauper" scholars increased because of a combination of the numbers of mature young men who were pushed off of family farms with little hope of amassing the capital needed to reestablish themselves in agriculture and the growing demand and support for a trained ministry. Thus demographic crowding, the economics of farming in New England, and the cultural habit of demanding that sons repay their rearing costs by working on the family farm forced those men into the colleges.[47] The high percentages of mature students in the Midwest places limits on Allmendinger's explanation. Why should so many older men have entered college in the Midwest where the economy and demography were so different from New England's? The Midwest was a flourishing agricultural area, and its frontiers gave a young man the chance to enter into farming with relatively little capital. The growth of towns offered employment in other occupations, and it certainly was not an overcrowded area. Furthermore, if the complaints of contemporaries and recent studies of the professions are correct, the Midwest did not have the social or educational restrictions on entry into the professions, including the ministry, that made New England, to many, an advanced and modern area.[48] Something more than a universal "push" thesis will have to be developed before the age and urbanity patterns of the Midwest may be explained. Perhaps cultural norms imported from New England played a role in patterns of retention of young men on the farms until they reached an older age. And perhaps the costs of education, especially for ministers, made the profession an economically advantageous career compared to farming.[49]

Another problem will have to be resolved. It is one that is more important than the explanation of the particular age distributions in the various regions. The findings on the backgrounds of students strongly suggest that young men of the period tended to make their occupational choices before they entered into the liberal arts colleges. Not only did future ministers create pressures on the colleges to provide preprofessional training, but those who entered other professions molded the colleges through both specific demands and the tone they imposed upon the institutions.[50] (Table 3.13)

The predetermined occupations of the students, along with regional influences, helped set the social as well as educational reputations of the various colleges. Behind the occupational choices of the students was the force of the social and class permeability of the various professions, the costs of training in each, and their recruitment systems.[51] These social and class influences resulted in significant differences among the students who entered the various occupations. These differences were reflected in the colleges through the mix of the projected professions of their students.

What remains unexplained is not the influence of the students on the institutions, but the causes of the different background characteristics of students with varied occupational destinations. Joseph Kett found similar differences in his study of all members of particular occupations. In his study of American youth of the nineteenth century he discovered signif-

Table 3.13

Background Characteristics of Students Entering Various Occupations By Region and Decade of Entry Into College, 1800-1860. A) Mean Age at Entry B) Percent from Large Cities C) Percent From Within State of College D) Percent From Within 100 Zip Codes of College E) Average Miles From Home to College F) Approximate Number of Cases for B-E

	1800's						1810's						1830's						1850's					
	A	B	C	D	E	F	A	B	C	D	E	F	A	B	C	D	E	F	A	B	C	D	E	F
New England																								
Ministers	18.45	11	64	29	49	75	19.89	6	48	17	83	123	20.45	15	53	25	83	273	21.14	11	51	22	82	193
Doctors	17.84	23	69	43	77	31	20.16	37	70	47	25	67	19.43	40	63	35	82	136	20.08	19	61	29	65	136
Lawyers	16.94	10	66	28	70	125	18.35	13	53	27	88	85	17.54	20	64	32	60	147	19.11	17	59	23	89	220
Businessmen	16.38	27	69	25	30	16	18.11	43	67	38	48	21	17.51	19	73	29	60	52	18.64	28	73	46	62	152
Middle Atlantic																								
Ministers	16.38	32	66	24	46	29	18.66	20	70	14	50	58	20.24	25	61	17	93	259	20.13	26	60	17	110	301
Doctors	17.72	42	63	26	66	19	17.66	50	88	55	37	34	17.77	48	68	43	70	113	18.92	46	54	29	87	233
Lawyers	15.74	42	70	23	55	44	16.43	38	75	29	55	59	16.79	41	60	22	81	144	17.71	36	55	24	115	238
Businessmen	14.75	86	43	43	28	7	15.00	60	100	80	13	5	16.47	48	63	33	60	50	17.29	49	59	31	100	177
South Atlantic																								
Ministers	-	0	50	17	46	6	17.71	29	48	10	237	21	19.90	17	48	16	118	76	19.01	13	59	14	115	125
Doctors	-	9	64	55	119	11	22.66	13	67	21	119	25	17.53	22	74	16	141	101	18.59	16	66	12	151	197

Table 3.13 (Cont'd)

	1800's						1810's						1830's						1850's					
	A	B	C	D	E	F	A	B	C	D	E	F	A	B	C	D	E	F	A	B	C	D	E	F
South Atlantic (cont)																								
Lawyers	15.41	4	44	15	253	27	19.33	11	58	21	191	19	16.62	14	69	15	148	98	17.83	15	69	14	129	178
Businessmen	–	–	–	–	–	–	18.00	–	–	–	–	–	15.38	23	50	18	122	28	17.48	23	68	21	166	80
Southwest																								
Ministers	–	–	–	–	–	–	–	–	–	–	–	–	18.55	33	43	23	268	22	19.91	11	58	23	241	62
Doctors	–	–	–	–	–	–	–	–	–	–	–	–	16.22	25	29	13	382	24	18.77	16	57	22	283	103
Lawyers	–	–	–	–	–	–	–	–	–	–	–	–	16.37	31	48	14	418	44	17.10	25	65	18	302	134
Businessmen	–	–	–	–	–	–	–	–	–	–	–	–	16.33	30	60	10	274	10	17.01	29	49	20	319	79
Midwest																								
Ministers	–	–	–	–	–	–	–	–	–	–	–	–	19.91	6	34	0	174	32	20.86	19	50	18	169	132
Doctors	–	–	–	–	–	–	–	–	–	–	–	–	18.20	0	79	36	197	14	20.22	26	44	18	224	73
Lawyers	–	–	–	–	–	–	–	–	–	–	–	–	17.69	13	56	20	187	27	18.50	10	53	19	175	145
Businessmen	–	–	–	–	–	–	–	–	–	–	–	–	19.40	56	56	33	209	9	18.92	21	53	21	235	79

icant differences of age–of–entry into various occupations. He explained these through the varied years of education (whether formal or apprenticeship) demanded by each profession. But the data on the entrance ages of students in the liberal arts colleges indicate that there were significant age differences before a young man even began his professional training. Nothing as simple as years of required professional education can account for these differences; a much more subtle social process was at work in all the regions, sorting out who would become a doctor, minister, or lawyer.[52]

There were significant and historically important differences in the ages of those who entered the liberal arts colleges and then went into different professions and occupations. These relationships held across time and regions and, if age is accepted as an indicator of socioeconomic background, the colleges, because of different balances in the students' envisioned occupations, were shaped by class differences. Those who became ministers, regardless of the region of their college or their home, were significantly older when they entered the liberal arts colleges than the students who would enter the other professions or business. Depending upon the professions to which that of the ministry is compared, the estimates place their average age at one to two years greater than others. The future ministers had significantly higher percentages of mature young men and significantly lower percentages of those who entered college at or below sixteen years of age. Those who became physicians appear to have had the next highest age of entry, with estimates which placed them one year younger than future ministers, and one year older than lawyers and businessmen. But beginning in the 1830s, the age distribution of physicians changed. Appreciable percentages of older students, as well as significant numbers of those who entered college below seventeen years of age appeared. The change in the age distribution of future physicians was especially noticeable in New England and the Midwest, perhaps due to the opening of the profession to lower–status men as the control of medicine passed from the alleopathic elite. Except in New England, future lawyers and businessmen had similar average ages at entry into college. The groups which entered these occupations tended to have low percentages of those who began liberal education at the age of maturity or greater, and comparatively high percentages of those who entered at sixteen or below. The estimates of percentages of younger entrants for physicians and lawyers typically were twice those for ministers and the proportion of the older men was less than one–half. The admittedly small sample size for those who ever became college professors or presidents indicated an unexpected age distribution. The existing estimates suggest that those who became part of academia, though usually ministers, were significantly younger than their strictly clerical counterparts. And the percentages of the academics who entered the liberal arts colleges below the age of seventeen, by the 1850s, was twice as great as for the ministers in all regions except the South.

The interaction of regional and occupational differences extended its influence to other background characteristics of the students. Although the differences were not as pronounced as in the case of ages, they reflect the impact of occupational aspirations filtered through a complex web of family resources, cultures, and professional restrictions. Ministers were more likely to have come from rural homes than were those who entered the other occupations. Perhaps because the nonurban environment was one in which the ministry was the most visible profession, it was the most attractive to rural young men. But more than role models and the tendency for ministers to recruit and train young men is needed to account for the high percentages of future ministers from rural areas. The ministry did hold out a promise of economic support for young men regardless of their backgrounds. The rural men must have felt welcome in the ministry because it needed to attract those who would be satisfied with a rural life without the possibilities of extremely high incomes.[53] Throughout the country, the colleges that produced significant numbers of ministers not only faced the challenge of adjusting to older and poorer students, but to a student body with a rural background and, perhaps, careers. This type of challenge was generated to some degree by students who became lawyers. The nature of the controls over the profession and the increasing demand for lawyers in all areas of the country made prospective lawyers the second ranking rural and small–town group in the colleges. These men were always more likely to have come from a nonurban background than were the physicians, academicians, or businessmen.[54]

Although many claimed that the business world was the major avenue for social mobility in nineteenth–century America, because it had no restrictions on entry and an objective measure of performance, business did not offer a great opportunity for mobility to liberal arts students. Both the ages and the rural–urban indicators suggest that future college–bred businessmen were from a more elite background than ministers, lawyers, or physicians. Those who entered business from the colleges were very likely to have come from established urban families. Colleges did not have the help of outside social and economic support or the pressures on future businessmen to allow them to attract large numbers of nonelite young men and channel them into the commercial or industrial world.[55]

Only one other significant background difference based upon future occupation emerged from the information on the students. Future ministers were more likely to have migrated to another state for their liberal arts education than those who chose the other professions and occupations. Lawyers, physicians, and especially businessmen appear to have been much more attracted to the colleges within their state, region, and immediate areas. Future ministers may well have moved to a greater extent because of denominational influences which led them to seek an institution known to support their established beliefs and because ministers had the need of and opportunity for economic support during their college years.

Unfortunately, it was impossible to isolate statistically those who became professional teachers from other occupations because of the habit of ministers and all other professionals in the early nineteenth century to teach during some period of their careers. But the impressionistic evidence is that, like ministers, professional primary and secondary teachers tended to be both older and more "rural" than those in the other secular professions.

Because of the influence of region and projected occupation it is impossible to isolate a pure denominational effect or to continue to use the concept of denominational colleges in respect to student backgrounds. Such categories as Baptist or Methodist or Presbyterian colleges have little specific meaning, and only a few denominations had student populations with any characteristics that seem to transcend the importance of region, college location, or the precollege occupational choices of their students. Quaker, Episcopal and Catholic colleges across the country seemed to have served students who were somewhat younger than the average student of the period. But part of this difference may be explained by the more than typical urban population and location of these denominational colleges. Congregational institutions did have students older than the average and more students who had begun their higher education at or above the age of majority. But the distinctive characteristics of the Congregational institutions were partially due to the exclusive Northern location of their college. While some of the minor denominations may have had more rural and local students, the samples for their colleges were too small to justify more precise generalizations. No significant denominational patterns were found for other background characteristics of students.

Chapter 4

Student Careers

Although the traditional histories of the antebellum colleges relied upon the supposed background characteristics of the students, the most important judgments of the colleges were based upon generalizations concerning the careers of the alumni. To show the dysfunctional nature of liberal education and the inability of the colleges to adjust to modernizing America, the numbers of ministers, the localism, and the conservatism among the alumni were emphasized. Critics stressed the few scientists, farmers, technologists, and politicians produced by the liberal arts schools to demonstrate that the antebellum college was incapable of contributing to American intellectual, scientific, or economic development.[1]

The generalizations about the occupations and contributions of the early students were based on little systematic evidence, and the information that was available was interpreted in an ahistorical manner. The critics applied the same sets of assumptions to the students' careers as they used to evaluate their background characteristics. The static, ideal–polar type was the basic conceptual framework, and it was embellished by the assumptions of educational autonomy, constant socioeconomic conditions, and infinite intellectual and educational resources. The study of careers was distorted by the projection of an occupational distribution on the antebellum period that fit the mid–twentieth rather than the nineteenth century.[2]

The liberal arts colleges were serving a changing student population because students adjusted to the alterations in the opportunities in and requirements for the various professions. Just as backgrounds of students began to differentiate and to represent a broader spectrum of the American population, occupational destinations and career patterns altered. And these changes were not a simple product of differences in educational programs, but were the result of the interaction of shifts in job markets and associated entry requirements, the socioeconomic backgrounds of students, regional economies, and the social and professional connections of the colleges and their alumni.

As occupational and career patterns changed, so did the colleges. The occupational aspirations of students had an immediate impact on the institutions, but the professional, social, and regional destinations of the alumni exerted subtle pressures upon the colleges. The alumni created college reputations, established recruitment and hiring channels, and set limits to the possibilities for fundraising and the political influence of the various colleges. While the colleges developed differing alumni and public images, there was a general trend towards the secularization of careers. Even as many institutions took advantage of the demand for ministers, the majority of their students entered other professions, and the link between the colleges and the secular world remained strong. Despite the increased numbers of students from nonelite and rural backgrounds, almost all indicators suggest that the contributions of the liberal arts students to business, technology, and science increased and that the students were a major force in American politics.

However, the colleges did not reproduce the distribution of occupations among the general population of the antebellum period. Students of the colleges chose professions with relatively high social or economic status, and they did not, as some populistic critics desired, become laborers or craftsmen. Rather, students increasingly chose to enter occupations more directly connected to social and economic modernization. Law, business, and science, as well as academia and engineering, became the professional destinations of more students as these occupations became appealing to those who planned investments in higher education.

Most indicators suggest that the students were geographically mobile and were more likely to be at the rural and urban frontiers of America than was the general population. Extremely important to an evaluation of the historical literature on the colleges were the contributions of those who entered the ministry. Ministers, perhaps more than other professionals, played important multiple roles in American society. The ministry was becoming the destination of fewer of the antebellum students, but these men continued to act as educators, social workers, and community leaders, and it was the ahistorical assumptions of the historians rather than the actual behavior of the ministers which made them appear to be conservative and ineffectual.

Many of the misconceptions about the careers of the antebellum students were due to an absence of systematic and comprehensive information. Bailey Burritt's historical study of the single major occupation of the graduates of some thirty–seven larger Northern colleges was essentially correct. But its focus on the famous Northern institutions and its interest in the single occupation for which each graduate was remembered (with a very limited number of occupational categories used in the study) left later analysts with an incomplete and somewhat biased view of the experiences and contributions of the alumni.[3] For the biographical sample used in this study, a relatively successful effort was made to include students from all regions and colleges. Furthermore, students were traced throughout their lives, allowing for up to four different occupations and associated locations to be coded for each subject, as well as other career information. Room was allowed for ninety–nine different occupational categories, including such occupations as laborer and retiree, but slightly over forty were used because of the nature of the categories found in the biographical sources.[4]

The new information on careers indicates that Burritt's effort not only understated the students' involvement in business and industry, but his method of categorization led to low estimates of those in the traditional professions. His focus upon a single major occupation, a very modern notion, distorted the history of the careers of the alumni. Such restricted categories as lawyer, physician, and minister, abstracted from other information on careers, hid the differences in the lives of the students of the various colleges and regions. As importantly, the absence of information on Southern students masked the influence of regional cultures and economies on activities after graduation.[5] However, even Burritt's series pointed out that occupational distributions were not static and uniform. The American colleges were adjusting to the changes within the occupations in the different regions, but the underlying socioeconomic conditions of the areas and the nature of student populations did not change evenly; the result was a college system which may be categorized by the occupational and geographic destinations of the students by colleges and regions.

The use of the static type, the antebellum student, obscured many changes and differences. Central to that type was the production of ministers by the colleges. Historians, in order to contrast pre–and postbellum higher education, pictured the early colleges as ministerial enclaves and centered their evaluations and interpretations of the colleges around the thesis that the curricula and orientation of early higher education determined that the colleges could only attract future ministers. But the history of the numbers of clergymen and their actual roles indicates that the proportions of ministers and their lives were the result of much more than college policies.[6] The production of ministers varied over time and location and reflected differences in the demand for a trained ministry among the regions and denominations, the social tone of various colleges, and the rewards and costs of entry into the ministry for students from differing socioeconomic backgrounds. By the 1850s, the interaction of these factors meant that the American colleges were facing the inescapable pressures of adjusting to students who were selecting secular occupations.

New England's rather unique experience with the shifting demands for entry into the ministry is most important to an evaluation of the historical type and to an understanding of the forces working on the colleges. New England was the first region to have major changes in the occupational destinations of students, the shifts in that region were the most radical, and it was the region most frequently used as representative of the entire country by historians. But the changes in New England concerning occupational choices also made it a very special case in the history of American higher education. (Tables 4.1, 4.2, 4.3) Calculated either by grouping the students of the smaller colleges of the region or across institutions, the percentage of students who ever entered the ministry doubled between 1800 and 1810, as the percentages of future lawyers plummeted. By the middle of the 1810s, 40 percent of the students became ministers. However, Harvard and Yale continued with their 1800s proportions as their students found it easier to envision success through occupations which demanded more social credentials and economic self–sufficiency. But the attraction of the ministry in the early decades may have transcended the influence of the social background of students and the urban location of a college, for Brown followed the pattern of the smaller schools and doubled its 1800s percentage by graduating 30 percent of its students as ministers in the 1810s.

But Harvard and Yale did begin to change. Harvard had 20 percent of its alumni enter the ministry and Yale had 40 percent in the 1820s. But neither college felt the change that hit the other New England schools in the 1840s. The colleges had become accustomed to high percentages of future ministers in the 1810s, and there were only slight declines in the following decades. But the 1840s brought about challenging decreases. In that decade of enrollment decline many New England colleges had to accept a near 50 percent reduction of the proportion of their students who decided to become ministers. The majority of the small colleges experienced at least a one–third decrease in the 1840s or 1850s. Only Wesleyan, New England's Methodist college, escaped the shifts in occupational choice. The result of the changes of the 1840s and 1850s was that 25 percent of the students of the smaller New England colleges in 1850s entered the clergy at some point in their careers. Harvard had less than 10 percent and Yale had 20 percent.

The changes in the demand for preministerial training resulted in significant differences among New England's colleges. The history of the institutions, as well as their profiles in the 1850s, were affected by both the levels and changes in students' occupational choices. Harvard and Yale did not have the precipitous declines that threatened the other colleges in the later decades of the period. Harvard had always been well below the region's average for preparing future ministers because of its

Table 4.1

Estimates of Percent of Alumni and Former Students of Liberal Arts Colleges Who Entered the Ministry, By Various Colleges and Groups of Colleges and Decade of Entry Into College, 1800-1860 1) Ministers as Percent of Subjects With at Least One Known Occupation 2) Ministers as Percent of All Subjects 3) Number of Subjects With at Least One Known Occupation 4) Total Number of Subjects

College	1800's				1810's				1820's				1830's				1840's				1850's			
	1	2	3	4	1	2	3	4	1	2	3	4	1	2	3	4	1	2	3	4	1	2	3	4
Harvard	16	15	61	68	20	14	108	155	26	19	93	123	18	15	147	177	12	11	159	187	9	8	236	261
Yale	31	30	90	91	19	19	35	36	41	32	81	104	36	31	161	189	30	26	168	188	23	20	202	229
Other New England Colleges	27	21	149	187	46	39	183	217	48	42	293	338	43	38	464	532	30	27	505	567	28	26	655	713
Princeton	18	13	34	47	44	34	36	47	40	32	32	41	35	27	85	109	22	18	77	94	26	25	94	100
Union	23	14	30	49	42	37	71	81	41	38	104	113	41	37	130	142	32	30	132	141	24	21	102	121
Columbia	32	13	25	61	16	10	37	59	9	4	23	52	14	9	36	58	10	7	39	58	16	11	38	53
U. of Pennsylvania	36	36	14	14	22	20	23	25	22	20	32	34	15	13	93	108	18	16	159	186	13	12	124	137
Other Middle Atlantic Colleges	44	29	25	38	36	23	50	78	63	53	146	172	51	43	279	371	44	38	399	464	38	31	625	776
U. of Virginia	-	-	-	-	-	-	-	-	2	2	40	55	3	2	105	124	12	10	94	105	5	4	285	332
U. of North Carolina	13	7	15	27	26	17	27	40	23	20	55	65	20	16	55	67	5	4	78	105	8	6	157	210
U. of Georgia	-	-	-	-	-	-	-	-	12	3	8	30	21	10	29	57	3	2	37	57	2	2	41	61
Other South Atlantic Colleges	12	8	25	35	18	11	33	42	39	27	43	62	23	13	140	248	19	13	217	330	25	13	330	602

Table 4.1 (Cont'd)

College	1800's				1820's				1820's				1830's				1840's				1850's			
	1	2	3	4	1	2	3	4	1	2	3	4	1	2	3	4	1	2	3	4	1	2	3	4
U. of Alabama	–	–	–	–	–	–	–	–	–	–	–	–	3	2	37	48	0	0	34	35	1	1	72	101
Other Southwest Colleges	–	–	–	–	–	–	–	–	33	15	15	33	31	13	24	56	35	27	131	171	17	9	243	455
Oberlin	–	–	–	–	–	–	–	–	–	–	–	–	77	26	9	27	63	32	22	44	46	27	26	44
U. of Michigan	–	–	–	–	–	–	–	–	–	–	–	–	–	–	–	–	32	27	25	30	15	12	81	99
Other Midwest Colleges	–	–	–	–	–	–	–	–	16	10	21	33	40	24	137	215	39	26	243	366	29	18	448	708

Table 4.2

Selected Professions and Occupations as Percent of the United States' Workforce 1860

Professions and Occupations	Percent of Workforce
Ministers	0.450
Lawyers	0.400
Physicians	0.600
Scientific Occupations	0.180
Related Scientific Occupations	0.336
Editors	0.036
Professors	0.030

urban location, its high tuitions, and its association with Unitarianism, a denomination that generated a low demand for ministers. Yale, despite its tie to conservative Congregationalism, had regional and alumni connections which compensated for its decline in ministerial students. Brown's urban location provided some but not quite enough of an advantage to adjust to its reduction from close to 40 to less than 20 percent in three decades.[7] But other colleges had faced both the threatening sudden reductions and, at the same time, a continued high proportion of students who desired the curricula and services which would allow them to enter the ministry. Amherst and Wesleyan ended the period with 40 percent of their students becoming clergymen and Williams and Middlebury had 30 percent.

Similar trends appeared in the other regions, as did the growing differentiation among colleges. But in spite of the parallel histories of the education of ministers, significant differences among the regions remained at the beginning of the Civil War, reflecting the variance of regional economies and societies. Despite the same phenomena of surge and decline in the percentage of ministers among the alumni, the timing of change and the percentages opting for the ministry varied over the regions, leaving New England's experience as unique.

Biographical samples for the Middle Atlantic states during the first three decades of the century were less satisfactory than New England's, but the data strongly suggests that the smaller Middle Atlantic colleges

Text continues on p. 151

Table 4.3

Estimates of Percent of Students With at Least one Known Occupation Who Were Ever Once in Various Occupations For Various Colleges and Groups of Colleges, 1800-1860 By Decade of Entry Into College

Colleges	OCCUPATIONS 1 Lawyers	2 Physicians	3 All Business	4 Manufacturing	5 Banking & Finance	6 Teachers	7 Principals & Superintendents	8 Professors	9 College Presidents	10 Agriculturalists	11 Science & Technology	12 Judges	13 Military	14 State-Local Government	15 National Government	16 Diplomatic Services	17 Editors
								1800's									
Harvard	49	18	(12)	3	2	8	3	3	0	3	0	6	8	3	2	3	2
Yale	49	8	(14)	3	1	23	13	7	0	7	1	14	0	3	0	0	5
Other New England Colleges	45	12	(10)	3	2	17	6	5	2	4	(1)	12	4	8	5	1	1
Princeton	44	20	(9)	3	0	0	3	6	0	9	0	6	6	6	6	3	3
Union	39	16	(10)	0	0	3	0	3	0	3	0	3	0	0	0	0	0
Columbia	32	20	(19)	0	5	4	0	12	4	0	0	8	4	0	4	4	0
U. of Pennsylvania	43	7	(35)	14	0	7	7	0	14	0	0	0	14	14	7	0	0
Other Middle Atlantic Colleges	20	19	(0)	0	0	12	4	4	8	15	(4)	0	4	11	4	4	
U. North Carolina	27	33	(0)	0	0	0	0	7	7	27	0	13	13	20	7	13	0
Other South Atlantic Colleges	24	20	(15)	0	4	12	0	0	0	28	0	8	12	8	0	0	1

Table 4.3 (Cont'd)

Colleges	OCCUPATIONS 1 Lawyers	2 Physicians	3 All Business	4 Manufacturing	5 Banking & Finance	6 Teachers	7 Principals & Superintendents	8 Professors	9 College Presidents	10 Agriculturalists	11 Science & Technology	12 Judges	13 Military	14 State-Local Government	15 National Government	16 Diplomatic Services	17 Editors
	1810's																
Harvard	24	32	(18)	2	1	13	5	4	0	6	7	0	3	0	1	2	6
Yale	37	17	(9)	0	3	6	·0	8	0	6	14	8	0	6	0	3	0
Other New England Colleges	31	14	(16)	1	1	21	2	9	3	5	(1)	7	1	5	3	2	4
Princeton	19	19	(3)	0	3	0	5	14	3	11	3	5	3	0	3	0	5
Union	48	8	(9)	3	1	1	4	7	3	3	0	8	3	4	4	0	1
Columbia	38	32	(20)	3	3	0	3	8	0	3	0	5	0	0	0	3	3
U. of Pennsylvania	39	35	(8)	0	0	0	0	13	0		4	0	0	0	4	4	0
Other Middle Atlantic Colleges	22	28	(6)	0	0	6	2	2	2	2	(0)	10	2	4	2	2	0
U. of North Carolina	33	26	(4)	0	0	7	0	7	0	30	0	15	4	7	4	4	0
Other South Atlantic Colleges	15	24	0	0	0	0	0	6	0	51	6	0	6	0	0	0	0

Table 4.3 (Cont'd)

Colleges	1 Lawyers	2 Physicians	3 All Business	4 Manufacturing	5 Banking & Finance	6 Teachers	7 Principals & Superintendents	8 Professors	9 College Presidents	10 Agriculturalists	11 Science & Technology	12 Judges	13 Military	14 State-Local Government	15 National Government	16 Diplomatic Services	17 Editors
	OCCUPATIONS																
	1820's																
Harvard	22	21	(20)	8	6	6	6	2	2	2	(4)	2	1	2	2	1	5
Yale	31	18	(13)	1	4	22	11	5	1	3	(1)		0	7	0	1	1
Other New England Colleges	17	18	(13)	2	2	24	10	9	4	7	(2)	3	1	4	1	1	4
Princeton	11	13	(12)	2	0	13	4	7	2	7	(6)	2	4	11	2	0	2
Union	33	13	(5)	0	0	8	2	7	2	4	(2)	2	2	0	0	0	4
Columbia	–	–	–	–	–	–	–	–	–	–	–	–	–	–	–	–	–
U. of Pennsylvania	28	15	(24)	3	6	6	0	9	0	6	(9)	9	3	6	0	6	3
Other Middle Atlantic Colleges	18	8	(2)	0	1	17	3	4	2	6	(0)	4	2	6	1	1	1
U. of Virginia	47	20	(7)	0	0	5	0	0	0	37	(0)	0	0	0	0	0	5
U. of North Carolina	23	25	(12)	2	4	15	5	9	0	18	(0)	5	7	4	4	0	0
U. of Georgia	33	15	(12)	4	4	11	4	7	4	29	(0)	15	4	8	0	0	0
Other South Atlantic Colleges	14	25	(4)	0	2	14	7	5	7	19	(0)	0	7	2	5	0	7

Table 4.3 (Cont'd)

Colleges	1 Lawyers	2 Physicians	3 All Business	4 Manufacturing	5 Banking & Finance	6 Teachers	7 Principals & Superintendents	8 Professors	9 College Presidents	10 Agriculturalists	11 Science & Technology	12 Judges	13 Military	14 State-Local Government	15 National Government	16 Diplomatic Services	17 Editors
							OCCUPATIONS										
							1830's										
Harvard	21	31	(21)	5	3	11	6	9	0	2	(5)	4	4	3	1	0	1
Yale	25	19	(20)	1	4	19	8	9	1	8	(4)	6	2	2	2	3	1
Other New England Colleges	22	15	(21)	4	4	26	13	7	2	4	(4)	4	2	8	4	1	4
Princeton																	
Union	34	14	(26)	5	11	8	4	5	2	2	5	6	1	4	1	0	3
Columbia	36	19	(17)	0	6	5	3	5	0	3	(3)	0	11	0	0	0	3
U. of Pennsylvania	21	45	(15)	3	2	4	1	9	0	3	1	1	4	4	5	2	1
Other Middle Atlantic Colleges	17	9	(15)	2	3	12	6	8	3	4	(3)	3	3	3	2	1	5
U. of Virginia	30	25	(12)	3	0	5	2	3	0	41	(0)	9	0	10	2	0	4
U. of North Carolina	35	24	(12)	2	2	2	5	4	2	18	(0)	2	2	4	2	0	4
U. of Georgia	35	9	(6)	0	3	0	6	0	3	29	(0)	3	0	3	3	0	0
Other South Atlantic Colleges	23	22	(8)	0	1	9	3	7	4	26	(2)	3	1	4	1	1	1
U. of Alabama	39	19	(15)	0	3	3	0	0	0	54	(0)	13	13	0	0	0	3
Other Southwest Colleges	38	0	(8)	0	4	4	8	8	4	16	(0)	8	0	4	0	0	0
Other Midwest Colleges	24	15	(12)	2	2	20	8	12	3	6	1	7	1	10	5	1	4

Table 4.3 (Cont'd)

Colleges	OCCUPATIONS 1 Lawyers	2 Physicians	3 All Business	4 Manufacturing	5 Banking & Finance	6 Teachers	7 Principals & Superintendents	8 Professors	9 College Presidents	10 Agriculturalists	11 Science & Technology	12 Judges	13 Military	14 State-Local Government	15 National Government	16 Diplomatic Services	17 Editors
							1840's										
Harvard	40	27	(45)	11	17	5	2	11	2	7	(2)	5	2	2	1	1	6
Yale	30	25	(27)	5	4	23	11	6	0	7	(4)	5	1	3	2	1	2
Other New England Colleges	26	21	(25)	5	3	25	10	8	1	5	(7)	4	2	7	2	0	3
Princeton	27	35	(16)	1	6	9	6	8	0	9	(3)	6	1	4	1	1	8
Union	30	25	(18)	3	6	15	10	8	1	9	(5)	1	0	2	1	1	4
Columbia	18	46	(19)	3	8	3	0	3	0	3	(5)	0	3	0	0	0	0
U. of Pennsylvania	25	31	(30)	7	4	7	7	8	1	32	(6)	2	5	1	2	2	1
Other Middle Atlantic Colleges	21	13	(24)	2	2	21	9	6	3	5	(2)	4	2	3	1	1	5
U. of Virginia	22	35	(18)	3	0	11	1	2	0	24	(3)	2	3	4	1	0	3
U. of North Carolina	28	36	(8)	3	1	4	5	4	3	23	(5)	4	1	5	2	2	3
U. of Georgia	51	11	(20)	3	3	3	5	0	3	29	(0)	0	3	3	3	0	3
Other South Atlantic Colleges	19	27	(10)	1	1	15	4	3	1	21	(3)	1	2	5	1	1	1
U. of Alabama	21	21	(27)	0	0	12	3	0	0	26	(3)	0	0	0	0	0	0
Other Southwest Colleges	21	12	(7)	0	1	11	6	9	2	25	(6)	4	1	5	1	0	0

Table 4.3 (Cont'd)

Colleges	1 Lawyers	2 Physicians	3 All Business	4 Manufacturing	5 Banking & Finance	6 Teachers	7 Principals & Superintendents	8 Professors	9 College Presidents	10 Agriculturalists	11 Science & Technology	12 Judges	13 Military	14 State-Local Government	15 National Government	16 Diplomatic Services	17 Editors
Oberlin	9	14	(27)	4	9	14	14	23	0	9	(9)	0	0	0	0	4	14
U. of Michigan	43	12	(24)	0	4	16	20	12	8	0	(4)	16	4	12	0	0	8
Other Midwest Colleges	25	14	(17)	3	3	18	6	10	3	11	(10)	7	1	5	2	1	3
							1850's										
Harvard	31	15	(51)	10	11	17	10	11	2	8	(14)	2	5	2	2	2	0
Yale	33	21	(36)	10	8	13	10	10	9	8	(7)	4	3	3	1	1	7
Other New England Colleges	23	18	(32)	5	6	24	15	8	3	5	(5)	3	3	5	2	1	5
Princeton	28	26	(22)	2	7	8	6	7	1	7	(6)	3	4	4	2	1	4
Union	41	15	(15)	3	7	13	7	8	2	6	(3)	4	2	4	2	2	8
Columbia	05	55	(19)	0	3	3	0	10	0	3	(6)	0	5	16	0	0	0
U. of Pennsylvania	24	31	(37)	10	8	2	2	7	0	6	(14)	0	2	0	4	0	2
Other Middle Atlantic Colleges	19	11	(25)	4	5	16	8	6	2	7	(3)	3	2	4	4	1	5

Occupations 1–17 are grouped in the header under OCCUPATIONS.

Table 4.3 (Cont'd)

Colleges	OCCUPATIONS 1 Lawyers	2 Physicians	3 All Business	4 Manufacturing	5 Banking & Finance	6 Teachers	7 Principals & Superintendents	8 Professors	9 College Presidents	10 Agriculturalists	11 Science & Technology	12 Judges	13 Military	14 State-Local Government	15 National Government	16 Diplomatic Services	17 Editors
U. of Virginia	27	29	(15)	2	2	11	5	4	0	26	(1)	3	9	2	1	2	2
U. of North Carolina	36	18	(12)	3	3	6	2	6	1	22	(4)	4	4	4	1	0	4
U. of Georgia	22	22	(13)	0	4	10	2	0	0	34	(0)	5	0	2	2	0	2
Other South Atlantic Colleges	17	16	(18)	1	3	22	8	5	2	24	(2)	2	2	2	1	1	4
U. of Alabama	19	19	(43)	1	1	4	1	0	3	36	(1)	4	1	1	3	0	5
Other Southwest Colleges	30	17	(13)	2	1	10	5	4	1	22	(1)	3	1	2	1	0	1
Oberlin	19	19	(16)	4	4	8	19	8	0	4	(4)	0	0	0	8	8	0
U. of Michigan	37	21	(37)	6	4	8	7	12	1	8	(4)	9	1	4	3	1	6
Other Midwest Colleges	23	18	(23)	3	4	15	8	6	3	16	(3)	3	3	4	2	1	5

had a different history than their New England counterparts. The great increase of the percentage of students entering the ministry occurred a decade later than in New England, the proportions of ministers was greater, and the serious declines came in the 1850s. Furthermore, there appears to have been more diversity among the small Middle Atlantic colleges. As in New England, the famous schools ended the period with fewer students preparing for the ministry. Considered as a single group, the students of the smaller colleges were more likely to become ministers than those of Columbia, Pennsylvania, Union, or even Princeton. The newer institutions had perhaps a one–third proportion in the 1800s and 1810s, and then a sharp increase in the 1820s when one–half of their students became clergymen. The decline for the small colleges during the 1850s resulted in their having 30 percent of their students intending to become ministers. In contrast, the large colleges of the Middle Atlantic states ended the period producing between 10 and 20 percent ministers. However, there was great variation among the small colleges of the region. Because of the presence of colleges representing denominations with different cultural and economic histories and the associated demands for ministers, the small schools had a wide range in the percentages of clergy they enrolled. The samples for the individual colleges ranged from zero to over 70 percent during the 1850s. Quakers, because of their beliefs, did not have professional ministers, but the rural, Presbyterian Jefferson College and the Baptists' Madison College did continue to act as ministerial "factories."

The famous Middle Atlantic colleges had important differences among them. Columbia and the University of Pennsylvania, both urban and with ties to higher–status denominations, did not have significant changes in the percentages of future ministers, and in the 1850s continued to have perhaps 10 percent of their students entering the ministry. But Princeton and Union followed the typical trends of surge and decline. They more than doubled their percentages in the first two decades of the century, then faced significant decreases in the 1840s. However, they served approximately twice the percentage of future ministers as Columbia and Pennsylvania by the 1850s.

Although the Middle Atlantic colleges remained somewhat different from New England, the American South was a distinct region even in respect to the numbers of ministers serviced by its colleges. The most distinctive feature of its schools was the small percentages of ministers they produced. The American South has been described as a major center of revivalism in America and the dispersion of its population might suggest a high demand for ministers to serve in the many isolated congregations. But the expectation that the smaller Southern colleges served as ministerial seminaries was not supported by the samples taken for this study. Probably because of the social and economic systems of the South, which did not provide the pressures or inducements necessary to generate a strong link between liberal education and the ministry, the percentage of Southern students who entered the clergy was surprisingly low, perhaps a half that of New England's small colleges. The culture, politics, and social structure of the slave society may help explain the low proportions. The only areas in the South having institutions enrolling percentages of future ministers close to those in the North were located in the border states. The migration patterns of Southern students indicate that many of them had to move to the Northern border areas for denominational education.[8]

Although the samples and the success of the attempt to trace the students of Southern colleges were much less satisfactory than for the North, enough information was obtained to draw a general picture of the relationship between the colleges and the ministry. The data suggests that the small Southern colleges produced fewer ministers than their Northern counterparts and that the region followed a different pattern over time. But, as in the North, there was a growing differentiation among its colleges. The estimates for the grouped students of the small colleges exceeded 15 percent in only one decade. The small sample for the 1820s suggests that 20 percent of the students entered the ministry. There were no long–term trends or sudden changes in the South, even in the 1840s and 1850s when the region had so many college failures and foundings. However, the percentages across the institutions indicates that the colleges were differentiating. The mean percentage remained close to that of the grouped sample, but the reported scores ranged from 100 percent for a new Lutheran institution to zero for the Baptists' Columbian College in Washington, D.C. These scores must be interpreted with caution because of sampling variance and because there was a decided tendency for recently founded colleges to have high percentages of ministers, although some denominational institutions, such as Duke, began with ministerial percentages which were significantly lower than those in Northern colleges.

The estimates for the larger colleges of the South Atlantic and Southwest also suggest that the economic and social rewards for the ministry in the South were comparatively low and that the accessibility of higher education for the lower–status persons such as New England's "pauper" scholars of Allmendinger's study was limited. The only Southern institutions with consistent estimates suggesting that they graduated great numbers of future ministers were located in the border regions of the South. Colleges such as Cumberland, representing lower–status denominations and groups, had estimates of over 50 percent. The large colleges of the South had even smaller percentages of students who became ministers than the large institutions of the North. But the estimates may indicate that the state institutions of the South were not completely removed from denominational and religious influences. The University of North Carolina, the University of Georgia, and the University of Viriginia ended the period with perhaps 5 percent of their alumni entering the ministry. The large colleges of South Carolina had 1850s estimates of over 10 percent, but the state institutions of the Southwest had a 5 percent estimate. In almost every case, the large institutions had one previous decade in which the percent of future ministers was double that of the 1850s.

The Midwest was more like the East. But many of its states produced fewer ministers through their liberal arts colleges than did the New England colleges. The samples for the small colleges of the Midwest and for their grouped students suggest that, by the 1850s, the percentage of their students who became ministers was slightly less than that of the small New England colleges. However, there may have been more diversity in the Midwest. The estimates for the 1850s were 18 percent for the grouped students and 23 percent for the colleges of the region. Although there are indications that the percentages of ministers was declining in the region (and perhaps there was a significant drop in the 1840s and 1850s) the small colleges of the Midwest appear to have remained more diverse than those of New England. Many of the institutional samples had well over 50 percent of their alumni and nongraduates entering the ministry while several had less than 5 percent. Further investigation of the smaller Midwestern institutions is necessary. Many of the sample sizes were too small, because of the tiny regular student bodies, to serve as the basis for statistical inferences (unfortunately, Burritt's work was confined to a few Western colleges and was marred by great numbers of missing cases for the region).[9]

One surprising finding from the samples for the Midwest was the absence of significant differences between the grouped small college samples and those for larger institutions in the area. Oberlin and Michigan, colleges with very different reputations, seem not to have been significantly different from each other or from the grouped small colleges in the 1850s. And Miami, a large college with some claim to being a state institution, continued to have a very high proportion of its students becoming ministers.

Although the changes in the numbers of clergymen produced by the colleges in the various regions challenges the concepts of a static and uniform student body in the antebellum colleges, the history of the other occupations chosen by the students and secondary activities of the alumni and former students are a more direct means of rejecting the old concept of the antebellum student. The traditional historiography was intent upon showing the premodern nature of the colleges, and thus the number of ministers was emphasized, although some populistic critics also decried the high percentages of students who entered the other professions.[10] Such concepts as the "Great Retrogression," were centered about the influence of religion on the intellectual life of the colleges and the ministerial–bound students seemed to be a direct indicator of the denominational motives and the limitations of the colleges. The clergymen were proof of the inability of the established leaders of higher education to adjust to the new character of American life. But the critics' view of the occupational distribution of the students was distorted by the focus on the ministers and by their concept of what the distribution of occupations for college–trained individuals should have been in the nineteenth century. They overlooked the great numbers of students entering other occupations, and they assumed that the colleges could have quickly altered the numbers and natures of the professions in America.

The antebellum colleges, even in the 1830s when young men were very likely to choose the ministry, produced a majority of students who entered the secular occupations; by the 1850s the system was generating a predominantly nonclerical alumni. Bailey Burritt's study, because of its focus upon the occupation for which a student was remembered, underestimated the numbers of students who pursued secular careers—especially those who were active in business, technical, and industrial pursuits. Because this study allowed up to four occupations for each student, the estimates of those involved in science, business, industry, and government were consistently higher than Burritt's, as were the estimates for the percentages of students who entered the traditional professions. Also, allowing for multiple, concurrent, or sequential occupations and activities for the students highlighted how different the professional and occupational world of the nineteenth century was from the ideal of the critics of the colleges. (Tables 4.4, 4.5, 4.6)

For example, ministers did not confine themselves to purely religious duties, but served as educators and community builders; lawyers served as community leaders, were highly involved in the shaping of the laws that allowed the development of large–scale enterprise, and were directly involved in business activities; and even physicians, despite the specialized nature of their profession, held multiple positions and performed a great number of social services. And many students who did engage in the types of activities desired by the critics, such as teaching, crafts, and farming, found them to be unrewarding and took advantage of the opportunities of the traditional professions. Even those who opted for science or invention or engineering found it necessary, because of the lack of social and economic support for such occupations, to depend upon other means of livelihood.

Text continues on p. 183

Table 4.4

Percent of Urban Career Locations of Students of Various Colleges, Regional Locations of Career Locations and Characteristics of Home Areas of Students, 1800-1860 by Decade of Entry into Liberal Arts Colleges
Percentages are for: A) Ever-Once in an Urban Area or Region B) All Non-Repetitious Geographic Locations*

College		1 % Urban	2 New England	3 Middle Atlantic	4 South Atlantic	5 Southwest	6 Midwest	7 West	8 Foreign Countries	9 % Urban	10 % in Home State	11 % in Home Region	12 % Within 100 Zip Codes of Home	13 Number of Subjects
						1800's								
Harvard	From	20	94	2	2	0	0	0						
	To	42	A95 B80	6 5	5 4	3 3	5 4	0 0	5 4	37	60	82	34	62
Yale	From	19	81	10	8	0	0	0						
	To	43	A65 B44	53 36	10 7	5 3	9 6	0 0	7 5	32	38	54	24	87
Other New England Colleges	From	10	94	4	2	0	0	0						
	To	33	A72 B54	30 23	12 8	5 4	12 8	0 0	3 8	22	26	60	13	142
Princeton	From	33	2	61	33	4	0	0						
	To	33	A3 B2	67 52	39 30	8 7	6 4	0 0	6 4	32	52	69	25	36

Table 4.4 (Cont'd)

College		1 % Urban	2 New England	3 Middle Atlantic	4 South Atlantic	5 Southwest	6 Midwest	7 West	8 Foreign Countries	9 % Urban	10 % in Home State	11 % in Home Region	12 % Within 100 Zip Codes of Home	13 Number of Subjects
Union	From	42	11	85	0	2	0	0						
	To	38	A12 B11	82 76	0 0	6 5	6 5	0 0	3 3	32	64	80	38	33
Other Middle Atlantic Colleges	From	28	5	65	26	0	4	0						
	To	32	A3 B3	79 61	17 11	7 5	28 21	0 0	0 0	19	50	58	19	28
University of North Carolina	From	0	0	0	100	0	0	0						
	To	31	A0 B0	6 5	94 71	25 19	0 0	0 0	0 5	22	54	67	32	16
Other South Atlantic Colleges	From	7	0	3	96	0	0	0						
	To	13	A4 B4	4 4	71 61	38 29	0 0	4 4	4 4	12	50	71	12	23
1810's														
Harvard	From	33	83	1	9	6	0	0	-					
	To	62	A79 B62	17 13	14 11	8 6	3 3	0 0	7 5	47	65	76	33	122

Table 4.4 (Cont'd)

College		1 % Urban	2 New England	3 Middle Atlantic	4 South Atlantic	5 Southwest	6 Midwest	7 West	8 Foreign Countries	9 % Urban	10 % in Home State	11 % in Home Region	12 % Within 100 Zip Codes of Home	13 Number of Subjects
Yale	From	31	71	20	9	0	0	0	–					
	To	59	A44 B34	44 34	21 16	6 5	6 5	0 0	9 7	39	47	63	30	34
Other New England Colleges	From	10	90	6	2	1	1	0	–					
	To	31	A75 B51	22 14	20 13	9 6	17 11	0 0	6 4	20	26	58	11	183
Princeton	From	41	7	66	25	2	0	0	–					
	To	51	A5 B4	70 47	30 20	19 13	8 5	0 0	16 11	43	42	60	21	37
Union	From	33	16	75	6	4	0		–					
	To	47	A12 B10	73 63	12 10	4 3	12 10	1 1	1 1	36	49	65	19	74
Uhiversity of Pennsylvania	From	67	16	76	4	0	0	0	–					
	To	80	A0 B0	73 64	9 8	14 12	5 4	0 0	14 12	72	41	67	37	23
Other Middle Atlantic Colleges	From	22	8	68	17	3	0		–					
	To	37	A4 B3	74 52	26 16	9 7	24 19	2 1	2 1	26	53	61	14	54

Table 4.4 (Cont'd)

College		1 % Urban	2 New England	3 Middle Atlantic	4 South Atlantic	5 Southwest	6 Midwest	7 West	8 Foreign Countries	9 % Urban	10 % in Home State	11 % in Home Region	12 % Within 100 Zip Codes of Home	13 Number of Subjects
University of North Carolina	From	13	0	0	95	5	0	0	–					
	To	22	A4 B3	4 3	85 77	15 13	4 3	0 0	0 0	28	67	84	23	27
Other South Atlantic Colleges	From	8	2	0	97	2	0	0	–					
	To	23	A0 B0	11 10	77 63	26 22	0 0	6 5	0 0	20	50	71	5	35
						1820's								
Harvard	From	41	94	3	2	0	0	0						
	To	60	A85 B65	13 10	9 7	8 6	10 8	0 0	4 3	38	58	70	31	98
Yale	From	34	66	23	9	1	1	0						
	To	52	A59 B37	46 29	15 9	6 4	20 13	4 2	10 6	36	33	50	15	79
Other New England Colleges	From	14	82	10	3	1	2	2						
	To	40	A71 B44	32 21	13 8	13 8	21 13	1 1	7 5	22	26	53	12	299

Table 4.4 (Cont'd)

College		1 % Urban	2 New England	3 Middle Atlantic	4 South Atlantic	5 Southwest	6 Midwest	7 West	8 Foreign Countries	9 % Urban	10 % in Home State	11 % in Home Region	12 % Within 100 Zip Codes of Home	13 Number of Subjects
Princeton	From	28	2	72	12	13	1	–	–					
	To	52	A3 B2	70 52	23 17	17 12	9 7	8 6	5 4	34	44	65	21	96
Union	From	24	12	74	1	3	8	–	–					
	To	55	A12 B8	70 49	7 5	12 8	32 22	5 4	5 3	38	51	61	21	121
Columbia	From	89	8	93	6	2	0	–	–					
	To	86	A6 B4	89 68	14 11	8 6	0 0	3 2	11 19	70	55	65	43	36
University of Pennsylvania	From	93	0	97	2	2	0	–	–					
	To	91	A4 B3	85 68	19 15	9 7	4 3	0 0	5 14	68	54	70	46	130
Other Middle Atlantic Colleges	From	24	4	73	9	3	8	–	–					
	To	45	A5 B3	70 50	14 10	10 7	29 21	7 5	9 5	29	43	57	17	689
University of Virginia	From	18	0	1	74	24	0	–	–					
	To	32	A3 B1	4 4	70 61	33 28	2 2	3 3	3 2	28	64	77	38	297

Table 4.4 (Cont'd)

College		1 % Urban	2 New England	3 Middle Atlantic	4 South Atlantic	5 Southwest	6 Midwest	7 West	8 Foreign Countries	9 % Urban	10 % in Home State	11 % in Home Region	12 % Within 100 Zip Codes of Home	13 Number of Subjects
						1830's								
Harvard	From	36	86	3	10	1	1	0	–					
	To	64	A82 B59	13 10	13 10	5 3	7 5	5 3	14 10	51	56	64	34	177
Yale	From	36	57	25	10	5	3	0	–					
	To	59	A49 B29	43 25	19 11	16 9	22 13	6 4	15 9	40	34	48	17	161
Other New England Colleges	From	15	80	13	3	1	1	0	–					
	To	43	A64 B40	33 19	12 8	14 8	26 16	6 4	9 5	26	23	46	9	467
Princeton	From	42	2	63	26	9	1	0	–					
	To	56	A3 B3	60 46	24 18	22 16	14 10	3 3	6 4	40	44	61	23	88
Union	From	26	14	80	5	1	1	0	–					
	To	49	A12 B8	76 52	9 7	9 6	31 21	5 4	2 2	37	44	55	14	137
Columbia	From	53	0	93	0	7	0	0	–					
	To	83	A10 B9	86 76	7 6	10 9	0 0	0 0	0 0	81	81	81	76	29

Table 4.4 (Cont'd)

College		1 % Urban	2 New England	3 Middle Atlantic	4 South Atlantic	5 Southwest	6 Midwest	7 West	8 Foreign Countries	9 % Urban	10 % in Home State	11 % in Home Region	12 % Within 100 Zip Codes of Home	13 Number of Subjects
University of Pennsylvania	From	90	0	91	6	3	0	0	-					
	To	74	A8 B5	84 58	13 9	13 9	8 5	4 3	17 11	57	49	59	34	103
Other Middle Atlantic Colleges	From	27	7	77	10	1	5	0	-					
	To	42	A7 B5	67 47	18 12	12 8	32 23	4 3	4 2	30	52	67	8	313
University of Virginia	From	20	1	1	77	21	0	0	-					
	To	23	A0 B0	3 3	67 64	31 29	1 1	4 3	0 0	24	61	76	40	111
University of North Carolina	From	12	0	2	92	6	0	0	-					
	To	16	A0 B0	5 4	82 70	23 19	4 3	2 1	2 1	16	61	75	43	57
Other South Atlantic Colleges	From	25	0	6	85	8	1	0	-					
	To	26	A1 B1	9 8	79 69	23 19	1 1	1 1	1 1	20	50	72	19	131
University of Alabama	From	15	0	0	0	100	0	0	-					
	To	26	A0 B0	0 0	0 0	95 93	2 2	0 0	5 5	27	55	91	38	39

Table 4.4 (Cont'd)

College		1 % Urban	2 New England	3 Middle Atlantic	4 South Atlantic	5 Southwest	6 Midwest	7 West	8 Foreign Countries	9 % Urban	10 % in Home State	11 % in Home Region	12 % Within 100 Zip Codes of Home	13 Number of Subjects
University of North Carolina	From	10	0	0	76	21	1	–	–					
	To	19	A2 B2	2 2	73 67	28 25	1 1	1 1	3 3	21	65	83	38	157
University of Georgia	From	15	0	0	89	9	2	–	–					
	To	26	A0 B0	0 0	72 71	30 29	0 0	0 0	0 0	20	82	84	48	47
Other South Atlantic Colleges	From	18	1	3	86	10	1	–	–					
	To	19	A1 B1	4 3	83 71	25 21	2 1	1 1	2 2	17	65	77	36	370
University of Alabama	From	20	0	0	3	96	0	–	–					
	To	26	A0 B0	6 6	8 7	90 81	0 0	5 5	1 1	24	49	80	30	72
Other Southwest Colleges	From	17	1	1	3	91	5	–	–					
	To	33	A1 B1	1 1	5 4	90 83	9 8	2 2	1 1	30	64	82	41	279
Oberlin	From	16	9	23	0	0	66	–	–					
	To	37	A13 B9	23 16	18 12	13 8	62 42	10 7	8 5	25	14	36	6	39

Table 4.4 (Cont'd)

College		1 % Urban	2 New England	3 Middle Atlantic	4 South Atlantic	5 Southwest	6 Midwest	7 West	8 Foreign Countries	9 % Urban	10 % in Home State	11 % in Home Region	12 % Within 100 Zip Codes of Home	13 Number of Subjects
Other Southwest Colleges	From	26	0	2	14	86	0	0	–					
	To	19	A0 B0	0 0	13 13	87 83	3 3	6 1	6 0	10	52	85	17	31
Other Midwest Colleges	From	14	7	10	8	15	61	0	–					
	To	41	A7 B5	19 13	7 5	21 15	72 54	8 6	3 2	28	36	60	8	150
1840's														
Harvard	From	43												
	To	73	A81 B50	23 14	14 9	7 4	8 5	9 5	19 12	53	54	62	27	171
Yale	From	37												
	To	66	A51 B31	43 26	15 9	9 5	18 11	12 7	17 10	45	36	48	20	168
Other New England Colleges	From	14												
	To	44	A62 B40	31 20	12 8	9 6	26 17	6 4	9 6	29	35	52	17	545

Table 4.4 (Cont'd)

College		1 % Urban	2 New England	3 Middle Atlantic	4 South Atlantic	5 Southwest	6 Midwest	7 West	8 Foreign Countries	9 % Urban	10 % in Home State	11 % in Home Region	12 % Within 100 Zip Codes of Home	13 Number of Subjects
Princeton	From	31												
	To	49	A6 B4	63 42	32 21	14 9	21 14	4 3	12 8	39	37	55	24	78
Union	From	25												
	To	53	A17 B12	72 51	14 10	5 4	22 15	5 4	6 5	35	48	57	16	132
Columbia	From	63												
	To	80	A0 B0	88 78	3 2	8 7	8 7	0 0	6 5	76	86	87	50	39
University of Pennsylvania	From	89												
	To	80	A5 B4	88 63	17 12	4 3	10 7	3 2	10 8	64	50	64	36	172
Other Middle Atlantic Colleges	From	20												
	To	43	A6 B4	63 45	19 13	11 8	29 20	9 6	5 3	29	45	57	15	451
University of Virginia	From	16												
	To	27	A1 B1	4 4	69 68	27 24	4 1	1 1	4 2	29	65	79	31	94

Table 4.4 (Cont'd)

College		1 % Urban	2 New England	3 Middle Atlantic	4 South Atlantic	5 Southwest	6 Midwest	7 West	8 Foreign Countries	9 % Urban	10 % in Home State	11 % in Home Region	12 % Within 100 Zip Codes of Home	13 Number of Subjects
Princeton	From	40												
	To	45	A6 B5	77 57	32 23	13 9	6 5	3 2	0 0	29	44	60	23	31
Union	From	24												
	To	46	A19 B15	68 52	11 9	6 4	19 15	1 1	7 5	30	45	59	17	104
University of Pennsylvania	From	88												
	To	75	A6 B4	69 46	25 17	28 19	3 2	6 4	13 8	52	47	48	23	32
Other Middle Atlantic Colleges	From	17												
	To	35	A9 B6	69 47	22 16	9 7	29 21	2 1	4 3	20	37	53	5	158
University of North Carolina	From	11												
	To	15	A0 B0	4 3	82 70	24 20	4 3	0 0	4 3	14	61	71	47	55
Other South Atlantic Colleges	From	23												
	To	35	A4 B4	9 7	80 56	33 23	15 11	0 0	0 0	21	38	56	9	46

Table 4.4 (Cont'd)

College		1 % Urban	2 New England	3 Middle Atlantic	4 South Atlantic	5 Southwest	6 Midwest	7 West	8 Foreign Countries	9 % Urban	10 % in Home State	11 % in Home Region	12 % Within 100 Zip Codes of Home	13 Number of Subjects
University of North Caolina	From	16												
	To	21	A1 B1	4 3	69 63	27 25	4 3	1 1	4 3	22	66	75	38	81
University of Georgia	From	18												
	To	29	A0 B0	0 0	83 80	19 18	0 0	2 2	0 0	21	65	73	49	42
Other South Atlantic Colleges	From	23												
	To	27	A1 B1	12 10	78 64	21 17	4 3	2 1	3 3	21	55	70	32	235
University of Alabama	From	11												
	To	17	A0 B0	0 0	6 6	97 94	0 0	0 0	0 0	10	60	96	40	35
Other Southwest Colleges	From	18												
	To	29	A1 B1	5 4	3 2	88 76	10 9	6 5	3 2	26	51	72	28	143
Oberlin	From	7												
	To	39	A9 B6	18 13	9 6	9 6	82 57	12 9	3 2	24	22	36	7	33

Table 4.4 (Cont'd)

College		1 % Urban	2 New England	3 Middle Atlantic	4 South Atlantic	5 Southwest	6 Midwest	7 West	8 Foreign Countries	9 % Urban	10 % in Home State	11 % in Home Region	12 % Within 100 Zip Codes of Home	13 Number of Subjects
University of Michigan	From	14												
	To	64	A7 B5	25 18	7 5	4 3	82 61	7 5	4 3	39	28	38	14	28
Other Midwest Colleges	From	13												
	To	37	A8 B6	12 9	4 3	16 13	82 62	6 4	3 2	22	35	55	16	261
						1850's								
Harvard	From	39	80	10	4	1	4	–	–					
	To	77	A72 B43	29 17	9 6	6 4	18 11	8 5	25 15	53	49	55	28	257
Yale	From	37	51	30	6	5	7	–	–					
	To	69	A49 B28	55 31	16 9	14 8	17 10	6 4	17 10	51	38	50	18	203
Other New England Colleges	From	17	72	17	2	2	3	–	–					
	To	49	A59 B38	36 22	8 5	9 6	29 19	9 6	8 5	32	33	50	19	696

Table 4.4 (Cont'd)

College		1 % Urban	2 New England	3 Middle Atlantic	4 South Atlantic	5 Southwest	6 Midwest	7 West	8 Foreign Countries	9 % Urban	10 % in Home State	11 % in Home Region	12 % Within 100 Zip Codes of Home	13 Number of Subjects
University of Michigan	From	19	3	11	0	2	83	–	–					
	To	54	A2 B2	11 8	6 5	15 11	81 59	15 11	6 5	37	33	53	18	93
Other Midwest Colleges	From	13	4	12	3	8	70	–						
	To	36	A4 B3	13 8	6 4	18 13	77 58	12 5	5 4	29	36	54	16	526

Table 4.5

Geographic Characteristics of Home Areas, Career Locations and Mobility Patterns of Students of Liberal Arts Colleges Who Entered Various Professions and Occupations by College Region, Occupation and Decade of Entry Into College, 1800-1860 - (Career Location Percentages Based Upon Non-Repetitious Locations) (Home Category Indicates Relationship Between Home Area and College Area or Location)

COLLEGE REGION AND OCCUPATIONS			1 % of Locations in Larger Cities	2 Home State of Student or College	3 % of Locations in Home Region of Student or College	4 % of Locations Within 100 Zip Codes of Home or College	5 % of Location Within Student's Home County	6 Average Distance in Miles From Student's Home	7 No. of Subjects	8 % To or From New England	9 % To or From Middle Atlantic	10 % To or From South Atlantic	11 % To or From Southwest	12 % To or From Midwest	13 % To or From West	14 % To or From Foreign Countries
						Decade: 1800's										
New England																
	Ministers	Home	45	70	96	32	25	49		96	4	0	0	0	0	0
		Career Locations	14	33	65	19	15	127	75	56	24	4	3	9	0	4
	Lawyers	Home	37	67	100	27	18	70		100	0	0	4	0	0	0
		Career Locations	34	40	61	24	19	180		57	22	7	0	7	0	2
	Physicians	Home	31	76	100	45	37	77	125	100	0	0	0	0	0	0
		Career Locations	32	37	68	21	23	134	31	65	21	6	0	9	0	0

Table 4.5 (Cont'd)

COLLEGE REGION AND OCCUPATIONS		1 % of Locations in Larger Cities	2 Home State of Student or College	3 % of Locations in Home Region of Student or College	4 % of Locations Within 100 Zip Codes of Home or College	5 % of Locations Within Student's Home County	6 Average Distance in Miles From Student's Home	7 No. of Subjects	8 % To or From New England	9 % To or From Middle Atlantic	10 % To or From South Atlantic	11 % To or From Southwest	12 % To or From Midwest	13 % To or From West	14 % To or From Foreign Countries
						1800's (Cont'd)									
New England (Cont'd)															
Agriculturalist	Home	-	-	-	-	-	-	-	-	-	-	-	-	-	-
	Career Locations	-	-	-	-	-	-	-	-	-	-	-	-	-	-
Businessmen	Home	-	-	-	-	-	-	-	-	-	-	-	-	-	-
	Career Locations	-	-	-	-	-	-	-	-	-	-	-	-	-	-
Middle Atlantic															
Ministers	Home	52	79	86	34	32	46		14	86	0	0	0	0	0
	Career Locations	26	42	64	20	16	155	29	3	59	19	0	19	0	0
Lawyers	Home	57	70	77	29	24	55		23	77	0	0	0	0	0
	Career Locations	43	62	71	42	39	115	44	10	71	2	6	10	0	2
Physicians	Home	42	63	79	26	11	66		21	79	0	0	0	0	0
	Career Locations	50	67	75	42	39	142	19	0	74	9	9	0	0	9
Agriculturalists	Home	-	-	-	-	-	-	-	-	-	-	-	-	-	-
	Career Locations	-	-	-	-	-	-	-	-	-	-	-	-	-	-

Table 4.5 (Cont'd)

COLLEGE REGION AND OCCUPATIONS		1 % of Locations in Larger Cities	2 Home State of Student or College	3 % of Locations in Home Region of Student or College	4 % of Locations Within 100 Zip Codes of Home or College	5 % of Locations Within Student's Home County	6 Average Distance in Miles From Student's Home	7 No. of Subjects	8 % To or From New England	9 % To or From Middle Atlantic	10 % To or From South Atlantic	11 % To or From Southwest	12 % To or From Midwest	13 % To or From West	14 % To or From Foreign Countries
Middle Atlantic (Cont'd)															
Businessmen	Home	-	-	-	-	-	-	-	-	-	-	-	-	-	-
	Career Locations	-	-	-	-	-	-	-	-	-	-	-	-	-	-
						Decade: 1810's									
New England															
Ministers	Home	23	54	94	26	23	85		93	7	0	0	0	0	0
	Career Locations	22	28	54	11	10	221	75	49	21	12	4	11	0	2
Lawyers	Home	22	58	93	28	19	88		93	7	0	0	0	0	0
	Career Locations	38	43	57	29	22	188	125	56	18	8	5	6	0	5
Physicians	Home	34	77	97	50	47	35		95	5	0	0	0	0	0
	Career Locations	36	57	74	35	36	104	31	72	11	2	4	5	0	5
Agriculturalists	home	-	-	-	-	-	-	-	-	-	-	-	-	-	-
	Career Locations	-	-	-	-	-	-	-	-	-	-	-	-	-	-

Table 4.5 (Cont'd)

COLLEGE REGION AND OCCUPATIONS		1 % of Locations in Larger Cities	2 Home State of Student or College	3 % of Locations in Home Region of Student or College	4 % of Locations Within 100 Zip Codes of Home or College	5 % of Locations Within Student's Home County	6 Average Distance in Miles From Student's Home	7 No. of Subjects	8 % To or From New England	9 % To or From Middle Atlantic	10 % To or From South Atlantic	11 % To or From Southwest	12 % To or From Midwest	13 % To or From West	14 % To or From Foreign Countries
		Decade: 1830's													
New England															
Ministers	Home	32	61	89	31	25	83		89	7	1	0	3	1	0
	Career Locations	19	22	48	10	6	331	273	42	19	8	5	19	2	4
Lawyers	Home	24	74	96	39	26	60		96	3	1	0	0	0	0
	Career Locations	47	33	49	23	19	364	147	45	13	8	8	13	4	9
Physicians	Home	40	71	98	46	36	82		98	2	0	0	0	0	0
	Career Locations	49	40	50	26	28	290	136	51	16	5	4	8	6	9
Agiruclturalists	Home	-	-	-	-	-	-	-	-	-	-	-	-	-	-
	Career Locations	-	-	-	-	-	-	-	-	-	-	-	-	-	-
Businessmen	Home	23	85	98	31	29	60		98	2	0	0	0	0	0
	Career Locations	47	35	48	32	32	443	52	43	10	10	6	10	11	11

Table 4.5 (Cont'd)

COLLEGE REGION AND OCCUPATIONS		1 % of Locations in Larger Cities	2 Home State of Student or College	3 % of Locations in Home Region of Student or College	4 % of Locations Within 100 Zip Codes of Home or College	5 % of Locations Within Student's Home County	6 Average Distance in Miles From Student's Home	7 No. of Subjects	8 % To or From New England	9 % To or From Middle Atlantic	10 % To or From South Atlantic	11 % To or From Southwest	12 % To or From Midwest	13 % To or From West	14 % To or From Foreign Countries
New England (Cont'd)					1810's (Cont'd)										
Businessmen	Home	-	-	-	-	-	-	-	-	-	-	-	-	-	-
	Career Locations	-	-	-	-	-	-	-	-	-	-	-	-	-	-
Middle Atlantic															
Ministers	Home	50	86	91	36	34	50		9	91	0	0	0	0	0
	Career Locations	26	38	52	13	13	170	58	7	51	15	9	13	1	4
Lawyers	Home	71	76	88	32	28	55		12	88	0	0	0	0	0
	Career Locations	47	60	66	34	31	232	59	1	66	4	9	15	1	3
Physicians	Home	55	85	94	48	46	37		6	94	0	0	0	0	0
	Career Locations	64	64	72	56	53	132	34	3	72	8	3	6	0	8
Agriculturalists	Home	-	-	-	-	-	-	-	-	-	-	-	-	-	-
	Career Locations	-	-	-	-	-	-	-	-	-	-	-	-	-	-
Businessmen	Home	-	-	-	-	-	-	-	-	-	-	-	-	-	-
	Career Locations	-	-	-	-	-	-	-	-	-	-	-	-	-	-

Table 4.5 (Cont'd)

COLLEGE REGION AND OCCUPATIONS		1 % of Locations in Larger Cities	2 Home State of Student or College	3 % of Locations in Home Region of Student or College	4 % of Locations Within 100 Zip Codes of Home or College	5 % of Locations Within Student's Home County	6 Average Distance in Miles From Student's Home	7 No. of Subjects	8 % To or From New England	9 % To or From Middle Atlantic	10 % To or From South Atlantic	11 % To or From Southwest	12 % To or From Midwest	13 % To or From West	14 % To or From Foreign Countries
					1830's (Cont'd)										
Middle Atlantic															
Ministers	Home	38	69	79	26	26	93		18	79	0	0	4	0	0
	Career Locations	26	31	47	9	9	297	259	9	46	8	6	24	2	4
Lawyers	Home	54	63	77	27	26	81		20	77	1	0	1	0	0
	Career Locations	38	54	59	31	33	273	113	4	59	5	10	11	5	6
Physicians	Home	62	70	83	43	42	70		14	83	2	0	1	0	0
	Career Locations	56	53	62	37	35	185	50	4	62	6	6	10	4	8
Agriculturalists	Home	-	-	-	-	-	-	-	-	-	-	-	-	-	-
	Career Locations	-	-	-	-	-	-	-	-	-	-	-	-	-	-
Businessmen	Home	41	69	80	33	24	60		20	80	0	0	0	0	0
	Career Locations	50	37	48	24	22	270	76	9	50	9	9	21	3	0
South Atlantic															
Ministers	Home	14	51	60	16	19	118		7	26	60	1	4	0	0
	Career Locations	21	30	54	17	10	285	76	2	20	53	16	7	2	1

Table 4.5 (Cont'd)

COLLEGE REGION AND OCCUPATIONS		1 % of Locations in Larger Cities	2 Home State of Student or College	3 % of Locations in Home Region of Student or College	4 % of Locations Within 100 Zip Codes of Home or College	5 % of Locations Within Student's Home County	6 Average Distance in Miles From Student's Home	7 No. of Subjects	8 % To or From New England	9 % To or From Middle Atlantic	10 % To or From South Atlantic	11 % To or From Southwest	12 % To or From Midwest	13 % To or From West	14 % To or From Foreign Countries
South Atlantic (Cont'd)					1830's (Cont'd)										
Lawyers	Home	12	68	86	15	5	148								
	Career Locations	21	60	73	45	39	186	98	1	1	73	19	4	0	2
Physicians	Home	62	70	83	43	42	70		6	12	79	0	1	0	0
	Career Locations	31	54	71	35	33	211	101	2	9	71	13	1	2	3
Agriculturalists	Home	8	77	92	8	7	114		2	6	92	0	0	0	0
	Career Locations	6	75	81	63	60	112	62	0	2	83	15	2	2	0
Businessmen	Home	14	57	71	25	32	122		0	17	60	17	0	7	0
	Career Locations	47	50	58	41	41	195	28	0	11	60	21	2	4	2
Southwest															
Ministers	Home	14	50	50	27	18	268		0	14	14	50	23	0	0
	Career Locations	34	32	63	10	8	309	22	6	12	6	58	15	3	0
Lawyers	Home	14	41	45	14	9	418		9	14	23	45	9	0	0
	Career Locations	44	50	77	32	28	229	44	2	0	8	73	8	4	6

Table 4.5 (Cont'd)

COLLEGE REGION AND OCCUPATIONS		1 % of Locations in Larger Cities	2 Home State of Student or College	3 % of Locations in Home Region of Student or College	4 % of Locations Within 100 Zip Codes of Home or College	5 % of Locations Within Student's Home County	6 Average Distance in Miles From Student's Home	7 No. of Subjects	8 % To or From New England	9 % To or From Middle Atlantic	10 % To or From South Atlantic	11 % To or From Southwest	12 % To or From Midwest	13 % To or From West	14 % To or From Foreign Countries
		1830's (Cont'd)													
Southwest (Cont'd)															
Physicians	Home	33	21	33	4	0	382		4	8	42	33	13	0	0
	Career Locations	25	50	64	28	30	322	24	3	3	8	64	3	8	11
Agriculturalists	Home	7	43	50	20	14	438		10	0	37	50	3	0	0
	Career Locations	3	75	85	51	48	93	30	0	3	10	84	3	0	0
Businessmen	Home	-	-	-	-	-	-	-	-	-	-	-	-	-	-
	Career Locations	-	-	-	-	-	-	-	-	-	-	-	-	-	-
Midwest															
Ministers	Home	9	63	75	11	16	174		6	19	0	0	75	0	0
	Career Locations	26	28	54	9	7	214	32	10	20	4	14	49	2	2
Lawyers	Home	12	60	70	28	15	187		7	22	0	0	70	0	0
	Career Locations	39	45	68	26	26	224	27	0	13	10	8	60	8	3
Physicians	Home	7	86	86	29	23	197		14	0	0	0	86	0	0
	Career Locations	36	45	59	9	10	254	14	5	24	0	5	57	10	0

Table 4.5 (Cont'd

COLLEGE REGION AND OCCUPATIONS	1 % of Locations in Larger Cities	2 Home State of Student or College	3 % of Locations in Home Region of Student or College	4 % of Locations Within 100 Zip Codes of Home or College	5 % of Locations Within Student's Home County	6 Average Distance in Miles From Student's Home	7 No. of Subjects	8 % To or From New England	9 % To or From Middle Atlantic	10 % To or From South Atlantic	11 % To or From Southwest	12 % To or From Midwest	13 % To or From West	14 % To or From Foreign Countries
Midwest (Cont'd)														
Agriculturalists — Home	-	-	-	-	-	-	-	-	-	-	-	-	-	-
Agriculturalists — Career Locations	-	-	-	-	-	-	-	-	-	-	-	-	-	-
Businessmen — Home	-	-	-	-	-	-	-	-	-	-	-	-	-	-
Businessmen — Career Locations	-	-	-	-	-	-	-	-	-	-	-	-	-	-
Decade: 1850's														
New England														
Ministers — Home	22	62	93	28	25	83		93	2	1	0	4	0	0
Ministers — Career Locations	21	27	51	12	8	349	193	46	18	4	6	15	6	5
Lawyers — Home	26	71	92	30	23	89		92	5	0	2	0	0	0
Lawyers — Career Locations	44	33	42	20	17	323	220	43	18	5	6	21	5	3
Physicians — Home	31	63	95	34	18	65		96	3	0	1	1	0	0
Physicians — Career Locations	47	35	48	18	17	291	136	47	17	3	3	13	5	11
Agriculturalists — Home	25	75	88	56	57	56		88	13	0	0	0	0	0
Agriculturalists — Career Locations	14	50	54	27	26	332	16	55	14	9	5	18	0	0

Table 4.5 (Cont'd)

COLLEGE REGION AND OCCUPATIONS		1 % of Locations in Larger Cities	2 Home State of Student or College	3 % of Locations in Home Region of Student or College	4 % of Locations Within 100 Zip Codes of Home or College	5 % of Locations Within Student's Home County	6 Average Distance in Miles From Student's Home	7 No. of Subjects	8 % To or From New England	9 % To or From Middle Atlantic	10 % To or From South Atlantic	11 % To or From Southwest	12 % To or From Midwest	13 % To or From West	14 % To or From Foreign Countries
					1850's (Cont'd)										
New England (Cont'd) Businessmen	Home	27	80	99	52	35	62		99	0	0	0	1	0	0
	Career Locations	50	35	42	24	20	308	152	44	18	5	7	15	5	7
Middle Atlantic Ministers	Home	34	66	78	19	18	110		15	78	1	0	6	0	0
	Career Locations	25	31	47	9	7	310	301	9	45	6	5	24	5	5
Lawyers	Home	50	58	71	26	24	115		23	70	3	0	5	0	0
	Career Locations	56	53	60	33	31	136	238	3	59	12	5	14	4	4
Physicians	Home	46	61	72	35	34	87		21	72	3	1	4	0	0
	Career Locations	55	60	71	36	37	158	233	4	69	5	6	8	2	7
Agriculturalists	Home	24	71	95	33	29	68		0	95	0	0	0	5	0
	Career Locations	13	31	47	13	10	233	21	4	48	24	4	12	8	0
Businessmen	Home	48	63	70	35	28	100		24	70	1	0	5	0	0
	Career Locations	56	53	65	36	35	205	177	5	65	5	5	13	2	5

Table 4.5 (Cont'd)

COLLEGE REGION AND OCCUPATIONS		1 % of Locations in Larger Cities	2 Home State of Student or College	3 % of Locations in Home Region of Student or College	4 % of Locations Within 100 Zip Codes of Home or College	5 % of Locations Within Student's Home County	6 Average Distance in Miles From Student's Home	7 No. of Subjects	8 % To or From New England	9 % To or From Middle Atlantic	10 % To or From South Atlantic	11 % To or From Southwest	12 % To or From Midwest	13 % To or From West	14 % To or From Foreign Countries
					1850's (Cont'd)										
South Atlantic															
Ministers	Home	13	58	73	14	8	115		5	18	72	2	3	3	0
	Career Locations	19	41	63	16	13	280	125	1	10	61	16	6	6	4
Lawyers	Home	17	71	87	15	7	129		4	6	88	2	0	0	0
	Career Locations	34	66	79	43	43	168	178	1	3	79	11	2	2	2
Physicians	Home	22	66	82	13	10	151		6	8	82	3	2	2	0
	Career Locations	26	53	61	26	23	230	197	2	9	61	17	3	3	5
Agriculturalists	Home	14	79	92	13	7	127		3	3	93	3	0	0	0
	Career Locations	8	81	85	61	63	112	127	0	2	83	13	1	1	1
Businessmen	Home	21	67	85	17	11	122		0	13	83	0	0	0	0
	Career Locations	41	59	74	44	43	140	80	0	11	71	10	1	1	3
Southwest															
Ministers	Home	6	53	64	24	14	241		5	8	6	65	16	0	0
	Career Locations	19	38	55	17	9	326	62	2	9	7	51	19	3	9

Table 4.5 (Cont'd)

COLLEGE REGION AND OCCUPATIONS		1 % of Locations in Larger Cities	2 Home State of Student or College	3 % of Locations in Home Region of Student or College	4 % of Locations Within 100 Zip Codes of Home or College	5 % of Locations Within Student's Home County	6 Average Distance in Miles From Student's Home	7 No. of Subjects	8 % To or From New England	9 % To or From Middle Atlantic	10 % To or From South Atlantic	11 % To or From Southwest	12 % To or From Midwest	13 % To or From West	14 % To or From Foreign Countries
					1850's (Cont'd)										
Southwest (Cont'd)															
Lawyers	Home	15	48	63	18	9	302		2	7	24	65	2	0	0
	Career Locations	32	68	86	39	36	201	134	0	3	7	83	2	4	1
Physicians	Home	22	55	66	22	10	283		4	5	21	66	3	0	1
	Career Locations	21	53	85	31	26	227	103	0	4	4	82	4	8	3
Agriculturalists	Home	13	48	59	19	11	331		3	1	34	59	2	0	0
	Career Locations	10	71	87	53	52	129	91	0	0	10	86	2	0	1
Businessmen	Home	20	50	70	18	12	166		1	5	26	70	4	0	0
	Career Locations	24	54	82	38	31	152	79	1	4	7	78	4	2	3
Midwest															
Ministers	Home	10	58	72	29	16	169		8	20	1	0	71	0	0
	Career Locations	25	24	58	5	3	371	103	8	15	6	9	49	9	5
Lawyers	Home	11	65	80	26	12	175		6	12	1	1	81	0	0
	Career Locations	45	43	66	22	20	262	145	2	4	4	15	63	8	4

Table 4.5 (Cont'd)

COLLEGE REGION AND OCCUPATIONS		1 % of Locations in Larger Cities	2 Home State of Student or College	3 % of Locations in Home Region of Student or College	4 % of Locations Within 100 Zip Codes of Home or College	5 % of Locations Within Student's Home County	6 Average Distance in Miles From Student's Home	7 No. of Subjects	8 % To or From New England	9 % To or From Middle Atlantic	10 % To or From South Atlantic	11 % To or From Southwest	12 % To or From Midwest	13 % To or From West	14 % To or From Foreign Countries
Midwest (Cont'd)		1850's (Cont'd)													
Physicians	Home	13	56	74	22	11	224		18	4	1	1	74	0	1
	Career Locations	36	38	56	18	18	268	73	4	14	6	10	53	7	6
Agiruclturalists	Home	5	74	74	42	35	64		0	24	0	0	76	0	0
	Career Locations	7	42	76	41	37	347	21	8	4	0	12	72	4	0
Businessmen	Home	14	58	78	26	17	319		11	9	0	1	78	0	0
	Career Locations	48	41	62	20	21	304	79	1	9	4	12	58	13	3

TABLE 4.6

Career Mobility of Liberal Arts College Students Who Left Their Home Region to Attend College (Movers) and For Those Who Remained Within Their Home Region for Higher Liberal Education, 1800-1860 A) Percent of Non-Repetitious Careers Locations in Students' Home Region B) Average of Percent of Career Locations in Other Regions C) Number of Subjects

Home Region	1800-1829						1830-1860					
	Movers			Stayers			Movers			Stayers		
of Student	A	B	C	A	B	C	A	B	C	A	B	C
New England												
Large Colleges	55	13	37	84	9	390	34	23	118	81	20	797
Other Colleges	34	21	34	77	12	563	38	21	117	73	14	1290
Middle Atlantic												
Large Colleges	83	10	52	84	7	298	64	14	287	87	8	914
Other Colleges	61	16	64	81	10	146	62	15	427	77	11	994
South												
Large Colleges	88	8	124	100	2	305	91	10	269	100	2	1057
Other Colleges	90	12	52	100	4	111	78	13	361	100	3	1055
Midwest												
Large Colleges	-	-	-	-	-	-	58	18	62	78	7	111
Other Colleges	77	15	28	100	12	5	71	12	181	87	7	717

Although a study of the multiple occupations of students aids in understanding the history of higher education and serves as a means of differentiating the colleges, it is also misleading unless other information about careers is included. The lives of young men who entered similar occupations were very different depending upon their social backgrounds, the areas in which they pursued their careers, the level at which they entered their profession, and even the age at which they began their career. Thus, colleges which might appear to be similar because they produced the same percentages of lawyers or businessmen were really quite different because of the specific career patterns of their students.

As the focus upon ministers tended to locate causation in the colleges rather than in the society and economy, a consideration of the other professions might imply that colleges rather than regional and local economies and cultures caused professional distributions. But just as forces outside the colleges were the major determinants of the percentage of their students who became ministers, the distributions of other occupations were only partially caused by the efforts of educators.

Before examining the results of the survey of careers, a methodological aside is necessary. The search for information on the history of the students revealed a serious bias in the reporting of occupations. When individuals were traced from the short college biographical sketches to complete biographies or when those whose occupations were not recorded by the colleges were linked with other sources, it was found that secondary occupations were underreported and secular pursuits went unnoticed by the colleges. There was a bias towards a complete reporting of ministers but an under–reporting of those in the secular pursuits, especially business. Therefore, the estimates for business, science, agriculture, and industry and other professions are minimum estimates, and the cited percentages should be prefaced with the term, "at least." Because complete biographies revealed consistent concurrent occupational patterns, the lives of students who entered various occupations are interpreted with the help of the complete biographies.

The legal profession was the dominant choice of New England's students after the Revolution and until the 1810s, then, the general decline in enrollments and the increase of the percentage of students who became ministers was accompanied by a very significant decrease in the numbers and percentage of students entering the legal profession. Before 1800, the region's colleges were dominated by men who pursued careers in law and its corollary, political influence. In 1800, most of the smaller colleges had between 30 and 50 percent of their students entering the legal profession: the pooled estimate for the smaller colleges was 45 percent. Harvard and Yale had approximately 50 percent of their students becoming lawyers. The shift of choices by students in the 1810s, perhaps because of a "crowding" of the legal profession at the same time that it opened to those from lower social backgrounds, affected all the colleges. Harvard and Yale dropped to 30 percent, and among the smaller institutions similar reductions were accompanied by an increase in the differences among them. The pooled estimate for the smaller colleges dropped to 30 percent, but the range increased from perhaps 10 to 35 percent. However, the percentages remained relatively stable until the Civil War. Harvard and Yale ended the period with one–third of their students becoming lawyers. The smaller institutions in the 1850s produced from 15 to 30 percent and their pooled sample reached approximately 25 percent.

The other regions had a more consistent history concerning students who entered the legal profession. The small Middle Atlantic colleges, despite some shifting of percentages among them, had a fairly constant proportion of students who became lawyers. There was no significant drop for the grouped samples and the range was restricted. Beginning with approximately 20 percent in 1800 and with a low point in the 1820s of 17 percent, the period ended with perhaps, as in New England, 25 percent of the students of the smaller institutions becoming lawyers at some point in their careers. Among the larger colleges, the percentages were significantly higher, but like the small schools, the famous institutions in the Middle Atlantic states did not have to face the great shifts that hit New England. Princeton was the only large college that seems to have had a significant reduction in the numbers of students who intended to become lawyers; dropping from approximately 40 to 20 percent between 1800 and 1820. The other large colleges began the period with close to 40 percent intended lawyers, but their decline to one–fourth was relatively smooth. Union College, however, seems to have maintained the older high percentages of those who would become lawyers.

In the South and the Midwest, the small institutions began and ended the period with approximately 20 percent of their students entering law, and the variance over time in both regions was small compared to New England. However, the larger colleges did have a tendency to enroll somewhat higher percentages. And in the Midwest it appears that Oberlin and Michigan students did attend their colleges to pursue different occupational careers. Oberlin had perhaps between 7 and 10 percent and the University of Michigan probably sent a majority of its students into law.

Perhaps because of the growth of towns and business in the regions, the areas outside of New England were able to maintain rather constant percentages of lawyers; although the West and South were probably less stringent as to the qualifications for entry into law, many students continued to invest in liberal education before entry into the field.[11]

But the disproportionate percentages of lawyers, relative to the occupations of the general population, did not mean that the colleges were removed from direct contact with the business world. Through the primary occupations of their students and the concurrent interests of those who were remembered for other professional activities, the schools, by the 1840s, were as connected to business as they were to the ministry, at least in respect to the destinations of their alumni. The known business activities of the New England graduates and ex–students more than doubled over the sixty years and it appears that the 1840s were years of significant change for the smaller colleges. By the 1850s, at least 20 percent of the alumni and former students of the smaller institutions were engaged in some business activity. Harvard, Yale, and Brown, after slow and consistent growth, had over one–third of their students of the 1850s enter into the business world.

Despite the similar levels for the rural and urban colleges of the region, there were important differences between the types of schools, perhaps reflecting the social backgrounds and the urban connections of their students. Harvard's and Yale's students were much more involved with finance, banking, and manufacturing than those at the smaller colleges—20 versus 10 percent in the 1850s. The students of the smaller colleges were more likely to engage in general business, such as merchandising and real estate, than were Harvard's or even Yale's students. For example, Middlebury's sample for the 1850s yielded an estimate of 4 percent in banking, finance, and manufacturing compared to the 21 percent estimate for Harvard.

The unexpectedly high numbers of students of New England's colleges who entered business were probably matched by those in the Middle Atlantic's schools, but reported activity always fell somewhat below New England's. The region's samples for the 1800s suggest that its students became much less involved with business than those from New England, but by the 1830s the numbers who would enter business after leaving the small colleges approached those of New England. However, the small Middle Atlantic colleges did not keep pace with the changes of the 1840s and 1850s in New England. The percentages of students who went into general business remained close, but the Middle Atlantic's percentages for banking and industry fell below New England's. The large and famous institutions of the region followed their New England counterparts. Their percentage of graduates and ex–students who entered business grew slowly over the sixty years, exceeded that of the small colleges, and was nearly as great as New England's. Their students were closer to the centers of economic power than those of the smaller colleges. Perhaps, as in New England, the family backgrounds and urban connections of the students of the large colleges allowed them greater access to finance, banking, and the emerging railroad and manufacturing enterprises.

Despite the obvious underreporting of occupations in the South and the importance of its agricultural economy, the estimates indicate that Southern students were involved in business at levels at least two-thirds those of New England. Even with the economic activity, planter, excluded from the calculation of rates of business activity, the South's history paralleled the North's. There was consistent and slow growth over the six decades and the larger and famous colleges had more students engaged in financial and industrial pursuits than the region's other colleges.

Similar levels and trends emerged from the samples for the Midwest. The reported percentages grew from the 1830s until the Civil War, reaching approximately two-thirds of New England's. But in the Midwest another puzzle concerning the University of Michigan and Oberlin was indicated by the life histories. These two supposedly different institutions were not only quite similar in respect to the business activities of their students, but they appear to have been significantly different from the smaller colleges.

The desires of students who wanted to enter the medical profession had less impact on liberal education than did the wish to enter law or the ministry. While the traditional curricula of the colleges was of some practical benefit to those in fields where classical learning and public speaking were important, the best the colleges could do for future physicians, partially because of the low stage of development of medical knowledge, was to certify their general abilities and to grant them some degree of social status. Furthermore, the medical profession was changing rapidly during the early nineteenth century. The field was marked by great controversy over the correct school of practice because of the absence of a developed science of medicine. Medicine had been opened to those from lower socioeconomic backgrounds and it had become a very crowded profession without the relatively high rewards of medical practice in the twentieth century. There were more physicians in the United States in 1860 than ministers or lawyers; the number of physicians per person was the highest in known American history.[12] Despite the unique nature of the medical profession, a significant proportion of liberal arts students entered medicine. The percentages never equalled those for law or the ministry, but perhaps 20 percent of the early nineteenth-century students became doctors.

New England students do not seem to have been affected by the opening of the profession, and many young men decided that there was an economic reward from an investment in liberal education before entering medicine. The restrictive entry requirements in New England and the expectations on the part of the region's population for the social standing of physicians may have led to the relatively consistent percentages of students becoming physicians. There were no long–term trends or great shifts in the percentages of future doctors in New England's schools. The grouped samples for the small colleges suggest a range of 15 to 20 percent over the six decades without any clear trends. By the 1850s approximately 20 percent of the students selected the profession, and the individual colleges had percentages ranging from 30 to close to zero percent future phsyicians, as, for example, at Williams College. Harvard's and Yale's history of enrolling students who became physicians was similar to the grouped sample for the smaller colleges of New England, but the two institutions had significantly different percentages. Harvard usually had more aspiring doctors than Yale or most other New England colleges. But in the 1850s it had 15 percent and Yale had 21 percent future physicians.

The other regions had different relationships between liberal higher education and the medical profession. Although formal entry requirements for the profession may have been similar, the social demands, the competition among physicians and schools of practice, and the rewards of extended liberal education probably varied over areas of the country. In the Middle Atlantic states the smaller liberal arts colleges seem to have begun the century with 20 percent of their students becoming doctors. But there may have been a significant drop in the 1830s which led to the schools serving one–half the New England percentage of future physicians in the 1850s. The small colleges' 10 percent rate was exceeded by the larger colleges of the Middle Atlantic states. Pennsylvania, with its location in the leading center of medical training in the country, ended the period with estimates of over 30 percent, but the other large schools continued their period averages and had approximately 15 percent of their 1850s classes entering the medical profession.

The small colleges of the South may also have had a significant decline, probably because of the expansion in their numbers in the 1850s. The estimates dropped from 25 to 15 percent physicians among the alumni between the 1840s and 1850s, but even the ending percentage of future doctors indicates that the South still provided rewards for those who combined liberal education with their practice of medicine. The famous institutions of the region, those connected with the elites of the South, not only had slightly higher percentages than did the smaller schools, but did not experience a significant change in the 1840s and 1850s.

The Midwest, however, seems not to have demanded or supported extended education for physicians. Both the grouped sample for its smaller colleges, and the samples for Oberlin and the University of Michigan, indicate percentages of physicians a half of New England's. The Midwest's approximately 10 percent rate was close to that for the Middle Atlantic region with its ethnic diversity and abundance of doctors. But, as in New England, the admittedly biased samples for the physicians indicate that those who had invested in college education were tending towards homoeopathy and were becoming disenchanted with the older heroic medicine.[13]

The importance of regional, social, and economic conditions is more clearly seen through the history of the selection of agriculture as an occupation. There were always significant differences between the North and South, but not among the Northern regions. The small Southern schools always had students who were at least four times as likely to use agriculture as an income producing activity as those of the small Northern colleges. In the state institutions of the South, at least one–quarter of the students became planters or large farmers, and their samples indicated that the students of the secular institutions found it much easier to become planters than those of the region's denominational colleges.

In the North there was great consistency over time and within the three subregions. Throughout the early nineteenth century the estimates for the percentage of Northern students who engaged in agriculture for some part of their career, including retirement, hovered around 8 percent. This figure applied to both large and small colleges (with the exception of Columbia Univesity) and also to the expanding agricultural Midwest where farming might generate significant profits. In the Midwest, the college with a seeming mandate to reproduce the occupational distribution of the region, the University of Michigan, had a sample which suggested that it was unable to return students to agriculture in greater proportions than the other colleges of the area.

Although the colleges did not develop direct ties to farming through the careers of their alumni and the aspirations of their students, they were always integrated with the lower educational system in America. But regional influences, as well as the income and status potentials of lower education as a career, made the relationships different from those between higher and lower education in the twentieth century. Although a majority of Northern college students taught school or college at some point in their lives, the primary and secondary systems did not provide the economic rewards and social status commensurate with the goals of many of the antebellum students. It would not be until the late nineteenth century, when the economics of the United States and of its educational systems improved, that the colleges would orient themselves directly to the production of high numbers of professional educators. However, well over 10 percent of the students in the North did become principals or superintendents of primary and secondary systems, indicating that the colleges were connected to the system and that their students were involved with the growth of popular education in the country. Well before normal schools developed pretentions to educate for more than classroom instruction and before educators claimed a separate and distinct profession, the antebellum colleges served as a major source of leadership for the educational system of the nation.[14]

Perhaps a majority of the students of New England's colleges taught school at some time in their careers, and the students of Harvard and Yale, who might have had less economic need to teach before or during their college years, seem to have been similarly involved. The estimates for the percentage of students who ever taught school increased over time, perhaps because of changes in the reporting of occupational activities of the students (it appears that teaching and the ministry were assumed to be synonymous in early decades) and because of the changes in the social and economic backgrounds of New England's students. By the 1830s, New England's estimate for the students who taught school reached 40 percent, about double that for 1800, and, despite a decline in the 1840s, the period ended with an estimate above 40 percent. Much of the educational activity of the New England students was of a temporary nature. Students used college vacations to teach in local schools and others entered teaching for a few years after college while they prepared for the professions. Many ministers established private schools, or managed academies, or became superintendents of a public system as an expected part of their ministerial duties. Others, especially students of Harvard and Yale, spent a year or so acting as tutors for the children of Southern planters.

A significant number of the students of New England's colleges devoted much of their life to education and probably were America's first "professional" educators. Burritt's study indicates that perhaps 15 to 20 percent of the students of the smaller colleges became career teachers. The biographies for this study suggest that well over 10 percent of the students became principals or superintendents.[15] And the estimates increased over time; from 7 percent in 1800 to 13 percent in the 1850s.

New England's reported percentages of its students in education were the highest in the nation, but, by the 1850s, the students of the other regions seem to have become as involved as New England's alumni. However, the trends for teaching as an occupation do not appear to have been as consistent as in New England, and in the other regions there were significant differences among the samples for the large and small colleges.

In the South the newer colleges seem to have made a much more significant and direct contribution to secondary and primary education than did the established colleges, but the University of Virginia may have been an exception. However, in the 1840s and 1850s the reported percentages for all teaching activity by Southern students were significantly below the New England estimates. The effect of the rise of the new colleges of the South in the 1840s and 1850s was to provide an important number of teachers for its emerging but still deficient lower educational system. Such denominational colleges as Duke and the once giant, but struggling, Transylvania University, were oriented to the production of teachers in the 1850s, but the South continued to be distinguished from the rest of the nation. The reported percentages for college professors and presidents continued to be significantly lower than in the North, although the 6 percent estimate (including medical professors) was impressive. The Southern institutions seem to have produced fewer men who remained actively in education. The slow development of both public and private education in the region may account for the signficantly lower percentages of educators.[16]

The percentages for those ever engaged in education for the Middle Atlantic and Midwestern states did begin to approach the New England levels in the 1840s and 1850s. With the exception of Oberlin, the large institutions of both regions had estimates significantly lower than those for the smaller colleges. The rural institutions and those which produced relatively high numbers of ministers had greater percentages of students who became temporary and professional educators, perhaps reflecting the social and economic backgrounds of their students.

As with teaching, science and engineering tended to be temporary and secondary occupations in the early nineteenth century. This conditioned both reporting of students' occupations and the apparent relationship of the colleges to science and technology. Because of the nature of employment in those fields, such activities were underreported in the brief biographies of the alumni and nongraduates. It was not only the underreporting of such activities that distorted the view of the colleges and science and industry; the known participation levels were misinterpreted because it was assumed that engineering and science had evolved as established and stable professions before the Civil War.

As with Burritt's study, the samples for this project indicate an increasing level of participation by the liberal arts students in science, invention, and engineering. The data from the biographical samples strongly suggest that Burritt's work significantly underestimated the degree of involvement. A comparison of the occupational distributions of students with those in the general population suggests that the colleges were enrolling students who engaged in science–related activities at levels equal to those for physicians, lawyers, and, perhaps, ministers.[17] Using Burritt's low estimate of the percentage of the students of the 1850s who were recognized for their activities in engineering, approximately 2 percent, leads to the conclusion that the colleges were producing engineers at a rate at least thirty times expectation, while ministers were graduating at close to fifty times expectation. However, the estimate for engineers is probably very low, because the results from this study were twice as great as Burritt's, and the adjusted figures for numbers of engineers from the census are probably too high.[18]

The reported involvement of students in science, invention, and engineering increased over the six decades. The estimates suggest that participation more than doubled, reaching perhaps 5 percent in the 1850s. The samples also suggest that great differences remained among the regions at the beginning of the Civil War. In the 1850s, the estimates ranged from 10 percent in New England, to 5 percent in the the Middle Atlantic states and Midwest, to less than 3 percent in the South.

New England seems to have led the nation. Its students were always more involved in technical occupations, invention, and scientific societies. Within the region, the governmental and business connections of its students and its advanced stage of industrial development probably explain the higher levels of involvement. The estimates of science–related activities were always significantly greater in New England. And throughout the country, urban colleges and students with an urban background had a greater probability of pursuing science, invention, manufacturing, or engineering. Harvard, Columbia, and the University of Pennsylvania, for example, had significantly higher percentages of their students engaging in such activities than did other colleges in their areas. But the estimates for the smaller schools suggest that they were not far behind the urban institutions. New Englands' small colleges' estimates were close to Harvard's percentages; the smaller institutions of the Middle Atlantic states and the Midwest were not significantly different from the University of Michigan's; and in the South, the University of Virginia's estimates were not statistically greater than those for the denominational institutions.

However, the technical and scientific activities of the students were of a particular type. The students did not become involved with the hands–on operation of machinery. Their activities were usually those of surveying, civil engineering, invention, or supervisory and managerial tasks in industry. Many of the students who engaged in these activities found them unattractive and, perhaps, unrewarding. Most of those who had a chance to make such occupations their careers turned to the traditional professions.

The positive involvement of the colleges with the development of modern America was not confined to occupations. The antebellum students were more "urban" than the general population and were more likely to be found in new areas of the country than the average American. As with the distribution of occupations, the location patterns and mobility of the students were the product of the interaction of student backgrounds, regional economies and culture, and the professional and social connections of the colleges and their alumni. The large cities of America, such as New York, Chicago, New Orleans, San Francisco, and Washington, and the some three hundred others identified by the Zip Code system as areas with a code ending in double zero were home to the nineteenth-century students. Even the small colleges of New England, which were so dependent upon students from farms and small towns, sent a majority of their students to the leading cities. The largest of these were always the usual destinations of American college students. The centers of power and change, such as Boston, New York, and Philadelphia, attracted students at rates far higher than expected. (Table 4.4)

For the small colleges of New England, the percentage of students who ever once worked in a large city rose from 30 to over 50 percent between the 1800s and the 1850s. In terms of all recorded nonrepetitious places for the small colleges' students, with the apparent exception of the urban Brown and Trinity, the percentage of large-city locations rose from 20 to 30 percent.[19] Although a calculation of the percent of the general population in the large cities has not been done, some indication of the relative urbanity of the antebellum students may be gained from general statistics.

In 1800 1 percent of the American population lived in places of fifty thousand or more. By 1860, 10 percent lived in such cities, and by 1900, 22 percent. Although the percentage of New England's students who worked in large urban centers did not increase as fast as that for the general population, a student was always more likely to have been in a large city than were members of the general population. But the difference between the growth rates for the general and the student populations may indicate that one function of the emergence of the new colleges of New England, and one of the reasons for the critics dislike of them, was that they were producing men who served the small towns and rural areas. For example, Harvard and Yale, the established and famous colleges of New England, had higher percentages of students who spent their careers in urban centers than did the small colleges throughout the nineteenth century. Despite the different constituencies of the two colleges and their students' occupational differences, both had 40 percent of their 1800s and 70 percent of their 1850s students living in a major city at least once during their careers. Of all recorded non-repetitious career locations, 50 percent were in large cities, approximately twice the rate for the students of the majority of the small colleges. However, Harvard's and Yale's estimates were exceeded by those for

Brown and Trinity. Those two colleges, which enrolled mainly students with urban homes, sent significantly higher percentages to the large cities. The differences between the estimates for all nonrepetitious career stops and the percentages of those who worked in a large city at least once during their careers suggest that the students of the large and small colleges had very different career patterns, despite similar occupations. Harvard students, for example, were less likely to begin their careers or spend other periods in small towns and rural areas than were those from the small colleges. The students of the smaller colleges seem to have had to work their way through their occupational hierarchies by spending many years in nonurban areas, perhaps because of their socioeconomic status, the established connections of family and college, and the greater probability that they came from nonurban homes.

Similar career patterns appeared in other regions. The newer institutions of most areas seemed to have influenced students in the same way as did those in New England, causing students with rural backgrounds to move to the large cities. In the 1850s 45 percent of the Middle Atlantic's new colleges' alumni and former students worked at least once in a large city, although only 20 percent had come from urban homes. Princeton and Union do not seem to have had a much higher percentage than did the small schools, but approximately 90 percent of the students of Columbia and the University of Pennsylvania worked at least once in an urban center.

Southern society created mobility patterns significantly different from the North's. Its colleges had students who were less urban; the differences between its large and small colleges were slight; and the Southern colleges were not able to influence moves by their students from rural to urban areas. The percentage of students from either the small or large colleges in the South who worked in urban areas was about one–half that of the North's, as might be expected from the distribution of the population in the South. But the force of Southern social and economic life seems to have altered the relationship between type of college attended and career location. Aside from the University of Virginia, there were no significant differences between the large and small colleges of the region. Students of the state institutions were no more likely to migrate to urban areas than were those from the denominational colleges, probably because of the plantation culture which generated rural–based elites. And, in the South, the colleges had less influence over the desire or ability of students to alter their location. Among the small institutions the percentages of students to and from rural or urban areas were equal. Despite the elite connections of the large colleges, their students remained in rural areas at far greater rates than the students of the Northern schools.

Perhaps the economic system and the social backgrounds of students in the Midwest caused them to move to urban areas much more than did the students of the Southern colleges. Although the Midwest was a rural area in the 1850s and although its colleges had many Southerners, its students located in urban areas at rates which were surprisingly high. The samples for the grouped students of the small colleges and Oberlin gave estimates of 40 percent urban career locations, and the University of Michigan's sample yielded a 50 percent estimate.

The Midwest's colleges had patterns of rural to urban migration similar to New England's. Students began their careers, many times, in rural areas rather than, as did Harvard students, starting their postcollege lives in large cities. As in New England, the percent of students who ever worked in a large city was usually two to three times the proportion who entered college from urban areas. As well, the samples for the small colleges suggest that there were few significant variations of the percent of urban locations.

The differences among the regions and the colleges within them are evident from a study of the patterns of geographic distribution. As with location in an urban or rural area, the known geographic distribution and geographic mobility of the alumni reflected the influence of region and student background and provides another basis for the differentiation of the colleges. Unfortunately, precise quantitative estimates of the geographic mobility of the American population are unavailable. By the 1840s the census did ask individuals to give their state of birth and current residence, but, as with recent studies of residential persistence, such statistics are incomplete because they do not trace individuals throughout their lives. Because of these problems, direct comparisons between the college students and the population are impossible. Only gross comparisons can be made between the two groups.[20] (Tables 4.5, 4.6)

However, there is every indication that the movement of the students paralleled the migration patterns of the general population, but the rates of geographic mobility were significantly higher for the students. Significant differences between the regions and colleges emerged from the biographical samples. These differences indicate that the social and economic backgrounds of students superseded, in many instances, the general regional and occupational determinants of mobility and location.

The students of New England's smaller colleges had extremely high mobility and regional "circulation rates".[21] And their mobility increased over time. The samples strongly suggest that the students of 1800 had over 50 percent of their occupational locations outside of their home states and less than 60 percent in their home region (if students from the South are eliminated, the mobility rates increase significantly). By the 1850s, after a smooth trend, less than one–third of the occupational locations were in home states and less than 50 percent were within home regions. These were much higher rates than those reported by the census for the general population.

Although Yale's students were as mobile as those from the smaller colleges of New England, Harvard's were significantly different. Its students were less mobile. The estimates suggest that 82 percent of its students of the 1800s pursued their careers in their home regions and over 60 percent in their home states. There was little change in Harvard's mobility history until the 1830s, when the percentage of its students who stayed within their home regions and states significantly dropped. But even with this change, Harvard remained a distinct college. By the 1850s, perhaps 55 percent of the career locations were within students' home states and 65 percent within home regions.

Harvard remained unique in other aspects of migration. The small colleges and Yale had few students who found it possible or attractive to work within the immediate areas of their homes or colleges. In 1800, the schools, the families, and the local economies could not provide work close to home for the students. Less than 20 percent of the students of the small colleges or Yale located within the immediate areas of their homes and less than 10 percent located close to their college. These estimates did not change over the period.

But the economy of Boston and the backgrounds of Harvard students led to much greater localism. Harvard students were three times as likely to have worked within the immediate area of their college as were the other students. Despite the changes in the student population at Harvard, its 1850s students remained more than twice as likely to work within their hometowns than were the students of the other New England colleges.

Similar patterns developed among the students from colleges of the Middle Atlantic states. The migration rates were somewhat lower than those in New England, but the differences between Harvard students and the others of New England were matched by the large and small colleges of the region. The grouped sample for the small Middle Atlantic schools suggests that the percentage of in–state occupational locations was halfway between that for New England's small colleges and Harvard's; approximately 45 percent. The estimate of the percentage of career locations being within the students' home region also places the colleges between Harvard and the other New England schools. Although the small sample for the new colleges of the Middle Atlantic states preclude definitive generalizations, it does appear that there was more variance in migration rates among its colleges than among those of New England.

The differences between the large and small colleges of the region are clear. The students of the large colleges were much less mobile than those of the smaller colleges. For the 1850s, when sample sizes were large enough, Princeton's, Union's, and Columbia's estimates indicate that their students remained in their locale much more than did those of the smaller schools. They had 50 percent in–state and 70 percent in–region nonrepetitive career locations. The students of the larger colleges had a much greater tendency to locate within the immediate areas of their homes. Columbia and the University of Pennsylvania had samples indicating that more than a majority of their students returned to their original locations. As with Boston, New York and Philadelphia were able to support large numbers of students.

The localism of the students from the colleges of the Middle Atlantic states was more than matched in the South. The mobility of the Southern students was more limited than that of students from the large urban colleges of the North. The geographic provincialism of Southern students seems to have been so great that it is difficult to understand how the South, even with its slave economy, could have provided so many relatively high–status positions for its students within the immediate areas of their homes.

The percent of students who remained in their home states was always twice as high as that for the students of the small New England colleges, and was, by the 1850s, 20 percent greater than Harvard's. Three–quarters of the known career locations of Southern students were within their home regions.

There were no significant trends for such mobility within the South, but there are some indications that the students of the larger colleges were more mobile than those from the smaller institutions. However, as with the data for Harvard's students, the greater mobility rates of the alumni of the large Southern schools are ambiguous indicators. The substance of the biographies of the students of the famous colleges indicated that the mobility they did experience was the result of earlier attainments close to their homes. Unlike students of the smaller colleges, who may well have had to move in order to gain any status, much of the mobility of the alumni of the larger schools was either optional or the product of obtaining political office or being assigned to the management of established enterprises or institutions.

The character of much of the mobility of Southern students is illustrated by the percentage of students who worked within the immediate area of their home. For both the large and small colleges of the region and for each decade, perhaps 40 percent of the students found themselves working at least once within their hometown, double the percentage for New England.

Unlike the Southern students, those of the Midwest were rarely found to have returned to their home areas to pursue their careers. Despite the growth of towns and the expanding economy of the Midwest, the region could not sustain the localism of the South or the urban migration of New England and the Middle Atlantic states. However, the Midwest was able to retain those it had trained. For the students of the 1850s, 45 percent of their nonrepetitive career locations were within their home states and 55 percent were within their home regions.

The two larger colleges, Oberlin and the University of Michigan, did not produce students who returned their investments in education to the Midwest at rates similar to those of the smaller colleges. Their students were more mobile. Oberlin's sample suggests that its students remained in their home states and regions at a level one–half that of those of the smaller schools, and the estimate for the University of Michigan's students was 10 percent lower than that for the alumni of the other schools.

Although mobility rates are an indicator of the differences among the regions and colleges, the movement of the students around the country and the identification of the specific regions where they lived and worked is even more informative. The colleges, because of the interaction of background characteristics, regional economies, and occupational influences had different histories of direct contact with and influence on the various regions.

The students of Yale and the small New England colleges settled most evenly across the country, moved most frequently, and thus always had the highest "index–of–circulation" scores. Although the sample for the less–populous schools of New England include the students of Trinity and Brown, who seem to have been immobile, the small colleges consistently had the greatest percentage of students who had come to college from one region but who later settled in another area.

As with the students of the other regions, those from New England's smaller schools followed the migration patterns of the general population of their areas.[22] But the students were more mobile. The regional destinations of New England students in rank order were: New England, the Middle Atlantic states, the Midwest, the South, and the West. For the educational cohort of 1800, 72 percent of the students worked at least once in New England; 30 percent in the Middle Atlantic states, 12 percent in the South Atlantic region; 12 percent in the Midwest; and 5 percent in the Southwest. This distribution slowly changed over the six decades. The major changes were that the Midwest became an important destination and significantly fewer students were able to find work within New England. The estimate for the small colleges during the 1850s strongly suggest that 30 percent migrated to the Midwest, while 20 percent fewer worked in New England. During the 1850s the opening of the Pacific coast resulted in 9 percent of the students locating there for some period of time. The alumni of the small New England colleges not only spread themselves across the country, but they were much more likely than others to move from their home regions. Their score on the "index–of–circulation", the summed differences between the home–region percentages and the percentage distribution of regional occupational locations, was always over 70, or approximately four times the score for Southern students.

Partially due to the regional backgrounds of their students, Harvard and Yale had different geographic profiles. Harvard students were more concentrated than those of the small colleges or Yale. Although Harvard had significant numbers of students from outside of New England, until the 1850s, it had 30 percent more of its students working in New England and significantly fewer of its students living in the Midwest than did the other colleges. And its students had less "geographic circulation".

Harvard did share one aspect of mobility with Yale. Both had greater contact with the South, through their students, than did the small colleges. However, Yale's students were more evenly spread over the nation. Its circulation scores approached those of the smaller colleges until the 1840s, and its students were found in all regions of the country, despite the comparative concentration of its alumni in the Middle Atlantic states and the South. Yale's students did not migrate to the Midwest at rates equal to those of New England's newer colleges.

The differences between the movement of the graduates of Yale, Harvard, and the small New England colleges were slight compared to those between the students of the various regions. The men who attended college outside of New England were much more likely to settle in their home regions. The result was that the circulation scores for the other areas were from one–half to one–third those of New England. Middle Atlantic students had one–half, the South had one–third, and the Midwest had one–half of New England's scores throughout the period.

In the Middle Atlantic states the pooled sample for the smaller institutions indicated that they educated students who were much more prone to leave the region for the Midwest and West than were those of the larger colleges. The students from Princeton, Columbia, and the University of Pennsylvania who left their home areas after college were oriented to the South. As with the students of the region's small colleges, they were more likely to work within their educational region than were the students of New England. But the students of the Middle Atlantic's established colleges, especially Union, were attracted to New England. Significantly more of their students worked at least once in the older region than did those of the smaller colleges.

The restricted geographic distribution of the students of the region's urban colleges appears cosmopolitan when compared to the record of

Southern students. Although the South received appreciable numbers of students who were educated in the North, the South sent few of its own to the other regions. There is some reason to believe that Southern college students, especially those from its prestigious institutions, travelled to Europe more frequently than they visited the other regions of the United States.

For the Southern students of the 1850s, the samples strongly suggest that less than 6 percent ever worked outside the South. The Southern students may have been less mobile than the general population of its two subregions. Only the migrations to and from the South Atlantic states and the Southwest, with a few temporary migrants to New York and Boston, prevented the South from being an isolated area.[23]

The immobility of Southern students makes the Midwest, by comparison, a producer of cosmopolitan alumni. But compared to other Northern regions, the Midwest's educational system was not enrolling students who would be highly mobile after leaving school. The samples for the Midwestern students of the 1850s indicate important flows to the Middle Atlantic states and the West, and perhaps as many as 5 percent of the students worked in New England. But the various regional percentages were significantly below those of New England and its "index–of–circulation" scores were lower. However, the Midwest, possibly because of the numbers of its students from the South, did have as strong a connection with that region as did New England. Many Midwestern students migrated to cities such as St. Louis and New Orleans both before and after the Civil War.

The varied migration, mobility, and urban location rates of the students of the various regions were not only a product of general regional forces, but of the occupational and professional choices of the students. Occupational forces interacted with student backgrounds to produce significantly different mobility and location patterns. The original decision by a student or his family to move out of his home region for higher education had an important impact upon his later migration history.

The rise in demand for ministers in new areas, the organizational revolutions within the denominations and the home missionary movement made ministers the most mobile, the least urban, and the most "cosmopolitan" professionals.[24] Even among the young men who attended college in the 1800s, students whose careers were begun well before the full impact of the bureaucratization of the denominations and the expansion of the American population to the West, ministers of all regions were the least likely of the alumni to settle near their homes. They were more prone to move away from their home states and regions and were the most likely of all the professionals to be found in nonurban areas during some part of their careers. These differences held firm over the period, with the influence of the formalization of the ministry keeping the clergy more mobile than doctors, lawyers, or other former students.

Doctors and lawyers were less mobile than ministers and were somewhat more "urban". They were more frequently found working close to their homes, but they were more cosmopolitan than liberally educated businessmen. Perhaps because of the socioeconomic backgrounds of the college–educated businessmen, they were very likely to be urban, to stay within their states and regions and to settle very close to their homes.

The precollege backgrounds of students were also important to the determination of the location patterns of the alumni. The consistent 0.70 correlation between the percent of students with an urban home and the percent which settled in an urban area suggests, again, that background characteristics of students had as much or more influence than college policies or curricula and conditioned the impact of occupational and regional influences. The importance of precollege decisions and influences are also illustrated by the impact of a student moving from his home region for liberal higher education. The social and occupational connections provided by the colleges and their alumni and sponsors, the prior connections of the students and their families, and, perhaps, discontent with the culture of a student's home region led those who moved to other regions to have significantly different migration patterns than those who stayed closer to home for higher education. The impact of this migration appears to have been the same for those who attended large or small colleges, but regional forces continued to exert their influence and the mobility patterns of Southern students remained distinct from migrants from other areas.

The samples for the students of the period between 1830 and 1860 strongly suggest that migration out of New England for higher education meant that the "movers" were one–half as likely to work in New England during their careers as those who had remained within the region. The migrants had twice the probability of locating in the Middle Atlantic or Midwestern states, but as with other Northern–bred and trained students, the initial migration had no effect upon migration to the South.

Middle Atlantic and Midwestern young men were more influenced by the decision to leave their home regions for higher education. Attending a New England college increased the probability of locating in that region four times for Middle Atlantic and over ten times for Western students. For many coming from those two regions, the migration to New England was permanent. Once they left, they were two–thirds as likely to relocate in their original regions as those who had remained at home for higher education.

Southern students were also affected by leaving their home region for college. The migrants were five times as likely as their counterparts who remained close to home to locate in New England, ten times more likely to settle in the Middle Atlantic states, and had nearly four times the probability of pursuing their careers in the Midwest and West. But the strength of Southern life and culture led the Southern students who left the region to return home. Unlike the students of the North who had left their home region to attend college, the Southerners who had left their area for higher education showed approximately the same likelihood of locating at least once during their careers in the South as did Southern students who remained in the region.

The use of biographical materials involves a methodological problem. Some biographical volumes are unbiased complete lists, but others are marked by significant faults. For example, the compendia for the members of the United States Congress contain the names of all members and enough biographical information to allow unambiguous matching of the college alumni with Congressmen and Senators. Other lists and compendia, however, are marred by biased inclusion or too little information to allow a correct identification of individuals. Many of the lists were oriented towards New England students or those who had been members of a national organization. For example, lists of physicians, lawyers, bankers, engineers, and scientists tended to be based upon membership in urban–centered and national organizations and, therefore, are indicators of connection with the urban and formally professional world rather than a pure measure of social contribution.[25]

A complex problem is that state and local nineteenth–century commerical surveys of outstanding individuals, "mugbooks", were the product of an uncoordinated effort, leaving many areas without such volumes. New England and the Midwest seem to have been the targets of the compilers of these volumes, leaving the South in general and many cities throughout the country without such historical records. Also, some complete lists proved of little value because of insufficient information. Registers of Civil War personnel, social registers, state registries for physicians, and Federal and state governmental registers usually did not include enough biographical material to precisely identify subjects.[26]

Thus, although all such biographical materials for the nineteenth century were surveyed during this study, many could not be used for a comparison among the regions and colleges. For example, a college–by–college comparison of participation in the Civil War was intended, but the problems of matching students and military men precluded such an analysis of contribution and leadership.[27] Therefore, while there are strong indications that the young college–bred Southerners had close to a 100 percent probability of serving in the armed forces during the Civil War and a very high probability of being killed or wounded, thus affecting the history of Reconstruction, truly defensible and precise estimates cannot be stated. The seeming tendency of the students of the urban and rich colleges of the North to participate in the Civil War at levels lower than those of the rural institutions cannot be fully documented because of the matching difficulties and the absence of complete studies of participation for all of the colleges.[28] The incomplete information in Federal and state registers also indicate that the connection of the colleges with the emerging civil services was higher than currently recorded in student computer profiles, but this is also impossible to defend formally. A similar limitation was encountered during the study of the membership lists of the American Association For the Advancement of Science. Name matching, aided by coincidence of location of subjects on the computer file and those on the association list, indicated that a high percentage of the association's members were college alumni. But the absence of other identifying information for the subjects prevented a formal use of the association's roster.[29]

The biases and the incomplete information in the biographical materials cannot be adjusted by any codified and precise techniques. Only the realization that the materials were biased towards the urban population, the members of national organizations, and, it seems, New England, provide any compensatory aid. But the recognition of these biases should lead to the conclusion that the already high levels of inclusion are understatements of the worth of higher education to the alumni and of the connection of the colleges to modernizing America. (Table 4.7)

Besides mobility patterns, occupational distributions, and contact by the students with both the urban world and the developing communities of frontier areas, there are other indicators which challenge the old image of the antebellum student and which show the influence of region and occupation. The alumni were very involved in politics, institution building, and science, and their contributions were recognized by the nation and later historians. The number of students included in national, state, and local biographical compendia, which were oriented towards the noteworthy of the nineteenth century, are a reflection of the positive contributions of the alumni of the early liberal arts colleges.

Despite the biases and the influx of new types of students there was no significant trend for the percentage of New England's college students included in major national biographical studies. For the grouped sample of the students of the small colleges, at least 10 percent were subject of a biography in every decade. The highest recorded percentage was for the 1810s, the decade of the "pauper" scholars and the begin-

Table 4.7

Percent of Students of Various Colleges and Groups of Colleges Who Were Traced to Various Biographical Volumes and Professional Registers and Who Are Known to Have Held Various Social Positions - By Various Colleges and By Decade of Entry Into College for the 1800's, 1830's and 1850's

Colleges	1 % Traced to National Biographies	2 % Traced to State-Local Biographies	3 % Traced to Medical Biographies	4 % Traced to Other Biographies	5 % Traced to Professional Registers	6 % Members of Phi Beta Kapa	7 % With Known Fraternity Memberships	8 % Known to Be Members of AAAs	9 % Known in U.S. Congress	10 % Known to Participate in State-Local Government	11 % Known to Participate in National Government	12 % Known to Participate in the Civil War	13 Number of Subjects
					Decade: 1800's								
Harvard	17.9	16.4	2.9	0	0	20.8	0	0	2.9	20.8	7.4	2.9	67
Yale	17.5	10.9	0	0	0	34.0	2.1	1.0	6.5	40.6	9.8	2.1	91
Other New England Colleges	11.2	12.9	0	5.3	1.6	14.5	0.1	0.5	7.5	22.5	6.9	0.5	187
Princeton	12.7	0	4.2	2.1	0	0	2.1	0	0	27.6	6.3	2.1	47
Union	2.0	4.0	0	0	0	6.1	0	0	2.0	4.0	2.0	2.0	49
Columbia	4.9	0	0	0	0	0	0	0	1.6	3.2	1.6	0	61
U. of Pennsylvania	-	-	-	-	-	-	-	-	-	-	-	-	-
Other Middle Atlantic Colleges	2.6	2.6	0	2.6	0	0	0	2.6	2.6	10.5	2.6	0	38
U. of Virginia	-	-	-	-	-	-	-	-	-	-	-	-	-
U. of North Carolina	11.1	14.8	0	3.7	3.7	0	0	0	11.1	32.3	14.8	0	27

Table 4.7 (Cont'd)

Colleges	1 % Traced to National Biographies	2 % Traced to State-Local Biographies	3 % Traced to Medical Biographies	4 % Traced to Other Biographies	5 % Traced to Professional Registers	6 % Members of Phi Beta Kapa	7 % With Known Fraternity Memberships	8 % Known to Be Members of AAAs	9 % Known in U.S. Congress	10 % Known to Participate in State-Local Government	11 % Known to Participate in National Government	12 % Known to Participate in the Civil War	13 Number of Subjects
U. of Georgia	–	–	–	–	–	–	–	–	–	–	–	–	–
Other South Atlantic Colleges	5.7	2.8	0	8.5	0	0	2.8	0	0	17.1	2.8	0	35
U. of Alabama	–	–	–	–	–	–	–	–	–	–	–	–	–
Other Southwest Colleges	–	–	–	–	–	–	–	–	–	–	–	–	–
Oberlin	–	–	–	–	–	–	–	–	–	–	–	–	–
U. of Michigan	–	–	–	–	–	–	–	–	–	–	–	–	–
Other Midwest Colleges	–	–	–	–	–	–	–	–	–	–	–	–	–
Decade: 1830's													
Harvard	15.8	6.7	0	0.5	0	29.9	3.3	1.6	0	11.8	0	12.9	177
Yale	11.6	8.9	1.0	0	0	22.2	4.7	1.0	2.6	16.9	4.2	11.6	189
Other New England Colleges	11.2	4.6	0.1	2.4	0.9	10.7	9.3	0.7	0.9	17.6	3.0	5.6	532
Princeton	11.9	1.8	0	0	0.9	0	0	0.9	0.9	10.0	4.5	15.5	109
Union	6.3	8.4	0.7	0.7	1.4	29.5	21.8	0	0.7	23.9	3.5	12.6	142
Columbia	3.4	3.4	0	1.7	0	1.7	6.8	1.7	0	6.8	0	0	58

Table 4.7 (Cont'd)

Colleges	1 % Traced to National Biographies	2 % Traced to State-Local Biographies	3 % Traced to Medical Biographies	4 % Traced to Other Biographies	5 % Traced to Professional Registers	6 % Members of Phi Beta Kapa	7 % With Known Fraternity Memberships	8 % Known to Be Members of AAAs	9 % Known in U.S. Congress	10 % Known to Participate in State-Local Government	11 % Known to Participate in National Government	12 % Known to Participate in the Civil War	13 Number of Subjects
U. of Pennsylvania	15.7	1.8	3.7	7.4	0.9	3.7	1.8	0	0.9	7.4	0.9	23.1	108
Other Middle Atlantic Colleges	6.1	3.7	0	1.8	1.6	1.8	3.7	0.5	1.0	8.0	1.3	6.4	371
U. of Virginia	4.8	3.2	0.8	8.0	0	0.8	0	0	4.8	20.1	7.2	13.7	124
U. of North Carolina	5.9	2.9	0	7.4	1.4	1.4	1.4	0	2.9	19.4	2.9	14.9	67
U. of Georgia	5.2	0	0	8.7	1.7	0	0	0	3.5	17.5	5.2	8.7	57
Other South Atlantic Colleges	4.8	0.8	0	2.0	0.4	0.4	1.2	0.4	2.0	9.2	3.2	9.2	248
U. of Alabama	2.0	6.2	0	33.3	0	0	2.0	0	2.0	25.0	6.2	20.8	48
Other Southwest Colleges	0	5.3	0	0	1.7	0	3.5	0	0	7.1	0	10.7	56
Oberlin	3.7	3.7	0	0	0	0	0	0	0	3.7	0	0	27
U. of Michigan	-	-	-	-	-	-	-	-	-	-	-	-	-
Other Midwest Colleges	6.5	3.2	0.4	1.3	0.4	2.7	6.5	0.9	3.7	13.4	4.1	8.8	215
Decade: 1850's													
Harvard	21	5.7	1.1	0.3	0.7	16.0	21.0	4.9	4.2	20.3	4.5	38.3	261
Yale	17.4	6.9	1.3	0	1.3	18.3	42.3	0.8	1.0	20.9	3.0	29.2	229
Other New England Colleges	9.8	6.3	0.5	2.5	0.8	16.4	37.4	0.8	0.4	28.3	1.5	30.8	713

Table 4.7 (Cont'd)

Colleges	1 % Traced to National Biographies	2 % Traced to State-Local Biographies	3 % Traced to Medical Bio-graphies	4 % Traced to Other Biographies	5 % Traced to Professional Registers	6 % Members of Phi Beta Kapa	7 % With Known Fraternity Memberships	8 % Known to Be Members of AAAs	9 % Known in U.S. Congress	10 % Known to Participate in State-Local Government	11 % Known to Participate in National Government	12 % Known to Participate in the Civil War	13 Number of Subjects
Princeton	11.0	7.0	0	0	1.0	3.0	22.0	2.0	1.0	15.0	2.0	34.0	100
Union	9.9	3.3	0	1.6	0.8	19.8	34.7	0.8	1.6	14.8	1.6	27.2	121
Columbia	3.7	0	1.8	0	3.7	0	26.4	0	0	13.2	0	18.8	53
U. of Pennsylvania	14.5	3.6	3.6	6.5	0	0	36.4	2.9	0	15.3	1.4	46.7	137
Other Middle Atlantic Colleges	7.0	4.3	0	1.0	1.0	3.0	22.0	0.1	0.9	10.5	1.9	20.6	776
U. of Virginia	3.9	3.9	0.9	7.2	0.3	0	9.6	1.2	0.6	11.7	7.5	54.5	332
U. of North Carolina	3.8	4.7	0.4	7.6	0	6.4	23.8	0.4	2.3	21.4	3.8	72.8	210
U. of Georgia	3.2	1.6	0	6.5	0	0	0	0	3.2	13.1	3.2	50.8	61
Other South Atlantic Colleges	2.4	2.9	0	2.3	0.3	0.4	2.1	0.1	0.4	5.1	0.6	23.2	602
U. of Alabama	0.9	0	0	27.7	0.9	2.9	11.8	0	0	12.8	0.9	67.3	101
Other Southwest Colleges	2.4	1.0	0	0.8	0.2	0	7.6	0	0.6	6.3	1.0	14.7	455
Oberlin	4.5	4.5	0	0	0	0	4.5	2.2	2.2	13.6	2.0	18.1	44
U. of Michigan	6.0	11.1	0	0	0	0	37.3	1.0	3.0	23.2	6.0	35.3	99
Other Midwest Colleges	3.3	2.9	0.1	0.8	0.1	2.6	10.4	1.9	1.4	8.4	2.2	15.8	708

nings of the "Great Retrogression." Harvard and Yale usually had significantly higher percentages of their students included in the national compendia and both colleges received more attention in the 1840s and 1850s than in earlier decades. The 1850s students of the two colleges had estimates which were approximately double those for the grouped smaller schools, perhaps reflecting the urban bias of the biographers.

The students of the Middle Atlantic colleges also appeared in the national biographical works much more frequently than those who had not attended the colleges, again suggesting that students were playing a major role in the development of American society. There were not significant statistical differences between the estimates for the Middle Atlantic and New England students.

As with New England's alumni, there was no trend for the mention of the students of the Middle Atlantic's colleges. However, there was an important difference between the two regions in respect to the inclusion of former students in major biographical works. There were no statistically defensible differences between the estimates for the large and small colleges of the Middle Atlantic states—with the important exception of the University of Pennsylvania's students of the 1850s. The students of the larger colleges did have reported percentages higher than the 7 percent for the grouped students of the other schools, but small sample sizes dictated the formal statistical insignificance.

Although the Middle Atlantic and New England students received similar levels of contemporary and historical recognition, the editors and compilers of the national compendia seem to have paid much less attention to the students of the South and Midwest, leading to lower frequencies of inclusion. The sample for the small Southern colleges of the 1850s did yield an estimate not significantly different from those of the Middle Atlantic states, but the proportions of Southern students traced were usually lower than for the Northern region's colleges. Surprisingly, the former students of the famous institutions of the South had lower estimates of inclusion than did the the alumni of the region's smaller colleges. The estimates for the University of Virginia and the University of North Carolina, for example, had percentages approximately one–half those of the grouped denominational colleges of the South.

Perhaps the stage of social development of the Midwest and its lack of an established elite led to comparatively low rates of inclusion in national biographical works. But the estimate of 3 percent indicates that the students of its smaller colleges received more recognition than did the common man of the region. Oberlin and Michigan did receive national acclaim through their students. The 6 percent estimates for the two colleges suggest that these institutions attracted and shaped students who became associated with national cultures and groups.

Unfortunately, the uneven geographical coverage of local, state, and city biographical catalogs and the different time periods covered by such works negates their usefulness for a comparison of the college students to each other or to the general population. However, the percentages of students recorded in such works were usually higher than those in the national compendia, as would be expected. The biographical histories of the college fraternities, including Phi Beta Kappa, suffered from similar problems of uneven coverage.[30] However, biographical volumes of famous physicians and attorneys did indicate two facets of nineteenth-century education. First, was the high percentage of liberal arts alumni found in such works and, second, was the advantage of students who had attended larger, urban colleges and who had spent most of their career in urban centers.[31]

Inclusion in national compendia and professional biographical works reflect national attention and, to some extent, the biases of the editors and contributors to the volumes. But membership in Congress was dependent upon local forces and the reporting of membership was complete. Therefore, it is a better indicator of the local influence of the college alumni.[32]

Although there were significant differences over time, colleges, and regions, the search through the biographical volumes for the United States Congress yielded estimates of participation and recognition for the college men far above those expected. The liberal arts alumni were always much more likely to join Congress than the general population of adult males. The samples for New England and the Middle Atlantic colleges indicated a sudden and large change in the relationship between liberal higher education and national office–holding. This change, which accompanied the alterations of the social background and occupational choices of the students, may be one reason for the perception of "retrogression" among the antebellum colleges by historians.

For New England's smaller colleges, there was a sudden and permanent downward shift in the percent of alumni and former students who entered Congress between the educational cohort of the 1800s and that of the 1810s. A drop of similar magnitude, and which was also statistically significant, marked the history of the classes of the 1810s and 1820s in the Middle Atlantic states. The New England estimates declined from 7 percent for the students of the 1800s to four–tenth of 1 percent for the succeeding group, where it remained for the rest of the period. The Middle Atlantic colleges dropped to a similar level in the 1820s and had generally stable estimates until the Civil War.

One significant difference among the colleges that affected their future histories and, possibly, the level of influence of their students, was the higher percentages of Congresmen and Senators generated by the larger and established colleges of the two regions. Harvard and Yale had somewhat higher percentages throughout the six decades than did the other colleges, but the students who attended Harvard and Yale during the 1850s seem to have been significantly different from earlier students. For the students of the 1850s, the samples yielded an estimate of 4 percent for Harvard and approximately a 1 percent particiption rate for Yale. A similar increase for the students of the 1850s was not found for the famous colleges in the Middle Atlantic states, but their former students had, like those from Yale, a 1 percent probability of becoming a member of Congress.

Because of missing student lists for the early decades it is impossible to rely upon sampling methods to estimate absolute levels of the Congressional membership of Southern students. However, it appears permissible to make some statements concerning Southern students' relationship to national political life after the 1820s.[33] As in the North, the percentages of Southern college students who became members of Congress exceeded expectations based upon numbers of Congressmen relative to the numbers of adult males in the United States. As might be expected from the general image of the elite character of society in the South, the percentage of Southern students who became members of Congress was greater than that for Northern students. However, two findings did not match the image of the elite nature of Southern society. The Southern percentages were not statistically significantly different from the North's, and, among the larger colleges, only the University of Virginia's estimate was significantly greater than that of the sample of the grouped students of the smaller colleges of the South in the 1850s.

More surprising were the great numbers of college–educated members of Congress from the Midwest. The percentages for the Midwest were the highest of all the regions by the 1850s. And unlike the other areas, the smaller colleges' students seem to have participated at the same rate as those of the large schools, Oberlin and the University of Michigan. The membership percentages for the smaller colleges of the region were significantly higher than those for the students of the 1850s from New England's smaller colleges.

Political influence was not confined to the national level. State and local politics were a major concern of the college students. Unfortunately, a formal estimate of the levels of participation at those governmental levels is impossible to make because many students were traced only to short biographies. The estimates from the coded data ranged from 20 percent in New England to 10 percent in the South. Although these indicate high levels of participation, they are gross underestimates of the influence of the college students. When students were traced to relatively complete biographies, the percentages of mayors, aldermen, governors, and other state and local office holders, especially for those in occupations such as law and business, were more than double the levels cited above. While lawyers were always more likely to hold local, state, and national offices, many ministers were found who participated in the management of governments by holding, at least, appointive offices.

These and other indicators, such as the membership of ministers in the American Association for the Advancement of Science and the high level of participation of the alumni and former students in the national and state civil services and the diplomatic corps, all challenge the static, ideal type of the antebellum student.[34] By every measure, the students were more "modern" than the general population, and they played a positive role in American life in both the urban and rural areas of the country. And what evidence there is on the political affiliations of the students reflects the diversity of the college system; the college educated did not form a monolithic and conservative political force in America. Students were Federalists, Jeffersonians, Democrats, Free Soilers, and Republicans, and the colleges usually contained a mixture of political affiliations within their student bodies, although regional forces conditioned the distribution of political choice.[35]

Some institutions had student populations which appeared more modern than others to historians of higher education. Harvard, Columbia, and Pennsylvania, among the liberal arts colleges of the period, seemed to be producing more "urban" men who would become famous for their contributions to government, industry, and science. But their students, like those of Yale, Princeton, and Michigan were not just the product of the colleges, but were more "urban" and more secular in orientation because of their backgrounds. Their achievements were not just the result of their higher education. Their family backgrounds, the connections of their kin, and the influence of the faculty and alumni conditioned their careers. But these students, especially those who remained for advanced study in the colleges with such programs, would become the new ideal student for American higher education—a new myth would emerge. That normative model of the well–prepared, urban, career–oriented mature student was enmeshed with the polemics of the university movement. This new myth of the university combined the intellectual demands of Hofstadter and the egalitarianism of Ross into an ideal which was the polar opposite of the the concept of the antebellum college and the antebellum student, and it has shaped the historical perception of post–Civil War higher education and the goals and structure of modern higher education in America. This new ideal, the university, set definitions of what higher education is for and who it is for, and because of the assumption of revolutionary change following the Civil War it shaped the writings about the history of higher education in America.

What changes did take place were treated as the product of the colleges themselves, rather than of the society and the economy.

The changes within the colleges were perceived as radical and the new ideal postbellum student was considered not only as the norm for American higher education but as the natural and inevitable result of the supposed institutional changes. Colleges and the public expected students to meet new standards of preparation, orientation and precollege achievement. They required that students conform to the new institutional configurations and attitudes because the changes within the colleges seemed to meet the needs of a modernized economy and society. And the colleges came to be evaluated, by both academics and the public, on the basis of the number of alumni they produced who matched the worldly achievements of the students who attended the institutions noted for their leadership in defining the university ideal.

Chapter 5

The Colleges in Perspective

The traditional view of antebellum education was made credible by a description of American higher education after the Civil War that was interwoven with the generalizations concerning the oldtime colleges and their students. The failure of the old institutions and their alumni was brought into sharp focus by an interpretation of the postbellum era which saw not only unprecedented growth in the numbers of students but a qualitative change in the nature of higher education and the students it attracted and trained. And central to those changes and to the history of American higher education since the Civil War were two types of institutions, the technical school and the research university with its new type of president. The unquestioned success of these new forms and their ability to achieve all the goals the critics of the antebellum schools had sought meant that condemnation of the old colleges was inescapable.[1]

But the image of the pace, nature, and causes of change after the Civil War is as incorrect as the accepted view of the earlier period. The historical record of the new institutions favored by the historians has been distorted, especially in respect to the curricular choices of students, leading to a distorted interpretation of the context and causes of change. And more importantly, the almost exclusive focus on the new university and technical education turned attention away from questions which would have led historians and even contemporaries to reevaluate the success of these institutions in achieving their stated goals.

The historical view of the post–Civil War era treated as irrelevant to higher education the old liberal arts colleges and relatively new institutions for postsecondary education, the normal school, the private business college, the nursing school, the private trade school, and even private correspondence instruction. The arbitrary disregard of these institutions and their students prevented educational, social, and even intellectual historians from asking significant questions about the shape of higher education in the mid and late nineteenth century. And, by not asking why so many students chose to attend such schools and by not examining the curricular choices of students within the major institutions, the history of postbellum higher education was significantly misinterpreted by historians. Evidence which has always been available would have revealed the facts and pointed to valid generalizations and evaluations if historians had asked questions as simple as, why did so many students choose to attend the old–fashioned colleges and the new "shadow" institutions of postsecondary education, and, why did so many students in the reformed recognized colleges continue to select old–fashioned curricula? The predetermined irrelevance of such institutions and questions could only lead to an idealistic view of the educational record. Instead of seeing how many social functions the recognized institutions were not fulfilling; instead of seeing that the higher educational system was becoming more stratified and perhaps elitist, instead of confronting questions concerning the need for new educational models, the two dominant reform institutions, the technical college and the research university, were treated as unqualified successes and the causes of change and democratization.

The misinterpretation of the changes that took place in the colleges before and after the Civil War was not intentional, and there was some evidence which might still be seen as indicating both a revolution within the educational institutions and a change in their relationship to American society. Because many of the changes demanded by reformers seemed to have been accomplished, or at least attempted, after the Civil War, it appeared to be logical to divide the history of higher education into two periods, termed the premodern and the modern. The temptation to divide the history of higher education into two simplictic time periods was encouraged by what were believed to be facts about ante–and postbellum education. The traditional image of antebellum education was one of conservatism, elitism, unstable colleges, and declining enrollments, but statistical series for the postbellum period seemed to show an amazing growth of enrollments and a diversification of programs even within the institutions classified as colleges. Sufficient funding, flexibility, and permanence dominated the image of the postbellum colleges. Enrollments in higher education were reported by the new Bureau of Education to be sixty–two thousand in 1870 and two hundred fifty thousand in 1900. Attention was turned to the successes of the state and private universities which reported their enrollments in the thousands, rather than the hundreds, and which seemed to be the realization of the institutional goals of those who had been so dissatisfied with the old colleges. From such general "facts" it was natural to assume that a new era had begun and that changes within the colleges had been the cause of increased enrollments and stability. It also was easy to assume that the system was democratized.[2]

There were many impressive changes after the Civil War which caught the attention of the public and historians. Technical schools arose across the country. The Morrill Act and increased state aid led to new colleges and universities seemingly committed to teach agriculture, engineering, science, and even the science of homemaking and to admit students without regard to socioeconomic background, ethnic roots, or preparation in the classics. Job specific training was made avialable to undergraduates, tuitions were eliminated in many schools, and scholarships were offered to those interested in careers in agriculture and business. Programs were altered and students were allowed more and more options during their college years. Not only were thirty–nine different academic degrees established by 1900, but the old regulations concerning student behavior were relaxed.[3]

At the same time a new generation of educational leaders came to power who were able to draw upon the vast riches of the industrial leaders of the nation and who seemed to be the embodiment of the scientific "metaculture" needed to make higher education rational, efficient, and above politics. Millions were given by the mercantile and industrial elite of the country for the creation of the university. The Eliots, Harpers, and Butlers forged the definitions and structures of the new higher education and with the help of huge endowments they created a research–oriented, professionalized faculty which was free from denominational control and many of the burdens the old college teachers had to bear. These new institutions and faculties were the academic realization of what historians have come to call the "culture of professionalism".[4]

The historical focus on these types of changes led to the conclusion that the new "university" and the technical and agricultural schools had solved all the major problems of American postsecondary education. But the changes in postbellum higher education provide a test case for the assumptions of the critics of the earlier colleges rather than direct evidence that the rise of technical training and the university set the necessary and successful patterns for education in modern America.

An examination of enrollments, the backgrounds and careers of students, and the numbers of colleges after the Civil War indicates that the same constraints that hampered reform in the antebellum period worked against reform in the later nineteenth century, giving much continuity to the history of higher education. Students did not appear in great numbers, and they did not select the curricula or occupations predicted by the reformers. There is little evidence that the system became egalitarian or democratized in the way usually pictured, but there is evidence that, by at least the early twentieth century, the colleges served a very special student.

The enrollment levels cited in standard statistical works such as *Historical Statistics of the United States* and the reports of enrollments at the major universities in the late nineteenth century are deceptive. Enrollments in all of the redefined higher education, including normal, female, and medical–related schools, did increase from some thirty thousand to two hundred fifty thousand between 1860 and 1900, but enrollments in the regular colleges, including women, who constituted 24 percent of the students in 1900, increased from sixteen thousand six hundred to eighty–two thousand. And in all of higher education at the beginning of the twentieth century at least 40 percent of the students were women.[5] (Table 5.1)

Despite the broadening of curricula, the relative reductions of average college costs, and changed admissions standards, the number of students in the undergraduate programs of the regular colleges was below that predicted by the growth of male enrollments in standard college programs during the 1850s.[6] The result of all the changes in higher education and the social and economic orders after the Civil War was that the number of male students enrolled in undergraduate programs in all the academic colleges and universities in 1900 was 2.4 percent of the native white males in the United States between either fifteen and twenty or twenty and twenty–five years of age. The more than three hundred fifty regular colleges, including the state colleges and universities, had increased the proportion of young men enrolled by less than 1 percent in the forty years after the Civil War. And it was not until the 1890s that a significant increase over the 1860 proportion was achieved. But even then, and with females included in the college statistics, the undergraduate schools were not keeping pace with the increase in the number of students who attended high schools. While college enrollments increased over 90 percent between 1890 and 1900, the number of high school graduates more than doubled, even as attendance in private, college preparatory schools remained at a high level.[7] (Tables 5.2, 5.3)

Many of the reports of attendance at the major colleges and universities were misleading. State colleges and universities and some of the famous private universities inflated their enrollment statistics by including students in the medical and law schools, teacher's colleges, associated female schools and even summer schools. For example, the University of Michigan reported over four thousand students in 1901–2, a figure which might lead one to believe that its low tuition and varied programs had rescued its undergraduate college. However, its undergraduate attendance was approximately twelve hundred students, with over 50 percent being women—not a great increase over 1860. Columbia University included the students in its associated and well–attended teachers' college, its women's college, and its professional schools. Harvard's reported six thousand students would be reduced to less than two thousand if pro-

Table 5.1

Enrollments in Various Types of Higher Educational Institutions, 1800-1900

	1800	1810	1820	1830	1840	1850	1860	1870	1880	1890	1900
Liberal Arts	1156	1939	2566	4647	8328	9931	16600	23000	33000	44000	82000
Law	21	50	48	116	306	621	1489	2000	3000	4000	13000
Medical	50	541	1032	2349	3321	5996	7890	7000	14000	22000	49000
Theological	10	32	226	710	1009	1008	1553	3000	5000	7000	8000
Normal	-	-	-	-	-	-	3210	10000	41000	45000	76000
Military	-	-	-	-	-	-	-	-	-	-	-
Scientific	-	-	-	-	-	-	1612	-	-	-	-
Technical	-	-	-	-	-	-	-	4000	10000	10000	12000
Women's	-	-	-	-	-	-	-	12000	12000	13000	16000

Table 5.2

Average Tuition and Fees as Percent of Estimated Income for Various Occupations 1840's and 1880's

	% 1840's	1880's
Urban Male Teacher	15	3
Rural Male Teacher	34	8
Mason	13	6
Common Laborer	25	7

fessional, female, and summer school enrollments are eliminated. It appears safe to assume that one–third to one–half of the reported enrollments in the larger Northern universities were in the regular undergraduate programs in 1900.[8]

Graduate programs in the academic departments were also not as well attended as is indicated by general statistical series which added all professional degree students to those in academic programs. Less than three thousand graduate students were enrolled in all of the United States in 1890–91. Athough the number of doctoral degrees awarded doubled to close to four hundred between 1890 and 1900, masters–degree candidates increased at a much lower rate.[9]

The small liberal arts colleges continued to admit a large proportion of the undergraduate population and they shared in the expansion of enrollments in the 1890s. Bailey Burritt's tabulation of graduates in the regular programs of the colleges between 1870 and 1900 provides a means of circumventing the problem of the overreporting of students in the major institutions. His work reveals that many colleges, not just the research universities, shared in the growth during the 1890s. A random check of attendance reports for the small liberal arts colleges after the Civil War suggests that many of the smaller and rural institutions also expanded enrollments in the 1890s.

Columbia had an increase in the number of graduates of less than 110 percent between 1870 and 1900, and 11 percent between 1890 and 1900. Harvard had a sharp decrease between 1870 and 1880, making its growth between 1870 and 1900 slightly greater than 100 percent and 183 percent between 1890 and 1900. The University of Michigan's male

Table 5.3

Enrollment in Undergraduate Programs in American Colleges and Universities as Percent of Native White Males in the United States Age 20-24, 1870-1900.
A) Unadjusted for female enrollments
B) Adjusted for female enrollments with 25% estimate of female enrollments

	% A	% B
1870	1.70	1.28
1880	1.84	1.38
1890	1.98	1.49
1900	3.20	2.40

graduates increased 79 percent in the 1890s, but this was less than the increase at Dickinson College. The relatively new University of Chicago, University of Wisconsin, and University of California more than tripled the numbers of their graduates, including an unknown proportion of females, between 1890 and 1900, but respectable growth marked the history of the remaining thirty–seven colleges studied by Burritt. Conservative Yale's antebellum growth, for example, was greater than Harvard's. A random sample of attendance at the smaller liberal arts colleges indicated that they also shared in the enrollment explosion of the 1890s, and, even without discounting the numbers of women among the graduates of the state universities, it appears permissible to assume that at least one–half of regular undergraduate enrollments in 1900 were in the smaller private colleges of the nation.[10]

The increases in total enrollment in higher education were also inflated. It was not just the liberal arts colleges and departments that failed to meet the expectation of the reformers and the predictions based upon enrollments in the 1850s. If enrollments at women's colleges and normal schools during the 1870s are subtracted from total enrollments for that decade and the estimate that 40 percent of the students enrolled were female is used for 1900, total enrollment in American higher education increased approximately 280 percent between 1870 and 1900; not the apparent 312 percent. If the 1870s enrollments are used as reported, the growth was 148 percent.[11]

The selection of programs by the undergraduate students also deviated from the hopes and predictions of the reformers. Within the regular colleges of the country during the 1880s and 1890s, more than a majority of students chose the standard bachelor's degree program (which still included classical language requirements) twenty percent enrolled for bachelor of science degrees, less than 8 percent opted for the short PhB programs, and 6 percent selected a bachelor of law curricula.[12] And the youth of America did not rush to enroll for a technical education. Technical schools and technical education cannot account for the growth of enrollments. The technical schools, dedicated to the teaching of practical industrial skills, were those most in conformity with the Jacksonian and the 1850s demands for the training of the common man. They had the potential to be completely free from premodern social and cultural influences, and it seemed that their students would be in high demand and have immediate economic returns from their training because of the changing nature of production in America. But at the level of what was regarded as higher education by historians, enrollments in technical schools did not grow as expected. They did increase from four thousand to ten thousand between 1870 and 1880, but in spite of the emergence of large and well–funded schools such as the Armour Institute, overall attendance remained constant until 1900. The cost of some of the technical schools and the development of industrial training at the high school level partially account for the relatively sparse attendance, but other factors were more important as illustrated by the attendance record at some of the colleges designed for technical and scientific training.[13]

One of the most successful "technical" colleges was highly selective, theoretically oriented, and very expensive. The students at the land–grant supported Massachusetts Institute of Technology were asked to pay more than students in Harvard's undergraduate program and the school demanded that students have traditional academic skills as well as the knowledge of a modern foreign language. The orientation of the institution soon turned to theoretical, rather than applied and practical training. But the land–grant institutions which charged no tuition, were dedicated to direct training, and which had more liberal admittance standards, such as Pennsylvania State College and the Massachusetts Agricultural College, had comparatively low enrollments.[14]

Within the regular colleges and universities, relatively few students selected either pure or applied programs. Estimates of the percent of students in the 1880s and 1890s who selected some engineering course are in the 10 percent range while approximately 4 percent of the graduates of the major northern colleges during those decades became professional engineers. Even an institution such as Cornell had less than 20 percent engineers among its graduates; its law and education alumni outnumbered them. The leading state universities in all regions of the country found it very difficult to match Cornell's record, and in the 1890s the number of students in theological seminaries was at least one–half the number of students in purely technical schools plus those in engineering programs in the regular colleges and universities.[15]

Agricultural training was even less attractive, although students were offered free tuitions and, in many states, scholarships covering other direct costs of education. Many colleges, especially those supported by the Morrill funds, were committed to the training of future farmers and continued the many attempts made during the antebellum years to institutionalize agricultural education. But most of the agricultural departments languished, and few students took advantage of the many scholarships and the low admissions standards of the agricultural schools. Perhaps 2 percent of the students of the late nineteenth century selected agricultural programs and, according to Burritt, students of the major colleges did not enter farming as an occupation. By 1900, Wisconsin, Michigan, Cornell, and other leading land–grant colleges and major universities reported that less than 2 percent of their alumni chose agriculture as a profession. In fact, the percentage of students entering agriculture diminished rather than increased between the Civil War and 1900, as illustrated by the history of the University of Illinois.[16] (Table 5.4)

Business courses and related training within the recognized institutions of higher education also were relatively unattractive to students. In the 1890s, perhaps 8 percent of the students chose some business–oriented programs and Burritt's estimates for business careers among the students of the thirty–seven major colleges were no greater than this study's estimates for the antebellum period. However, the pre–Civil War trend for the rise of private business colleges continued. Private and public business schools enrolled somewhere between one hundred thirty thousand and two hundred thousand students in the 1890s and early 1900s, almost as many students as enrolled in all of recognized higher education. But such schools and the skills they taught were not regarded as part of higher education during the period.[17]

However, the teaching of abstract science and research skills were among the most important goals of progressive educational leaders before and after the Civil War. Science in undergraduate programs was increased, and special institutions, such as Johns Hopkins, that offered very attractive economic benefits to students, were opened. But very few students selected professional science programs and even fewer became professional scientists or researchers in private industry.[18]

Table 5.4

Percent of Students Enrolled in Agricultural Programs at Selected Land Grant Institutions 1870-1900

	1870	1880	1890	1900
University of Illinois	21.0	7.0	4.0	1.1 (1892-4)
University of Michigan	2.9	1.1	0.6	0.9
University of Wisconsin	4.9	1.7	1.2	1.3
Cornell University	-	-	-	3.0

The schools, programs, and occupations that account for the growth of attendance in all of higher education and in the undergraduate institutions were not the ones predicted by the early reformers. Changes in two of the traditional professions, law and medicine, the emerging profession, education, and the increased number of women students were the reasons for the increases in the numbers of students in the colleges and universities.

Law and medically related enrollments remained close to their levels of the 1860s for some years and may even have declined during the decade of the Civil War. Then attendance began rising at an astounding rate. The undergraduate institutions that tied themselves to such newly extended training, either through undergraduate programs or by directly recognizing the old connections between college and professional school, experienced significant growth. Between 1870 and 1880, all attendance at medical schools doubled while law enrollments remained constant. At the same time, the number of schools for medical training increased. In 1860 there were some ninety medical schools for physicians and surgeons in operation, but by 1900, after years of repetition of the antebellum history of high failure rates, there were one hundred sixty such medical schools. Nursing schools grew from fifteen in 1880 to over four hundred; dental schools from three to fifty–four; and after their faltering antebellum history, veterinary colleges were established in most areas of the country.

Enrollments of students in law and medical specialties grew in the 1880s, but it was the 1890s that experienced the great rise in demand for formal training in the two fields, primarily due to the increased number of years of required professional study. Attendance at law schools increased more than 300 percent and at medical and nursing schools, more than 200 percent. Law schools and departments were opened to meet the profitable demand for legal training. From perhaps twenty–five law schools in 1860, over one hundred were in operation in 1900. The growth of the number of law schools and departments began in the 1870s, but the last decade of the century witnessed approximately thirty foundings.

By 1900, the number of students in medical and nursing schools was almost twice that of all technical and engineering students, and the enrollments in medical and law schools amounted to almost three–fourths of the number of students in the undergraduate colleges and universities. Attendance at medical and nursing schools increased seven fold in the forty years after the coming of the Civil War; attendance at schools for physicians and surgeons grew by 300 percent; and law school attendance increased from approximately fifteen hundred to over thirteen thousand.[19]

But the curricula that brought about most of the growth of enrollments, outside of that in the "shadow" institutions, was education itself. Combined with the new role of women in higher education, the training of teachers and professors accounts for most of the increase in attendance and helps explain the nature of college programs, if not the rhetoric of the period. Normal schools, begun before the Civil War, had 4 percent of total enrollments in 1860, 16 percent in 1870, and 30 percent in 1900. Within the regular collges, Burritt's study of graduates indicates that one–fourth of them became teachers or professors, but this understates the importance of the provision of teacher training within the major institutions. The state colleges and universities had become even more dependent upon the training of teachers and professors, and this increased their need to attract females.[20] The University of Michigan's history illustrates the dependence upon female enrollments, education as an occupational destination, and the need to compete for female students. Over half of its undergraduate population was female and 45 percent of its alumni became teachers by the 1890s.[21] It and other state and private institutions appear to have successfully competed with both women's colleges and normal schools for women and future teachers. The normal school enrollment growth slowed after the 1870s, and women's colleges maintained an almost constant number of students in the postbellum period. Although the more highly–endowed private universities, such as Harvard, segregated their female students and only small numbers of their male students became teachers, most private colleges produced over 25 percent teachers and other educators and in some way had become involved with the education of women.[22]

A factor analysis of Burritt's series for the period between the Civil War and the early twentieth century revealed that the only major shift in occupational choice within the major Northern colleges was that to education in the 1890s.[23] But the dependence upon the teaching of teachers was not confined to undergraduate colleges. A survey of the careers of the graduate students at Johns Hopkins, America's first research university, indicated that the main function of its program was the training of college educators, not the preparation of students to be experts directly employed in private industry. It seems reasonable to conclude that the emergence of graduate studies (including the new social sciences) at other leading universities served the same purpose.[24]

Just as in the antebellum era, recognized higher education was tied to an upgrading of the entire educational system. Graduate schools taught professors, who taught future high and normal school teachers, who taught primary teachers. By 1900, close to 40 percent of all those in American higher education were in some type of program for the training of educators. Despite the rhetoric aimed at the new sponsors of higher education, businessmen, industrialists, and agricultural interest groups, the American higher educational system and most colleges were attuned to students who entered three of the traditional professions. Medicine, law, and education, the focus of antebellum colleges, besides the ministry, were higher education's link to the new industrial order of America before 1900. The continuity of the history of higher education was not confined to enrollments and occupational choices. Not only did the postbellum years fall short of fulfilling the expectations for enrollments and a change in the careers of students, but increased inequality among the colleges and regions, continued foundings and failures, and the skewed distribution of students' backgrounds argue against the thesis of an educational revolution caused by the actions of the leaders of the new universities and state–sponsored colleges after the Civil War.

At very minimum, as many colleges were founded between 1861 and 1900 as were in operation in 1860. There has not yet been a study of the exact number of foundings and failures during the era, but a random check of national lists of colleges and universities for the period between 1870 and 1900 revealed a great number of institutions which were started after the Civil War but that did not survive into the early twentieth century.[25]

The founding of new colleges, the upgrading of academies and normal schools to college status, and the establishment of women's colleges continued in the pre–Civil War patterns. Perhaps with more direct aid and supervision from the denominations, colleges to service small towns and rural areas were begun despite the existence of the supposedly liberal and democratic government–sponsored colleges in every state. And many new state institutions had to concern themselves with the despised preparatory training. Just as in the antebellum years, the areas with the most inadequate lower educational systems turned to the combination college and preparatory school, but their enrollments were in the hundreds rather than in the tens, as in the antebellum era.[26]

Specialized educational institutions continued to be founded. More medical, nursing, and law schools were started and theological education was expanded. In 1898–99, America, partially because of the expansion of the Catholic church, had more than one hundred sixty theological seminaries, compared to the some fifty in 1860 and the eighty of 1870. Theological enrollments did not keep pace with the expansion of all of higher education, and the training of ministers accounted for 3 percent of all enrollments in 1900, compared to the 5 percent of 1860.[27]

The competition which resulted from the increase in the number of colleges that were founded in the postbellum era was not confined to or caused simply by the development of small towns and the denominations' fears concerning a loss of faith among the young. Stanford University was opened a few miles away from the University of California; Johns Hopkins soon competed for undergraduates with the sprawling Maryland state college; and the expansion of the University of Chicago was threatening to the University of Illinois.

As well, the colleges continued to differentiate. And resources remained unequally distributed, perhaps more than in the antebellum era. In 1900 the productive funds of the regular colleges and universities ranged from zero to twenty million dollars. The highly–endowed and perhaps most progressive institutions continued to charge high tuitions and fees while the poorer colleges attempted to pursue their antebellum subsidization policies.[28] (Table 5.5)

Inequalities in college enrollments as well as resources continued. Although most states offered students at least one low–tuition state institution and a wide range of options as to colleges and programs within their borders, students increasingly tended to migrate out of their home states for higher education.[29] (Table 5.6)

There were important increases in the percent of the young who attended college, especially in the Midwest and West, but inequalities remained and there were continuities in enrollment percentages despite the changes of institutional profiles in the states and the migration of students. Michigan, with its famous state university, continued to educate fewer of its own young men and women, either within or without the state, than did Ohio. Massachusetts and Connecticut remained educational centers for the nation. But they had comparatively low enrollments from among their own native populations.

Table 5.5

Instructors per Student and Expenditures for Instructional Purposes at Several Universities Circa 1909

	Ratio Student/Instructor	Income per Student	Salary Expenses per Student	Salary per Member Instructional Staff
Columbia	7.3	$409	$280	$2,050
Harvard	7	456	210	1,470
Chicago	17.4	257	138	2,400
Michigan	15	252	125	1,880
Yale	9	529	159	1,440
Cornell	7.1	298	140	1,007
Illinois	8.7	333	136	1,183
Wisconsin	10.4	321	157	1,650
Pennsylvania	9.8	158	117	1,186
California	8.5	282	137	1,180
Stanford	10.7	510	219	2,500
Toronto	9.5	179	93	881
Princeton	8.2	340	237	1,950
Mass. Institute	6.7	359	213	1,427
Minnesota	12.8	133	68	867
Ohio State	15.8	236	121	1,923
Nebraska	16.6	147	83	1,387
Missouri	14.3	317	115	1,660
McGill	6	365	194	1,176
N.Y. University	14.7	98	71	1,043
Northwestern	9.5	198	88	835
Johns Hopkins	3.7	479	325	1,226
Syracuse	15.3	97	63	904
Temple C.	11.8	31	23	274

What is most striking about the 1890s and post–Civil War enrollments are the relative decreases of the percentages of Southern young men and women in undergraduate higher education. The South had the lowest enrollments of any section of the nation. The University of Virginia, among many other Southern colleges, did attempt to encourage attendance. It had one of the most liberal tuition and scholarship policies in the country and a relatively attractive program, but the university and the state had enrollment levels which were less than before the Civil War. Maryland, with its new state college and its virtually (at times) free education, could not attract students, and the old pattern of students leaving the state and low enrollments continued. If the attendance of students from outside of Maryland at Johns Hopkins is controlled, Maryland's enrollment ratio becomes one-half that presented in Table 5.6, not much greater than in the 1860s.[30] Although one goal of the establishment of state-sponsored educational institutions was to retain

Table 5.6

Enrollments, 1890-91, in 361 Colleges and Universities of the United States by State. A) All Students from State in Any U.S. College or University as Percent of Native White Male Age 15-20 in Respective State. B) All Students Enrolled in a State as Percent of Native White Males Age 15-20 in the State. C) Students from a State Enrolled Within That State as Percent of Native White Males Age 15-20 in the State

%	A	B	C
Maine	2.30	1.80	1.48
New Hampshire	2.90	2.60	1.20
Vermont	2.90	1.60	1.22
Massachusetts	3.30	5.70	2.71
Rhode Island	3.00	3.50	1.82
Connecticut	2.80	6.16	0.92
New York	2.40	2.32	1.48
New Jersey	1.80	2.00	0.74
Pennsylvania	1.60	1.50	1.11
Delaware	2.80	1.30	1.21
Maryland	2.10	2.62	1.28
District of Columbia	4.30	4.00	1.84
Virginia	1.84	2.20	1.43
West Virginia	0.70	0.70	0.30
North Carolina	1.60	1.50	1.28
South Carolina	3.07	2.60	2.34
Georgia	1.43	1.21	1.13
Florida	1.32	0.81	0.78
Kentucky	1.49	1.34	1.13
Tennessee	2.13	2.62	1.89
Alabama	1.61	1.80	1.40
Louisiana	3.94	3.50	3.29
Texas	1.12	0.89	0.87
Arkansas	0.36	0.01	0.01
Oklahoma	0.01	0.01	0.01
Ohio	2.25	2.30	1.79
Indiana	1.50	1.40	1.15
Illinois	1.56	1.27	0.95
Michigan	1.52	2.14	1.26
Wisconsin	1.51	1.36	1.13
Minnesota	2.32	2.17	1.80
Iowa	2.34	2.20	1.87
Missouri	1.39	1.25	1.09
Nebraska	1.24	0.92	0.84
Kansas	1.50	1.23	1.35

students within each state, the movement of students from their home state was probably more likely than before the Civil War. (Table 5.7)

Student migration rates increased, perhaps helping to further nationalize America's middle and upper classes, but the predicted radical change in the socioeconomic backgrounds of the students of the undergraduate colleges and universities did not occur. In many institutions the results

Table 5.7

Number of Students from a State in Higher Education In that State for Each Student From the Respective State Enrolled in a College or University Outside of the State, 1890-91. For 361 Colleges and Universities.

Maine	3	Florida	2
New Hampshire	2	Kentucky	4
Vermont	2	Tennessee	9
Massachusetts	5	Alabama	7
Rhode Island	3	Louisiana	6
Connecticut	3	Texas	5
New York	3	Arkansas	1
New Jersey	2	Oklahoma	0
Pennsylvania	3	Ohio	5
Delaware	2	Indiana	5
Maryland	3	Illinois	3
District of Columbia	2	Michigan	6
Virginia	4	Wisconsin	4
West Virginia	2	Minnesota	4
North Carolina	5	Iowa	5
South Carolina	5	Missouri	5
Georgia	5	Nebraska	2
		Kansas	4

of the modernization of faculty and curricula were the opposite of the antebellum reformers' predictions. The American colleges and universities continued to differentiate on the basis of the background characteristics of their students, but few of the recognized institutions were able to attract students from the lower socioeconomic orders or from among the new ethnics of the country. With the possible exception of the normal schools and teacher–training programs within certain institutions (and store–front trade schools) American higher education was the domain of the Anglo–Saxon middle class. And if the results of the World War I era intelligence tests, examined later, are accepted as representative of the abilities of the students in the various types of postbellum institutions, the conclusion must be made that the colleges and universities were stratified more by socioeconomic background than by intellectual capabilities.

The failure of the land–grant colleges to fulfill earlier promises to attract the "industrial" classes was noticed by some observers before the turn of the century. Supporters of more aid to the new institutions responded to the critics by admitting some of the difficulties the Morrill colleges had encountered, but put emphasis upon the need to shape educational policies for economic and social advancement, rather than on egalitarianism. Data from educational surveys of the 1920s indicated that the criticisms of the new state universities were correct. One famous investigation, which used a representative sample of over fifty colleges, found that the social and economic backgrounds of students at various types of institutions were unequally distributed. Other surveys reinforced the conclusions in the Reynolds study. The system seems to have been stratified by the 1920s. And it was not the land–grant colleges or engineering programs that attracted students from the lower end of the socioeconomic spectrum. Among the types of institutions studied, the normal schools, teacher–training programs, and private coeducational colleges, enrolled most of the students from the "industrial" classes.[31] (Table 5.8)

Few complaints about the backgrounds of the state university students or direct recognition of the role being played by many of the smaller lib-

Table 5.8

Indicators of Socio-Economic Backgrounds of Students at Various Types of Colleges and Universities for the Period of the 1920's

	Non-state Co-educational Colleges	State Universities	Men's Colleges	Women's Colleges	Normal Schools
Median Parental Income	$2821	$3172	$4889	$5140	$1775 to $2665
Percent of Fathers who were College Graduates	14%	10%	25%	29%	--
Percent of Fathers with no Secondary Education	43%	27%	24%	13%	--

eral arts colleges, normal schools, or private practical training schools are evident in the literature on higher education in the early twentieth century. Perhaps this was due to what had evolved within the institutions that were usually taken as the representatives of the liberal arts college in America, the older colleges of New England. Many of them had become enclaves for the wealthy and the sons and daughters of the highly educated. By comparison, the state universities seemed to be fulfilling a social mobility function.

Median income of parents is only one indicator of social and economic stratification. The parental incomes of students at the various types of recognized colleges suggest that only the normal schools and some of the private coeducational colleges took students from families of unskilled and skilled workers. The median incomes of the fathers of state university students were above the level of male graduates of the land–grant colleges who had become clergymen, high school teachers, or farmers. Of the graduates of the land–grant institutions, however, only the highest level professionals earned enough to equal the median income of fathers of students in the famous private men's and women's colleges.[32] One report on the distribution of incomes among the parents of college students highlighted the growing inequalities among the schools. Yale was reported to have 47 percent of its students coming from families whose head earned over ten thousand dollars a year. Seven percent of these earned over fifty thousand dollars. But one–third were reported to have had incomes of five thousand dollars or less. Williams, one of the old ministerial colleges, had 68 percent of its students with fathers earning ten thousand dollars or more a year compared to 17 percent at Wabash.[33]

Another aspect of the socioeconomic stratification of the colleges was the educational background of parents. Again, a hierarchy developed with the private coeducational colleges serving a greater percentage of those from families with little education. But the reports on educational levels do suggest that both state universities and men's colleges, as well as the coeducational private institutions, were serving the sons and daughters of those who had been economically successful, although they had little formal education.[34] The occupations of the fathers of the students were similarly distributed. Students whose fathers were professionals were overrepresented in most types of colleges. Overall, the percentage of the student population from professional families was six times that expected on the basis of the proportion of professionals over forty–five years old in the American workforce, according to one survey of colleges and universities, and four times the expectation according to another survey which concentrated on state universities and private liberal arts colleges. Farmers were barely equally represented in the state universities. And private colleges had 6 percent fewer sons and daughters of farmers than the state institutions. Reports of other occupational backgrounds varied, but it is clear that those lower on the occupational ladder were underrepresented, with only the normal schools and the private trade schools acting as channels for the unskilled. A very unsatisfactory category used in one study, "manual labor", despite its ambiguity, indicates that, although public high schools and junior colleges had a much better record in enrolling the children of men in such occupations than private schools, state universities had approximately the same percentage of such students enrolled as did private colleges and universities.[35]

Place of birth and age are other socioeconomic indicators, and they suggest the same distributions among types of colleges. Almost all students were native born and the English and German elements of the population dominated the schools. Only the normal schools were enrolling first–generation students in significant numbers from outside these groups.

But one goal of the antebellum reformers did seem to be achieved during the era. The age of students who entered the colleges and universities was narrowed to the modern range of 18 to 20. The dependence upon high schools and changes in the American economy not only eliminated the very young student, the older potential students did not enroll in the colleges and universities. However, the older pattern of social–mobility through higher education being related to age at entry continued, and it was the familiar antbellum pattern. Teacher–training programs within the colleges and normal schools had the highest percentages of mature students. Within the land–grant colleges, teacher programs had greater percentages of students who had begun higher education when they were more than twenty years old than engineering or any other undergraduate program. These age groupings suggest that the modern college subjects were not attracting or holding the young men who had, perhaps, spent some years working and saving for higher education.[36]

There is also evidence that student behavior did not change as predicted. Religious conversions may have diminished, but immature conduct continued despite the increased age of entry. The narrow age group resulting from the dependence on the secondary schools may have, in fact, increased immature behavior, as indicated by the change of the nature of fraternities and student uprisings. However, the definitions of permissible behavior were altered and actions that would have led to major investigations of campus conditions in the antebellum period went unnoticed after the Civil War. Fraternities developed into organizations devoted to institutionalized misbehavior, college athletics and accompanying festivities were encouraged or tolerated, and riots continued. At

Michigan, President Angell had to quiet the aftereffects of a major battle between "town and gown" and rescue several hundred of his students from jail. But these and possibly many other disruptive actions were not given the attention they would have received in the antebellum period.[37]

> A change has taken place in the manner and measure of collegiate discipline. This is due not to the change of locality, but to the spirit of the age. It has come to be a maxim that the best government is that which governs least. We seek the minimum of restriction on liberty that is compatible with the ends of government, viz., order, morality and diligence. Formerly the dormitory system prevailed; students were required to be in their rooms during certain hours of the day and night; professors and tutors visited the buildings, seeking to surprise the inmates, in order to ascertain whether the rule was observed; there were many minute regulations which have since been abandoned. This continued exercise of authority and plan of watching provoked insubordination and evasion; the wits of the boys were set to work in order to deceive the teachers, and to break the rules without detection, or, at least, with impunity. The risk gave to mischief and lawlessness a relish they would not otherwise have possessed. Unwholesome suppers were stealthily brought to the rooms by negroes at late hours of the night; calathumps aroused the neighborhood with most hideous music; blackboards were greased; the bell–rope was cut, and old John had to blow his horn at daybreak in every row of the buildings, as a call to prayers and recitations. This provoked him greatly, and he used to say, "If you won't be rung up as gentlemen, I must blow you up as hogs." How heartily I have heard Dr. Smith laugh as he repeated the old negro's complaint at such times, "We have the worstest young men, and the mostest on 'em, I ever seed!" Practical jokes, sometimes of a very disagreeable sort, were played on professors in their nocturnal rounds of inspecting the premises. Calves were hauled up into lecture–rooms, and other silly tricks were perpetrated. I am glad that these follies have passed away, that faculty and students treat each other as gentlemen and friends, and that the public sentiment of the College would not tolerate any rudeness, though disguised under the name of fun. It is well to appeal to the conscience, gentlemanly propriety and honor, and generous and kindly sentiments of young men, rather than resort to espionage and multipled restraints.

The hated teaching methods also seem to have continued in many institutions. At MIT, students were subjected to daily "oral quizzes" and, in many institutions, the lecture method turned into a means of reducing faculty costs. The old patterns of instruction in the medical and law schools were transferred to the colleges. Great numbers of students were assigned to one lecture class and the old tutors, called by more modern names, continued to be the usual direct contact between faculty and student. In many modern colleges chapel attendance was encouraged, indicating that the socialization function was still a major duty of the administration and staff.[38]

Other predicted radical changes were not made. Although the new, wealthy, and research-oriented universities were able to pay very high salaries to their leading professional scholars, the relative economic status of college professors continued to decline, and greater inequalities of economic rewards developed among the faculties. It is difficult to state the income of workers and professionals with precision, but the trend of faculty salaries in the nineteenth and twentieth centuries indicates that many of the complaints about faculty renumeration in the antebellum period may have been guarded comments about the conditions in the later nineteenth century.[39] (Table 5.9) Although there are no systematic studies of the job security of later nineteenth-century faculty members, there are enough indications from the history of universities and the demands of faculty organizations to suggest that the professionalization of education did not mean that the new professors were protected against arbitrary action by administrators. Eliot's reign at Harvard was marked by firings and a sense of insecurity among the faculty, and later organizations such as the AAUP found it necessary to fight both for rules for promotion and tenure and independent retirment plans.[40]

> The most serious danger which threatens the continued and developing efficiency of our universities lies in the unattractive and utterly inadequate salaries paid the instructors. Is it not well to make the portals through which all must enter the collegiate teaching profession reasonably attractive to men of character, spirit and ability? The writer is well aware of the satisfactions and rewards of the teacher's life other than financial, but should not these men for the sake of efficiency of the institutions receive salaries somewhat commensurate with the long and expensive preparation for their life work, and adequate to insure the possibility of their intellectual development rather than retrogression?
>
> Is it to be expected, otherwise, that the field of university teaching will appeal to men of suitable quality? It has been seen that it is upon these men that the greater part of the burden of the instruction falls, and within the limitations of their ranks must develop those who are to recruit the higher positions. Nine hundred or a thousand dollars a year for doctors of philosophy! Why should uni-

Table 5.9

Average Salaries of Professors, Average Income of Unskilled Urban Workers, and Ratios. 1810-1970's U.S.A. Current Dollars

Decade	Average Professor Salary	SD	n Colleges in Sample	Unskilled Income	Ratio
1810	$ 1377	$593	13	$ 153	9.0*
1820	1085	446	19	118	9.2
1830	1401	561	34	149	9.4
1840	1277	564	31	157	7.8
1850	1269	615	46	170	7.5
1890	1470			281	5.2
1900	1481			322	4.6
1910	2108			523	4.0
1920	3151			953	3.3
1930	3237			993	3.3
1940	4221			1804	2.3
1950	5658			1902	1.9
1960	8993			4332	2.1
1970-1973	13144			6676	2.0**
1975-1976	17142			8500	

* For the years 1810-1860, Average Professor Salary was computed by: faculty salary per decade x average number of faculty in the college. For later decades, the results for professors and workers was computed by: the sum of the average yearly salary divided by number of years. Workers' incomes are based upon 2000 hours a year employment.

** This ratio is probably too high. To bias the data against the thesis, incomes for the unskilled were selected from categories of urban workers with relatively low income.

versities place so very low an estimate upon the value of their own product? As if to discredit the rank still more, the rules of the Carnegie Foundation refuse to recognize the years spent in it as a teacher toward the necessary twenty-five years of service entitling one to a retiring allowance. The writer has known of able men, loyal to their institutions, who have spent fifteen years and more in this rank before receiving deserved promotion. Furthermore, most institutions rob themselves of the younger men's natural desire to pursue advanced study and to grow, by loading them down with a heavy burden of entirely elementary work—and refusing to count years of service as instructor toward a sabbatical leave.

But one objective of the intellectual–meritocratic reformers seems to have been achieved. The intellectually deficient or ill–prepared student, if he really did exist in the antebellum period, was eliminated. Because of the selectivity of the secondary educational system and the increasing reliance upon formal admissions standards, an academically well–qualified student became the norm for recognized American higher education in the late nineteenth and early twentieth century. But even with this quality of students, attrition rates remained high, indicating continued deficiencies within the institutions and, perhaps, the socioeconomic system.[41] Intelligence tests, which are best interpreted as measures of conformity to academic norms, were given to students (usually those at larger and modernized colleges) as well as to a group representative of the young white population of the country during World War I. Because other tests were equated with the World War I Alpha and Beta, which were given to the members of the armed forces, it is possible to compare the students of the early twentieth century to the general population and to later students. The results of the tests, as they relate to college students, went unnoticed by historians, perhaps because of the difficulty of compiling the necessary statistics and because such achievement levels were assumed to be normal. However, the scores indicate that the larger colleges were enrolling a very special type of student.[42] (Tables 5.10, 5.11, 5.12, 5.18, 5.19) The average student may well have scored at or above the 90th percentile. One reason for such high scores was the selectivity of the high schools and another, indicated by the differences between freshmen and higher level students' scores within the colleges, was a process within the colleges which led lower–scoring individuals to withdraw.

However, the colleges did not fully achieve the meritocratic goal that became one of the justifications for and ideals of the university movement. Recognized higher educational institutions could have increased enrollments by 50 percent if all the relevant population that scored at or above the 94th or 95th percentile had been attracted to the colleges and universities. Enrollments could have been increased by 250 percent if all those at or above minus one standard deviation from the mean score had been admitted.[43]

The failure of the colleges, especially the state and private men's universities, to enroll students who came from lower–status families or to attract a majority of the academically capable was the result of more than internal college policy. A growing attitude of selectivity, a result of the need to fulfill the gate–keeper role, had something to do with the increased exclusiveness of many institutions. And conservatism did exceed its normal bounds when attitudes such as those reflected in the fol-

Table 5.10

Percentile Location of Average Scores of Various High Schools and High School Students on the Army Examinations (circa 1918-1925)

School Location	Level	Percentile on National Distribution	Percentile on State Distribution
California	All	91	88
Hartford, Ct	frosh	78	73
	junior	92	89
	senior	94	92
Michigan			
Small town	frosh	77	76
	sophmore	85	84
	junior	90	88
	senior	93	92
Detroit	senior	93	92
Detroit, 1st year teacher		98	97
New York State	frosh	79	78
	sophmore	86	85
	junior	91	91
	senior	95	95
IA, urban	frosh	93	90
	senior	97	95
Emporia, KA	frosh	71	65
	sophmore	86	83
	junior	84	80
	senior	89	86
Stanton, VA	frosh	75	85
	sophmore	89	95
	junior	96	98
	senior	91	96
5 Military Acad.	All	94	--
10 High Schools	All	95	--
IL, IA, MO	frosh	83	77
	sophmore	89	84
	junior	93	90
	senior	94	91
Native White Draft, WWI	4 years	88	--
White Officers WWI	4 years	97	--

Table 5.11

Percentile Location of Average Score of Various Normal Schools and Teachers Colleges on Army Examinations (Circa 1918-1925)

School Location	Sex	Level	Percentile on National Distribution	Percentile on State Distribution
Kansas	M	frosh	95	93
Illinois	M	all	94	94
Texas	F	all	76	83
Illinois	F	frosh	94	94
Colorado	F	all	93	89
Minnesota	M	all	95	93
	M	all	97	96
Missouri	F	all	93	94
Nebraska	F	all	94	95
Michigan	F	frosh	92	92
	F	sophmore	97	96
	F	junior	97	97
	F	senior	98	98
	M	frosh	94	94
	M	sophmore	97	96
	M	junior	98	98
	M	senior	99	99
Nebraska	F	frosh	94	94
	F	sophmore	95	95
	F	junior	97	97
	F	senior	98	99
Minnesota	M	all	95	94
	M	all	97	96
Pennsylvania	F	all	91	88
Kansas	F	all	90	87
7 Normal	F	all	88	--
4 Normal	M	all	89	--
Illinois	both	frosh	95	94
	F	frosh	94	94

lowing quotation from a speech given by one of America's most renowned new psychologists became influential.:[44]

> The university professor's experience renders him peculiarly receptive to the present day view of psychologists that among the so–called normal human beings there exists rather large differences in native intellectual ability....The general population covers the wide range from genius to vegative idiocy, the university only that

from genius to a point not considerably below the intelligence of the average individual of the northern, central, or western European races.... If the 1000 best endowed students in Stanford University were replaced by an equal number at the lower end of the university intelligence distribution, and if that situation were made perma-

Table 5.12

Percentile Location of Average Scores of Various Colleges and Universities on Army Examinations (Circa 1918-1925)

College	Sex	Level	Percentile on National Distribution	Percentile on State Distribution
U. North Dakota	F	all	94	95
Colorado	F	all	97	94
Ohio State	M	frosh	95	88
	M	sophmore	96	91
	M	junior	97	92
	M	senior	97	93
	M	graduate	99	96
Oberlin	M	frosh	98	95
	F	frosh	97	92
Dickinson	both	frosh	97	95
	M	frosh	97	95
	M	sophmore	99	98
	M	junior	98	97
	M	senior	98	97
U. Florida	M	frosh	92	97
Mass. Agricultural	M	?	98	97
Johns Hopkins	M	frosh	96	99
Virginia Polytechnic	M	?	80	96
U. Minnesota	M	frosh	94	93
U. Idaho	M	frosh	94	88
	F	frosh	91	84
Colorado	M	all	97	94
Notre Dame	M	all	96	97
Purdue	both	frosh	93	94
Rutgers	M	?	96	99
Purdue	M	engineering	96	96
U. Texas	M	all	94	97
Brown	M	frosh	98	98
Citadel	M	all	94	98

Table 5.12 con't

College	Sex	Level	Percentile on National Distribution	Percentile on State Distribution
20 Colleges	M	all	94	--
13 Colleges	F	all	94	--
U. Minnesota	F	frosh	94	92
Southern Methodist	?	all	93	96
	both	frosh	94	97
	both	sophmore	90	94
	both	junior	93	96
	both	senior	95	99
Ohio State	F	frosh	94	88
	F	sophmore	96	89
	F	junior	96	90
	F	senior	97	92
	both	graduate	99	96
Yale	M	frosh	99	98
U. California	M	all	96	93
Dartmouth	M	all	98	98
Hamline	M	all	94	--
	F	all	95	--
U. Illinois	both	frosh	98	98
	both	sophmore	97	97
	both	junior	97	97
	both	senior	98	98
	both	graduate	99	99
U. Arkansas	both	frosh	92	99
	both	frosh, eng.	96	99
	M	frosh	93	99
	F	frosh	91	98
Kansas	both	frosh	94	93
U. Chicago *	both	frosh	98	98
N. Western *	both	frosh	96	96
Large Universities *	both	frosh	99	--
Colleges *	both	frosh	97	--
Colleges *	both	frosh	98	--
Native White Draft WWI	M	4 years	97	--
White Officers WWI	M	4 years	99	--

nent, no amount of endowment or internal improvement could maintain our present rank in relation to other institutions of higher learning and professional training. On the other hand, if our 1,000 dullest students were replaced by an equal number, all of whom belonged above the lower limit of the top five percent of our present student body, and if that situation could be made permanent,

Stanford might hope to become one of the world's greatest universities within a few score of years.

Such attitudes help explain the changes within the colleges and the gap between expected and actual patterns of enrollments in the late nineteenth century. As well, other policies pursued by the universities held down the number of students and helped to determine the type of students who entered the various institutions. Many famous colleges, despite their riches, continued to charge high tuitions and fees. The social and economic backgrounds of the established student populations at some institutions made attendance uncomfortable for the poor and for those from different class or ethnic backgrounds. Some colleges became tied to markets for a very traditional curricula and others became overt representatives of a particular religious doctrine. But the major constraints on change and the causes of the failures of the famous reforms to accomplish their expected results, as in the antebellum period, were external to the colleges. Because of this, the attempts to change the nature of institutions and student populations, despite major experiments, did not produce the desired results. Outside forces were interfering with the possibilities of reform and were influencing the nature of the colleges and their students. More radical educational and social reforms than were attempted, and which would have endangered the financial and status positions of many institutions and faculties, would have been necessary to achieve the somewhat contradictory reform goals. Perhaps it was the frustration stemming from the failure to attract large numbers of students, competition from other institutions, and the intransigence of the American social and economic system that turned late nineteenth–century educational leaders away from the earlier focus upon students and teaching to the emphasis upon the other possible contributions of higher education and from an optimistic and democratic philosophy to one of pessimism and elitism. The failure to attract students to the new curricula, the nature of the markets for graduates, and the type of appeals necessary to gain funds from the business world led higher education's spokesmen, in self–defense, to emphasize research, specific training, community service, and the intellectually elite character of their students.[45]

Postbellum social and economic conditions were more supportive of higher education than those of the pre–Civil War period, but they continued to place constraints on educational reform, and they changed educational ideals. The major forces shaping higher education ranged from the economic to the intellectual and the ideological. The costs of higher education remained important because of the level and distribution of income and wealth in the nation. Tuition and direct cost reductions were ineffectual because of the level and distribution of disposable income and because of the major cost of both secondary and higher education, income foregone while attending school. Also important, but less direct, were the continued competitive advantage of apprenticeship, on–the–job training, and short professional courses that discouraged investments in recognized higher education, especially college, for students intending to enter many occupations. One reason for the competitive advantage of informal training was the difficulty of devising curricula to prepare students who wished to enter many of the new and attractive occupations of the period. Another was the absence of social and political inducements to invest in higher education for many occupations and professions. And a basic difficulty was the lack of a market for many occupations over which the colleges seemed to have a natural monopoly to train people. Thus, significant economic and social conditions needed to make regular higher education attractive and necessary to the new ideal student envisioned by the reformers such as Wayland did not exist during the postbellum years.

Although the average direct costs of going to college, tuition, fees, and books, became a smaller percentage of incomes of workers and others in the late nineteenth century, a significant barrier remained to the economic accessibility of even the free tuition colleges. Income foregone, the loss of income which might have been earned had an individual gone to work rather than to college or high school, remained an extremely important factor, especially to those whose families had limited economic resources. Income foregone while attending secondary and higher education was greater than the immediate costs of attending the most expensive colleges. In their effort to differentiate themselves from the high schools and to create a hierarchially organized educational system, the colleges, especially the new universities, increased student income foregone by demanding more formal preparation for entry into college. The informal modes of preparation, such as training by a local minister, became less effective means of ensuring acceptance by the colleges and universities.

Even if educational requirements had remained at antebellum levels, income foregone would still have been a major deterrent to college–going and an inducement to enroll in "trade" schools. Economically marginal individuals and their families, because of transportation systems and the location of colleges, had to carry both the direct and indirect costs of education through savings. Few students could find well–paying work during the school year and parents had to pay out part of their own income, as well as forego the income of sons and daughters who were finally old enough to make economic contributions to their families.

The ramifications of income foregone extend beyond the problem of immediate economic welfare. When foregone income is combined with the direct costs of education and the expected income stream from an investment in education, a rate of economic return from the investment may be calculated. Just as financial investors discount future interest and consider the opportunities lost when they commit their funds to a long-term note, those considering investments in themselves may compare their futures with and without formal training. They make predictions about future salaries and the security of employment. When they predict income streams with and without formal training and their associated costs are compared, a "rational" decision may be made. If apprenticeship, which pays a salary, or a practical course, which takes only a few months, seems to guarantee as high an income as attendance at school, the rational decision, at least for those who consider education a long-term investment rather than a consumption item, is to choose the informal mode of education.[46] The perceived and actual returns from formal training are determined by much more than pure economics, however. Societal norms and socialization may make one method of attaining a position appear to be more financially rewarding than it actually is. Advertising may affect the perceptions of students. Families might insist upon one mode of training, formal or informal, based upon their outdated perceptions of the occupational world. Social and cultural conditions might prevent particular groups from perceiving a possibility of entering a profession even through expensive formal education.

The objective conditions which set the returns to investments in education are also the result of more than the workings of a pristine marketplace. Social and political forces have had much influence over the economics of work and education. Interest groups may demand expensive formal education for entry into their allied occupations. Legislatures may make a specific number of years of formal training mandatory at the same time that unions or occupational groups make them more difficult to attain. Taxation and other disincentives may make the gains in income from the investment in one form of training uneconomic for a particular occupation or profession. And society may radically alter the educational investment environment through legislation which outlaws particular forms of training or which makes investment in formal education mandatory, such as a high school education.

Unpredictable technnological change and styles of management have also affected the rates of return from education. Increased competition, caused by transportation technology, may force increased investments in education as in the case of the country doctors whose practices were threatened by the increased use of the automobile in the 1920s. Bureaucratic reward systems can make formal education an absolute necessity for entry and advancement, although such training may not affect job performance.[47]

Although educators hope that investments in formal education always will assure greater rewards than informal education and that schools and colleges have the ability to devise inherently rewarding curricula for all occupations and societal tasks, the returns from investments in formal education have not always been the result of the substantive content of education. Just as formal regulations inducing and forcing investments in schooling make education appear to be contributing directly to economic growth, the admissions procedures, performance demands and the bureaucratic structure of education may act as "gate–keepers" and a means of presorting individuals for employment rather than as means of ensuring that those in most need of education attend schools and colleges. The apparently higher returns from formal education are assured by allowing only those relatively sure of success into the colleges, by eliminating those who had entered but who might damage the reputation of the college, by ignoring those with low potentials while they attend college, and by cultivating the promising students intending to enter the highly rewarding occupations and then focusing upon their later achievements.[48]

One of the reasons for the failure of many of the reforms of the postbellum era was that the new educational leaders, perhaps without being aware of the consequences of their philosophies and actions, encouraged the growth of the "gate–keeper" role for higher education. Combined with the new economic world of the postbellum era, which induced colleges to emphasize the economic rather than social or cultural rewards from higher education, the needs of institutions turned the reform philosophies into a conservative force. The postbellum era carried along with it disincentives for the democratization of higher education. Only those institutions which could seemingly guarantee high economic rewards to their students received acclaim, status, and adequate financial support.

The shift from emphasis upon character training and humanistic education to education for specialized skills did not mean that the colleges became free from outside influences or that they were able to institutionalize a means of overcoming the social and economic forces working against full democratization of the higher educational system—new but less obvious masters took the place of denominational sponsors and educational leaders shaped their policies to maximize their institutions' advantage within the framework of the political, social, and economic worlds of postbellum America. Legislatures which demanded proof of productivity, interest groups which demanded services from the new expert faculty, and donors who demanded evidence of a program's special contribution, shaped not only academic rhetoric but fundamental educational policies.[49]

Students and their families followed a similar logic as they began to perceive the changes in the American economy and society during the postbellum period. Given their financial resources, they sought the schools and colleges which could generate the highest possible returns on their investments. Those with the economic resources could treat higher education as, to some degree, a consumption item, but the majority of Americans looked upon it as an investment decision. The changes in the occupations and professions created new parameters for individual decisions and Americans responded in a predictable manner. The occupations that students desired and the general demand for higher education before and after the Civil War are explained by the role of college expenses, altered income levels, job markets, the social system, criteria for entry into professions, and the state of objective knowledge. And the history of various institutions is explained by their reactions to changing economic, social, and political conditions. Institutions pursued different policies and attracted different types of students depending upon their resources, their previous reputations, their alumni, their social and political influence and, to some extent, politically generated directives. And much of the educational in–fighting of the period is explained by the new competitive conditions established by socioeconomic changes.

The immediate results are most clearly seen in the professional schools, but the new inducements and constraints were felt in the liberal arts colleges and their departments. The occupations which college students usually chose were not only those with high returns or which were expanding, but those regulated by government or private organizations and which, through one means or another, had developed a formalized entry procedure. Enrollment growth and occupational distributions in the recognized institutions were tied to the formalization of the American social and economic orders. Institutions that were able to link themselves to occupations with relatively high rates of return and fixed entry criteria and that were able to seemingly be responsible for guaranteed student success became the most prestigious colleges.

At least in New England, the same institutions which were noted for high–status students during the antebellum period became the most respected colleges after the Civil War, indicating that within both periods the backgrounds of students, as much as direct educational influences, shaped the nature and image of colleges.[50]

Education was the occupation that offered the greatest opportunity for employment during the period, and it had the most direct ties to academic culture and power. As a new professional educational elite gained political control over primary, secondary, and even higher education, they were able to formalize training and to create new rules for entry which, in many instances, forced increased investments in higher education by prospective teachers. The new central bureaucracies of state and city educational systems and college faculties, such as those at the University of Michigan, which provided textbooks and set standards for the schools and teachers, created an expanded market for higher education, one that had only begun to emerge in the antebellum era. Even with the increased power over training for primary and secondary training, economic and social forces limited achievements by the new educational elite.

Despite the lowering of the immediate costs of formal education for the teaching profession, the availability of the new teacher–training schools, and even the direct subsidization of many students, higher education was unable to maximize the market potential of the expanding American educational system. The same forces that blocked the antebellum colleges frustrated the postbellum educators who had much more power over the educational market than the early college administrators.[51]

Eduction was an expanding industry, undergoing the pains of professionalization; the total number of teachers in public schools rose from two hundred one thousand to four hundred twenty–three thousand in just thirty years and the number of professors quadrupled. The increase in the number of teachers is, however, a great understatement of the number of individuals who engaged in teaching because turnover rates remained extremely high. Even with the great numbers of teachers, the growth of the student population in the schools exceeded the expansion of the teaching force. There was one teacher to thirty–three students in 1870 and less than one to forty in 1900.[52] (Table 5.13)

The low cost and accessible normal schools, teachers' colleges and teachers' programs in both public and private colleges were unable to attract all future teachers (in the 1890s 30 percent of New England's teaching force had any professional training). And women, rather than men, dominated the field. Women comprised 61 percent of the teaching force in 1870 and 71 percent in 1900, and they were always the majority of students in the normal schools. They were 60 percent of the students in 1870 and 70 percent in 1900. But within the higher cost private normal schools the numbers of men and women were evenly balanced.[53]

The reasons for these trends were economic and social, and with all the power of professional educators, the investments in higher education by future teachers and the socioeconomic backgrounds of students was not determined by the normal schools and colleges. Women tended to choose the lower–cost training schools, they dominated primary teaching, men chose higher investments in formal education and many avoided any formal training because of the reward systems in the society

Table 5.13

Percent of Teachers in Various States Who Were College Graduates and Who Were Normal School Graduates, 1918, and Percent of Massachusetts' Teachers Who Were College or Normal School Graduates, 1874-5 to 1920

	1918	
	College Graduates	Normal School Graduates
Massachusetts	17	68
Rhode Island	15	70
New Jersey	15	67
Connecticut	14	58
New Hampshire	21	37
Colorado	21	34
Minnesota	15	33
Montana	15	28
Wisconsin	13	29
Illinois	16	20
Virginia	7	26
North Dakota	9	23
West Virginia	8	22
Kansas	14	12

Massachusetts	Percent College Graduates	Percent Normal School Graduates
1874-5	--	19
1884-5	--	29
1894-5	6	36
1904-5	14	48
1913-14	16	55
1920	17	69

and the teaching profession. And students from high-status backgrounds opted for other occupations, programs, and schools.

The closure of the professions to women combined with other factors to determine the numbers of females in higher education and the types of schools and subjects they selected. The American economy was becoming wealthier and more families could afford to send their daughters to college without planning that their education would lead to employment. But women were not considered to be future breadwinners and most families with intentions to educate their daughters, or independent females, could not afford to select expensive education. While the focus on male children hindered female enrollment in higher education, the fact that women lost relatively little income while attending a college, because of the typical wages of female workers, increased the likelihood of their attendance. These factors interacted with new certification rules, subsidization policies, and bureaucratic procedures and norms to channel women into lower–cost education for teaching and nursing and into the traditional curricula in the regular colleges. Two pseudo–professions, nursing and teaching, were the usual careers of women who aspired to professional life. A few postbellum women entered the law. Medical schools for women physicians had been open since before the Civil War but they met with little success. Private business colleges admitted them, but the training was intended for low–status clerical positions. The traditional women's colleges, recently created from the older ladies' seminaries, realized the barriers to the professions for women and concentrated on the socialization of their charges for suitable marriages and a Victorian cultural role. A new curriculum, domestic science, was really a traditional subject with a new name and continued the old habit of education for consumption and, perhaps, welfare activities.[54]

Normal schools and a primitive form of nursing education had begun to emerge before the Civil War, and their development was partly a result of the general rationalization of American society. Both arose in conjunction with certification demands for entry and a search for a means to allow the expansion of education and hospitalization at relatively low economic cost. Because women sought higher–status but faced poor employment potentials, the two careers appeared rewarding to them, although primary education and nursing paid very little. To attract females and to ensure some degree of competency, minimal cost training for both occupations, especially teaching, was devised. Normal schools asked for relatively little preparation or tuition and had short courses as well as, in many cases, subsidies for other costs. The new nursing schools had similar policies and some provided room and board to students free of charge. In both types of schools, per student expenditures were held to the minimum.[55]

Women became predominant in normal school training because of these conditions and because once they entered teaching there was relatively small return on their investments in further education. Although not as fruitless as in nursing, increased or initially high–cost education was uneconomic for women. The bureaucratic rules in education were such that men were the most likely to be allowed to advance to higher teaching positions or administrative posts, and as bureaucratic demands for formal certification for such positions increased, men responded accordingly. However, over the century the possibility of women achieving higher roles improved, and it was rational for them to invest in the fulfillment of the escalating demands of the educational elites, especially for those who had already invested in secondary training. The regular colleges and universities benefited from decreased sexism in the school systems and the relatively lower opportunity costs of education for women. Because traditional undergraduate programs were in conformity with demands by the schools, women could invest in them for both self–satisfaction and career purposes.

However, for both men and women, the comparatively low economic rewards from teaching discouraged investments in higher education. Those who sought college posts normally chose to spend additional years in school but Johns Hopkins Unversity had to subsidize students to encourage graduate study for teaching. Other universities adopted similar policies to generate and sustain a demand for higher education. Only with the combination of increased demands for schooling by the educational bureaucracy and the guarantee of economic rewards through promotion procedures directly tied to certification by higher education, would a strong demand for advanced teacher training be generated. In areas of the country with poor economies, such as the South, little could be done either to force or entice increased educational levels for teachers.[56]

In more prosperous times and areas the formalization of teaching led to institutional changes. With great influence over certification standards and criteria, professional educators turned the old normal school into the teacher's college and then, because of vested interests as well as student demands, into an imitation of the university and a competitor of private commercial colleges.[57]

Achievements were also limited in professorial training. Despite the growing power of established professional academics over certification for entry into the role of professor and the more than fourfold increase in the number of college instructors, the market for advanced training remained limited. Between 1870 and 1900, some thirty–nine hundred doctoral degrees were awarded by American universities; less than one–fifth the number of college professors in 1900. Combining master's and doctoral degrees for the thirty–year period yields approximately the number of employed college professors in 1900, but it it doubtful that all master's degree holders entered college teaching.[58] Academia had begun to professionalize and to replace the minister, who spent part of his career teaching college, with full–time scholars and instructors who began to establish new disciplines and new definitions for entry into their fields. The 1890s were a critical turning point with the emergence of new intellectual specializations and accompanying organizations to encourage and enforce professional differentiation. Professors at the new research universities began to reshape old professional associations at the same time that they created new domains of study and sought to control the procedures for hiring academics. The one grand organization for the social sciences began to splinter and the resulting organizations became dominated by the professional, full–time scholar (who in many cases supplemented his low salary by a new form of the old ministers habit of outside lecturing, consulting). History, sociology, economics, and anthropology not only represented new intellectual disciplines, but new groups whose membership and conduct were defined by the reseach elite rather than the broader American community or even academia in general. It appears that the social sciences were not alone in moving towards the model of professional control which paralleled movements in medicine and law. The natural sciences, and even the humanities, tied themselves to formalism, "objective" criteria, and standards of productivity and competence which were defended by claims of merit as defined by the specialized group and the new mandates of science.[59]

In spite of the pretentions of professional status, investments in advanced education for academia remained limited. Relatively low salaries and the comparatively small number of positions in academia prevented advanced training from becoming a major source of direct income or students for higher education. The rate of return from the investment needed to qualify to teach in the colleges and universities continued to make advanced training a minor part of the college market. The average professor could expect a salary that was less than half that received by graduates in law and medicine in the early twentieth century, but he was asked to spend, if he fulfilled the new mandates for specialization and research productivity, as many or more years of income foregone as the physician or lawyer. As with lower education, the colleges could depend upon graduate training only when a combination of professional control, increased wealth in the nation, and a vastly expanded market for college education emerged later in the twentieth century.[60] And, administrators and professional interest groups had to devise new roles for professors which would allow at least a minority to achieve competitive income levels through outside activities. But only a few institutions and professors managed to balance such practical professional demands and the continued need for a focus upon teaching.

Similar forces limited the realization of one of the great hopes of modernizers of the colleges and universities such as Charles Eliot. Despite the attempts to define new criteria for specialists in governmental affairs and to create rules of entry into government bureaucracies in favor of those with college education, the idea of the civil service as a career for college students remained unfulfilled until the mid–twentieth century.

College–educated men may have continued to form a subculture within the higher levels of the Federal and state bureaucracies, but the size of government employment remained too low to provide the colleges with a significant destination for their growing alumni. Even with the meritocratic definitions and the demands for specialists in government, other educational means remained competitive with the colleges and universities, especially for the major portion of governmental positions. And the emergence of private research organizations failed to provide enough jobs to directly encourage enrollments.[61] (Table 5.14)

Higher education thus remained dependent upon the traditional occupations and professions because, as in the antebellum period, it was not the particular shape of the college and schools but outside forces which were the major determinants of attendance and the character of student populations. The influence of changes in the society and economy on enrollments is more evident for the two leading occupational choices of students besides education—medicine and law. Developments in the body of knowledge relevant to both professions, the nature of organizational controls and the context of work in the two professions illustrate the relative power of internal changes and social and market forces.

As with teachers, lawyers were in increasing demand in the nineteenth century. The formalization of business and government and the inclusion of more of the population in a formal and anonymous society created expanded opportunities in the profession. In the early decades of the nineteenth century the old means of control over entry and behavior of attorneys had broken down as Jacksonian demands tore away at class

Table 5.14

Percent of Applicants With Different Educational Backgrounds Passing Civil Service Examinations in 1892

Educational Background	Percent Passing
All Types	62.5
High Schools	74.8
Business College	69.9
Private High School	68.8
College	66.6
Common School	55.1

and cultural restrictions. Young men took advantage of the less-demanding entry requirements, which depended upon local judges and relatively weak bar associations, and became lawyers with little formal training or the old social credentials. A large percentage of college students became lawyers, but before the Civil War the lack of consensus or central controls and the nature of the law in America discouraged young men from attending either regular college or the adjunct to the apprenticeship system, the struggling law schools.[62]

As the American economy changed, the nature of American legal practice altered. At the same time, the profession began to reorganize and to gain increasing powers over entry to the bar. American law began to move from persuasion to prediction. As business became more complex and as the nation became integrated, legal practice turned from being centered about the swaying of juries or legislatures (in terms of local custom or advantage) to the knowledge and interpretation of an established and codified body of law. Judge-made law and precedents rather than local norms, the prediction of the legal consequences of future actions rather than open court debate or persuasion, and the processing of routine, but more complex, transactions within a large legal office rather than a court became the avenues of success for more attorneys. As the law was formalized and as lawyers were more frequently found in bureaucratic settings, it was possible to develop a rewarding link between formal education and the profession. Formal legal training became necessary for economic advancement, thus providing a further inducement to attend law school.[63]

At the same time that legal educators were developing an expanding curricula and techniques to turn legal training away from an emphasis upon common law and oratory and into a science focused upon specialized practice through the case method, the legal profession began to exert more control over admission to the bar and to require more formal education through bar examinations which were difficult to pass without contact with formal education or a modern practicing lawyer. The number of years of formal training increased threefold between 1860 and 1900 as law firms concerned with bureaucratic legal practice provided economic rewards for those who invested in the changed and extended professional education.[64] (Table 5.15)

The colleges developed new versions of old subjects to attract future lawyers and to maintain their traditional ties to the profession. The old senior-year seminar in political economy, with its moralistic overtones, was changed into undergraduate courses in political science and government, history began to focus upon constitutional law, and other social sciences compatible with a legal career were put into place. The universities improved their law schools by bolstering faculties and providing the

Table 5.15

Percent of Applicants From Different Educational Backgrounds Passing Bar Examinations at Their First Attempt. New York Bar Examinations, 1922-1931

Educational Background	Percent Passing
All Types	59
Colleges and Law School	70
Law School	55
No Law School, No College	48
Clerkship Only	33

environment for the creation of professional legal teachers and scholars. They lengthened the number of weeks in the school year, and the more prestigious schools, through formal and informal means, demanded more preparation for admittance.[65]

However, even with economic inducements and more stringent licensing requirements, the undergraduate colleges did not capture all of the new lawyers, and many aspiring attorneys continued to invest in relatively low-cost and short-term professional training. The concept that lawyers should have a college education did not take hold until the 1870s, and as late as the 1920s, the American Bar Association and the American Association of Law Schools were attempting to convince the profession that two years of college should be a requirement for admission to law schools and, perhaps, to the bar.[66] Many young men, those not envisioning the new bureaucratic practice, those attuned to rural life, or those without the resources to pay for college or the more expensive university law schools (or to pass their entrance requirements) attended the many small professional schools. In 1898–1899, 29 percent of law school students had a BA or BS degree.[67]

But the change in legal practice and the greater control over the profession by attorneys with more formalized education did have an effect upon both the colleges and professional schools. Attendance at both increased as longer and more formal education seemed to become necessary for professional survival, but probably at the cost of social mobility through the profession, especially after educators and professionals turned to politics to eliminate the many store-front law schools that had arisen after the Civil War.[68] (Table 5.16)

Table 5.16

Type of Law Practice and Educational Level of Attorneys, 1950's

Type of Practice	Attended Law School	Did Not Attend Law School
Solo	% 61.4	% 81.7
Firm	28.8	18.1
Associate	6.0	0.7
Employed	3.8	2.5

The medical profession and related fields experienced similar trends during the nineteenth century. Jacksonian destruction of older social criteria, opening of the profession, changes in knowledge and organization which created different professional cultures and goals, and then formal and informal pressures leading to a closure of the profession and a closer link to higher formal education and greater training costs, affected higher education. However, the medical profession sensed an even greater threat than did the law because of overcrowding, had more difficulty reaching a consensus concerning the fundamentals of medical practice, and the profession had a much less direct connection to undergraduate training. But it was more successful than the lawyers in regulating the profession and creating a necessity for the investment in higher education.[69]

Entry into the medical profession had faced some pre–meritocratic regulation before the Civil War and there were inducements to take some institutionalized professional training. But most aspiring doctors used the apprenticeship system and took perhaps sixteen to twenty–six weeks of schooling in the mostly small and unstable medical colleges. The body of formalized medical knowledge was inadequate, if not incorrect and dangerous, and short service with a practicing physician seemed to be a more rewarding if not less expensive education. Furthermore, the profession was torn between schools of practice, each with very different fundamental concepts of correct theory and application. Heroic medicine was challenged by new imports brought by immigrants and accepted by Americans fearful of the treatments and results of alleopathic practice. Homeopathics, botanics, eclectics, and native Thomsonians threatened the status of the medical establishment and secured the right to practice in most states. The power of the old local medical associations broke down, and competition increased with the ease of entry (through professional schools) into what appeared to many to be a profession with declining social and economic status. The profession became crowded during the antebellum period and it seems that at the beginning of the Civil War America had more doctors per capita than at any time in its history.[70]

At the beginning of the Civil War medical knowledge began to change and become more reliable, urbanization led to greater formalization of procedures, and the profession developed new organizations to control, standardize, and nationalize American medicine. The result of these changes was to increase the necessity for formal training, its economic returns and cost, and to restrict entry into the profession. Although the number of practicing physicians doubled between 1860 and 1900, the ratio of physicians to population dropped appreciably.[71]

By the beginning of the Civil War anesthesia, as well as some concepts of antiseptic and asceptic procedures, allowed the development of surgery and it became a means of attaining great wealth for many physicians. Physiology and biology became more relevant and as the pharmacopia became more formalized and as a realization of the role of bacteria in infectious diseases spread, chemistry became more important to physicians. The new doctrines of cause and effect and specific treatment learned from the French led to more formalized practice at the same time that increased use of hospitals and urban practice carried a need for education for standardized procedures. Medical societies and new professional medical professors, especially those tied to the new version of alleopathic medicine with its scientific justifications, turned these trends into entry criteria and used their political influence to revise licensing requirements and tests. The new practice of medicine spread in wealthy urban areas, and the influence of medical politics was effective. In 1860, 14 percent of medical enrollments were in nonalleopathic schools. In 1900, only 6 percent of the enrollments were in the schools representing the remaining "medical sect," homeopathy.

As a result of the new medicine, enrollments in medical schools climbed, as did the cost of becoming a physician; but the returns from the completion of the new requirements increased for physicians in many settings. The required number of weeks in a medical school term escalated and the number of years of formal study increased to become at least three times that of 1860. Instead of some eight thousand students in 1860, twenty–six thousand were enrolled in 1900.[72]

The impact of hospitals, revised medical knowledge, and formalization are even more evident in related medical fields. The mid–wife and neighbor were turned into the new professionally trained and licensed nurse. Enrollments in nursing schools increased fivefold between 1880 and 1890 and seven times in the 1890s. Formal training for pharmacists jumped from a few men in 1860 to forty–four hundred, and dental students were almost double that number by 1900. But veterinary schools remained small in number and had less than six hundred students in 1900.[73]

The universities had been able to tie themselves to medical training, especially for physicians, pharmacists, and dentists by emphasizing their old institutional connections and by developing some undergraduate programs that prepared students for professional training. It seems that college–trained men and those who were trained for medicine at university–related schools did have an advantage over those from the smaller medical schools. A report on the results of examinations for medical licensure for 1903 indicated that no matter what state a student chose for his test, attendance at institutions such as Harvard's medical school guaranteed passing. Failure was more probable for those from the unassociated schools.[74]

However, medical education remained competitive. Young men and women, without undergraduate education, continued to attend proprietary medical schools and selected shorter term and lower cost professional education than that offered at most universities. It was not until the full impact of the Flexner report and the further actions by professional organizations that the majority of students were both enticed and forced into the colleges and medical schools associated with universities. At the turn of the century, 21 percent of all students in medical schools for physicians had a B.A. or B.S. degree.

With the increase in the potential to enjoy a profitable medical practice, greater competition to enter the profession, and the urbanization and economic abundance which allowed college attendance, the undergraduate institutions became the major gate–keeper for the medical profession. As with legal training, the increased educational demands and the attempts to define entry criteria in terms of a value–free science may have led to less social mobility through the profession and to the creation of an insulated profession that became insensitive to all but the factors defined by the new science as relevant.[75] (Table 5.17)

The accessibility and attractiveness of higher education for the service occupations and professions traditionally related to formal education were limited by the social and economic conditions of the postbellum period. These constraints were slight compared to those working against higher education linking itself more directly to primary production. Agriculture, engineering, science, and business did not provide the colleges or higher technical schools with the expected numbers of students. Agricultural groups had been one of the major supporters of the Morrill Act and the movement for practical education for the industrial classes of the nation. An integral part of the hopes for such education was training

Table 5.17

Cumulated Frequency Distribution of Licensing Statutes for Selected Occupations in the United States

Occupation	UP TO 1870	1871	1876	1881	1886	1891	1896	1901	1906	1911
Accountants	0	0	1	1	1	1	4	9	22	39
Architects	0	0	0	0	0	0	1	4	7	11
Attorneys	10	11	11	11	12	12	16	18	21	22
Dentists	2	2	6	15	27	35	37	41	42	43
Engineers	0	0	0	0	0	0	0	0	1	1
Midwives	0	0	0	0	0	2	4	5	6	9
Pharmacists	0	3	7	20	31	38	41	44	45	45
Teachers	10	11	11	11	13	13	15	17	17	19
Veterinarians	0	0	0	1	2	6	9	17	25	34
TOTAL for 38 Occupations	24	34	47	78	111	149	195	278	370	480

Table 5.18

Scholastic Aptitude Test Score Averages for
College-bound High School Seniors
United States, 1966-67 to 1976-77

School Year	Verbal Score	Mathematical Score
1966-67	466	492
1967-68	466	492
1968-69	463	493
1969-70	460	488
1970-71	455	488
1971-72	453	484
1972-73	445	481
1973-74	444	480
1974-75	434	472
1975-76	431	472
1976-77	429	470

of prospective farmers within the new colleges and aid by the new faculties of agricultural departments and government agencies to established farmers. But training for agriculture did not attract students in great numbers and historians have noted that the direct services to agriculture by the colleges and government bureaus also fell short of original promises.[76]

Attendance was limited by the distribution of income and wealth among farmers and, as important, the absence of a body of specialized knowledge that could provide the basis for competition with informal training in agriculture. Also, as government agencies distributed more information to farmers, they reduced the comparative return from formal agricultural training. Unlike law, education, or even medicine, specialized agricultural training promised to deal with an activity that was fundamentally nature related, rather than societal. Law and education were concerned with relatively arbitrary bodies of knowledge and procedures, the parameters of which could be defined by sociopolitical means. Medicine was dependent upon science, but its success, to a great degree, was self-measured, compared only to the success of other medical practices. But agricultural success was more the result of natural forces, the economic system which was difficult for any interest or intellectual group to control, and the distribution of productive land and capital. Thus, even codification of the procedures of the most successful agriculturalists had little relevance to most farmers. And entry into farming was impossible to control through legislation. More immediately important was the lack of a body of established specialized knowledge in the field of agriculture. The development of an applied science of agriculture was highly dependent on the emergence of a new body of knowledge in chemistry and biology. Those two areas of investigation had not reached the stage of sophistication such that they could be made directly relevant to farming. Much of what was known could be disseminated through non–academic agencies, private producers of agricultural products and tools, railroads, and county and state agricultural service agencies.[77]

Academics thus found it very difficult to devise a viable agricultural curricula that was cost–effective for the public. The body of knowledge was so deficient that one of America's leading agricultural educators seriously stated at a national meeting of his illustrious colleagues in 1871:

> Again, we find as I mentioned this forenoon, when animals are first put up, they consume more feed in proportion to their weight than towards the close. We find they give a greater return for the feed consumed during the earlier stages of feeding than afterwards.

Table 5.19

Estimates of Alpha Scores or Equivalents for the Population and Various Educational Levels (White only)

Category	WWI	1940	1946	Korean War	1950's
Population	67.6	101	90		101
4th Grade	37	37	41		22
6th Grade		44			44
8th Grade	60	65	70		66
10th Grade	82	105	99		84
12th Grade	98	124	114		105
College, 1 year	130	143	143	133	138
1 & 2	130	147			120
3 & 4	137	153			130
all	130	147	138		130
graduate	155	155	151		138
U. Mo. frosh	--	--	--		138

> What is the cause of the variation? I apprehend there are three causes, and two of them I have no doubt about. The third, I am inclined to think, has an influence, yet it is an exceedingly difficult matter to determine. These peculiarities, or differences, are the age, the size and the ripeness. From the experiments we have already tried at the college, I have no doubt age has a very great influence on the result. The young animal seems to have an organization capable of deriving more nutritive material from the same feed, so that it gives a larger return for feed, other things being equal, than when it gets older....[78]

The difficulty of devising curricula also helps to explain the seeming conservatism of many faculties in the agricultural colleges and the apparent elitism of some of the agricultural professors. Many academics, realizing the deficiencies of established knowledge, found it difficult to approve of programs in agriculture and turned the schools toward the more traditional curricula to attract students. Others were discontented with the need to spend their time giving practical advice to farmers when more research seemed necessary for both their careers and their substantive contributions to agricultural development. The connection between the agricultural colleges and the emerging agribusiness is also explained by the state of knowledge. What the agricultural colleges could teach were organizational techniques and the use of high–cost materials. The problems of the small farmer were political and economic rather than technological given the available knowledge in the nineteenth and early twentieth century. These conditions also help explain why so many alumni of the early agricultural schools drifted away from farming to the processing and merchandising of agricultural products. Graduates of the land–grant colleges' agricultural programs who remained in agriculture reported incomes about a half lower than those of physicians and lawyers from the same schools and much less income than their fellow graduates who entered business or banking.[79]

Engineering was a term applied to a great number of occupations during the nineteenth century, perhaps encompassing much of what we now call vocational education. The United States census, for example, seems to have included in the category of engineer, operators, machinists, and many other skills which we do not associate with the term today. Partially because of the ill–defined nature of the field in the nineteenth century it was difficult to devise a successful curricula that could provide a high rate of economic return compared to that from informal or private short–course training. The field was so diverse and each activity within it was changing so rapidly that it was difficult for either industry or academia to establish and codify standard practices. The absence of entry controls prevented the codification of knowledge in an arbitrary manner. On–the–job training, because of the particularity of techniques, was as or more effective than formal training for many subfields, and even within civil engineering informal training had somewhat of an economic advantage. One study showed that one renowned formal training program did not provide a greater economic return than informal training for civil engineers educated in the antebellum era, and there is other evidence that a similar relationship continued after the Civil War.

A survey of the individuals listed in the directory of American railroad executives, foremen, and specialists in the late nineteenth century indicated that the industry did not place high value on formal education. The biographies in the volumes gave practical experience in detail but did not mention formal training. The registers of American engineers indicated a similar bias. The associations of engineers remained divided over the question of college and formal training down to the twentieth century. A 1934 study of the elite of the engineering field indicated that 9 percent of its members had not attended college and 13 percent had failed to complete college.[80]

Applied vocational skills in the field were even more difficult to link to higher education and to the colleges. Although justifications for technical decisions and perhaps economic returns could be gained from the study of theoretical physics and mathematics by those engaged in design and analysis, operatives and mechanics found that on–the–job training and short practical courses provided as much or more return than extended formal education. High schools, apprentice programs, private technical schools, as well as forms of in–house training, combined with the expansion of industry and the demand for employees, worked against higher educations' role in applied technical education. Attempts to force more education upon the craftsmen and applied technologists were also ineffective in America. In Germany, apprenticeships were regulated by strong laws requiring attendance at technical schools for the apprentices and forcing employers to ensure and subsidize such attendance. America's ability to control attendance through such means was comparatively weak.[81]

The nature of technical training and the relatively low rewards from formal education for applied technologists helps explain the policies of the more famous land–grant schools such as Cornell and MIT. They turned to abstract and theoretical training because those who could afford extended years of schooling aimed at the most renumerative and high–status positions within the field of engineering. Few graduates of MIT, for example, were found to be in applied positions; they sought and migrated to managerial roles. The growing exclusiveness of MIT and other schools such as Cornell followed the logic of the new ideology of higher education, and they became selective in order to guarantee the future of their students and the reputations of the institutions. But even with a selected student population and advanced and abstract training, the nature of engineering as a livelihood threatened the security of investments in higher education. Graduates of all land–grant university engineering programs, because of economic and social pressures, tended to waste their investments in specific training. One–third of the graduates reported, in the 1920s, that they were in occupations that had no direct relationship to engineering training—a proportion about equal to the graduates of other programs in the land–grant schools.[82]

It was also difficult to attract those who wished to pursue a career in business into the colleges and professional schools. High schools and private commercial schools taught the already codified business procedures: handwriting, essential bookkeeping, and other secretarial skills. Higher level schools found it difficult to devise competitive curricula, and the business community could not organize to define entry criteria such as those in the established professions. Social demeanor, character, general reasoning, and business ideologies could be enhanced or at least certified by the colleges, but little else could be done until business itself regularized practices and became large enough to generate demands for specialists in such fields as organization and marketing.

Even accounting was a disorganized and ill–defined occupation. The first certified public accountant regulations were a product of the 1890s. There were few high–paying positions within the general occupation, and as late as the turn of the century established accountants were discussing the possibility of requiring a high school diploma for entry into the status of a certified accountant. Accounting, as a profession linked to formal and specialized education, had to await the growth of large–scale business enterprises and the development of professional organizations to define entry criteria.

Economics and other academic subjects potentially useful to the business world, such as psychology and statistics, were in the developmental stage in the late nineteenth century. The Wharton School, America's first university–level business program, found it very hard to define a specialized curricula. It taught its own version of general courses for many years because of the inability to establish formalized business practices beyond those known to lawyers, engineers, or bookkeepers. Harvard, despite its reputation for relevant courses and established business connections, had a smaller percentage of its students entering business at the turn of the century than Yale, which was noted for its academic conservatism and its continued reliance upon a philosophy of transfer of training.[83]

An even more basic constraint faced the colleges in respect to a field which was a seeming monopoly of the colleges and universities by the late nineteenth century, scientific research. Government and business were generating relatively little demand for trained researchers. Research and development activities outside of academia were rare because American industry relied upon relatively crude methods and had not reached the stage of institutionalization necessary to allow investments in a continuous stream of new products from established concerns. Only when firms faced a limit to the consumption of their established products and at the same time could carry the costs of highly paid researchers could a significant demand for research in industry be generated. The hopes of the university leaders to train large numbers of students for high–status positions in science were not realized before the twentieth century because of market conditions. The hopes to turn the part–time interests of middle class intellectuals into careers for their sons had to await complex technological, economic and political changes in America. The market for professional scientists was so limited that, assuming a forty–year career span, all the professional scientists in America in 1900, including those in government, could have been produced by graduating less than one hundred per year from 1860 to 1900. In 1900, two hundred seventy–six chemists were employed full–time in American industry, and many of these men were the product of informal training. The limited market is illustrated by the demand for engineers, many of whom did not enter their profession through formal training. Again assuming a forty year career, the number of engineers cited by the census in 1900 (a very inclusive category) could have been produced by graduating nine hundred fifty men a year after the Civil War War.[84]

The clergy continued to be an important force in America and the ratio of clergy to the general population was more favorable for higher education in the 1890s than in 1870. In the earlier decade there was one cleryman for every eight hundred seventy–nine in the population but in 1890, there was one for every seven hundred ten. And at the beginning of the twentieth century, the clergy was the most highly educated of the major professions, with over 50 percent of theological students holding a bachelor's degree. The theological schools had arisen to train the expanding numbers of ministers and priests and, in some cases, to provide alternative educations for those who did not wish to or could not afford to attend college. But the importance of future clergymen to the colleges declined. One reason was that the economic and social status of the ministry was decreasing and many institutions did not wish to emphasize a vocation with low economic returns because of the resulting public image and the need for wealthy alumni. Another reason was that, as the socioeconomic system of the United States changed, the ministry became less attractive to many young men and those who might have entered the ministerial profession in earlier decades were drawn to more rewarding and, perhaps, less demanding professions. Among the universities and colleges studied by Burritt, the shift of the percentage of alumni into education as an occupation was accompanied by an almost exact decline in the percentages of men entering the ministry during the 1890s.

The forces determining the level of enrollments in ministerial programs were indicative of the causes of and limits on educational change in the later nineteenth century. The story of higher education can not be derived from idealistic and rhetorical salutes to university leaders and the emergence of a new round of state funding for higher education after the Civil War. Not only was change much more limited than the traditional histories pictured, but the causes of change did not lie within the colleges. In fact, the institutions usually cited as the advance agents of change were only the best at taking advantage of new educational market conditions. But the results of their policies were not, necessarily, democracy and egalitarianism or the servicing of an intellectually and academically typical student population.[85] And many of the internal policies the leaders of such institutions established, and the support they gave to external groups whose actions determined the shape of the professions and occupations, were inegalitarian. The new university and the famous technical schools were a leading part of a new politics of education which developed after the Civil War, a politics of education which determined the allocation of resources to various types of higher schools and, as a consequence, the future policies of such institutions as normal schools and junior colleges. The continuation of the attention of historians to the great universities and their leaders will only hide the more socially significant history of American higher education. And the continued use of the assumptions concerning educational autonomy and the interest–free benevolence of educational leaders will mask the realities of educational change in America. Focus has to be turned to the numerically more significant normal schools and "shadow institutions" as well as back to the liberal arts college, if we are to understand both the process and content of academic development. The next histories of higher education will have to confront the realities of academia in its political and social and economic context before we can profit from studying our educational past.

Notes

Introduction

1. Richard Hofstadter, *Academic Freedom in the Age of the College* (New York: Columbia University Press, 1955). Especially relevant is Chapter Five, The Old Time College. On the emerging reinterpretations of the antebellum colleges see the analyses, reviews, and bibliographies in the articles by James McLachlan and David Potts. McLachlan's, The American Colleges in the Nineteenth Century: Towards a Reappraisal, *Teachers College Record* 86 (December, 1978): 28–306, is somewhat more comprehensive and speculative than Potts', College Enthusiasm: A Public Response, *Harvard Educational Review* 47 (February, 1977): 8–42. A recent general interpretation of the history of American education contains elements of the traditional approach to higher education but also brings a fresh perspective to the rise of the university as an ideal and as a social and economic reality. See, Robert L. Church and Michael W. Sedlack, *Education in the United States: An Interpretive History* (New York: The Free Press, 1976). Historians of higher education in Europe and analysts of the relationship between education and modernization are also beginning to reinterpret the historical record. Not only are they questioning the initiating role of higher education in economic and technological change but they are reexamining the social impact of the rise of technical training and the university and, thus, the perhaps overly optimistic treatments of higher education and development put forward during the 1960s. See: Peter Lundgreen, Industrialization and the Educational Formation of Manpower in Germany, *Journal of Social History* 9 (Fall, 1975): 64–79; A.L. Peaslee, Education's Role in Development, *Economic Development and Cultural Change* 17 (1969): 293–319; and, Fritz Ringer, *Education and Society in Modern Europe* (Bloomington, Indiana: Indiana University Press, 1979).

2. Earle D. Ross, *Democracy's College: The Land Grant Movement in the Formative Stage* (Ames, Iowa: Iowa State College Press, 1942).

3. Earle D. Ross, *The Land Grant Idea at Iowa State: A Centennial Trial Balance* (Ames, Iowa: Iowa State College Press, 1958), p. 7.

4. Walter P. Rogers, *Andrew D. White and the Modern University* (Ithaca, New York: Cornell University Press, 1942), p. 44.

5. R. Freeman Butts and Lawrence A. Cremin, *A History of Education in American Culture* (New York: Henry Holt and Co., 1962), p. 279.

6. Frederick Rudolph, *The American College and University: A History* (New York: Alfred A. Knopf, 1962), p. 48.

7. Rogers, p. 1.

8. Donald G. Tewksbury, *The Founding of American Colleges and Universities Before the Civil War* (New York: Archon Books, 1965); Bailey B. Burritt, *Professional Distribution of College and University Graduates* (Washington, D.C.: Government Printing Office, 1912); Henry Barnard, *Annual Report of the President of Columbia College* (New York, 1870), pp. 40–62; Henry Barnard, *Two Papers on Academic Degrees* (New York: McGowan and Slippers, 1880). Also be aware that many more esoteric details concerning the colleges, such as calculations of total private and social investment in higher education during the antebellum period, are not contained in this work. For such calculations see, Colin B. Burke, The Quiet Influence: The American Colleges and Their Students, 1800–1860, Diss. Washington University, St. Louis, 1973.

Chapter 1

1. Donald G. Tewksbury, *The Founding of American Colleges and Universities Before the Civil War* (New York: Archon Books, 1965).

2. The concept, metaculture, was borrowed from psychological anthropology. It refers to a single set of ideas and values that organize and transcend cultural diversity by serving as common norms, referents, and values for diverse cultures. See the concept of the organization of diversity in, Anthony C.F. Wallace, *Culture and Personality* (New York: Random House, 1963). In the specific historical context the desired metaculture was one based upon a vague and naive concept of science. Educators hoped that the development of or pretentions to a science of education would allow educators and their institutions to develop professional mentalities and standards that would transcend the various cultural and socioeconomic differences in America. With such a culture–above–cultures, educators could achieve professional definition, power, and autonomy and at the same time appear to be fulfilling all achievable educational goals through an unbiased process. This search for what appeared to many to be a totally objective, rather than just an apolitical, and thus covertly conservative educational elite, was not confined to Columbia or higher education and the drive for such a professional and general culture began well before the Progressive era. See, Paul H. Mattingly, *The Classless Profession: American Schoolmen in the Nineteenth Century* (New York: New York University Press, 1975), on the early move towards such a philosophy and rationale among primary and secondary school leaders and the consequences, for both the schools and their students, of the urge to find a means of gaining professional definition, the appearance of being above politics, and institutional autonomy. James Axtell's, The Death of the Liberal Arts College, *History of Education Quarterly* (Winter, 1971): 339–352, contains insights into how such ideas transferred into the history of higher education in the form of the Whig philosophy of educational history. There is not a single adequate work on the Teachers College approach to higher education, but a glance through periodical indexes to educational literature in the early twentieth century will indicate the power of the school and the various approaches of its professors. Useful for the general contours of reformist thought in the Progressive Era are, Walter H. Dorst, *David Sneeden and Education for Social Efficiency* (Madison, Wisconsin, 1967), and, Raymond Callahan, *Education and the Cult of Efficiency* (Chicago: University of Chicago Press, 1962). A useful insight into the realm of ideas and values concerning higher education in the postbellum and Progressive years may be gained through a comparison of, William DeWitt Hyde *The College Man and the College Woman* (Boston: Houghton–Mifflin, 1906), Andrew Dickinson White, *The Autobiography of Andrew Dickinson White* (New York: The Century Company, 1905), and, Abraham Flexner, *Universities: American, English, German* (New York: Oxford University Press, 1930). Although directed towards lower education, the article by Lois Banner, Religious Benevolence as Social Control, *Journal of American History* 60 (1973): 23–41, contains an exploration of the assumptions behind the post–World War II sociological interpretations of the role of the denominations in American education which is applicable to many of the interpretations of the colleges.

3. Tewksbury, pp. 3–33; E.S. Dexter, *A History of Education in the United States* (New York: McMillan, 1904); E.P. Cubberley, *The History of Education* (Boston: Houghton–Mifflin, 1920); A.F. West, *The American College*, Nicholas Murray Butler, (ed.), *Monographs on Education in the United States*, Dept. of Education, United States Commission to the Paris Exposition (Washington, GPO, 1900). For the extrapolation of Tewksbury's findings and the population figures see, U.S. Bureau of the Census, *Historical Statistics of the United States, Colonial Times to 1957* (Washington, D.C.: GPO, 1960), Series A 71–85, p. 10.

4. Tewksbury, pp. 3–33 and p. 28. Although the histories of individual colleges have to be consulted to comprehend the differences in the regional distribution of aid, Frank W.

Blackmar, *The History of Federal and State Aid to Higher Education in the United States, Contributions to American Educational History, No. 9* (Washington, 1890), provides some help. The complexities of ties to the government, including the political and social issues, are explored in John S. Whitehead, *The Separation of College and State: Columbia, Dartmouth, Harvard, and Yale, 1776–1876* (New Haven, 1973).

5. *3rd Annual Report of the Committee of Statistics to the Governor of the State of Ohio* (Columbus, Ohio: Richard Nevins, State Printer, 1860), pp. 131–142; James S. Garland (compiler) *An Index to the State Laws of Missouri* (St. Louis: St. Louis Book and News Co., 1869), pp. 66–67; Frederick Eby, *The Development of Education in Texas* (New York McMillan, 1925), pp. 140–141. A helpful work on Tewksbury's method and the history of college founding in Pennsylvania is an article which appeared just after the completion of the original version of this study. See, Natalie Naylor, The Antebellum College Movement: A Reappraisal of Tewksbury's Founding of American Colleges and Universities, *History of Education Quarterly* 13 (Fall, 1973): 261–274.

6. Consult Naylor and, Colin B. Burke, The Quiet Influence: The American Colleges and Their Students, 1800–1860, Diss. Washington University, St. Louis, 1973, pp. 30–33.

7. Tewksbury, pp. 3–33.

8. Tewksbury, pp. 28 and 3–33.

9. Teachers College Library was contacted in 1969 and 1970 by phone and a personal visit was made by one of the researchers for the project in 1977 in order to secure a copy of Tewksbury's file. In each case, the file could not be located and librarians reported that the file had never been deposited. Other researchers have also been unable to locate the file. See Naylor's article on the problem of the file.

10. With funding from the Social Science Research Council, the National Library of Medicine, the Newberry Library, the National Endowment for the Humanities, the University of Maryland, Baltimore County and the Spencer Foundation (and private vacations), an exhaustive and sophisticated search of all relevant materials was conducted to locate operating as well as planned institutions. In the ten years of the project almost all major college libraries and archives were visited and all their holdings were surveyed. Many of the smaller colleges known to have been in existence before the Civil War were visited and their holdings of local–history materials and the published and unpublished sources on the history of particular colleges were examined. State and local historical societies, medical libraries, and professional and industrial association libraries were visited. The American Antiquarian Society Library's collection of directories was surveyed, most of the holdings of the Newberry Library on the antebellum period were examined, and visits to as well as inter–library loan use of the Center for Research Libraries were made. All the holdings of the Library of Congress were examined (including early encyclopedias) and all the relevant materials in its associated union catalog were obtained. Not only were all the materials in the National Library of Medicine surveyed but all relevant listings in the early Surgeon General's Catalog were examined. All local medical associations were contacted for information concerning biographical materials and official registers. The Smithsonian collection on engineers was used and all state histories in the Library of Congress were surveyed. Not only were all available periodicals and directories of the denominations used in the study, but all known articles on education in state historical journals were surveyed. Post Office and railway directories were sought and examined, U.S. and many state censuses and statistical reports were surveyed, and, to check the U.S. census reports on colleges (the census proved to be untrustworthy in many ways) the microfilm collection of census manuscripts at the National Archives was utilized. The holdings of the old Bureau of Education Library were surveyed but the new NIE Library was not visited because of its reported disorganization during its early years. *Dissertation Abstracts* and the old American Historical Association guides to historical literature were used for sources on the colleges

and the New York Public Library and Library of Congress guides to state and local–history were examined for indications of the existence of colleges and for sources on students. All the histories of the various colleges were read, including those in their catalogs down to the 1920s, and special attention was given to finding mentions of other institutions besides those which were the direct subjects of the particular history. All national, professional, and state and large city biographical volumes were examined and professional registers for ministers, engineers, lawyers, bankers, and physicians were used for the biographical search detailed in Chapter 3. Fraternity publications were also surveyed. When these biographical materials were examined attention was given to the mention of colleges besides those attended by the subjects in the biographical sample for this study. Of course, the Reports of the U.S. Commissioner of Education, its antebellum precursors, educational journals of the antebellum period, and the monographic studies associated with the Bureau of Education were utilized. One significant finding emerging from all this material was that contemporaries did make distinctions between various types of "higher" educational institutions. Both individuals and organizations saw differences between colleges and academies and there seems to have been a hierarchy developing well before the Civil War among the various types of higher educational institutions. Not only did the denominations make distinctions in their official publications but individuals behaved as if there was a hierarchy. During the search for biographical materials we found no cases where students moved from colleges to academies but we did encounter a distinct pattern of movement from academies to the colleges. For the postbellum period, the *Reports of the U.S. Commissioner of Education* and the Library of Congress collection of college guide books and college school directories as well as various encyclopedias were utilized to identify existing colleges.

11. The most useful sources on the various failures in these states are: George Gary Bush, *History of Education in Florida, Contributions to American Educational History, No. 6* (Washington, 1889); Josiah H. Shinn, *History of Education in Arkansas, Contributions to American Educational History No. 26* (Washington, 1900); and Frank W. Blackmar, *Higher Education in Kansas, Contributions to American Educational History, No. 27* (Washington, 1900). However, all these have to be supplemented by numerous local–history articles and books.

12. The history of education in Massachusetts, despite the image of its stability and the objectivity of its leaders, was marked by many political crises and decisions. In relation to the Catholic frustrations in Massachusetts and other areas of the country and the nature of most Catholic colleges of the period, see: T.A. Burn, et al., *History of Catholic Higher Education in the United States,* (New York: Benzinger Brothers, 1937); F.P. Cassidy, Catholic College Foundations and Developments in the United States , Diss. Catholic University of America, 1924; S.A. Erbacher, Catholic Higher Education for Men in the United States, 1850–1866 , Diss., Catholic University of America, 1931.

13. Again, the late nineteenth–century federal series on higher education in the various states serves as the best single introduction. See, Blackmar, *History of State and Federal Aid to Higher Education*; Andrew C. McLaughlin, *History of Higher Education in Michigan, Contributions to American Educational History, No. 11* (Washington, D.C.: 1891); George W. Knight and John R. Commons, *The History of Higher Education in Ohio, Contributions to American Educational History, No. 12,* (Washington, D.C.: 1891). But these should be supplemented by such works as Willis Dunbar, *The Michigan Record in Higher Education* (Detroit: Wayne State University, 1963), and William McGill, The Belated Founding of Alma College: Presbyterians and Higher Education in Michigan, 1833–1886, *Michigan History,* 57 (Summer, 1973) 93–120.

14. This and all other correlations are the standard Pearson product moment correlations. The voting statistics were from, *Historical Statistics of the United States,* Series y, 80–126, 688–9.

15. David Potts encountered similar problems during his study of Baptist colleges. He also found that strict denominationalism was a myth and that local influences and needs

were as strong or stronger than denominational forces. See, David Potts, American Colleges in the Nineteenth Century: From Localism to Denominationalism, *History of Education Quarterly*, II (Winter, 1971): 363–80, and, David Bronson Potts, Baptist Colleges in the Development of American Society, 1812–1861, Diss., Harvard University, 1967. In this study when there was doubt about the denominational affiliation of a college, Tewksbury's assignments were used.

16. See the appended lists of colleges in operation in the period and the list of institutions which were found, after intensive searching through both antebellum and postbellum materials, not to have opened or to have operated only as academies, primary schools, or professional schools. The difficulty of establishing the numbers of actual colleges in the antebellum era was minor compared to what an investigator will face when attempting to do a history of academies and grammar schools. For example, see, Lewis Joseph Sherrill, *Presbyterian Parochial Schools, American Education, Its Men, Ideas and Institutions*, (New York, 1969), pp. 73–83.

17. On the policies of the three states, besides the works already cited, see: George H. Calcott, *A History of the University of Maryland* (Baltimore, Maryland Historical Society, 1966); J.C. Leonhart, *100 Years of Baltimore City College*, (Baltimore, 1939); Bernard C. Steiner *History of Education in Maryland, Contributions to American Educational History, No. 19*, (Washington, D.C.: 1894); James Albert Woodburn, *Higher Education in Indiana, Contributions to American Educational History, No. 10*, (Washington, D.C.: 1891); Edwin Whitfield Fay, *The History of Education in Louisiana, Contributions to American Educational History, No. 20*, (Washington, D.C.: 1898).

18. For male population age 15–20, U.S. Census Office, *8th Census, 1860*. Tables for each state were used.

19. The model used for the calculation was: a = number of white males in Massachusetts divided by population per square mile in Massachusetts. b = a/number of colleges in Massachusetts, while expected colleges in other states = (population white males 15–20/density).

20. U.S. Office of the Census, *7th Census, 1850*, Religious Denominations of the United States, (Washington, 1850), lix–lxi; *Statistics of the United States, in 1860, of the Eighth Census* (Washington, D.C., 1866), pp. 497–501.

21. The data for the distribution of church property were from the census tables cited above.

22. The values for the churches were also taken from the census materials cited above. The linear correlation between property values and percent failures approached zero.

23. Census reports for each decade were used for number of males. In some decades interpolation was necessary to arrive at the size of the age group 15–20. In the absence of useful studies of the distribution of young men within broader age groupings, the total number in the category was divided by the number of years in the category. This result was multipled by five to arrive at the 15–20 year old estimates.

24. Census reports were used for the state distributions and the same interpolation methods were used.

25. U.S. Office of the Census, *7th Census*, Table XLIL, p. 1x and 1xi, U.S. Office of the Census, *8th Census*, Vol. 4, p. 505.

26. The calculations were based upon the tables cited in footnote 25.

27. Lee Soltow, *Men and Wealth in the United States* (New Haven: Yale University Press, 1975), Table 6.2, p. 152.

28. *Statistics of the United States in 1860* (Washington: GPO, 1866) Table 2, p. 295, The True Value of Personal Property According to the 7th Census and the 8th Census. The correlations between percentage failures and per capita property values was less than .10 in both decades.

29. The sources for enrollments are cited in footnote 25.

30. See footnote 25 for the sources of enrollment statistics.

31. See the catalogs of the high schools of Baltimore, Philadelphia and Brooklyn for curricular and age profiles.

32. The academies were so varied that it will take a new and major investigation to understand their nature and evolution. Some insights into the academies are found in: Theordore R. Sizer (ed.) *The Age of the Academies* (New York, 1964); James McLachlan, *American Boarding Schools* (New York: Charles Scribner's, 1970); Joseph F. Kett, *Rites of Passage: Adolescence in America* (New York: Basic Books, Inc., 1977); Robert Church, *Education in the United States*; and Paul Mattingly, *The Classless Profession.* For a more detailed picture in one area see, E.M. Coulter, The Ante–Bellum Academy Movement in Georgia, *Georgia Historical Quarterly* 5 (December, 1921): 11–42. For the involvement of the denominations in the academy–seminary–institute movement see, for example, *Methodist Almanac, 1858*, pp. 21–22.

33. Again, the extensive and intensive biographical search as well as tabulations such as those in the *Dictionary of American Biography* indicate that a hierarchy of status and perhaps curricula was developing among the institutions of higher education.

34. See footnote 25 for sources.

35. See footnote 25 for sources.

36. See footnote 25 for sources of expenditures per pupil. A principal in an established urban system received at least $1,000 a year. See, for salaries, *American Educational Year Book, February, 1858*, (Boston: James Robinson and Co., 1858).

37. U.S. Office of the Census, *8th Census*, Vol. 4, p. 505.

38. One of the reasons for the use of the term "university" found in the titles of so many small institutions were the legal ramifications of the status of a university. It allowed direct association with professional schools. See, on Oberlin, Robert S. Fletcher, *A History of Oberlin College From the Founding Through the Civil War* (Oberlin, Ohio, 1943). For the means and attempts to link with professional schools, see, George B. Manhart, The Indiana Central Medical College, 1843–1852, *Indiana Magazine of History*, 56 (June, 1960): 105–122. A thorough investigation of the financial benefits of college versus academy charters should be done.

39. Almost every small college operated in this manner. For just two examples see, Rev. William Nathaniel Schwarze, *History of the Moravian College and Theological Seminary...* (Bethlehem, Pennsylvania, 1910), Chpt 4, and Edward Dwight Eaton, *Historical Sketches of Beliot College* (New York, 1928).

40. James McLachlan, The Choice of Hercules: American Student Societies in the Early Nineteenth Century, Lawrence Stone (ed.) *The University in Society* (Princeton: Princeton University Press, 1976), and Thomas S. Harding, *College Literary Societies: Their Contribution to Higher Education in the United States, 1815–1976* (New York: Pageant–Poseidon, 1971), provide some insight into a still truly unexplored subject.

41. The survey of the curricula, courses, and acceptance of science by the colleges conducted for this study through catalogs and college histories reinforces the findings of Guralnick, Rudolph, and Bozeman: Stanley Guralnick, *Science and the Ante–Bellum College* (Philadelphia, 1971); Frederick Rudolph, *Curriculum: A History of the American Undergraduate Course of Study Since 1636* (San Francisco; Jossey–Bass, 1977); Theodore Dwight Bozeman, *Protestants in the Age of Science: The Baconian Ideal and Antebellum Religious Thought* (Chapel Hill: University of North Carolina Press, 1977); Albert W. Gendebein, Science the Handmaiden of Religion, *Pennsylvania History* 22 (1966): 127–152. On Howard College, see its Annual Catalogs for the late 1850s. Especially important to the history of the colleges are two institutions which were innovators but whose history was eclipsed by such institutions as Harvard and Yale despite their great innovations and their attempts to serve a varied student population. We need in–depth studies of New York University and Cumberland University which go beyond the very particular work produced in the 1930s. See, W. P. Boone, *A History of Cumberland University* (Lexington, Kentucky, 1935), and Theodore Francis Jones, *New York University, 1832–1932* (New York, 1933). For the problems involved in

establishing research universities during the antebellum period, many of which were caused by demands by professional academics, see, R. Silverman and M. Beach, A National University for Upstate New York, *American Quarterly* 22 (1970).

42. See the migration patterns of German trained scholars, most of whom were in the humanities in the antebellum period, detailed in Carl Diehl, *Americans and German Scholarship, 1779–1870* (New Haven: Yale University Press, 1978), especially p. 161.

43. Tuition and fees were gathered from the annual catalogs of the various colleges.

44. Harvard was charging about twice that of other New England colleges including a four hundred dollar security deposit. For some of the reasons for such a policy and its social consequences, see the forthcoming book on Harvard by Ronald Story of the University of Massachusetts, Amherst. For suggestions on the contents of his new book consult, Ronald Story, Harvard Students, the Boston Elite and the New England Preparatory System, *History of Education Quarterly* 15 (Fall, 1975).

45. See Burke, Quiet Influence, pp. 197, 244.

46. National Center for Education Statistics, *Digest of Educational Statistics, 1976 Edition* (Washington, D.C.: GPO, 1977), pp. 102 and 139.

47. Consult, Howard H. Peckman, *The Making of the University of Michigan, 1817–1967* (Ann Arbor, Michigan: The University of Michigan Press, 1967), for some of the policy decisions by Tappan. On the perception of the University and Tappan as socially and religiously biased see: William J. McGill, The Belated Founding of Alma College: Presbyterians and Higher Education in Michigan, 1833–1886, *Michigan History* 57 (Summer, 1973): 93–120.

48. See Burke, Quiet Influence, p. 198. The financial figures and the amounts of state aid were taken from many different sources for each college. Not only traditional histories but catalogs, broadsides, and governmental and denominational reports were used to compile the economic profiles of the colleges and regions.

49. For the average endowments in the American West, also compiled from hundreds of sources, see Burke, Quiet Influence, and Table 1.21 in this work.

50. Charles M. Perry, *Henry Philip Tappan: Philosopher and University President, American Education: Its Men, Ideas and Institutions,* (New York: Arno Press, 1971), pp. 172–173.

51. On the difficulties of college financing and the ingenuity used during the period see: Saul Sack, A Nineteenth Century Scheme for Financing Higher Education in Pennsylvania, *History of Education Quarterly* 1 (1961): 50–53, and, Daniel T. Johnson, Financing the Western Colleges, 1844–1862, *Illinois State Historical Journal* 65 (1972): 43–53.

52. *Union College, A Record of the Commemoration, June 21 to 27, 1895 ...* (New York, 1897); Lyman P. Powell, *The History of Education in Delaware, Contributions to American Educational History, No. 15,* (Washington, D.C., 1893).

53. The investment of college funds in the antebellum period has not been explored for more than a handful of colleges and it is difficult to tell if the many financial crises were due to general economic problems in America or to mismanagement by college leaders. On Amos Lawrence, see, Lawrence University, *Wisconsin Magazine of History*, 6 (December, 1922). One of the few economic studies of a college is Seymour E. Harris, *The Economics of Harvard* (New York: McGraw–Hill, 1970). See also, Peter D. Hall, The Historical Economy of Education, *History of Education Quarterly*, 14 (Winter 1974): 501–11.

54. James Findlay, The SPCTEW and Western Colleges: Religion and Higher Education in Mid–Nineteenth Century America, *History of Education Quarterly* 17 (Spring, 1977): 31–52; Natalie A. Naylor, The Theological Seminary in the Configuration of American Higher Education: The Ante–Bellum Years, *History of Education Quarterly* 17 (Spring, 1977): 17–30. On the distribution of per capita property values, U.S. Office of the Census, *18th Census, 1860,* Real and Personal Estate, p. 295. Also, Soltow, *Men and Wealth*, and Jeffrey C. Williamson, American Prices and Urban Inequality Since 1820, *Journal of Economic History*, 36 (June 1976): 303–333.

55. Burke, Quiet Influence, Chapter 3, pp. 122–50.

56. Burke, Quiet Influence, Chapter 3, pp. 122–50.

57. One of the most useful works encountered during this study and which included many facts on the economics of the colleges, including Columbia and Union was, Franklin B. Hough, *Historical and Statistical Record of the University of the State of New York During the Century, 1784–1884* (Albany, New York, 1885).

58. There is not one single source for the distribution of books and other resources. The profiles for each college were built from many references. Helpful, but sometimes misleading because of repetitions and errors, were the surveys of the colleges contained in the *American Almanac and Register.*

59. Unless the cause was a fire, epidemic, or natural disaster suspensions came about due to financial deficiencies. Those colleges in financial trouble would usually try to continue operations by lowering institutional costs. Faculty salaries were cut or suspended.

60. In most small colleges the president's salary during the 1850s was between fifteen hundred and two thousand dollars. Outstanding lawyers and physicians could make at least twice that amount. See Burke, Quiet Influence, pp. 69–80.

61. Burke, Quiet Influence, pp. 69–80.

62. Burke, Quiet Influence, p. 44.

63. The unfortunate focus by interpretive historians upon New England colleges during the antebellum period, especially Harvard, has masked the flexibility of the smaller schools. Without great fanfare or philosophical justifications they instituted engineering, chemistry, agricultural, and scientific programs and they allied themselves with legal and medical instruction. For just a few examples, see: Leonard G. Boone, *A History of Education in Indiana* (New York, 1892); J. A. Woodburn, *Higher Education in Indiana,* U.S. Bureau of Education Circular of Information 1, 1891; and, Albert W. Gendebein, Science the Handmaiden of Religion.

64. Burke, Quiet Influence, pp. 66–78.

65. Burke, Quiet Influence, pp. 66–78.

66. Williamson, Urban Inequality. But along with his work on income and wealth distributions and the other efforts he cites, Robert Gallman's comments in, Professor Pessen on the Egalitarian Myth, *Social Science History* 2 (Winter, 1978): 194–207, and, Craig Buettinger's, Economic Inequality in Early Chicago, 1849–50, *Journal of Social History* 11 (Spring, 1978): 413–418, should be consulted.

67. W. Carson Ryan, *Studies in Early Graduate Education* (Washington, D.C., 1930).

68. See Chapter 5 of this study.

69. On the beginnings of the University of Michigan and a plan as comprehensive and out–of–place for its time as any of the frontier adventures, see Charles M. Perry, *Henry Phillip Tappan.* A plan as or more grand for New York failed, but not because of a lack of great rhetoric. See, *Speeches in Behalf of the University of Albany, by Hon. Sam'l B. Rugles, Rev. Duncan Kennedy, Hon. Azor Taber, and Rev. Ray Palmer, Published By The Committee Of The Young Men's Association of the City of Albany, March, 1852,* (Albany, N. Y.: Charles Van Benthuysen, Printer, 1852).

70. See, Naylor, Ante–bellum College Movement.

Chapter 2

1. Among the many versions of the same theme, see: Henry A. Barnard, *Analysis of Some Statistics of College Education* (New York, 1870); Frederick A. P. Barnard, *Annual Report of the President of Columbia College* (New York, 1870); Henry A. Barnard, *Letters on College Government*

(New York: 1855); Francis Wayland, *The Education Demanded by the People of the United States* (Boston: Phillips, Sampson and Co., 185); and, Francis Wayland, *Thoughts on the Present Collegiate System in the United States* (Boston: Gould, Kendall and Lincoln, 1842).

There was a desire to compare the enrollments in American higher education to those in foreign countries but this was frustrated by the absence of comparable statistics for various European nations. Although new series on European higher education have appeared since the inception of this study, such as the *Historical Statistics of Europe* and the work of Fritz Ringer, valuable comparisons await a thorough investigation into the various categories of educational enrollments within the European nations. See, Fritz Ringer, *Education and Society in Modern Europe* (Bloomington, Indiana: University of Indiana Press, 1979), and, B.R. Mitchell, *European Historical Statistics, 1750–1970* (New York, 1975).

The enrollment statistics in this chapter are the result of searching through all college catalogs and histories as well as through the various almanacs and registers of the antebellum period that concerned themselves with the progress of education. An explanation of the nature and scope of the search for such materials is found in the footnotes to Chapter 1 of this work.

These estimates should be compared to those in Arthur M. Comey, The Growth of the Colleges in the United States, *Educational Review* 2 (1892): 124, and, his, The Growth of New England Colleges, *Educational Review* 1 (1891): 213.

2. For example, George P. Schmidt, *The Liberal Arts College: A Chapter in American Cultural History* (New Brunswick, New Jersey: Rutgers University Press, 1957), pp. 76–77. Although Schmidt mentioned the New England bias of the statistics of enrollments, he proceeded as if they applied or would have had to apply to the rest of the nation at some period or stage of development. Similar logic of specification is found in most of the traditional historiography.

3. Francis Wayland, *Thoughts on the Present Collegiate System*, is the most frequently cited of Wayland's writings on the antebellum system. For more on Wayland's logic and the acceptance of his thesis see, David Potts, College Enthusiasm as Public Response, 1800–1860, *Harvard Educational Review* 47 (February, 1977): 28–31. For a particular example of the acceptance of Wayland's predictions and explanation see, Schmidt, pp. 60–63.

4. As will be shown, Wayland's estimates for particular New England colleges may have been correct for the late 1830s and 1840s, but those were atypical years as were many of the New England colleges.

5. For example, Potts, College Enthusiasm, p. 41 and Schmidt, p. 76. The estimates of regular enrollments in this work are slight revisions of the estimates in the Burke dissertation (1973) and reflect the additional information gathered since the completion of the dissertation. If all the students in degree track programs are included and the numbers of those in professional schools and normal schools are added to the enrollments figures, the total number of students in 1860, exclusive of womens' colleges and seminaries, approaches the estimates cited by Potts and Schmidt. See Table 5.1 in this work.

6. Consult the tables of occupational distributions in the various decennial censuses of the United States, 1850–1870.

7. *Historical Statistics of the United States*, Series A 71–85, H 321–322 and D 123–572.

8. *Historical Statistics of the United States*, Series H 233.

9. Lee Soltow, *Men and Wealth in the United States 1850–1870* (New Haven: Yale University Press, 1975), p. 186, for the generalization concerning the percentage with enough wealth to support a student and see Williamson, *Urban Inequality*, p. 305 for inequality trends in wealth. Soltow's data on real estate values over time also indicate that the proportion of the population with significant amounts of real estate grew appreciably in the period between 1850 and 1860.

10. Burke, Quiet Influence, p. 69.

11. This drop may have been the result of the disruptions caused by the economic panic of the late 1830s, its long term impact on life plans, and the disruptions caused by the Mexican War. Wayland's work, *Thoughts on the Present Collegiate System,* which seems to have received much attention, was in response to the enrollment problems of the late 1830s and early 1840s.

12. See Chapter 5 in this work for the estimates of male students in 1900. The predicted numbers of students were based upon a compound rate of growth.

13. On the new types of students, see Chapter 3 in this work and David Allmendinger, *Paupers and Scholars: The Transformation of Student Life in Nineteenth Century New England* (New York: St. Martins Press, 1975), especially Chapter 1 and pp. 129–138.

14. On the famous Yale Report, see Melvin I. Urofsky, Reforms and Response: The Yale Report of 1828, *History of Education Quarterly* 5 (March, 1965): 447–469, but be aware of his misinterpretation of the consequences of the Report for the college curricula and student populations.

15. Wayland's, *Thoughts on the Present Collegiate System,* is still the best single source on the socioeconomic explanation.

16. The U.S. census tables for population age groups for each state from the appropriate decennial censuses were used to compile the New England age and nativity profiles. On the out–migration from New England see, L.K. Mathews, *The Expansion of New England* (New York: Russell and Russell, 1962), a reprint of the 1909 edition.

17. See Allmendinger, *Paupers and Scholars,* pp. 131–138 and Chapter 3 in this work for age trends among entering students.

18. The numbers of ministers were taken from the appropriate decennial U.S. census reports of occupational distributions.

19. The estimates of percentages of ministers are based upon the sample of students taken for this study which is described in Chapter 3 of this work. Also, see, Burritt, *Professional Distribution of College and University Graduates.*

20. Estimates of the percentage of out–of–state and out–of–region students are based upon the sample of college students described in Chapter 3 of this work.

21. Property values are from, U.S. Bureau of the Census, *Statistics of the United States, in 1860, of the Eighth Census,* Table 2, p. 295.

22. Correlations for such variables approached zero.

23. Urofsky, and Potts', Baptist Colleges in the Development of American Society, Diss. Harvard University, 1967, provide insight on Wayland but they both should be supplemented by the histories of each of the New England colleges to understand the liberalizing changes that most initiated in the late 1820s and 1830s in attempts to resolve their enrollment problems.

24. The best source of information on Harvard as well as the other New England schools are its annual catalogs but Samuel Eliot Morison's *Three Centuries of Harvard 1636–1936* (Cambridge, 1946) contains information on curricular and entrance requirement changes during the antebellum period.

25. Some of the more informative histories of the various New England colleges are: Charles T. Burnett, *Hyde of Bowdoin: A Biography of William DeWitt Hyde* (Boston, 1931); Louis C. Hatch, *History of Bowdoin College* (Portland, Maine, 1927); Nehemiah Cleveland and A.S. Packard, *History of Bowdoin College 1806–1879 with Biographical Sketches of Its Graduates* (Boston, 1882); Claude M. Fuess, *Amherst: The Story of a New England College* (New York, 1935); Gail Kennedy, *Education at Amherst: The New Program* (New York, 1955); Thomas Le Duc, *Piety and Intellect at Amherst College* (New York, 1946); Walter G. Bronson, *History of Brown University 1764–1914* (Providence, Rhode Island, 1914) (which contains a wealth of information on the other New England colleges); Carl F. Price, *Wesleyan's First Century* (Middletown, Connecticut, 1932); Ralph H. Gabriel, *Religion and Learning at Yale* (New Haven, 1958); and the very informative, Glenn Weaver, *The History of Trinity College* (Hartford, Connecticut, 1967).

26. The catalogs of Norwich and the various medical schools indicate that the 1840s also hurt their enrollments. But the timing of the impact was somewhat different for the professional schools. On Norwich, see: William A. Ellis, *Norwich University, Her History, Her Graduates, Her Roll of Honor* (Concord, New Hampshire, 1895); and, William A. Ellis, *History of Norwich University 1819–1911* (Montpelier, Vermont, 1911). Dartmouth's history still remains vague, see: *General Catalog of Dartmouth College and Associated Schools 1769–1910* (Hanover, New Hampshire, 1910–1911).

27. Glenn Weaver's, *The History of Trinity College* (Hartford, Connecticut, 1967) details the many attempts at creating successful liberalized programs at Trinity including partial, agricultural, civil engineering, and even work–study programs. Its experimentation began within a few years after its opening.

28. Again, catalogs are the most direct source of information, but Bronson, *History of Brown University*, goes into great detail about the history of Wayland's reforms.

29. See Brown's catalogs during the period for student costs and its facilities.

30. Bronson also points out that Latin and Greek were returned to the curricula and entrance requirements were changed back to the older standards after the demise of the experiment.

31. Very useful on Cornell are: *Proceedings and Addresses at the Twenty–Fifth Anniversary of the Opening of Cornell University* (Ithaca, New York, 1893); and, *Ten Year Book of Cornell University III, 1868–1898* (Ithaca, New York, 1898).

32. *The Ten Year Boook, III, 1868–1898*, contains details on course selection and enrollments during the early decades of Cornell's history as well as much detail on the activities of its students and professors.

33. See, *The Ten Year Book, III.*

34. *History of the Class of 1872, Cornell University* (np, nd.).

35. See the annual catalogs as well as: Russell H. Chittenden, *History of the Sheffield Scientific School of Yale University* (New Haven, 1928); and, Fuess, *Amherst.*

36. Consult, Morison, *Three Centuries of Harvard*, as well as its catalogs for curricular details.

37. The reasons for the increases at Dartmouth remain a significant puzzle. One supposed explanation was a change in the availability and costs of transportation to Hanover, but efforts by the staff of the library of the Association of American Railways in Washington, D.C. in 1979 indicated that there was not a change in its accessibility by rail in the 1850s.

38. Again, the catalogs of the various colleges provided the data on enrollments.

39. Burritt, *Professional Distribution of College and University Graduates.* Consult his tables for the individual colleges.

40. Data on tuition, fees and living expenses were taken from the author's file which was built from thousands of sources.

41. See Table 2.8 of this work.

42. The estmates of in–state and in–region percentages are based upon the sample described in Chapter 3 of this study.

43. Property values were from U.S. Office of the Census *Statistics of the United States in 1860*, p. 295. Enrollment percentages by states in New England were regressed on the per capita property values.

44. David Potts explored Union's history and seems to agree with its reputation as a haven for those who had not been able to adjust to the demands of other institutions. (private conversations with professor Potts.) Also, see the guarded hints in Andrew Raymond (ed.) *Union University* 3 vols., (Schenectady, New York, 1907).

45. The estimates of migrations are based upon the sample described in Chapter 3 of this work.

46. The estimates from the sample for this study conform to other data on Yale's attrac-

tion. See, for example, Ralph Gabriel, *Religion and Learning at Yale,* its yearly catalogs, and, Charles Warren, *An Inquiry Concerning the Vital Statistics of College Graduates,* Circular of the Bureau of Education March 1872, no. 1 of 2, (Washington, D.C., 1872) pp. 19–21, for birth places of the graduates of Yale, Harvard, Dartmouth, and Wesleyan.

47. The calculations for the South included the elimination of "outliers," such as Louisiana, but the relationships continued to be very slight.

48. The estimates of enrollment ratios are based upon the sample described in Chapter 3 of this study and the population statistics for each state are in the various decennial U.S. census volumes.

49. Again, the migration flows are estimated from the sample described in Chapter 3 of this work and they seem in conformity with the Charles Warren, *Vital Statistics of College Graduates,* data and with the tabulations of the geographic backgrounds of students sometimes included in annual catalogs of the various colleges.

50. For later nineteenth–century and twentieth–century migration patterns for the various states and regions, see: U.S. Commissioner of Education, *Education Report 1890–91, pp. 822–825, and, National Center for Education Statistics, Digest of Education Statistics, 1979,* p. 87. Note that the NCES statistics include junior and community college students.

51. The samples for the University of Virginia indicated few Maryland students attending.

52. On wealth distributions in the Southern regions, which seem to be close to those in the larger Northern cities, see: Gavin Wright, Economic Democracy and the Concentration of Agricultural Wealth in the Cotton South, 1850–1860, William N. Parker (ed.), *The Structure of the Cotton Economy of the Antebellum South,* (Washington, D.C., 1970), pp. 63–100. However, the inequality of wealth, occupational distributions, and the social and formal regulation of the professions in the South appear not to be able to fully explain the less than expected rate of college–going in the region. Southern states had, for example, as many professionals per white population (and in some cases more) than in the Northern states and, as Soltow demonstrates, many Northern states had as many propertyless adult males as did the South in 1860. (See the decennial census statistics on occupations by state and Soltow, *Men and Wealth,* p. 41). Perhaps, for many parts of the social–occupational world of the South, liberal education or even formal education in a profession was less necessary than in the North in the antebellum period and, perhaps, there was a different value and saving–consumption habit in the South. (See the very interesting work by James Sturm, *Investing in the United States 1798–1893* (New York: Arno Press, 1977), especially pp. 144–170 and 164.) As well, middle or moderate income young men in the South may have faced a different opportunity structure than in the North where farm–making was as or more expensive than entering a profession and where achievable statuses such as school teaching promised some economic and social rewards and, perhaps, a career. See, Clarence H. Danhof, Farm–making Costs and the 'Safety–Valve': 1850–1860, *Journal of Political Economy* 49 (1947) 317–359.

53. Although old and lacking explicit interpretive frameworks, the Contribution to American Educational History series provides the most facts about the states and education in a single volume. See, James A. Woodburn, *Higher Education in Indiana* (Washington, D.C., 1891).

54. Migration levels are based upon the sample described in Chapter 3 of this work.

55. Soltow, *Men and Wealth,* pp. 152, 149.

56. However, the geographic location of Union may well have been an important influence.

57. These estimates are based upon the reported denominational membership in, U.S. Office of the Census, *Statistics of the United States, in 1860,* pp. 497–501.

Chapter 3

1. The general interpretive works cited in the Introduction of this study are pervaded with this approach to the students of the colleges and a flavor of it may be found in more modern histories such as the usually insightful and scholarly work by Christopher Jencks and David Riesman, *The Academic Revolution* (New York: Doubleday and Company, 1968), pp. 1,4,7.

2. Bailly B. Burritt, *Professional Distribution of College and University Graduates,* U.S. Office of Education Bulletin No. 19 (Washington, D.C.: GPO, 1912) concentrated on institutions that were large and successful at the beginning of the twentieth century. He used a very small number of occupational categories (9) and the alumni were categorized by the single occupation or activity for which they were in Burritt's term, "remembered" (p. 11). Furthermore, he had high percentages of unclassified alumni in many of his tables of occupational distributions, and some suspicious categorizations such as almost thirty percent of Beliot's early 1850s graduates entering literature and journalism (p. 115). Charles Warren concentrated on New England colleges in his An Inquiry Concerning the Vital Statistics of College Graduates, U.S. Bureau of Education, Circular 1 and 2, (Washington, D.C., March 1872): 8–40.

3. Scholarly journals are publishing a host of studies on the social conditions and the nature of the professions in antebellum America which detail the different life context of even "respectable" segments of the native American population, groups, and individuals that might be categorized as "middle–class" today. At the same time, these works are beginning to show how subtle and complex the causes of socioeconomic change were during the period. Useful works introducing the reader to the newer social history are: Stephan Thernstrom, *The Other Bostonians: Poverty and Progress in the American Metropolis 1880–1970* (Cambridge, 1973), a work which covers a broader subject and longer time span than indicated by its subtitle; Tamara K. Hareven, (ed.), *Family and Kin in Urban Communities 1700–1930* (New York, 1977); Edward Pessen, (ed.) *Three Centuries of Social Mobility in America* (Lexington, Massachusetts, 1974); Joseph F. Kett, *Rites of Passage: Adolescence in America, 1790 to the Present* (New York, 1977); and, Theodore K. Rabb and Robert I. Rotberg, (eds.), *The Family in History* (New York, 1973). One article stands as almost "the" example of how the new social history should be related to the history of education: David F. Allmendinger, Jr., Mount Holyoke Students Encounter the Need for Life–Planning, 1837–1850, *History of Education Quarterly* 19 (Spring, 1979): 27–46. The newer perspectives on the history of the professions are cited in Chapter 5 of this study, but Richard M. Bernard and Maris A. Vinovskis', The Female School Teacher in Ante–Bellum Massachusetts, *Journal of Social History* 10 (1977): 332–345 stands as another example of how the history of education benefits fom new methods and perspectives.

4. Some more insightful work on student revolts may be found in Steven J. Novak, *The Rights of Youth: American Colleges and Student Revolt, 1798–1815* (Cambridge: Harvard University Press, 1977) and, Joseph DeMartini, Student Culture as a Change Agent in American Higher Education: An Illustration From the Nineteenth Century, *Journal of Social History* 9 (Summer, 1976): 526–541.

5. This set of assumptions is implicit in the traditional literature which, despite threats such as those of the McCarthy era, treat the problems of higher education as solved by the university ideal and which, by their use of the concept, antebellum college, treat the history of higher education as marked by revolutionary change which, somehow, came as the Civil War allowed new educational leaders to radically alter the colleges. James McLachlan explores these assumptions in his, The American College in the Nineteenth Century: Toward a Reappraisal, *Teachers College Record* 80 (December, 1978): 287–290.

6. It was also required that the list contain at least one other piece of information besides the name of the student that was usable for the biographical profile of the student.

7. The bibliography for the sources used to select subjects and to trace their lives contains thousands of items. Part of this bibliography, a small fraction of the total number of citations, is already mounted on a computer file which, when printed, runs to hundreds of pages. Some indication of the sources used to trace the subjects comes through the realization that all relevant materials cited in the following works were examined. (But with the exception of materials on physicians, only national, state, and large city collections and volumes were searched.)

National Union Catalog; *United States Local Histories in the Library of Congress*; New York Public Library, *U.S. Local History Catalog*; Robert B. Slocum, *Biographical Directories and Related Works*, Vol. 1 and 2 (Detroit, 1967 and 1972); and *Surgeon General's Catalog*.

As well, many volumes encountered during trips to various libraries were searched. All the medical journals of the nineteenth century were searched for obituaries, biographical materials, and registers and all relevant medical directories and registers of the various state and county medical associations were obtained and examined.

Local and county biographical materials were not examined because of the costs involved in such a project. Genealogical sources were ignored after an early attempt to use such materials revealed that they provided little information on the subjects relative to the expense of searching through sources such as the *New England Historical and Genealogical Register*. It was hoped that the manuscript census materials could be searched in order to obtain more precise information on, at least, the backgrounds of the students. But this hope changed into very painful frustration as it became more and more difficult to finance the project either through direct grants or the more typical means of support of academic research, the use of graduate assistants.

However, the biographical sample is prepared for an efficient search of both the U.S. census records and local biographical volumes. All geographic entries are ZIP coded, and through the use of the program GETDIS are coded for FIPS state and county codes. On the FIPS codes see: U.S. Dept. of Commerce, National Bureau of Standards, *County and County Equivalents of the States of the United States–Federal General Data Standard Representations and Codes* (Washington, D.C., 1973).

8. The sample of students began as a pure random sample. Names from the lists were chosen through the use of random number tables. However, it was soon found that researchers were unable or unwilling to continue to use this tedious process and a systematic method (one of every ten sequentially listed subjects) was used in many instances. Even the author, faced by the pressures of closing–times of libraries, slipped into this mode of selection. On sampling, see the introductory essay in Hubert M. Blalock, *Social Statistics* (New York, 1960), Chapter 22, and, Frederick Stephan and Philip J. McCarthy, *Sampling Opinions* (New York, 1958).

The sample should be considered a systematic proportionate sample but it is obvious that it is not pure because of missing information and the disappearance of lists for various colleges. The author found no techniques to formally compensate for the known and unknown missing information that were applicable to both the practical and theoretical problems of the sample. For more esoteric approaches to particular sampling problems, see, for example, Melvyn A. Hammarberg, Designing a Sample from Incomplete Historical Lists, *American Quarterly* 32 (October, 1971): 542–561.

A 10 percent sample was decided upon in order to obtain a relatively large proportionate sample but one which was manageable. A more sophisticated original sampling design was impossible because there was no knowledge, at the beginning of the study, of the exact nature of the available lists of college students. Some lists of college catalogs and alumni publications were available but they were obviously incomplete and they did not indicate the contents of the materials which were cited. Therefore, sampling designs based upon required absolute numbers were impossible. Furthermore, assumptions about the representative nature of particular student populations or years or decades of attendance which would allow more detailed designs could not be made. In fact, it was exactly the assumptions about the nature of students that were to be tested and specific apriori selection would have been illogical. The number of cases used in this work was 14,345. This was composed of the original sample of students in the colleges and some two thousand professional school students who were found to have attended the liberal arts colleges. The additional two thousand cases were included for two reasons. The first reason was practical. Some coders, despite instructions, did not always list the liberal arts college in the correct position in a subject's coded profile and time and cost factors did not allow a return to the original documentation to correct this problem. The second reason was that we could not identify specific and important biases caused by the miscoding that could not be at least partially compensated for by examination of the records of individual colleges.

The number of subjects per decade was:

1800:667, 1810:834, 1820:1372, 1830:2711, 1840:3393, 1850:5377.

The recovery of information on students is indicated by the following list of percentages of data recovered and validly coded:

Birth Date: 44 percent, Home Area: 90 percent, Death Date: 59 percent, Father's Occupation: 21 percent, Area, Occupation 1:77 percent, Occupation 1:76 percent, Area, Occupation 2: 59 percent, Occupation 2: 59 percent, Area, Occupation 3: 45 percent, Occupation 3: 45 percent, Area, Occupation 4: 34 percent, Area, Occupation 4: 34 percent.

9. There are no simple and codified methods for such problems of bias because each study will have its own unique sets of known and probable biases and most of them cannot be quantified. For examples of the exploration of the problems of collective biographies, see, Richard Jensen, Quantitative Collective Biography, Richard Swierenga, (ed.), *Quantification in American History* (New York, 1971).

10. An adequate discussion of sampling and statistical inference problems from a traditional perspective is in: Blalock, *Social Statistics* (New York, 1960), Chapter 22. One frustration encountered in this study was the absence of consideration of the problems of sampling from finite populations and the inferential power of such samples.

11. All statements of comparison in this and the following chapter are based upon tests of significant differences. The formula used was that in Hubert M. Blalock, *Social Statistics* (New York, 1960), p. 151. There was a great desire to use much more sophisticated methodology on the information such as automated typology techniques but two forces prevented a serious attempt to apply such methods. The first was the amount of missing data and the second was the immediate costs of computer time and the difficulties of securing adequate computer facilities with such programs in reliable working order.

12. At least thirty cases were demanded for t tests and point estimates are qualified with the terms mentioned in the text and the phrase, "strongly suggests". The college groupings used in this study were chosen after scores for each of the colleges were examined. The categories "small" or "other" colleges do contain institutions with differences among each other, but the patterns for these institutions indicate or suggest that they were more like each other than the various "large" colleges.

13. Burritt, *Professional Distribution of College and University Graduates*, and, Allmendinger, *Paupers and Scholars*, especially pp. 132–138.

14. Compare the findings in this and the following chapter with the data provided in Fritz Ringer, *Education and Society in Modern Europe* (Bloomington, Indiana, 1979), especially pp. 89, 169, 170, 243.

15. Richard Hofstadter, *Academic Freedom in the Age of the College* (New York, 1955), especially pp. 210.

16. See Chapter 4 of this work for details on the mobility patterns of students of the various colleges.

17. See Chapter 4 for details on the mobility of the various occupations.

18. See Chapter 4 of this book and the interesting study of the ministry by Donald M. Scott, *From Office to Profession: The New England Ministry, 1780–1850* (Philadelphia, 1978).

19. The data in this and the next chapter document the unique nature of New England students and their careers. Some works suggest reasons for the differences. Allmendinger, *Paupers and Scholars,* points to what were perhaps unique demographic–economic conditions and work on the professions in New England suggest that it was a region in which professionals were expected to make relatively great investments in education. See Gerald Gawalt's new book on New England professionals, *The Promise of Power: The Emergence of the Legal Profession in Massachusetts, 1760–1840* (New York, 1974).

20. Allmendinger, *Paupers and Scholars,* pp. 1–5.

21. Allmendinger, *Paupers and Scholars,* Chapter 1.

22. Consult Burritt's *Professional Distribution,* on occupational choice during the post Revolutionary period.

23. Allmendinger, *Paupers and Scholars,* Chapter 1 and the data presented in this chapter.

24. Allmendinger, *Paupers and Scholars,* p. 10.

25. See Table 3.2 in this study and Allmendinger, *Paupers and Scholars,* pp. 132–136, and W. Scott Thomas, Changes in the Age of College Graduation, *Popular Science Monthly* 3 (1903):159–171.

26. See Table 3.2 in this study and Allmendinger, *Paupers and Scholars,* pp. 132–136.

27. See Table 3.2 in this study.

28. See Table 3.2 in this study.

29. See the background profiles on Harvard students in this chapter.

30. Joseph F. Kett, *Rites of Passage,* pp. 18 and 21, and, Paul H. Mattingly, *The Classless Profession: American Schoolmen in the Nineteenth Century* (New York, 1975), pp. 154–155.

31. Kett, *Rites of Passage,* covers the emergence of concepts and structures. Especially pertinent are Chpts. 5 and 8.

32. The samples for Lawrence, Sheffield, Dartmouth, and Union, as well as Rennselaer and Norwich were small, but t tests showed them to not be significantly different from the college student samples.

33. Examine, for example, the official rules of the University of Maryland.

34. Allmendinger, *Paupers and Scholars,* Chpts. 3 and 5 are especially informative on this point.

35. See, Carl H. Hendershot, *Programmed Learning and Individually Paced Instruction–Bibliography* (Bay City, Michigan, 1973).

36. See the annual catalogs of the various colleges.

37. Allmendinger, *Paupers and Scholars,* Chapter 5.

38. For example, see, Rev. John J. Ryan, S.J., *Historical Sketch of Loyola College, Baltimore, 1852–1902: A Memorial of the Golden Jubilee of Fifty Years of Existence* (nd, np). This work is located at the Loyola Library.

39. See Table 4.7 in this work.

40. "Educator" might mean a low paying position such as rural school teacher or a very high–status position such as the head of a famous academy. The term "farmer" is so vague that it becomes useless unless precise economic information is available for each subject. The most that should be inferred from such categories is that the individual was in a position of some degree of respect in the community. Attempts to use modern quantified socioeconomic scales for the occupations of father's and of the students was soon abandoned because of the ambiguity of the categories.

41. Parental desire must have played a significant role in college selection by younger students. Perhaps college archives will yield letters from both parents and alumni substantiating this thesis.

42. For a very different interpretation of the nature and impact of the various colleges in the South, see, Hofstadter, *Academic Freedom in the Age of the College,* pp. 220–221.

43. The samples for the other Virginia colleges did indicate or suggest somewhat older students. These age profiles should be confirmed through a larger sample and if they are confirmed an explanation should be sought through an investigation of the state's school system, its society, and its wealth distributions.

44. The author made several attempts to use the records and archives of Southern colleges but time pressures and inaccessibility of records prevented a thorough investigation of the question.

45. See Table 4.3 in this study.

46. A useful history of the American economy that contains a relatively comprehensive bibliography, although not organized by region, is, Lance E. Davis, et al., *American Economic Growth: An Economist's History of the United States* (New York, 1975).

47. Allmendinger, *Paupers and Scholars,* Chapter 1.

48. On lawyers, compare William R. Johnson, *Schooled Lawyers: A Study in the Clash of Professional Cultures* (New York, 1978) who describes career styles and requirements in Wisconsin, with the findings of Gerald Gawalt in his study of New England. Also see, Gary B. Nash, The Philadelphia Bench and Bar, 1800–1861, *Comparative Studies in Society and History* 7 (1965): 203–220.

49. On farm costs, see, Clarence H. Danhof, "Farm-making Costs and the Safety Valve: 1850–1860," *Journal of Political Economy* 49 (1941): 317–359.

50. See Table 3.13 in this work.

51. The ministry, because of the demand for new ministers, the presence of a local clergy to recruit young men, and subsidies for ministerial education within the context of denominational "competition" may have been the most open of the professions with incentives for college training. The rise of professionals schools for ministers, physicians, and lawyers has been interpreted in various ways. Some saw them as means to circumvent the colleges and to break the hold of established professional elites over entry into the professions. For example, see, Naylor, The Theological Seminary, pp. 19–20, and, Nash, Philadelphia Bench and Bar, pp. 203–204. But in law and medicine, apprenticeships continued as a norm and usually a requirement for official sanction. Therefore, the impact of the rise of professional schools on the social backgrounds of practitioners remains unclear.

52. Kett, *Rites of Passage,* pp. 34, 158–159. Kett's data indicates that rurality and older age of entry went hand in hand during the period for professional–school students. The colleges were thus enmeshed in a larger social and demographic pattern which impacted upon all of American education during the era. The temptation to account for much of the difference between the large and small colleges (as defined in this study) through the sociodemographic differences between rural and urban areas was countered by the findings of Harvey J. Graff, Patterns of Dependency and Child Development in the Mid Nineteenth Century City, *History of Education Quarterly* 13 (Summer, 1973) 129–143. Class and ethnic background may have been as important as the rural–urban influence.

53. See Table 4.5 in this work for career locations of those in the ministry and the description of careers in Donald M. Scott, *From Office to Profession.*

54. See Table 4.13 in this work.

55. Young men from relatively affluent urban families may have been able to treat education as a consumption item. Young men with business occupations as their career goals had little incentive to invest in higher education because of the absence of specific entry

criteria for business occupations, especially at the managerial level or in the world of entrepreneurs. Those who sought bureaucratic positions could acquire the needed skills through academies and the growing number of private commercial schools in the country. On the question of social mobility through the business world, Pessen's, *Three Centuries of Social Mobility*, Part III, contains central articles and a sensitive introductory essay.

Chapter 4

1. For an example of the continued use of the assumptions concerning the dysfunctional nature of antebellum higher education and its supposed consequences for the careers of the students of the colleges see, Christopher Jencks and David Reisman, *The Academic Revolution in America* (New York, 1968), pp. 1–3. Also note that the work seems to assume a great effective demand for technological and specific training during the antebellum and postbellum years.

2. The old but still useful article by A. Ross Ecklar, Occupational Changes in the United States, 1850–1920, *Review of Economic Statistics* 12 (1930): 77–89 gives a general picture of the varying occupational profiles but does not detail the important changes within the professions and occupations in the seventy years.

3. Bailey Burritt, *The Professional Distribution of College and University Graduates*, U.S. Office of Education Bulletin No. 19 (Washington, D.C., 1912). For compatible findings for a somewhat later period see, Floyd Reeves, et al., *The Alumni of the Colleges*, University of Chicago Survey No. 6 (Chicago, 1933).

4. The categories used in the study were determined by the nature of the reporting in the biographical sources. The reports, even in the more complete biographies, were of a general nature concerning the occupations and professions of the students and their parents. This, combined with the brief descriptions in many biographies, made attempts to use highly refined categories or to assign quantitative weights to occupations a fruitless task. The temptation to attempt the quantification of social and occupational status was engendered by works such as, Otis D. Duncan, et al., *Socio Economic Background and Achievement* (New York, 1972). For a stimulating and imaginative use of collective biography consult, John N. Ingham, Rags to Riches Revisited, *Journal of American History* 63 (1976): 615–637.

5. Burritt, *Professional Distribution.* It remains unclear why Burritt did not include Southern institutions.

6. Consult Donald M. Scott, *From Office to Profession: The New England Ministry, 1750–1850* (Philadelphia, 1978), for the importance of influences outside of the colleges for the careers of ministers.

7. This estimate is in conformity with Burritt's tabulation.

8. See Table 3.6 and Table 3.12 in this work.

9. Consult Burritt's tables for the individual colleges of the Midwest.

10. Some of the flavor of the many speeches and broadsides against the liberal arts colleges may be gained through: Ann Keppel, The Myth of Agrarianism in Rural Educational Reform, *History of Education Quarterly* 2 (1962): 100–109; C.A. Bennett, *History of Manual and Industrial Education Up to 1870* (Peoria, Illinois, 1926); and, Burt E. Powell, *The Movement for Industrial Education and the Establishment of the University, 1840–1870* (Urbana, Illinois, 1918).

11. There are some hints that formal regulations for the professions, informal demands for higher education, and rewards from investments in training varied over the American regions. Compare Gawalt, *The Promise of Power*, and William Johnson, *Schooled Lawyers: A Study in the Clash of Professional Cultures* (New York, 1978) and see data in Frederick C. Waite, Ohio Physicians in the Nineteenth Century: A Statistical Study, *Ohio State Medical Journal* 46 (1950): 791–793 and 893–895.

12. U.S. Bureau of the Census, *Historical Statistics of the United States: Colonial Times to 1957* (Washington, D.C., 1960), Series B 181. William F. Norwood, *Medical Education in the United States Before the Civil War* (Philadelphia, 1944). American Medical Association, Report of the Committee on Medical Education, *Transactions of the American Medical Association* 4 (1851): 409–446.

13. Consult William Harvey King (ed.) *History of Homeopathy* (New York, 1905), for the rise of homeopathy and an invaluable list of homeopathic physicians. This four volume work is an historical treasure.

14. See Paul Mattingly's *The Classless Profession: American Schoolmen in the Nineteenth Century* (New York, 1975), on the beginnings of professional definition. Very informative on the development of job opportunities and careers in education is, David B. Tyack, Pilgrims Progress: Towards a Social History of the School Superintendency, *History of Education Quarterly* 16 (1976): 257–300.

15. Burritt, *Professional Distribution* pp. 67–73.

16. Consult the decennial U.S. census reports on Southern education and see, Irving Gershenberg, Southern Values and Public Education: A Revision, *History of Education Quarterly* 10 (1970): 413–422.

17. The nature of scientific activity and interest is being reexamined by historians of science and education. A useful work which seems to have stimulated much of the new interest is, George H. Daniels (ed.) *Nineteenth Century American Science* (Evanston, Illinois, 1972). For the occupational distributions in 1860 see, *Statistics of the United States, in 1860, of the Eighth Census* (Washington, D.C. 1866).

18. For estimates of the numbers of professional scientists and those in occupations directly related to science see: Nathan Reingold, Definitions and Speculations: The Professionalization of Science in America in the Nineteenth Century, Alexandra Oleson and Sanborn C. Brown (eds.) *The Pursuit of Knowledge in the Early American Republic* (Baltimore, 1976), pp. 57–60.

19. Brown and Trinity, probably because of their urban location and attraction for students from urban areas, had significantly greater percentages of urban destinations. On the urbanization of the general population, consult, *Historical Statistics of the United States*, Series A 181–209.

20. For example, *Historical Statistics*, Series C 15–24.

21. The regional circulation index is the summed and averaged difference between the percentage of students from each region and the percentage who ever once were in that region. The scores were not presented because the same information is conveyed by the tables of regional distribution.

22. Consult, *Historical Statistics*, Series C 15–24.

23. See the distribution of the Southern general population in *Historical Statistics*, Series C 15–24.

24. See the occupational distributions by states in the decennial censuses and Donald M. Scott, *From Office to Profession.*

25. For examples of the urban and national organization bias in professional volumes see, for example, *Great American Lawyers* (Philadelphia, 1907), and *Dictionary of American Medical Biography* (New York, 1928). Inclusion in such volumes is a measure of the relationship of higher education to modernization because of the bias.

26. For example, *Official Army Register for August, 1862* (Washington, D.C., 1862). A requirement imposed on the search for information on the students was that the prior information on the subject and the biography match on more than just the name of the individual. Information on education, occupation, birth or death dates, or mobility patterns had to coincide.

27. Some institutions such as Yale and the University of Virginia did make serious at-

tempts to identify all their students who participated in the Civil War. But the materials at their archives seemed to indicate that they also faced identification problems.

28. This generalization concerning the different participation rates for the urban and rural institutions is based upon the impression gained while searching through the various catalogs for the alumni.

29. *Proceedings of the American Association for the Advancement of Science Fourteenth Meeting* (Cambridge, 1861): xxv–xiviii, and *Twenty-Seventh Meeting, 1880* (Salem, 1881): xxix–lxxvii. There are innumerable studies of the individuals listed in national biographical catalogs such as, *The Dictionary of American Biography, Who Was Who, Appleton's Cyclopedia of American Biography, National Cyclopedia of American Biography, American Men of Letters, Notable American Women, American Men of Science* and *Herringshaw's Encyclopedia of American Biography*. And many scholars have investigated the lives of famous scientists and engineers. All of these studies of elites point out that college attendance was highly correlated with national recognition. Unfortunately, controls to establish the causal influence of education are rarely found in this literature. Among the more interesting studies of national elites are: Stephen Sargent Visher, *Geography of American Notables,* Indiana University Studies No. 79, 1928, which also highlights the number of ministers and sons of ministers who were noted for their scientific activities; George W. Pierson, *The Education of American Leaders* (New York, 1969); Donald Beaver, The American Scientific Community, 1800–1860, Diss., Yale University, 1961; Clark Albert Elliott, The American Scientist 1800–1863, Diss. Case Western University, 1970. And a most interesting summary of early works on elites is, Caswell A. Ellis, The Money Value of Education, Bureau of Education Bulletin, No. 22 (Washington, D.C., 1917), pp. 14–52.

30. *Baird's Manual of American College Fraternities* was consulted for a list of Greek Fraternities in operation at various colleges before the Civil War. All the biographical volumes for the various fraternities were then obtained and searched. Debating society catalogs were not searched for two reasons. The first was the difficulty of obtaining them. The second reason was that the items which were examined either contained little information or their biographical profiles had been merged with the regular college biographical materials. However, the archives and published materials for the literary and debating societies should be the subject of an investigation by a future researcher.

31. For example, see *Martindale's U.S. Law Directory,* Haupt's *American Engineering Register,* and *Medical Register of New York and Vicinity.*

32. For example, see *Biographical Directory of the United States Congress 1774–1961* (Washington, D.C.: GPO, 1961).

33. The information on Southern Congressmen in *The Biographical Directory of the United States Congress,* may not include all the educational experiences of the Southern Representatives. However, studies of the backgrounds of Congressmen indicate that Southern members had very high educational levels for their time. See, for example, Frank E. Coburn, The Educational Level of the Jacksonians, *History of Education Quarterly* 7 (1967): 515–520.

34. See the titles associated with the names in the AAAS lists cited in footnote 29.

35. Consult, Francis Gordon Caffey, Harvard's Political Preferences Since 1860, *Harvard Graduates Magazine* 1 (1893): 407–415. The undigested material in Thomas S. Harding, *College Literary Societies* (New York, 1977), should be analyzed.

Chapter 5

1. The deterministic thesis is found in most stark form in, Earle D. Ross, *Democracy's College: The Land Grant Movement in the Formative Stage* (Ames, Iowa, 1942). But note that such literature tended to contradict itself when it joined authors such as Richard Hofstadter, *Aca-*

demic Freedom in the Age of the College (New York, 1955), in voicing demands for the autonomy of higher education and the direction of higher education by professional educators.

2. The source for most statistical series on higher education is, U.S. Office of Education, Report of the Federal Security Agency: Office of Education 1867/68–1951/52, *Report of the Commissioner of Education* (title varies). This series, during the nineteenth century, included normal schools and female seminaries and "colleges" within the category, higher education, but excluded high schools. For some insight into the Reports see, Donald R. Warren, *To Enforce Education: A History of the Founding Years of the United States Office of Education* (Detroit, 1974). The continued use of the summary statistics from the *Report(s) of the Commissioner of Education* is shown in, U.S. Bureau of the Census, *Historical Statistics of the United States, Colonial Times to 1957* (Washington, D.C., 1960), Series H 321–326.

3. On the varied degree offerings consult the various reports on higher education in the *Report(s) of the Commissioner of Education,* especially that of 1900. An informative work on financial aid to students, especially those in technical schools is, *Report(s) of the Commissioner of Education, 1893–94,* pp. 791–807.

4. The best survey, to date, of the changes in higher education, although written from the perspective of intellectual history, is Laurence R. Veysey's, *The Emergence of the American University* (Chicago, 1970). For another interpretation of the motives and ramifications of the changes in higher education and an exploration of the rise of a new definition of professionalism both inside and outside of academia, see, Burton Bledstein, *The Culture of Professionalism,* (New York, 1976).

5. The enrollment estimates cited in the text and in Table 5.1 are the result of a thorough reworking of the enrollment statistics presented in the *Reports,* various U.S. census publications and statistics presented in various encyclopedias and journals such as *The American Year Book and Register.* The estimates of the number of females enrolled came from the many special articles in the *Report(s) of the Commissioner of Education.*

6. For the predicted enrollments, based upon the growth of attendance during the antebellum period, see Chapter 2, in this work. The percentage of the young males in the colleges is, admittedly, an understatement of the growth of higher education because of the narrowing of the range of the age of attendance after the Civil War. Although there are some studies of the age of students in the colleges after the Civil War, they are not comprehensive enough to allow a precise estimation of age controlled ratios for the antebellum and postbellum periods. The exact age distributions would be significant for several questions relevant to the history of the growth of higher education but in respect to the testing of the growth intimated in the traditional history of higher education in the nineteenth century, the enrollment percentages used in this work seem acceptable. Also, compare this estimate with the view of change in A.M. Comey, Growth of Colleges in the United States, *Educational Review* 3 (1892):120–131.

7. For population trends and the increase of high school graduates see *Historical Statistics* Series H 232–233 and A 74–75. The estimates of the relative costs of higher education cited in Table 5.2 are based upon evidence presented in Colin B. Burke, The Quiet Influence: The American Colleges and Their Students, 1800–1860, Diss. Washington University, St. Louis, 1973, pp. 243–244.

8. Compare the reports of enrollments in the *Report(s) of the U.S. Commissioner of Education* with those in the annual catalogs of the various colleges.

9. *Historical Statistics,* Series H 327–338.

10. Consult the tables for the various colleges in Bailey Burritt, *Professional Distribution of College and University Graduates,* U.S. Office of Education Bulletin No. 19 (Washington, D.C., 1912). On enrollments in the "small" colleges see the series in the *Report(s) of the Commissioner of Education.*

11. See Table 5.1 in this work.

12. *Report of the Commissioner of Education*, 1890–91, pp. 820–821.

13. The best single source for enrollments in the schools mentioned are the *Report(s) of the Commissioner of Education*, but such series as that in the *American Almanac*, 1902, pp. 614–621 are very useful. See Table 5.1 in this work for general trends in enrollments. The Armour Institute in Chicago should be investigated by historians because of its size and rapid growth. Its students, however, may have been of "high school" age. For a romantic view of technical education see, Burt E. Powell, *The Movement for Industrial Education and the Establishment of the University* (Urbana, 1918). But for a much more enlightening view of technical and agricultural training see, Mary Jean Bowman, The Land Grant Colleges and Universities in Human Resource Development, *Journal of Economic History* 22 (1966):523–546.

14. Consult the annual catalogs of MIT for the entrance requirements and its costs. There is, as yet, no satisfactory history of MIT. For enrollments in other land–grant colleges see the *Report(s) of the Commissioner of Education.*

15. Enrollments in the various programs were estimated from the series in the *Report(s) of the Commissioner of Education* and Burritt, *Professional Distribution.* Particularly useful sources for enrollments in the programs and institutions were: *Report of the Commissioner of Education*, 1890–91, pp. 820–821. But see the changes in the 1920s as noted in, U.S. Dept. of Interior, Bureau of Education, *Statistics of State Universities and State Colleges*, 1922, Bulletin, 1923, No. 49 (Washington, 1923), pp. 6–9.

16. Joseph R. DeMartini, Student Culture as a Change Agent in American Higher Education: An Illustration From the Nineteenth Century, *Journal of Social History* 9 (1976):528; Burritt, *Professional Distribution*; U.S. Dept. of the Interior, Office of Education, Bulletin (1930) No. 9, *Survey of Land Grant Colleges and Universities.*

17. The estimates of attendance at such schools and in such programs varied from report to report and the basis for the distinction between business education as "higher" or "secondary" education remains unclear. Note that the *Report(s) of the Commissioner of Education* did not include commercial schools in the statistics of enrollment in higher education. Because enrollments in private and public institutions for business training were so high, historians should turn attention to them, especially the private schools and national chains of business "colleges" which appeared even before the Civil War. Edmund James, *Commercial Education*, Nicholas Murray Butler (ed.), *Monographs on Education in the United States* (Washington, D.C., 1900) is not very useful for the history of training for business. Such institutions as St. Stanislaus Commercial College at Bay St. Louis, Mississippi, have to be investigated not only for their own history but for their impact upon enrollments in the colleges.

18. *Register of Graduates, Massachusetts Institute of Technology, 1868–1909*; *Register of Graduates, MIT* (Boston, 1904).

19. *Report of the Commissioner of Education*, 1898–1899, and, James Russel Parsons, Jr., *Professional Education*, Nicholas Murray Butler (ed.), *Monographs on Education in the United States* (Washington, D.C., 1900), pp. 470–477.

20. See Table 5.1 and Burritt, *Professional Distribution.*

21. Consult Burritt, *Professional Distribution*, and the various histories of each of the colleges and universities as well as their annual catalogs.

22. For example, see, Burritt, *Professional Distribution*, p. 143.

23. The factor analysis was done with the program Factan. For details see, Colin B. Burke, The Quiet Influence: The American Colleges and Their Students, 1800–1860, Diss. Washington University, St. Louis, 1973, pp. 273–281.

24. For example, see, W. Norman Brown, *One–Half Century Catalog of Officers, Students, Graduates, and Non–Graduates 1876–1926*, (Johns Hopkins University, Baltimore, 1926).

25. Besides the lists of colleges cited in the *Report(s) of the U.S. Commissioner of Education*, the Library of Congress' collection of college guides and encyclopedias were used to trace the colleges.

26. For the distribution of colleges and their increasing enrollments consult the *Report(s) of the U.S. Commissioner of Education,* and such series as those in the *American Almanac.*

27. See Table 5.1 in this work.

28. On the general distribution of endowments and college income consult the *Report(s) of the Commissioner of Education; American Almanac,* 1902, pp. 614–620. The source for Table 5.5 was, Guido H. Marx, Some Trends in Higher Education, *Science* 29 (1909): 784.

29. U.S. Office of Education, *Executive Documents, 1891–2,* vol. 2, pp. 822–826.

30. See the catalogs of Johns Hopkins for out-of-state students.

31. Some of the more informative works on the socioeconomic backgrounds of students in the early twentieth century are: O. Edgar Reynolds, *The Social and Economic Status of College Students* (New York, 1927); Leonard V. Koos, *The Junior–College Movement* (Boston, 1924); *The Social and Economic Background of State Teachers College Students* (Greeley, Colorado, 1925); L.D. Coffman, *The Social Composition of the Teaching Population* (New York, 1911); Edward L. Thorndike, *The Teaching Staff of Secondary Schools in the United States* (Washington, D.C., 1909); U.S. Department of the Interior, Office of Education Bulletin (1930) No. 9, *Survey of Land Grant Colleges and Universities.* These should be supplemented by: George S. Counts, *The Selective Character of American Secondary Education* (Chicago, 1922); Paul Mattingly, *The Classless Profession* (New York, 1975); William G. Spady, Education, Mobility and Access: Growth and Paradoxes, *American Journal of Sociology* 7 (1967):273–289; and, William C. Landis and Louis C. Solmon, Compulsary Schooling Legislation, *Journal of Economic History* 32 (1972):54–91. As well, other analyses of attendance in primary and secondary education are helpful in understanding the continued class and ethnic biased character of higher education. For example, see, Colin Greer, *The Great School Legend* (New York, 1972).

32. *Survey of Land Grant Colleges and Universities,* p. 382.

33. Reynolds, *Social and Economic Status,* pp. 23–24.

34. For example see Reynolds, *Social and Economic Status,* pp. 42–47.

35. Koos, *The Junior College Movement,* p. 158.

36. For example, see, Allmendinger, *Paupers and Scholars,* p. 10; Coffman, *The Social Composition of the Teaching Population,* p. 17.

37. For example, consult, Howard H. Peckham, *The Making of the University of Michigan 1817–1967.* For the continued distance between the cultures of faculty and students see, in addition to DeMartini, Student Culture, the findings presented in Bessie Lee Gambrill, College Achievement and Vocational Efficiency, Diss. Columbia University, New York, 1922, especially pp. 34–35 where college marks and income are shown to have little relationship and business students received low grades.

38. On many of these points and for an early but very important article on postbellum higher education see, Merle Borrowman, The False Dawn of the State University, *History of Education Quarterly* 1 (1961): 6–22. The quotation is from, Richard Irby *History of Randolph Macon College, Virginia,* (Richmond, Virginia, nd), pp. 112–113.

39. Note that the estimates for academic salaries in the nineteenth century are for the average college faculty member while the twentieth century estimates are for associate professors. Although data for both average and assistant professors are available for the modern period, the series for associate professors was chosen in order to bias the evidence "against" the hypothesis of declining status. An attempt to prevent bias in the opposite direction for the nineteenth century data was made in that information was included only for those colleges reporting salaries for all their instructors rather than just the president or leading professors.

The estimates for professors' salaries in the 1800–1860 period have varied over the years as new data was found. But the estimates have never broken the bounds of being seven to nine times those of the unskilled worker. The lowest recorded average faculty salary for any college before the Civil War was three hundred dollars, an income, relative to the worker that was the average salary of associate professors in the United States in the 1970s.

There is some data for the two decades after the Civil War, but the sample is small and biased. Fortunately, W.R. Harper conducted a survey of professors' salaries in the 1890s. The results were printed in his, The Pay of College Professors, *Forum*, 16 (1893): 97. His estimates are consistent with those presented by Guido H. Marx, Some Trends in Higher Education, *Science* ns XXIX No. 750 (1909):759–784.

The implicit definition of unskilled worker and the data for the category was taken from the work of one of America's most respected economic historians, Jeffrey G. Williamson. He and his coworkers handled the thorny problems of definition and estimation in their brilliant piece on relative incomes in the United States. See, Peter H. Lindert and Jeffrey G. Williamson, Three Centuries of American Inequality, Institute for Research on Poverty, University of Wisconsin–Madison, March 1976. The data in the Lindert and Williamson effort was checked against other sources before a decision was made to take advantage of their work. Their estimates proved highly compatible with the other sources. Examples of other estimates used for both the nineteenth and twentieth–century series for the professions and occupations cited in this note are: Randolph Burgess, *Trends in School Costs* (New York: Russell Sage Foundation, 1920); Walter B. Smith, *Wage Rates on the Erie Canal, 1828–1881, Journal of Economic History*, 23 (1963):268–311 Donald R. Adams, Jr., *Wage Rates in Philadelphia* (New York, 1974); Sidney G. Tickton, *Teaching Salaries Then and Now: A Second Look* (New York, 1960); AAUP, *Bulletin* 51 No. 3 (1965), and 63 No. 3 (August, 1977). More sources were used to bring the Lindert–Williamson series up to the mid–1970s. See, W.V. Grant and C.G. Lind, *Digest of Education Statistics: 1976 Edition* (Washington, D.C. , 1977); U.S. Bureau of the Census, *Statistical Abstract of the United States: 1976* (Washington, D.C., 1976); U.S. Dept. of Labor, Bureau of Labor Statistics, Bulletin 1966, *Handbook of Labor Statistics* (Washington, D.C., 1977); U.S. Dept. of Labor, Bureau of Labor Statistics, *Employment and Earnings, U.S., 1909–1975* (Washington, D.C., 1977). An example of how a short time span can alter the perceptions of the status of college teachers is the otherwise excellent article by Howard R. Bowen, Faculty Salaries: Past and Future, *Educational Record*, 49 (1968):9–21.

For the salaries of teachers and professors in the 1970s, see, *Digest of Education Statistics*, tables 55, 56 and 105. As in a comparison with classroom teachers, the calculation of rates of return to investments in the education necessary for college teaching and for unskilled work would make the position of the professor look even worse. There have been significant changes in the salary structure of higher education since the Civil War. One change of importance is the regularization of payment and another is the equalization of salaries among colleges. If the spread between high–and–low paying schools in the antebellum period had been maintained until 1965, the average Harvard professor would have received some forty–five thousand dollars a year (instead of fourteen thousand five–hundred dollars) while the instructors at American International College would have been paid twelve hundred dollars rather than seven thousand six–hundred sixty–one dollars. (AAUP, *Bulletin*, 1965, p. 281).

The most startling change has been the one away from equality within the college and university. In the early nineteenth–century college professors were equals–among–unequals. The typical college president made about 30% more than the average faculty member but by at least the 1890s the situation had changed. The presidents then made 101% more than the faculty. (Harper, p. 97) This relationship seems to have held since the modernization and professionalization of higher education. In 1973–74, the presidents of four–year colleges and universities made 104 percent more than assistants. The average associate professor, in terms of salary, now stands further from his president than the unskilled worker stands from the professor. Little needs to be said concerning the relative position of the young assistant professor. (*Digest of Education Statistics*, tables 105 and 106).

Fringe benefits for professors have also regularized in the twentieth century but it is questionable whether they have really increased since the antebellum period when subsidized housing was the norm. Today, fringe benefits are about 15 percent of faculty salaries. (AAUP, *Bulletin* 1977). The amount of income from outside work by professors is somewhat difficult to specify and it is also questionable whether such income should be included in a discussion of salaries. But the returns from writing and consultation in the 1920s, when higher education was still an elite operation, was not only unequally shared by professors but was a relatively small part of total income. Returns from writing were 5 percent of salaries and consultation added 2 percent. (Trevor Arnett, *Teachers' Salaries in Certain Endowed and State Supported Colleges and Universities in the United States,* Publications of the General Education Board, Occasional Papers, No. 8 (New York, 1928), p. 71.) For the salaries of assistant professors and those offered to accounting and business majors just out of college, compare, *Digest of Education Statistics,* table 105, and, Mary A. Golladay, *The Condition of Education* Vol. 3 Part 1 (Washington, D.C.: 1977), table 219.

These conclusions concerning the relative standing of faculty salaries should be compared with other studies which redefine professional categories (from physicians to "health professionals") and which redefine the work–load expectations for faculty members so that summer teaching, teaching in addition to the regular teaching load and income from consulting (very unequally distributed) are considered normal. Such studies pay little attention to the results for quality education and teaching if such definitions become the norms for faculties, as the nineteenth–century university ideal seems to have intended.

See, How Earnings in Academia Compare with Other Fields *Chronicle of Higher Education,* October 18, 1979.

40. The quotation is from Marx, Some Trends, pp. 777–778. Consult John McCaughey, The Transformation of American Academic Life: Harvard University, 1821–1892, *Perspectives in American History* 8 (1974): 239–330, not only for the continued insecurity but the much earlier emergence of new faculty conditions than previously pictured. AAUP, Report of the Committee on Academic Freedom and Academic Tenure, *AAUP Bulletin* 1 (1915):15–43.

41. The turnover in the colleges, especially in the state institutions, should be thoroughly investigated especially for the question of why the public did not react to the problem.

42. The primary report on the army tests, Robert M. Yerkes (ed.), *Psychological Examining in the United States Army* (Memoirs of the National Academy of Sciences, Vol. 15; Washington, D.C., 1921), contains great amounts of data on the mental tests of World War I and also relfects some of the interpretive biases of the new professionals. It appears that the original data from the tests has been lost or misplaced (conversations with various U.S. Army departments) but the numerous tables in the report provide more than enough information for the purposes of this study. A second report on the army tests is also very useful because it goes into more detail on some subjects than the primary publication. See, Margaret V. Cobb and Robert M. Yerkes, Intellectual and Educational Status of the Medical Profession as Represented in the United States Army, *Bulletin of the National Research Council,* Vol. I, Part 8 (February, 1921), 484–532. The context in which the tests were developed and interpreted and the ideologies of the test–builders is revealed in: Leon J. Kamin, *The Science and Politics of I.Q.* (New York, 1974); C.C. Brigham, *A Study of American Intelligence* (Princeton, 1923); C.S. Yoakum and R.M. Yerkes, *Army Mental Tests* (New York, 1920); W.V. Brigham, Army Personnel Work, *Journal of Applied Psychology* 3, No. 4 (1919):1–12, Lewis M. Termin, *The Intelligence of School Children* (New York, 1919). A brilliant survey of our present knowledge of intelligence with a title that does not reflect its scholarship and sensitivity is, John C. Loehlin, Gardner Lindzey and J. N. Spuhler, *Race Differences in Intelligence* (San Francisco, 1975). On scores by occupation see, *Psychological Examining,* Chapter 15, and, Douglas Fryer, Occupational Intelligence Standards, *School and Society,* 16 (1927):273–277. Henry E. Garrett's and Matthew R. Schenck's, *Psychological Tests, Methods and Results*

(New York, 1933), provides a detailed history of the various tests as well as a discussion of the assumptions and methods of the early testing movement. On testing in higher education see; Ben D. Wood, *Measurement in Higher Education* (New York, 1923), and A.H. MacPhail, *The Intelligence of College Students* (Baltimore, 1924). To understand the testers' beguilement with statistics and how they could move from a very tempered position in respect to the validity of IQ testing to almost unquestioning acceptance, see: Edward L. Thurstone et al., *The Measurement of Intelligence* (New York, nd); Lewis M. Terman, *Measurement of Intelligence* (Boston, 1916); *The Twenty First Yearbook of the National Society for the Study of Education: Intelligence Tests and Their Use,* (Bloomington, Ill., 1923); Guy M. Whipple, The National Intelligence Tests, *Journal of Educational Research* 4 No. 11 (1921):16–31; Henry Herbert Goddard, *Human Efficiency and Levels of Intelligence* (Princeton, N.J., 1920). The nature of the army sample is discussed in: *Psychological Examining,* especially Chapter 1; C.C. Brigham, xix–xxv; and, W.V. Brigham. A brief description of the samples used for other intelligence tests is, Walter S. Neff, Socioeconomic Status and Intelligence: A Critical Survey, *Psychological Bulletin* 35 (1938):752–753.

The testers frequently admitted the dangers in attempting to measure adult intelligence but, as with intelligence testing in general, proceeded as if the problems did not exist. On the practical and theoretical problems of adult measurement see: Frank S. Freeman, *Theory and Practice of Mental Testing* (3rd ed.; New York, 1964), 197–210 and 241–245; E.A. Doll, The Average Mental Age of Adults, *Journal of Applied Psychology* 3 (1919):317–328; K.P. Bradway and Clare W. Thompson, Intelligence at Adulthood, *Journal of Educational Psychology* 53 (1962):1–14; and W.A. Owens, Age and Mental Abilities, *Journal of Educational Psychology,* 57 (1966):311–325. On the problems of comparing scores from various tests (compounded when only MA or IQ are reported) see, Grayson N. Kefauver, Needs of Equating Intelligence Quotients Obtained from Group Tests, *Journal of Educational Research,* 19, 2 (February, 1929), 92–101. The many studies of the intelligence level of college students are summarized in, Paul Taubman and Terence Wales, Mental Ability and Higher Educational Achievement in the Twentieth Century, *Education, Income and Human Behavior* ed., F. Thomas Juster, et al. (New York, McGraw Hill, 1974), 47–69. This work contends that the intelligence level of college students increased since the early 1920s, but it also indicates the beginnings of a decline in the early 1960s (p. 51). The most important studies summarized in Taubman and Wales are: Charles W. Odell, *Are College Students a Select Group* (University of Illinois, Bureau of Educational Research Bulletin No. 34; Urbana: University of Illinois Press, 1927); F.P. O'Brien, Mental Ability with Reference to Selection and Retention of College Students, *Journal of Educational Research,* 18 (1928):136–143; F.H. Finch, Enrollment Increases and Changes in the Mental Level of the High School Population, (Applied Psychological Monographs, No. 10; London: Oxford University Press, 1946); and, Leo T. Phearman, Comparisons of High School Graduates Who Go to College With Those Who Do Not, *Journal of Educational Psychology* 40 (1949):405–414.

On WWI recruitment and test assignment procedures see, *Psychological Examining,* especially Chapter 1. Unfortunately, scores were not presented by age for all the groups in the army sample, only for some officers. The seven percent estimate was calculated from Table 366. When Alpha scores below twenty were eliminated (Table 286) the average was lowered by three points, or four percent.

To compensate for possible biases in the army sample, Negro scores were excluded and the effects of including officers at a ratio of one to fifteen was evaluated. Adding white officers raised the median by three points (four percent) and the Combined Score for the population from 13.54 to 13.87. The population average was computed in three different ways: by the Alpha score for the native white draft *Psychological Examining,* Table 281 ; by the combined score for the native white draft (Tables 281 and 159); and by the combined score for the white draft (Tables 281, 282, 159 and 162). The distribution for the combined white draft (including foreign born, Alpha and Beta) yielded the smallest distance scores. This national combined score was calculated by a weighted mean of the Alpha and Beta scores as transformed into combined scores by Tables 159 and 162. The mean and standard deviation were computed for each score category in Tables 159 and 162 and interpolation was used to find the transformed score. The standard deviation for the resulting combined score was estimated at twenty percent of the mean (C.C. Brigham, 80). State population scores were calculated by a similar process using Tables 200 and 201 for the raw Alpha and Beta scores. Standard scores for the college averages were found by: College Score–Population Mean/SD Population. These were then transformed into percentile scores by the use of the normal curve table in, Hubert M. Blalock, *Social Statistics* (New York, 1960) p. 441. These results were checked against the empirical score distribution, *Psychological Examining*, Table 281. The empirical distribution gave scores (for Alpha) one percentile less, on the average, than did the assumed normal distribution for the combined scores.

In 1926, E.O. Bergman published a percentile equivalent table for Alpha in, On Converting Scores on Army Alpha Examinations into Percentiles of the Total Population, *School and Society*, 23, (1926):695–696. The table was held to be the product of E.L. Thurstone. It combined the native white draft and officers at a ratio of twenty to one. This table reduced the percentiles cited herein by five points in the midnineties range. The table was not used for this study because it was so different from a reconstruction of the same two groups in, *Psychological Examining*, and because the methods used to arrive at the table were not described. The Bergman table also differed from a reconstruction of the table in C.C. Brigham, *A Study of American Intelligence*, p. 80. The reconstructed table from the Brigham estimates yielded higher percentiles than those presented in this work. A weighted mean score from, *Psychological Examining*, (Tables 280 and 281) revealed that, for officers at the twenty to one ratio, the Thorndike table was at great variance with the army data. The 50th percentile for the combined weighted mean was 70 from the army data and 61 from the Thorndike–Bergman conversion.

While it is reasonable to assume that the schools and colleges reporting their test scores were ones with relatively high scores, there was such a wide range of institutions reporting that the data may be held to be representative. Further, data from the army testing, by level of education, indicate that the institutional scores were not significantly higher than the national average for high school and college students (*Psychological Examining*, Table 281 and Chapter 10). Data for the high schools, normal schools, colleges and universities was taken from: *Psychological Examining*, pp. 163–171; E.L. Noble and F.G. Arps, University Students' Intelligence Ratings According to the Army Alpha Test, *School and Society* II (1920): 233–237; J.F. Anderson, Intelligence Tests of Yale Freshmen, *School and Society* II (1920): 417–420; C.F. Arps and H.E. Burtt, Correlation of Army Alpha Intelligence with Academic Grades in High Schools and Military Academies, *Journal of Applied Psychology* 5 (1920):289–293; S.S. Colvin and A.H. MacPhail, The Value of Psychological Tests at Brown University, *School and Society* 16 (1922):113–122; Moehlman, S.D. Hill, Results of the Intelligence Tests at the University of Illinois, *School and Society* 9 (1919):542–545; G.L. Roberts and C.C. Brandenburg, Army Intelligence Tests at Purdue University, *School and Society* 10 (1919):776–778; A.M. Jordan, Some Results of Correlations of Army Alpha Tests, *School and Society* II (1920);354–358; E.S. Jones, The Army Tests and Oberlin College Freshmen, *School and Society* II (1920):389–390; C.M. Whipple, Sex Differences in Army Alpha Scores in Secondary Schools, *Journal of Educational Research* 15 (1927):269–175; H.T. Hunter, Intelligence Tests at Southern Methodist University, *School and Society* 10 (1919):437–440; M.V. Cobb, Limits, H.P. Fling, I.N. Madsen and R.H. Sylvester High School Students' Intelligence Ratings According to the Army Alpha Test, *School and Society* 10 (1919):407–410; G.P. Walcott, Mental Testing at Hamline University, *School and Society* 10 (1919):57–60; H.A. Peterson and J.G. Kudorna, Army Alpha in the Normal Schools, *School and Society* 13 (1921):476–480; Lewis M.

Terman Intelligence Tests in Colleges and Universities, *School and Society* 13 (1921):481–Homer Davis, Army Alpha and School Grades, *School and Society* 14 (1921):223–227; M.J. Van Wagenen, Our Schools as Measured by the Army Tests, *Educational Administration and Supervision,* 5 (April, 1919): 163–176; M.J. Van Wagenen, Has the College Student Reached His Mental Maturity When He Enters College, *School and Society* 9 (1919):663–666; C.L. Stone, Intelligence and Scholarship, *Dartmouth Alumni Magazine* 12 (March, 1920):686–690. Odell, p. 31 did provide some raw Otis scores.

43. The estimates were based upon the distribution in Yerkes, *Psychological Examining,* Tables 280 and 281, with officers included at a 20 to 1 ratio.

44. The quotation is from, Lewis M. Terman, Intelligence Tests in Colleges and Universities, *School and Society* 13, 330 (April 27, 1921):481.

45. Laurence Vesey, *The Emergence of the American University* (Chicago, 1970), Chapters 2 and 3, cover the rise of the concepts of utility and research and some of their institutional ramifications. Also see the contemporary statement on "utility" in Charles McCarthy's, *The Wisconsin Idea* (New York, 1912), and for the university ideal and professional training see the works of Abraham Flexner. An interesting and important type of education which became a step–child of some colleges and universities after the Civil War is education by correspondence. Despite its relevance to modernization through the widespread distribution of knowledge it appears that it never received great attention from the new sponsors of higher education. The study of such education should be begun not only for the nineteenth but the twentieth century. A few works on education by mail and adult education by some of the colleges and universities exists but there is need for the study of both private and public efforts. See, for examples of the existing literature: John F. Noffsinger, *Correspondence Schools, Lyceums, Chatauquas* (New York, 1926); Chester A. Feig, The Effectiveness of Correspondence Study, Diss., Pennsylvania State College, 1932; J.J. Clark, The Correspondence School: Its Relation to Technical Education and Some of Its Results, *Science* 327 (1906); Alfred Lawrence Hall–Quest, *The University Afield,* (New York, 1926); and W. Bittner and H.F. Mallory, *University Teaching By Mail* (New York, 1933).

46. Economists have written extensively on the conceptual and theoretical aspects of the economic returns to education. One of the most readable and thorough works for those unfamiliar with basic concepts and techniques is John Vaizey, et al., *The Political Economy of Education* (London, 1972), which also surveys the problems of evaluating the social returns from educational investments. Also consult, Robert Campbell and R.N. Seigel, The Demand for Higher Education in the United States, 1919–1964, *American Economic Review* 57 (1967):482–494.

47. The first Jencks study, Christopher Jencks, et al., *Inequality: A Reassessment of the Effect of Family and Schooling in America* (New York, 1972), summarizes much of the literature on the relationship between training and achievement.

48. On the gate–keeper role see the sophisticated argument in Paul J. Taubman and Terrence J. Wales, Higher Education, Mental Ability and Screening, *Journal of Political Economy* (1973):28–53. But the ability of the higher educational system to perform this function and to generate high rates–of–return to its students is, to a great degree, dependent upon its ability to be selective. For a temperate view of the role of social and economic status see the more recent work by Christopher Jencks, et al., *Who Gets Ahead?: The Determinants of Economic Success in America* (New York, 1979).

49. One does not have to accept either Thorstein Veblen or the more radical commentators on primary and secondary education in the late 1960s and early 1970s to see the consequences of the emphasis on job training. No matter what the general political or economic system, a focus upon job training has many consequences for the nature of educational institutions.

A fascinating literature on the rate of return to higher education, including technical training, emerged in the early twentieth century. The burst of such studies indicates that educators were concerned, perhaps fearful, about the impact of the new education and that the public or elite sponsors were not accepting the idea that higher education did produce high economic rewards. The early rate of return literature is vast but the following works are some of the more interesting of the many studies. See: James M. Dodge, The Money Value of Education, *Transactions, American Society of Mechanical Engineers*, 25 (1903); David E. Rice, The Study of Income, Technically Trained Men, *Scientific American* 109 (1913):116; E.H. Thompson and H.M. Dixon, *A Farm Management Survey of Three Representative Areas in Indiana, Illinois and Iowa* (Washington, D.C., 1914); C.A. Ellis, The Relation of Higher Education for Economic Development of the State, *Journal of Education* 78 (1912):198–202; Bureau of Education Library Leaflet, *List of References on the Money Value of Education* (Washington, D.C., 1924).

50. See Chapters 3 and 4 in this work for information on the antebellum students at Harvard, Columbia and the University of Pennsylvania.

51. On the general contours of change in the organization of the teaching force consult, among many, many works: Bernard E. McClellan, Education for an Industrial Society, Diss., North Western University, 1972; U.P. Gordy, *The Rise and Growth of the Normal School Idea in the United States*, U.S. Bureau of Education Circular of Information, No. 8, 1891; Carl F. Kaestle, *The Evolution on the Urban School System: New York City, 1750–1850* (Cambridge, Massachusetts, 1973); and Marvin Lazerson, *Origins of the Urban School: Public Education in Massachusetts, 1870–1915* (Cambridge, Massachusetts, 1971); Edward C. Elliot, *State School Systems* (Washington, D.C., 1907); U.S. Bureau of Education, Circular of Information, 1, 1883, *Legal Provisions Respecting the Examination and Licensing of Teaching* (Washington, D.C. 1883.

52. *Historical Statistics*, Series H 236–238, H 229, H 317. Maris Vinovskis and Richard M. Bernard, Women in Education in Ante–bellum America, Working Paper 73–7, University of Wisconsin Center for Demography and Ecology, 1973, and, Tyack, Pilgrims Progress are useful for an understanding of the turmoil within teaching.

53. *Historical Statistics*, Series H 236–238, gives an overview of the sex ratios but the various *Report(s) of the Commissioner of Education* and the many state surveys of teachers should be consulted. On the enrollments in the normal schools and their costs, Statistics of Normal Schools, *Report(s) of the Commissioner* (1870–1900).

54. On women's options, John K, Folger and Charles B. Nam, *Education of the American Population* (Washington, D.C., 1967):78–79. On women's education two traditional works, Thomas Woody, *A History of Women's Education in the United States* (New York, 1929) and James T. Monroe, *Before Vassar Opened* (New York, 1924), should be supplemented by J.M.E. Blandin, *History of Higher Education for Women in the South to 1860* (New York, 1909) and more recent work on the social nature of women's education in the periodical literature. A very rewarding article is, David Allmendinger, Mt. Holyoke Students Encounter the Need for Life Planning, *History of Education Quarterly*, (1979) 27–46. Also see, Deborah Jean Warner, Science Education for Women in Antebellum America, *ISIS* 69 (1978):58–67.

55. On nursing education consult: U.S. Bureau of Education, Circular of Information, 1882, *The Inception, Organization and Management of Training Schools for Nurses* (Washington, D.C., 1882), and, Helen E. Marshall, *Mary Adelaide Nutting, Pioneer of Modern Nursing* (Baltimore, 1972).

56. Table 5.13 is from W. Randolph Burgess, The Education of Teachers in Fourteen States, *Journal of Educational Research* 3 (1921):161–172. On the relative rewards to men and women from increased training, see L.D. Coffman, *The Social Composition of the Teaching Population* (New York, 1911), especially pp. 40–47. Randolph Burgess, *Trends of School Costs* (New York, 1920) should also be consulted.

57. There is not yet an adequate account of such changes and all the reasons for them but the process may be seen through a tracing of institutions in college lists from the early twentieth century to the present. The alterations in the junior colleges during the same period has also not been explored. See Koos, *The Junior College Movement* for some idea of the reasons for the emergence of those institutions in the early twentieth century.

58. *Historical Statistics*, Series 327–338.

59. Sally Gregory Kohlstedt, *The Formation of the American Scientific Community: The American Association for the Advancement of Science, 1848–1860* (Urbana, 1976); Thomas L. Haskell, *The Emergence of Professional Social Science: The American Social Science Association and the Nineteenth–Century Crisis of Authority* (Urbana, Illinois, 1977); Anthony Oberschall (ed.), *The Establishment of Empirical Sociology: Studies in Continuity, Discontinuity and Institutionalization* (New York, 1972); L.L. Bernard and Jessie Bernard, *The Origins of American Sociology* (New York, 1965); and, see, Howard S. Miller, *Dollars for Research: Science and Its Patrons in Nineteenth–Century America* (Seattle, 1970).

60. For one example of studies showing the relative incomes see, *Survey of Land Grant Colleges and Universities*, p. 382.

61. Paul P. Von Riper, *History of the U.S. Civil Service* (Westport, Connecticut, 1958) provides data on the relationship between higher education and the Civil Service. Table 5.14 is from, *U.S. Civil Service Commission, Report*, 1893, pp. 130–132.

62. On early conditions in the legal professions see, Daniel Calhoun, *Professional Lives in America* (Cambridge, Massachusetts, 1960), and, William R. Johnson, *Schooled Lawyers: A Study in the Clash of Professional Cultures* (New York, 1978).

63. Charles Warren, *A History of the American Bar* (New York, 1966); James W. Hurst, *The Growth of American Law* (Boston, 1950); Alfred Z. Reed, *Training for the Public Profession of the Law* (Boston, 1921).

64. On increased time in formal training, Parsons, *Professional Education*, p. 475. Table 5.15 is from, James W. Hurst, *The Growth of the American Law: The Law Makers* (Boston, 1950), pp. 272–274.

65. Parsons, *Professional Education.*

66. Albert P. Blaustein and Charles O. Porter, *The American Lawyer: A Summary of the Survey of the Legal Profession* (Chicago, 1954), pp. 181–195.

67. The estimates of the number of professionals and those in professional school who had college training vary but all the estimates are fairly close for lawyers and other professionals. See: Parsons, *Professional Education*, p. 474; J.P. Shaw, Statistics of College Graduates, *Journal of the American Statistical Association* 10 (1910); and E.G. Dexter Training for the Learned Professions, *Educational Review* 25 (1903):30–35.

68. Table 5.16 is from, Blaustein and Porter, *The American Lawyer*, p. 193.

69. A general survey of the medical profession in the nineteenth century is found in: Richard Shryock, *Medicine and Society in America 1669–1860*; Joseph F. Kett, *The Formation of the American Medical Profession* (New Haven, 1968); and William Rothstein, *American Physicians in the Nineteenth Century* (Baltimore, 1972). Edward Atwater's work, The Medical Profession in a New Society, *Bulletin of the History of Medicine* 47 (1973):221–235, is important because it demonstrates the competitive position of the forgotten practices because of the absence of an established and viable science of medicine.

70. A more than adequate survey of changes in medical practice is John Duffey, *The Healers: The Rise of American Medicine* (New York, 1976). On the number of physicians, *Historical Statistics*, Series B 181.

71. *Historical Statistics*, Series B 181.

72. On comparative enrollments for the various schools of practice see, J.K. Scudder, Numerical Strength of the Different Schools of Medicine in the United States, *Eclectic Medical Journal* 54 (1894): 396. On the evolution of medical education, Robert P. Hudson, Abraham Flexner in Perspective: American Medical Education 1865–1910, *Bulletin of the History of Medicine* 46 (1972):545–561, and Parsons, *Professional Education* are important.

73. Parsons, *Professional Education.*

74. Charles McIntire, Results of the Examination for Medical Licensure in the United States in 1903, *Bulletin of the American Academy of Medicine*, 6 No. 13 (1904):709–792.

75. The source for Table 5.17 is, Council of State Governments, *Occupational Licensing in the States* (Chicago, 1952).

76. Among the revisionist historians who have shown the difficulty of devising a viable agricultural education and of providing adequate services to farmers are: Mary Jean Bowman, The Land Grant Colleges and Universities in Human Resource Development, *Journal of Economic History* 22 (1966):523–546; Margaret W. Rossiter, *The Emergence of Agricultural Science*, (New Haven, 1976); James Whorton, *Before Silent Spring: Pesticides and Public Health in Pre DDT America* (Princeton, 1974); and, Roy V. Scott, *The Reluctant Farmer: The Rise of Agricultural Extension to 1914* (Urbana, Illinois, 1970). Douglas Hawr, Agricultural Education in Nineteenth Century Ontario, Michael B. Katz and Paul H. Mattingly (eds.) *Education and Social Change: Themes From Ontario's Past* (New York, 1975), pp. 169–192, found difficulties of a similar nature in Canada's attempt at agricultural education.

77. Consult the works in footnote 76. Also see, L.F. Haber, *The Chemical Industry During the Nineteenth Century* (Oxford, 1958), and, Edgar F. Smith, *Chemistry in America* (New York, 1914).

78. *An Early View of the Land Grant Colleges* (Urbana, Illinois, 1967), p. 13.

79. Consult John L. Shover, *First Majority–Last Minority: The Transformation of Rural Life in America* (DeKalb, 1976) for the economic and political aspects of farming. On incomes see, for example, *Survey of Land Grant Colleges and Universities*, p. 382.

80. On the antebellum engineers trained at West Point see, Terry Mark Aldrich, Rates of Return on Investment in Technical Education in the Ante–bellum American Economy, Diss., University of Texas, Austin, 1969. *Biographical Directory of Railway Officials of America* (Chicago, 1887). *Haupt's American Engineering Register.* Also see the low relative income of graduates of Sheffield in the first decade of the twentieth century as cited in A.C. Ellis, *The Money Value of Education.* The 1934 study of education of civil engineers is, Society for the Promotion of Engineering Education, *Report of the Investigation of Engineering Education, 1923–29*, (Pittsburgh, 1934), I. General works citing the division within the engineering field and its different branches are: Daniel Calhoun, *The American Civil Engineer*, (Cambridge, Massachusetts, 1960); Edwin T. Layton, Jr., *The Revolt of the Engineers* (Cleveland, 1971). On the relationship between modes of training and innovation see, D.L. Burn, The Genesis of American Engineering Competition, *Journal of Economic History* 60 (1935): 292–311.

81. Wm. A. Wickersham, *A Comparative Study of Engineering Education in the United States and In Europe* (Lancaster, Pa., 1929); Paul R. Douglas, *American Apprenticeship and Industrial Education* (New York, 1921); Charles R. Mann, *A Study of Engineering Education* (New York, 1918).

82. *Register of Graduates, MIT, 1868–1909. Survey of Land Grant Colleges and Universities*, p. 368. A.M. Wellington, The Supply and Demand of Engineers, *Engineering News* (1892), p. 111.

83. John L. Carey, *The Rise of the Accounting Profession* (New York, 1969–70); Edmund J. James, *Commercial Education* (Washington, D.C., 1900); and, Roy J. Sampson, American Accounting Education, Textbooks and Public Practice Before 1900, *Business History Review* 34 (1960). On the Yale and Harvard students, Burritt, *Professional Distribution.*

84. On the needed production of scientists and engineers, Nathan Reingold's estimates were used for the numbers of men. See his, Definitions and Speculations, Alexandra Oleson and Sanborn C. Brown (eds.), *The Pursuit of Knowledge in the Early American Republic* (Baltimore, 1976), pp. 57–58. On the chemists, Beardsley, p. 193. On the limited demand for scientists in industry and some of the reasons for the rise in demand during and after World War I see: David Noble, *America By Design* (New York, 1977) and A.P.M. Fleming, *Industrial Research in the United States of America* (London, 1917).

85. For the SAT scores in Table 5.18, *Digest of Education Statistics 1977–8*, p. 63, and, Timothy R. Sanford, Test Score Decline: An Overview, *High School Journal* 60 (1977):302–306. On the evolution of the high school and some of the reasons for the divergence of the colleges and the secondary system see Edwad Krug, *The Shaping of the American High School*, 2 vols.

(Madison, Wisconsin, 1964, 1972), and Paul Mattingly, *The Classless Profession*. The Alpha estimates for the World War II period and for the postwar era in Table 5.18 are from: Read D. Tuddenham, Soldier Intelligence in World War I and II, *The American Psychologist* 3 (1948):54–56; Bryon E. Fulk and Thomas W. Harrell, Negro–White Army Test Scores and Last School Grade, *Journal of Applied Psychology*, 36 (1952):34–35; Tolan L. Chappell, Note on the Validity of the Army General Classification Test as a Predictor of Academic Achievement, *Journal of Educational Psychology* 46 (1955):53–55; Walter V. Bingham, Inequalities in Adult Capacity—From Military Data, *Science* 104, No. 2694 (Friday, 16 August 1946):147–152; Staff, Personnel Research Section, The Adjutant's Office, The Army General Classification Test; With Special Reference to the Construction and Standardization of Forms 1a and 1b, *The Journal of Educational Psychology*, 38, (1947):385–420; Staff Personnel Research Section, The Adjutant General's Office, The Army General Classification Test, *Psychological Bulletin* 42 (1945):767; E.F. Fuchs, Army Test Scores vs Education Since World War I, unpub. paper presented at the American Psychological Association Convention, 1957; U.S. Army, Personnel Research Branch, Relation Between Amount of Acceleration or Retardation in School and GCT–1a Scores, 2/27/42, p. 2; U.S. Army, Personnel Research Branch, AGCT Scores for Level of Educational Attainment, 2/7/42, p. 2; Henry Chauncey, The Use of the Selective Service Qualification Test in Deferment of College Students, *Science*, 116 (July 25, 1952), 73–79; Bernard D. Karpinos, Mental Test Qualification of American Youth for Military Service and Its Relation to Educational Attainment, American Statistical Association, *Proceedings*, 1966, pp. 92–111, Table 5; Staff, Personnel Research Section, The Army G.C.T., *Psychological Bulletin*, 42 (December, 1945), 760–768; Dael Wolfe, *America's Resources of Specialized Talent* (New York, 1954); Dael Wolfe, Intellectual Resources, *Scientific American* 185 (1951): 42–46; Dael Wolfe and Toby Oxtoby, Distribution of Ability of Students Specializing in Different Fields, *Science*, 116 (Sept. 26, 1952):311–314.

Tuddenham tested a World War II sample with a revised form of the Alpha test. To convert this into original Alpha scores, the work by Irving Lorge, A Table of Percentile Equivalents for Eight Intelligence Tests With Adults, *Journal of Applied Psychology*, 20 (1936):392–395, was used. The regression of the original Alpha on the Wells revision used by Tuddenham was: a = –10.675, b = 1.023, r = .99. The other WWII scores were transformed from AGCT scores to the Wells revision by: a = –90.33, b = 1.96115, r –.98 (AGCT, 417–420). The estimate used for the average college Alpha score in WWI was a very conservative, 130. This was probably the average for college freshmen and freshmen scores were usually lower than those for upperclassmen.

The AGCT (WWII) results are biased upwards because of the very effective techniques to eliminate illiterates and the mentally incompetent. But it still seems that the colleges and universities were able to double the percentage of the population entering college to 16 percent in the years from 1920–1940 without lowering intellectual standards. The World War II tests also indicate that the majority of the "competent" persons had not gone to college. W.V. Bingham estimated that 25 percent of the young adults could go to college without lowering standards and that the college population could be doubled if all those one–half a standard deviation above the army mean were admitted (*Inequalities*, p. 148).

The W.V. Bingham and the Fulk estimates for the average scores of college students (AGCT standard scores of 130 and 119.5) are very different. Bingham's estimate seems to be too high because the scores of two very select college groups are close to it—fourth year West Point cadets and students from the elite colleges tested by ACE. The estimate by Fulk matches the score for University of Missouri freshmen (Chappell, 54). The Fulk estimate places the average college student (including graduates) at about one standard deviation above the mean for the population; at the eighty–fourth percentile. Data in Kaprinos, Table 5, indicates that by the mid–1950s the average white college student (including graduates) stood lower than the seventy–fifth percentile on the national white distribution. In the same publication, W.B. Schrader, Educational Data from Large Scale Testing Programs, pp. 112–117, has estimates for PSAT verbal (p. 116) indicating that the early 1960s saw a further decline. Male college entrants were .61 SD above the tested high school seniors, or the the seventy–second percentile when 75 percent of the 17 year–old population was graduating from high school. Chauncey reported on the college deferment tests of the 1950s, an upwardly biased sample. The mean score of the 1950s college freshmen in terms of WWI Alpha was 138. The table of estimates of the absoslute values of Alpha scores for college students and other population categories for the 1950s to the late 1960s indicates that while the scores for the population in general increased significantly, the college scores, at best, remained stable. The estimates from World War I through the mid–1950s should be considered highly reliable because a number of scholarly investigations provided information on the test results in a form translatable into Alpha scores. For the period after that, unfortunately, the reports of armed forces testing programs are very difficult to interpret. The nature of the reports themselves, the frequent revision of the tests that were used from the early 1950s until the end of the draft, and the complex interaction between test item–selection and the use of the World War II mobilization base as the norm for standardizing test scores, lead to very confusing estimates. But with the aid of reports on other tests, some of the armed forces materials proved of use through estimation procedures based upon deviation measures. (Table F.1)

Table F1

Estimates of Alpha Scores or Equivalents for the Population and Various Educational Levels (All Races)

Category	1951	1953	1960's
Population	94	94	108
8th Grade			
10th Grade			
12th Grade		118	117
College, 1 yr.		127	
College, 1 & 2			
College, 3 & 4			
College, all			126, 132 White
College, grad	137	140	
U. Mo. frosh			
4th grade			
6th grade			
PhD's	166		
H.S. Entrant		108	
Grad. Std.		145	

Evidence from studies of ACE test results from the 1930s and 1966–67 and the results of Wechsler adult tests given to college students provide some parameters for estimating Alpha from the 1960s armed forces data. The study of A.W. Tamminen, A Comparison of the Army General Classification Test and the Wechsler Bellevue Intelligence Scales, *Educational and Psychological Measurement,* II (1951):646–655, and those by, Rev. John B. Murray, College Students' IQs, *Psychological Reports,* 20 (June, 1967):743–7, and D.P. Campbell, A Cross Sectional and Longitudinal Study of Scholastic Abilities Over Twenty–Five Years, *Journal of Counseling Psychology,* 12 (1965):55–61, show that the administration of tests designed for adults (which allow the achievement of high scores by the most able) resulted in stable scores from the 1930s on. These studies used students from select colleges and universities, schools where major increases should have appeared if they did occur. Further, they indicate that, at the more prestigious schools in the 1960s, the students were about one standard deviation above the population mean.

Collaborative studies between Project Talent and the armed forces also provide some boundaries for the use of the armed forces data from the 1960s. Lonnie D. Valentine, Jr., Relationship Between Airman Qualifying Examinations and Armed Forces Qualifying Test Norms, Personnel Research Division, Air Force Human Resources Laboratory, Air Force Systems Command, July, 1968, and Ernest R. Tupes and Marion F. Shaycroft, Normative Distributions of AQE Aptitude Indexes for High School Age Boys, Personnel Research Laboratory, Aerospace Medical Division, Air Force Systems Command, July, 1964, have similar estimates. Both point to a one–fourth SD increase in the scores of eighteen–year–olds over 1946, and a one SD increase for high school seniors for the same period.

Another collaborative effort, between the Selective Service System and the Educational Testing Service, yielded startling results. The tests given to college students for deferments from the early 1950s through the late 1960s are puzzling. The test was supposedly designed to pass the same proportion of college students on the SSCQT as would have made a score of 120 (1 SD above the mean) on the standard army tests (AGCT–AFQT) if they were undergraduates and 130 (1–1/2 SD) if they were opting for graduate status. In the first administration of the test, the results indicated that the college freshman was about one standard deviation above the population. In 1951, 53 percent of the freshmen scored at or above the passing mark. But within three years the percentage of freshmen and other students achieving the passing grade climbed to over 80 percent and remained at about that level until the program was discontinued in the late 1960s.

There may be several explanations for these results but the need for historical investigation seems evident. There was a bias in respect to who took the test. Those with higher class standing seemed to take the SSCQT in greater proportions than others, but it seems unlikely that this alone could account for the high scores. Perhaps the test was compromised, perhaps the students were extraordinarily motivated, and the norms for the test may have been set too low. In any case, it is surprising that there is no evidence of a governmental investigation of the results during the period. On the SSCQT, see: Chauncey, Educational Testing Service, A Summary of Statistics on Selective Service College Qualifying Test, Princeton, N.J., 1951; Educational Testing Service, Candidates Who Took the Selective Service College Qualification Test in the Fall of 1966, Princeton, N.J., July 1967; Educational Testing Service, reports on test results, mimeo, 1955, 1958, 1959, 1960, 1961, 1962.

With the boundaries suggested by the above–mentioned studies, Karpinos' article was used to estimate Alpha scores for the 1960s. However, his work, one much more useful for this study than most of the armed forces reports in the 1960s, still had to be manipulated. Scores for various educational levels were estimated by combining the raw scores mid–points of the percentile classifications with the score percentile category estimates for each educational level group. (Karpinos, p. 97 and Table 5, all regions, all races, and all regions, white). The mid–point raw score for each category was multipled by the category frequency to arrive at the categories' AFQT score. This resulted in estimates indicating (AFQT to AGCT via Uhlaner, p. 52) that the 1960s average score for all draftees was one–half a standard deviation higher than in 1946, that the college students were one–half a standard deviation above the average (compared to the 1–1/2–2 SDs in WWI), and that the college students were one–fourth a standard deviation above the draftee who had three to four years of high school. The standard deviation equivalents in Alpha scores were added to the 1946 Alpha estimates for the population to arrive at the 1960s scores.

For examples of the armed forces reports of the 1960s testing see, besides the works already cited, U.S. Army, Surgeon General's Office, Supplement to the Health of the Army; Results of the Examination of Youths for Military Service, 1966, (Washington: GPO, March, 1967), and, Supplement to the Health of the Army, Results of the Examination of Youth for Military Service, 1965, (Complementary Analysis, September, 1966), (Washinton: GPO, 1966). On the AFQT tests, see *Development of the Armed Forces Qualification Test and Predecessor Army Screening Tests, 1946–1950,* by J.E. Uhlaner, Personnel Research Branch, The Adjutant General's Office, Dept. of the Army, PRB Report 976, 1968; Dept. of the Army, *Army Personnel Tests and Measurements,* Pamphlet 611–2, June 1962; U.S. Army Behavior and Systems Research Laboratory, Technical Report 1161, *The Armed Services Vocational Aptitude Battery,* by Abram G. Bayroff and Edmund F. Fuchs, Feb. 1970; U.S. Army, Personnel Research Note 150, December, 1964, Evaluation of the New Test Structure for the AFQT, by A.G. Bayroff and U.R. Graham; U.S. Army Behavior and Systems Research Laboratory, Technical Research Note 228, May 1971, Effects of Ability, Education, and Racial Group on Aptitude Test Performance, by Milton H. Maier; U.S. Army, Personnel Research Office, Technical Research Report 1132, *Development of Armed Forces Qualification Test 7 and 8,* by A.G. Bayroff and Alan A. Anderson, May, 1963; Milton H. Maier, Changing Role of General Ability in the Army Classification System, *74th Annual Convention of the American Psychological Association,* 1969; 4 (pt. 2), 699–700.

APPENDIX A

Schools in Operation 1800–1860

Liberal Arts Colleges in Operation 1800–1860, By States.

ALABAMA.

University of Alabama. Located at Tuscaloosa, this college was legally founded in the 1820s, but did not come into operation until the early 1830s. It was coded as a state college in this study.

Florence Wesleyan. Located in Florence, it did not operate at the college level until the late 1850s after it inherited the endowment of Lagrange College. It was coded as a Methodist college.

Howard College. At Marion, it began operation as a college in the mid–1840s. It was coded as a Baptist college.

Lagrange College. Founded in the 1830s and first located at New Tuscaloosa, this Methodist college moved to Lagrange and, perhaps, Florence. It appears to have taught some college level students but it closed its doors in the mid–1850s when its staff and endowment went to Florence Wesleyan.

Spring Hill College. At Spring Hill, near Mobile, this Catholic college began operation in the 1830s but was perhaps not teaching at the college level until the 1840s.

Southern University. Coded as a Methodist College and located near Greensboro, this school began some college level work in 1859. It was chartered in 1856.

CALIFORNIA.

St. Ignatius. Located in San Francisco, this Catholic school probably was a preparatory level institution.

Santa Clara. This was a Catholic Jesuit college which began operation in the late 1850s. There remains some question as to whether or not it actually taught at the college level during the period.

University of the Pacific. This study found this school to have more of the character of a nondenominational than a Methodist college during the era, but it was coded according to Tewksbury's designation. It began operation in the mid–1850s and survived into the twentieth century at a new site as the College of the Pacific.

CONNECTICUT.

Washington–Trinity College. Located in Hartford and coded as an Episcopal institution, Trinity started in the late 1820s as Washington College, then became known as Trinity in the 1840s.

Wesleyan University. This Methodist college began operation in 1831 at Middletown.

Yale. Founded in the Colonial era and coded as a Congregational college for the entire period, Yale was always located in New Haven.

DELAWARE.

Newark–Delaware. Located at Newark, this college was coded as Presbyterian for the 1830s, then as a state institution in the 1840s and 1850s.

St. Mary's. Founded in the 1830s as a preparatory school and receiving a college charter in 1847, this Catholic Diocesian school began college level work in the 1850s only to fail in 1868. Tewksbury did not list it as surviving into the twentieth century and, as with most Catholic colleges of the antebellum period, there is some question as to whether it was regarded as a college before the Civil War.

WASHINGTON, D.C.

Columbian/George–Washington. This was a Baptist college that began college level work in the 1820s and that survived into the twentieth century.

Georgetown. This Catholic college was founded in the 1790s and survived into the twentieth century. It is not certain when it began to teach students in a diploma track.

Gonzaga College–Washington Seminary. Founded in the 1820s as a "preparatory" school, this Catholic Jesuit institution appears to have done some college level work in the late 1850s. However, several sources claimed that it did not engage in college teaching until 1868 or 1874. Tewksbury did not list it as surviving into the twentieth century.

GEORGIA.

Christ College and Episcopal Institutute. Located in Montpelier, this Episcopal school began some college level work in the 1840s but seems to have failed by the end of the decade. Tewksbury did not list it as surviving into the twentieth century.

Emory. Coded as a Methodist institution and located in Oxford, this college began operation in the late 1830s.

University of Georgia. Founded before 1800, this state institution came into operation in the first decade of the nineteenth century under the name, Franklin College. It was always located at Athens.

Mercer University. This was a Baptist college at Penfield which began operations in the mid–1830s.

Oglethorpe. This Presbyterian college opened in the late 1830s at Midway, then moved to Milledgeville in the early 1850s.

ILLINOIS.

Eureka/Abingdon. This college was the product of a merger with a school which was probably an academy, Abingdon College. Opened in the late 1850s and located at Eureka, this Disciples college survived into the twentieth century. However, it is not certain that Eureka operated or was regarded as a college before the Civil War.

Hillsboro College/Illinois State University. Treated as a Lutheran institution, Hillsboro was founded in the late 1840s at Hillsboro, then moved to Springfield in the early 1850s. Tewksbury did not include it in his list of surviving colleges. It survived the Civil War to fail in 1868.

Illinois College. In operation by the early 1830s, this college at Jacksonville was founded with a combination of Congregational and Presbyterian support. In this study it was coded as a Presbyterian institution.

Illinois College/Illinois Wesleyan University. This was a Methodist college founded in the 1850s at Bloomington.

Jubilee College. Coded as an Episcopal institution, it was in operation by the mid–1840s near Peoria. While it would survive the antebellum period, it closed by 1900.

Knox Manual Labor College. Founded as a Congregational–Presbyterian school, it was coded as Presbyterian. It began operation in the mid–1840s and survived into the twentieth century.

Lombard College. This was a Universalist–sponsored school which was in operation in the mid–1850s. It survived into the twentieth century at Galesburg.

Marshall College. Established by Episcopalians at Henry in 1855, little is known about the nineteenth–century history of this college.

McDonough College. There is some evidence that this college, which was located at Macomb, operated as a college in the late 1830s and the 1840s. It disappeared by 1845 and no particular denominational support could be identified.

McKendree (McKendrie) College. Located at Lebanon, it began operation in the late 1830s under Methodist sponsorship.

Monmouth College. This institution at Monmouth may have conducted some college level work by the late 1850s under some degree of Presbyterian control.

North Western University. Although there is some debate about when this Methodist institution began as a liberal arts college, it is known to have had some graduates before 1861.

Shurtleff. Evolving from the Rock Spring Academy at Alton, this Baptist–sponsored school began college work in the late 1830s.

Wheaton College. While there is some indication that this school was first sponsored by Methodists, then by Congregationalists, it was coded as a Congregational institution for its five or six years of operation before the Civil War at Wheaton. It survived into the twentieth century although it closed for some years in the 1860s.

INDIANA.

Bloomington/Indiana College/University of Indiana. Coded as a state institution, Bloomington's many–named college began operation at the collegiate level in the late 1820s.

Butler College/Northwest Christian University. Located at Irvington, near Indianapolis, this Disciples school may have offered some college level work in the 1850s.

Earlham College. Founded in the 1850s, this Friends institution had college level students by the end of the decade. It was located at Earlham, near Richmond.

Franklin College. Although organized in the mid–1830s, this Baptist school did not begin continuous college level work until the mid–1840s. It was located at Franklin.

Hartsville College. Evolving from an academy at Hartsville, this United Brethren institution may have had some college students in the late 1850s. It was not listed by Tewksbury as surviving into the twentieth century, but it is known to have been in operation in the 1870s.

Indiana–Asbury/DePauw. This Methodist college at Greencastle was founded and in operation in the late 1830s.

Moores Hill College. This appears to have been a Methodist institution established at Moores Hill in the mid–1850s. Although there is no record of its demise before the Civil War, Tewksbury did not list it as being in operation in the 1920s. It was regarded as an academy by its sponsors as late as 1859.

Notre Dame. While mainly serving as a preparatory school, this Catholic college appears to have provided some college level work after its founding in the early 1840s.

St. Gabriel's. Located at Vincennes and chartered in 1843–44, this Catholic college seems not to have survived into the 1850s. It is not clear if it ever offered college level work. It was founded in 1836.

South Hanover/Madison University/Hanover College. An old–school Presbyterian institution founded in the late 1820s, in operation by the early 1830s and located at South Hanover, this school went through three reorganizations between its founding and 1849. It survived into the 1920s.

Territorial University/Vincennes. This state institution was open between 1820 and 1824, but died when state support was withdrawn.

Wabash. Located at Crawfordsville, this new–school Presbyterian college began operations in the mid–1830s.

IOWA.

Alexander College. Located at Dubuque, this school was affiliated with Presbyterianism. It seems that it was essentially a preparatory school. It was in operation by the mid–1850s, but would not appear on Tewksbury's list of survivors into the twentieth century. It is known to have closed its doors in 1857.

Burlington University. In operation by the mid–1850s and located at Burlington, this Baptist affiliated school appears to have taught some college students before the Civil War. In 1864 it was called "Burlington Collegiate Institute." It died in 1901.

Cornell College. A Methodist school at Mt. Vernon, it was in operation by the late 1850s.

Central College of Iowa. This was a Baptist aided institution which evolved from an academy. It opened its collegiate department in 1858 and survived into the twentieth century.

Des Moines College. Although founded in the late 1840s, this institution does not seem to have even made a claim to college level work until the mid–1850s. It has a very confused history and may have been sponsored by Presbyterians, then Lutherans, and for a time may have been located at West Point. It appears to have survived until the Civil War, but Tewksbury did not list it as alive in the twentieth century. It is known that the Lutherans started a college at Des Moines in 1855 which failed in 1862 to be revived by the Baptists only to die in 1916.

Iowa College/Grinnell. Located at Grinnell, this college opened in the late 1840s under Congregational–Presbyterian sponsorship but was listed in this study as Congregational. There are some indications that it was only a preparatory school.

Iowa State University. Before the Civil War this institution was probably a normal school, but may have instituted some college work in the late 1850s. Its operations were suspended (despite its state affiliation) but it did stay alive into the twentieth century.

Iowa–Wesleyan. Located at Mt. Pleasant, this Methodist affiliated school evolved from a preparatory institution founded in the early 1840s. College work may not have been offered until the mid–1850s.

KENTUCKY.

Augusta College. Located at Augusta, this Methodist affiliate opened in the late 1820s and failed in the late 1840s.

Bacon College/Kentucky University/Collegiate Institute and School for Civil Engineers. This Disciples–Christian school opened in Georgetown in the mid–1830s, then moved to Harrodsburg. It closed in the 1850s and merged with Kentucky University.

Bethel College. A Baptist College opened for college work in 1856, it was not included in Tewksbury's list of survivors. It was located at Russellville.

Bethel College. This Methodist–sponsored institution opened in 1790 and received a charter in 1803. It failed in 1812 after what had probably been a history as an academy.

Centre College. Opened for college level work in 1822, this Presbyterian affiliate survived into the twentieth century at its Danville location.

Cumberland College. In operation in the late 1820s, this Cumberland Presbyterian college was alive until the mid–1840s when it failed and merged with Nashville University.

Georgetown College. It is somewhat unclear as to when this Baptist affiliated school began college level work. Although in operation in the early 1830s, it may not have had college students until its reorganization in the late 1830s. It was, however, on Tewksbury's list of survivors.

Paducah. This institution, for which no denominational affiliation could be established, may have been only a preparatory school during its first decade of operation, 1852 to the war. It was listed as a failure by Tewksbury.

St. Joseph's. Located at Bardstown, this Catholic Jesuit college was probably a preparatory school. While there is some evidence that it may have had college level work in the late 1830s, other indicators suggest its being a preparatory school from its founding in 1819 until the Civil War. Tewksbury listed it as a failure.

St. Mary's. A Catholic Diocesan college in Marion county, it opened as a preparatory school in 1822 and offered some college work beginning in 1837. The evidence found during this study indicated that the college failed in the late 1840s. But Tewksbury listed it as a survivor in the twentieth century.

St. Thomas Aquinas. Located at Bardstown, this school was known to have been open in 1807 and 1808.

Shelby College. Surviving until at least the Civil War, this institution began some college work in 1841 after reorganization under Episcopal auspices. It may have lost the strict denominational influence it had in a reorganization in the mid–1850s. It was considered a failure by Tewksbury.

Southern College. Located at Bowling Green, this Presbyterian school failed within a decade after its 1820 opening.

Transylvania University. This famous college at Lexington was founded in 1798 and would at least formally survive into the twentieth century. Despite its advanced programs it passed through the hands of several denominations during the antebellum era and declined and became a normal school in the mid–1850s. For the tabulations in this study it was listed as Presbyterian, then Methodist, although some Episcopal and state influences were present during its history.

LOUISIANA.

Baton Rouge. This institution seems to have offered some college work in the 1840s and 1850s. It failed in 1856, possibly because it was not strongly affiliated with a denomination. This may have been St. Peter's and St. Paul's.

Centenary/College of Louisiana at Jackson. Although Tewksbury claimed that this was a semi–state institution, it was found to be a Methodist school. The Methodists had taken over the old Mississippi College and brought it to the old College of Louisiana. For this study it was coded as a state institution in its early years, the 1820s, then as a Methodist college. As did Centenary, it survived into the twentieth century.

College of Immaculate Conception. Located in New Orleans, this Catholic institution was chartered in 1847 and may have conducted some college work in the late 1850s.

College of Orleans. This school is an example of the failure of state aid in the early nineteenth century. Open as a state institution between 1807 and the 1820s, but perhaps not pursuing college level work, it failed when the complex social and ethnic politics of Louisiana led to the withdrawal of state support.

Franklin College. At Opelousa, this nondenominational and state school of the 1840s and 1850s probably never operated as a college.

Homer College of Louisiana. Located at Claiborne and founded in 1850, this Methodist institution may not have been regarded as a college before the Civil War. It was not listed as a Methodist college in the denomination's publications of the mid–nineteenth century.

Holy Cross. This New Orleans Catholic school was probably not regarded as a college by contemporaries.

Immaculate Conception. Located at Iberville, this school was another example of a Catholic "college"

Jefferson. This institution had a very complex history and was another example of the failure of state aid in the Southwest. It began as a nondenominational school with much state aid in the late 1830s at St. James then moved to Baringiers (sic.) to close in the mid–1840s because of a fire. It seems to have had Catholic leanings and was regarded by many as a preparatory school. Catholics took over what was left after the fire and declared it to be an academy. In 1907 a Catholic "Jefferson" College, claiming 1868 as its founding date, was listed in various compendia.

Louisiana College. A Catholic institution at Jackson which was open between 1830 and the 1840s, it was listed as a failure by Tewksbury.

Paydras College. Located at Point Coupee, this unchartered Catholic school opened in 1854. It probably was not a college during the 1850s.

University of Louisiana. Beginning college work in the early 1850s, this state institution at New Orleans survived into the twentieth century, but under different sponsors and names. It essentially failed when state aid was withdrawn in the late 1850s.

MAINE.

Bowdoin College. Organized in the 1700s, but with its first graduate in 1805–6, this Congregational College survived into the twentieth century at its old site in Brunswick.

Waterville/Colby College. Located at Waterville, this Baptist college opened in the early 1820s.

MARYLAND.

(Maryland's higher educational history was the most difficult to trace or understand. It was especially hard to categorize its institutions as to college level operation, and, in many cases, to trace through the history of its institutions.)

Baltimore College. This elusive and mercurial school was open for a few years in the 1830s and then in the 1850s. It was an attempt to create a liberal arts college within the Maryland state system. However, it probably was never regarded as a college.

University of Maryland. This product of a once grand state plan for higher education had a very checkered career after its formal organization in the 1810s. Although Tewksbury listed it as a survivor into the twentieth century and although there were some claims that college level work was done in the early decades of the nineteenth century, this study treated the college as in operation only in the 1850s as a state institution, and this was done by merging the semi–private Maryland Agricultural College with the history of the University of Maryland.

Mount Hope. Located close to Baltimore, this school was open for a short time in the 1830s. It is not certain that any college work was done. It was associated with the Presbyterians.

Mount St. Mary's. This was a Catholic institution founded in the eighteenth century and which may have been regarded as a college during its long history of serving the Maryland and Pennsylvania areas.

New Windsor/Calvert College. Located at New Windsor, this school passed through many hands. In the 1840s it was sponsored by the Old School Presbyterians. It failed soon after its chartering in 1843 to be revived by the Jesuits in the 1850s. It probably never operated as a college before the Civil War.

St. James. Located at Hagerstown and emerging from a preparatory school in the mid–1840s, this Episcopal institution lasted until 1863.

St. Johns. This Episcopal school in Annapolis was founded before the turn of the century but was coded as engaging in college level work in the mid–1840s. It survived into the twentieth century.

St. Mary's/Loyola College. Located at Baltimore, St. Mary's failed during the early 1850s, just as it may have begun to be regarded as a college. It was replaced by Loyola which, as with other Catholic schools, probably was not a college before the war.

Washington. Formally organized in the 1780s and located at Chestertown, the instituton received much state aid during its early years. However, it was coded as an Episcopal institution.

MASSACHUSETTS.

Amherst. Opening in the the mid–1820s, this Congregational college at Amherst survived to become one of the famous colleges of the twentieth century.

Harvard. Located at Cambridge and founded in the seventeenth century, Harvard was coded as a Congregational college for the antebellum period although its Unitarian connections are well known.

Holy Cross. This Catholic institution at Worcester was probably a preparatory school from its opening in the mid–1840s until the Civil War. Tewksbury did not include it in his list of surviving colleges.

Tufts. This Universalist institution at Medford was predominantly a preparatory school from its beginnings in the mid–50s until the Civil War.

Williams. Located at Williamstown, this Congregational "country" college was founded in the 1780s.

MICHIGAN.

Adrian/Michigan Union. Located a Leoni, then Adrian, this school grew from an academy. It seems to have begun college work in the mid–1850s after changing from Presbyterian to Methodist sponsorship.

Hillsdale/Michigan Central. Under Free Will Baptist's and moving from Spring Arbor to Hillsdale, this institution seems to have had some college students as early as the mid–1840s. It began as an academy in 1835.

Kalamazoo/Michigan–Huron Institute. Growing from a preparatory school which began in 1836, this Baptist college at Kalamazoo began college level work about 1855.

Marshall. Located at the town of the same name, this nondenominational school opened for college work in the 1830s but failed before the end of the decade without granting any college degrees. It did have strong Congregational–Presbyterian connections.

University of Michigan. This state institution opened in the early 1840s at Ann Arbor.

St. Phillips. A Catholic school, it began in the 1840s in Detroit to close about 1850 and may not have had any college students.

MINNESOTA.

Hamline College. Located at Red Wing, this Methodist school educated a few, if any, college students. It faced severe financial problems after the Civil War but stayed alive into the twentieth century.

MISSISSIPPI.

Jefferson. Organized in 1802 and in operation at least at the preparatory level by 1815 at Washington, this school appears to have been relatively nondenominational and to have taught some college students between 1815 and the 1840s. It is uncertain if college work continued in the 1840s and 1850s. The school does not appear on Tewksbury's "survivors" list.

Madison. Located at Sharon, this Methodist college lasted until at least the Civil War. However, it was classified as a failure by Tewksbury. It was reclaimed by the state in 1869.

Mississippi. Located at Clinton, in operation by the late 1830s, and probably experiencing some suspensions in its early years, it lasted through the period. It was classified as a Baptist institution although there appears to have been some strong Presbyterian support at different stages of its history.

University of Mississippi. This state institution was located at Oxford and had both a large endowment and large annual subsidies from the state. It opened its doors in the late 1840s.

Oakland. Opening in the mid–1850s and surviving the era, this Presbyterian college at Oakland did not appear on Tewksbury's list of surviving colleges.

Planter's College. This school at Port Gibson, which was open for a few years during the late 1850s, may have taught at the academy level only.

Semple–Broaddus. Located at Centre–Hill and sponsored by Baptists, it opened in the late 1850s. Tewksbury did not classify it as a survivor.

MISSOURI.

Central College. An institution probably located at Fayette before the Civil War, Central opened in the mid–1850s. It may have assumed the assets of Fayette College. Tewksbury listed it as a survivor and as a Methodist institution. The information for this study indicated Baptist support, then Methodist sponsorship before the war.

Fayette. Opened in the late 1830s, this school probably failed in the 1850s. No denomination could be associated with the school.

Kemper. This was an Episcopal school in St. Louis which opened and closed in the 1840s.

Marion–Masonic. Located at New Palmyra, then Lexington, this school went from Presbyterian sponsorship to become nondenominational. It began in the late 1830s and lasted to at least the Civil War. It was coded as a Presbyterian college. Tewksbury categorized it as a failure. The school has a fascinating history because of its abolitionist position and its communal nature.

McGee College. Founded by the Presbyterians in the mid–1850s at College Mound, it survived the era but, according to Tewksbury, failed to see the twentieth century.

Missouri University/Columbia College. Beginning at Columbia in the late 1830s, this school became Missouri's approximation of a state college in the 1840s. It survived through the century.

Mt. Pleasant College. Located at Huntsville, this Baptist institution seems to have served some college students during the 1850s. Although it survived the antbellum era, Tewksbury classified it as a failure because it could not be directly traced into the twentieth century.

St. Charles. This college opened in the late 1830s. It graduated a few college students before the war but relied upon academy students for its income. The school was claimed by both Baptists and Catholics.

St. Louis University. Opened in St. Louis as a Jesuit institution in the 1830s, this robust school survived into the twentieth century.

St. Mary's. Moving from Barrons to Cape Giradeau, this Catholic college of the 1830s and 1840s may well have contented itself with preparatory training. Its demise was probably followed by a reorganization which led to St. Vincents' expansion.

St. Vincents. Found in the mid–1840s, this Catholic school at Cape Girardeau survived to at least the Civil War but Tewksbury did not include it in his list of twentieth century survivors.

Westminister College/Fulton/Cumberland. This Presbyterian school at Fulton began in the 1850s and survived into the twentieth century.

William–Jewell. Open in 1850, this Baptist college faced temporary closings during its first decades but continued into the 1900s at Liberty.

NEW HAMPSHIRE.

Dartmouth. Although much of the evidence concerning this famous school indicated that it was not dominated by a single denomination, it was classified as a Congregational institution to conform to Tewksbury's and other historians' mandates.

NEW JERSEY

Burlington. This Episcopal institution at Burlington was founded in the mid–1840s and may have conducted some college level work. It was listed as an operating college until the Civil War but, according to Tewksbury's genealogy of higher education, did not survive into the twentieth century.

Princeton. This Colonial Presbyterian college was treated as a denominational school in this study.

Rutger's/Queen's College. This Dutch Reformed college was founded before the Revolution and weathered several suspensions during the first three decades of the nineteenth century. The college's complex history needs clarification.

NEW YORK.

Alfred University. Growing out of Alfred Academy, this Baptist school began college work in the late 1850s.

Central College. Located at McGrawville, this school opened in 1849 and survived until at least the Civil War as an anti–slavery Baptist college. Tewksbury considered it as a failure because of his twentieth century criteria.

Columbia University. Although receiving much financial support from the state during the Colonial period, this New York City institution was coded as being Episcopal.

Genesse. Located at Lima and having Methodist connections, Genesse opened in the 1850s to merge, later in its history, with Syracuse.

Geneva–Hobart. An Episcopal school which opened in the mid–1820s at Geneva, it survived into the twentieth century.

Hamilton–Madison. This Baptist college began to teach college students in the 1830s. It was renamed Colgate after receiving significant funds from important businessmen .

Hamilton. This was a Presbyterian school at Clinton which began in the 1810s.

University of the City of New York. Founded in the 1830s with support from Presbyterians and others, this was one of the most flexible and innovative schools of the antebellum period and its history as an early "urban" college should be detailed and explained.

St. Paul's. Located on Long Island at College Point, St. Paul's may not have survived more than ten years after its opening in the early 1840s. It may not have taught any college students.

University of Rochester. A Baptist institution, it began in the early 1850s.

St. John's/Fordham. Situated at Rose Hill near New York City, St. John's was a Catholic college which began in the mid–1840s.

St. Lawrence University. This Universalist college and seminary opened in 1859 and survived into the twentieth century at Canton.

Troy University. Located at Troy and having Methodist support, it started in the mid–1850s. Tewksbury called it a failure.

Union College. Founded before the nineteenth century, this Presbyterian college is still in operation.

OREGON.

Pacific University. Founded in 1853–54 in Forest Grove and with Congregational encouragement, this school may well have done some college level work before the Civil War.

Williamette. As with other institutions in Oregon during the antebellum era, this Methodist school is included in this list of operating "colleges" with great hesitation. It may have taught some college students before the Civil War and it may have been regarded as a college by contemporaries in the area, but no evidence of stable and continuous college work was found. It may have enrolled some college students in the early 1850s but some commentators have claimed college work in the school as early as 1842.

NORTH CAROLINA.

Davidson. A Presbyterian institution located in the town of the same name, Davidson began in the late 1830s and survived into the twentieth century.

Duke. Duke was a Methodist institution with a paradigm history of the migration from academy to college during the nineteenth century. It may have taught some college students as early as the 1840s although its official transformation from academy–normal school status to college did not come until the late 1850s.

University of North Carolina. Founded shortly after the Revolution, this state college at Chapel Hill had an illustrious nineteenth century history despite the financial ravages of the Civil War.

Wake Forest. Baptists helped this school begin operation in the mid–1830s.

OHIO.

Antioch. The Christian denomination began this Yellow Springs school in the 1850s but it soon received support from Congregational and Unitarian sources. It was coded as a Congregational college in this study.

Baldwin. A Methodist college connected to German ethnic groups and first known as Baldwin University–German–Wallace College, it opened in the mid–1850s.

Capital University. This German Lutheran college and seminary at Columbus was founded in the 1830s but did not have college students until the 1850s.

Cincinnati College–University. This nondenominational school had fascinating origins in the 1810s but seems to have closed its college department in the late 1840s after suspending operations in the 1820s and 1830s. It was classified as a failure by Tewksbury.

Farmer's/Belmont College. Located at College Hill and evolving from a private academy in the late 1840s, this institution was classified as nondenominational. It survived to at least the Civil War but was called a failure by Tewksbury.

Geneva College. This college began in Northfield Village, Ohio, in 1849 only to have its Reformed Presbyterian sponsors move it to Pennsylvania.

Franklin/Alma College. Founded in the mid–1820s, this school at New Athens had Lutheran support and survived until the Civil War if not longer. Tewksbury classified it as a failure.

Granville/Denison. Located at Granville and supported by the Baptists, this school opened in the late 1830s.

Heidelberg/Tarlton College. A German Reformed institution with a varied curricula, it opened in the early 1850s.

Iberia College. Founded in the early 1850s and probably being a nondenominational school, it had a non–classical and co–educational course. Located at Iberia–Mellow Springs, it may have restricted itself to preparatory training. Tewksbury listed it as a failure.

Hiram College/Western Reserve Eclectic Institute. While this Free Soil Disciples' school conducted most of its work at the preparatory level during the 1850s, it did provide some college instruction. It lasted to at least the Civil War but was considered a failure by Tewksbury.

Kenyon College. This school was begun by Episcopalians in the 1820s.

Marietta College. With Congregational support, Marietta began in the mid–1830s. It did receive aid from the Presbyterians but it was coded as a Congregational school in this study.

Miami University. Located at Oxford and opened in the mid–1820s it was classified as Presbyterian despite Tewksbury's indication that it was a state school.

Mt. Union. Located at Alliance, this Methodist academy seems to have confined its early years as a college to conducting normal training. It seems to have failed during it first decade, the 1850s. Tewksbury classified it as a survivor, however.

Muskingum. Located at New Concord, this Presbyterian school was started in the late 1830s.

Oberlin. Founded in the mid–1830s and chartered in the 1850s, this radical Congregational school has never had an adequate history. Its role in producing teachers for the Midwest and its wide ranging activities need to be explored.

Ohio University/American Western University. Opened at Athens in the mid–1820s, this state institution suffered a suspension in the 1840s but survived into the twentieth century.

Ohio Wesleyan. This was a Methodist college at Deleware which opened in the mid–1840s.

Otterbein College. Located at Waterville and initiated by the United Bretheren, this mostly preparatory school began in the late 1840s.

Urbana University. Founded by the Swedenborgians in the mid–1850s, this school survived the decade but was classified as a failure by Tewksbury.

St. Xavier. Located at Cincinnati and begun by the Jesuits in the early 1840s, the school probably functioned as a preparatory school before the Civil War as well as having to close its doors from some time in the early 1850s until the end of the Civil War.

Western Reserve. Open at Hudson in the late 1820s as a Congregational and Presbyterian venture, it was coded as a Congregational school in this study.

Willoughby University. Begun at Chagrin in the late 1830s and without denominational support, this school seems to have failed before 1838.

Wittenberg. This German Evangelical Luthern school was founded at Springfield in the late 1840s.

Woodward. Begun at Cincinnati in the late 1830s as a nondenominational institution and having mostly preparatory students, Woodward failed in the mid–1850s despite the enrollment boom of the decade.

Xenia. This was a Methodist affiliated school which probably confined itself to theological training. It was included in this list of active colleges only because of its cloudy history and the attempt to bias the evidence against the theses in this study.

PENNSYLVANIA.

Alleghany. Located at Meadville, this college was opened in the late 1810s. Although it was coded as a Methodist institution for the antebellum period, there was Presbyterian influence and there was much evidence indicating that it was a nondenominational school.

Bucknell/Lewisburg. This Baptist college began in the late 1840s.

Bristol. Established at Bristol in the mid–1830s, it disappeared by the end of that decade. It was sponsored by Episcopal interests and it may have confined itself to academy work.

Dickinson. Begun at Carlisle in the 1780s, this school probably had college students as early as 1804. It was coded as being Presbyterian from 1800 to 1829 and as Methodist from 1830 to 1860.

Duquesne. A Presbyterian school, Duquesne was chartered in 1844 but was not given the power to grant degrees. It seems to have done what was regarded as college work for the five or six years of its existence.

Marshall/Franklin and Marshall. This German Reformed school was founded in the 1850s at Lancaster.

Gettysburg College. Founded in the early 1830s and open by the mid–years of the decade, the school was aided by the Lutherans.

Haddington. Located near Philadelphia, this Baptist school appeared in the mid–1830s then disappeared by the end of the decade. It may have never served college level students.

Haverford College. Although receiving its charter in the mid–1850s, this Quaker school may have begun work in the mid–1830s. The school appeared on few contemporary lists of colleges.

Jefferson College. Located at Canonsburg and founded in the early 1800s, this Presbyterian school survived into the twentieth century without the historical attention it richly deserves as a major nineteenth century institution.

Lafayette College. Opening in the early 1830s, this Presbyterian school at Easton survived the nineteenth century.

Marshall/Franklin–Marshall. Founded in the late 1830s, Marshall merged with Franklin College to represent the German Reformed Church in the 1850s.

Madison. Located at Uniontown, this elusive school began as an academy in the 1790s. It seems to have done some college work in the late 1820s and did receive some state support. It closed in 1832 and an attempt to revive it in the 1850s failed. It had some degree of association with the Methodists.

St. Thomas of Villanova. Opening in the late 1840s near Philadelphia, this Catholic school failed in 1857. However, Tewksbury listed it as a twentieth century survivor.

University of Pennsylvania. This Colonial college received much state support in its early years but it had connections with Episcopalians, then Methodists. It was coded as a Presbyterian school for the antebellum period.

Washington. Located at Washington, this college emerged from an academy in 1806. It received state support in its early years but was coded as a Presbyterian institution for this study.

Western University. Evolving from the Pittsburg Academy, this school opened in the 1820s. The original coding for this study classified it as a nondenominational institution but the final "runs" used Tewksbury's Presbyterian classification. The school had to suspend operation during the late 1840s and early 1850s.

Westminister. Located at New Wilmington and opened in the early 1850s, there are doubts about its denominational affiliation and whether it ever operated as a college. Claims were made that it was nondenominational, United, Associate Presbyterian and Quaker. Although the best evidence points to the Presbyterian connection, Tewksbury's classification was followed.

Waynesburg. This school was chartered in 1850, had Cumberland Presbyterian support, and is known to have awarded degrees to both men and women before the Civil War.

RHODE ISLAND.

Brown. This Baptist Colonial college in Providence followed a nondenominational admittance policy.

SOUTH CAROLINA.

Charleston. This Colonial school not only weathered several suspensions in the early nineteenth century, even though it had a strong economic position, but it passed through the hands of several supporters. It began as Episcopal, received municipal support and, in the 1840s, turned to the Baptists. Although Tewksbury classified it as a municipal school, this study categorized it as Episcopalian from 1800–1839 and Baptist from 1840–60.

Erskine. Located at Abbeville, Erskine evolved from an academy. It began college work in the late 1830s under Presbyterian influence but its formal beginning as a college is sometimes dated as 1840.

Furman. This Baptist school opened in 1852 and was situated at Grenville.

College of South Carolina. This college received much support from the state from its mid–1800s opening at Columbia.

Mt. Zion. Located at Winnesboro, this school is known to have been chartered as a college and to have been open from before 1800 to the 1820s.

Wofford/Limestone. This Methodist institution opened in Spartansburg in the early 1850s.

TENNESSEE.

Cumberland University. Under Cumberland Presbyterian influence and located at Lebanon, this 1840s school prospered before the Civil War.

East Tennessee. Although planned in the 1790s, this institution opened in the 1820s. There is much confusion concerning the denominational affiliation of this college. In this study it was first coded as nondenominational, but for final tabulations it was coded as a state institution following Tewksbury's classification. The college was located at Nashville.

Enon College. This Baptist school may have operated as a college before the Civil War.

Franklin College/Elm Creek Agricultural School. Founded in 1845 and located at Nashville, this Church of Christ–Disciples school is another example of how alternative schools of the period drifted to the liberal arts model because of educational markets, problems of curricula, and status aspirations. It had agricultural courses and taught physical education from its inception but may not have been fully recognized as a college in the 1840s. It was destroyed by fire in 1866.

Greenville. This was a 1790s institution founded, it appears, under Presbyterian auspices. Its history is cloudy and it may have been closed in the 1840s and the early 1850s. It was first coded as nondenominational but Tewksbury's Presbyterian classification was used in the final computer runs. Greenville merged with Tusculum.

Hiwasse College. Located at Monroe, this nondenominational college survived to at least the Civil War but became one of Tewksbury's non–survivors.

Jackson College. This school was at Columbia and was, most likely, a preparatory school until the late 1840s. However, it was listed as an operating college in the 1830s for this study. Some sources called it a Masonic college but others listed it as a nondenominational school with some financial support from the state. It did not appear on Tewksbury's list of surviving colleges.

Lagrange–Masonic. Opened at Lagrange in the mid–1850s with some Presbyterian support, this college was categorized as Presbyterian. It was not listed by Tewksbury as a survivor.

Maryville College. This was a Presbyterian institution which was open for operation in the late 1820s, but its official status might not have been granted until the 1840s.

Madison College. Located at Spring Creek, this Baptist school began in the late 1850s. It is not certain that it taught college work but it was listed as a failure by Tewksbury.

University of Nashville. With origins in the 1790s, this college had some relationship to Presbyterians but was regarded as a nondenominational school. It was classified as Presbyterian in this work even though it instituted a quasi–military curricula for its students in the 1850s.

Stewart/South West Presbyterian–Masonic. Opening at Clarksville in the early 1850s, this Presbyterian school did not survive into the twentieth century.

Tusculum. Evolving from an academy, this Greenville school began some college work in the mid–1840s. It had some ties with the Presbyterians but was usually cited as being nondenominational.

Union College. This was a Baptist school at Murfreesboro which opened in the early 1840s. It is not certain if it survived into the twentieth century because Tewksbury listed a Baptist Union College at Jackson, not Murfreesboro.

Washington. A nondenominational college which failed in 1856, this school probably opened in the mid–1830s in Tennessee but moved to Washington County, Louisiana, in the late 1850s. It may not have functioned as a college while in Tennessee.

TEXAS.

Austin. This Old Presbyterian college at Huntsville began as an academy and offered college level work in 1852.

Baylor. This Baptist institution began some college level instruction in the mid–1850s.

Larissa College. With Cumberland Presbyterian support, this school was chartered before the Civil War. It is not certain that it produced, as claimed, some college graduates before 1865.

Rutersville College. This interesting effort by Methodists, with the help of state land grants, led to the founding of an all–purpose educational facility which enrolled over 800 students between 1841 and its failure in 1856.

Waco University. Typical of Texas' educational policies which demanded the name "university" in almost every school's title, this small institution seems to have opened just before the Civil War and to have gained a charter in 1861. It is not certain that it was regarded as a college.

VERMONT.

Middlebury. Founded in 1800, this Congregational college more than survived into the twentieth century.

Norwich University. Evolving from a preparatory institution, this semi–military school offered college level courses by the mid–1830s. Although it was nondenominational it received support from Episcopal sources in the 1840s and 1850s. It was coded as an Episcopal institution despite Tewksbury's classification of the college as Universalist.

University of Vermont. Despite its name, this institution was a Congregational affiliate and received little state support during the antebellum years. However, it did well from its founding in the 1800s and remained a significant school in New England's educational system.

VIRGINIA–WEST VIRGINIA.

Bethany. Located at Bethany, West Virginia, this Disciples college, with Alexander Campbell as its president, opened in the mid–1840s.

Emory–Henry. Opened in the very late 1830s, this Methodist institution at Glade Springs survived into the 1920s.

Hampden–Sidney. This Presbyterian college began in the years just after the American Revolution.

Marshall College. Chartered in 1858 and opened in 1859, this institution grew out of the old Marshall Academy. It was under the nominal control of West Virginia Methodists. It was not on Tewksbury's list of surviving colleges.

Randolph–Macon. Located at Boydton, Virginia, and opened in the mid–1830s, this Methodist school survived into the twentieth century.

Rector. This Baptist school was opened in the last years of the 1830s at Harrison, Taylor County, West Virginia. It was destroyed by fire in 1851.

Richmond College. Located at Richmond, Virginia, this Southern Baptist college began in the mid–1830s and survived into the twentieth century.

Roanoke College. Opened in the mid–1850s at Roanoke, this college was coded as a Lutheran institution although there were a few indications of early Presbyterian influence.

University of Virginia. Opening in 1825 at Charlottsville, this university was a state institution which survived the ravages of the Civil War. Its history has to be rewritten and young scholars should examine its fascinating policies during Reconstruction.

Washington. This was a Colonial college that received most of its support from Presbyterians. It survived into the twentieth century.

William and Mary. This Colonial college was under Episcopal guidance in the nineteenth century.

WISCONSIN.

Beliot. A Congregational–Presbyterian college, coded as Congregational in this study because of the relative weight of support, it opened in the late 1840s.

Carroll. Located at Waukesha, this was another joint Congregational–Presbyterian educational effort. Again, it was coded as Congregational because of the proportionate influence of each denomination. The school opened in the late 1850s but suspended operation in 1860. It was revived and lasted into the twentieth century.

Lawrence University. Opened in the mid–1850s under Methodist sponsorship, Lawrence survived into the twentieth century.

Racine College. This was an Episcopal school which began in the early 1850s. Tewksbury did not list it as surviving into the 1920s.

University of Wisconsin. A state institution, though deprived of funds before the Civil War, it began operations in the early 1850s.

Medical Schools in Operation 1800–1860, By States

ALABAMA.

Alabama Medical Institute. An alleopathic school located at Watampka, this small institution was founded in the mid–1840s and appears to have lasted less than five years.

Graffenberg Medical Institute. Founded and in operation in the mid–1850s, this school was located at Dadeville and Montgomery and taught regular medicine.

Medical College of Alabama. Located at Mobile, this alleopathic school was started in the late 1850s. It appears to have begun with capitalization funds of over one hundred thousand dollars from the state and the city.

CALIFORNIA.

University of the Pacific Medical Department. Opened in San Francisco in 1858 or 1859, this regular medical school was nominally associated with the University of the Pacific, a liberal arts college. It became Cooper Medical College.

CONNECTICUT.

Yale Medical School. Connected with Yale and located at New Haven, this institution taught regular medicine and received much aid from the state during its first decade of operation during the 1810s.

DISTRICT of COLUMBIA.

National Medical College/Columbian College Medical Department. Begun in the late 1820s with little aid from the parent college, this regular practice institution suspended operation in the late 1830s but rebounded in the 1840s.

Georgetown Medical. Nominally associated with the Catholic liberal arts college, this 1850s school taught regular medicine.

GEORGIA.

Atlanta Medical College. Founded in the mid–1850s to teach regular medicine, this school received significant aid from the state during its first decade.

Botanic Medical College/Thompsonian Medical College. Located at Barboursville, this Botanic school began operations in the early 1850s only to fail by the end of the decade.

Medical College of Georgia/Medical Academy of Georgia. Receiving a large amount of state financial aid to continue its operations, this regular medical school began in the late 1820s, perhaps not taking students until the 1830s, and was located at Augusta.

Oglethorpe Medical College. Located in Savannah and founded in the mid–1850s, this regular medical college failed by 1861.

Reformed Medical College of Georgia./Southern Botanic Medical College. Opened in the late 1830s, even this school received state aid. Although it survived until the Civil War, it did have to move from Union to Forsythe.

Savannah Medical College./Savannah Medical Institute. Opened in 1852, this regular school was located at Savannah.

Savannah Springs Medical College. Teaching alleopathic medicine, this very small school opened in 1856 to close within a few years. It was located in or near Savannah.

Middle County Medical College, Griffin. Incorporated in 1859, this projected school seems never to have opened—perhaps because of the war.

ILLINOIS.

Lind University Medical Department/Chicago Medical College/Northwestern Medical School. Located at Chicago and teaching regular medicine, it opened in 1859.

Chicago College of Pharmacy. This school was chartered in 1859 but was difficult to trace.

Franklin Medical College. Located at St. Charles, this regular school was open from the early 1840s to 1849 when it failed.

Hahneman Medical College and Hospital. A homeopathic school in Chicago, this institution may not have had students before 1860.

Medical Department of Illinois College. At least nominally associated with the Presbyterian college, this regular school opened in 1843 to close early in 1848.

Rush Medical College. Opened in the early 1840s in Chicago, this famous school taught regular medicine.

Rock Island Medical College. Along with a fascinating history and faculty this early 1840s school was open for a year or two in Illinois before it moved to Davenport, then Keokuk, Iowa. It was treated as a failure in Illinois.

IOWA.

Keokuk Medical College/College of Physicians and Surgeons of the Iowa University. This school, teaching regular medicine, was perhaps the example of a school in search of a home. It moved, within a space of two years, from Madison, Illinois, to Rock Island, then to Davenport, Iowa and Keokuk.

Iowa Medical College. Located at Keokuk and open in 1858, the school failed by 1860.

INDIANA.

Dr. Chapman's Practical School of Anatomy. Located at Davenport, this one–man school taught regular medicine. It lasted for a year or two during the 1850s.

Indiana Central Medical College. Connected with the Methodist's Asbury University, this regular school opened in the late 1840s and failed in the early fifties. It was located at Indianapolis.

Medical College of Evansville. This regular school opened in 1849 to close in the early 1850s. It was revived in the 1870s.

Laporte University Medical Department/Indiana Medical College. This alleopathic school at Laporte opened in 1842 and seems to have disappeared by 1856. It held some of its sessions at St. Charles, Illinois and Lafayette, Indiana before settling down at Laporte.

Modesa Medical Institute. Open in 1843, this school had no graduates.

New Albany Medical College. Chartered in 1833, this remained as the earliest example of an American diploma mill.

KENTUCKY.

American Reformed Medical Institute/Eclectic Medical College. Located at Louisville, this irregular school was open for about two years in the late 1840s.

Kentucky School of Medicine. Open in 1850 in Louisville, this school survived the Civil War and the trauma of Reconstruction. It was an alleopathic school.

Louisville Medical Institute/University of Louisville Medical Department. Abundantly subsidized by the city and the state, this 1837–38 institution became affiliated with the University in 1845.

Medical Department of Transylvania University. This famous school, associated with the university, was opened in the late 1810s with much support from local and state sources. It was a regular school and held its last antebellum class in 1858.

Transylvania School of Dental Surgery. Also located at Lexington, this school opened in the early 1850s.

LOUISIANA.

Medical College of Louisiana/University of Louisiana Medical Department. Receiving almost one hundred thousand dollars in state aid before the Civil War, experiencing a fascinating conflict between English and French doctors, and becoming perhaps the third largest medical school in the country, this regular institution, which was founded in the mid–1830s, was severely hurt by the Civil War.

New Orleans School of Medicine. A very modern and innovative regular practice school, it opened in the late 1850s only to be killed by the war.

MAINE.

Maine Medical/Bowdoin. Located at Brunswick, this alleopathic school, nominally associated with the college, opened in 1820.

Portland Medical and Preparatory Institute. This school was founded in the mid–1850s. It may have been innovative because descriptions of it drew a picture of a school attempting to be a direct substitute for the old medical apprenticeship. Its history should be explored.

MARYLAND.

Baltimore College of Dental Surgery. Apparently open in the 1840s, this school survived until at least the Civil War.

Maryland College of Pharmacy. Opened in the early 1840s, this Baltimore school suspended operations several times before the Civil War.

University of Maryland Medical School. Opened in the late 1800s and with somewhat tenuous status, this alleopathic school was located in Baltimore.

Washington University Medical School. Opened in the late 1820s, this regular practice school ended the 1850s in suspension. It was located in Baltimore and was revived after the Civil War.

MASSACHUSETTS.

Berkshire Medical Institute.(Williams College). As with the other New England colleges with allied professional schools, Williams' attempts to become a university in fact, if not in name, has not received enough attention from historians. This Pittsfield school received substantial aid from the state and, for unknown reasons, dropped its tie to Williams which had been established at its opening in the 1820s.

Boston Female Medical School/New England Female Medical. Open in 1852, this homeopathic school was helped by the state. It appears to have been known under both names.

Boylston Medical School. Located in Boston and opened in the late 1840s, this regular school probably served as a supplement to the Harvard medical lectures.

Massachusetts Medical College/Harvard Medical Department. Founded before the nineteenth century, this was a regular practice school which dissolved its formal ties with Harvard but remained closely associated with the university. It was located in Boston after 1810. Again, the pattern of early association with professional schools then disassociation has not been adequately explained.

Tremont Street Medical School. Founded in the late 1830s, this Boston alleopathic school served to give supplemental lectures. It eventually became Harvard's official medical summer school.

Worcester Medical School/New England Botanico Medical College. This was a Botanic institution which opened in the late 1840s and which failed in 1859.

MICHIGAN.

University of Michigan Medical School. This alleopathic school, which opened in 1850, was unique. It was the only medical school in Michigan during the period, it had free tuition and its professors were on salary rather than being dependent upon student fees. It was located at Ann Arbor and was supported by the state. There is no history which integrates the medical school with Tappan's policies in a realistic manner and there is little to explain how this political–educational coup developed.

MISSOURI.

Homeopathic Medical College of Missouri. Opened in 1859 in St. Louis, the school had to suspend operations during the Civil War.

Humboldt Institute. Located at St. Louis, this regular medical institute gave its instruction in German. It began in 1859.

Franklin Medical and Literary Institute. Open for a few years in St. Louis, the regular school closed before 1845.

Kemper College Medical Department/Medical Department Missouri State University/Medical Department Missouri Institute of Science/Missouri Medical College/McDowell's College. This group of medical teachers in search of a sponsor began their school in the early 1840s and were able to carry this proprietary institution into the twentieth century. It was an alleopathic school.

O'Fallan Preparatory Medical School. This was a regular school which began in St. Louis in 1859.

St. Louis College of Medicine and Natural Science/Humboldt Medical. Opened in St. Louis in 1855, the school may not have survived to the Civil War. It was a regular practice institution.

University of St. Louis Medical Department/St. Louis Medical College. Opened in the early 1840s, this regular school was also known as Pope's Medical College.

NEW HAMPSHIRE.

New Hampshire Medical School (Dartmouth). Opened in the 1810s and located in Hanover, this was a regular practice institution. It received some support directly from the state in its early years.

NEW YORK.

Albany Medical College. This alleopathic institution began in the mid–1830s with state financial assistance.

American College of Medical Science. Located at New York City, this regular school seems to have opened in 1858–59.

Bellevue Medical College Hospital. Chartered in 1861 and perhaps opened in that year, this New York City school was one of the first to link hospitals and teaching.

Botanic Medical College. Founded in 1836 and never receiving an official charter, this school failed in 1846.

University of Buffalo Medical Department. This alleopathic school began in the mid–1840s.

College of Pharmacy. Located at New York City and with a charter dating from 1829, this school opened in the early 1850s.

College of Physicians and Surgeons. Opened in the 1800s and with some affiliation with Columbia University, this regular practice school received much financial support from the state.

Central Medical College of New York/Rochester Eclectic. Opening in 1850, the school died by 1852.

College of Physicians and Surgeons: Western District/Fairfield Medical School. This "rural" medical school was sponsored by the state for some time after its opening in the 1810s. It was alleopathic and did manange to survive until the early 1840s.

Medical Department of Genessee College. Located at Lima, this regular practice school began in the early 1850s.

Long Island College of Medicine. Located in Brooklyn, this alleopathic school was chartered in 1858 and had its first graduate in 1860.

Geneva College Medical Institute/Hobart Free College Medical Institute. Receiving some state aid, this regular practice school opened in the mid–1830s at Geneva.

Homeopathic Medical College. Located at New York City, this school was chartered in 1859 and may have begun operation before the war.

Metropolitan Medical College. Although incorporated in the late 1840s, this New York City botanic school seems to have opened in the late 1850s.

New York School of Medicine. Located at New York City, this school may have been open from 1831 to 1833.

New York Medical College. This regular school began in the early 1850s. It had a very expensive building in New York City.

New York College of Dental Surgery. Opened in Syracuse in the early 1850s, the school appears to have survived to at least the Civil War.

University of New York Medical Faculty. This very rich school was opened in the 1830s and received aid from the state at critical moments.

New York Central Medical College/Randolph Medical Eclectic Institute/Medical School of Fredonia New York. Under these various names the school survived to at least the Civil War. It was open in the early 1840s.

Excelsior Medical College. Located at New York City and incorporated in 1857, this school disappeared from historical records. It was not in operation in 1879.

New York College of Veterinary Surgery. Chartered in 1857 and located at New York City, the school may not have opened before the war.

New York Homeopathic Medical College. This school was open in the 1850s.

New York Therapeutic College. This irregular practice school was open in New York City from 1857 to 1861.

Reformed Medical College of New York City. This was a botanico–eclectic institution without a charter. It was open in New York City from the mid–1820s to 1838.

New York Ophthalmic School. Founded in 1852, this New York City school may not have had the power to grant degrees and perhaps confined itself to lectures to interested physicians.

Rutgers Medical Faculty/Queens College Medical Department. This school was also associated with Geneva College. It opened in the early 1810s to face several suspensions and its final demise in the late 1830s. It was located in New York City and was alleopathic in orientation.

Syracuse Medical College. This school was organized in 1850 and died by 1855.

New York Infirmary for Women and Children. This institution, not included in the numbers of antebellum medical schools, taught some females before 1860 but did not grant degrees until 1868.

OHIO.

American Medical College of Ohio. Lasting about three years, this eclectic school was opened in Cincinnati in the mid–1850s without leaving much for interested historians. See Worthington Medical College.

Botanico Medical College of Ohio. Located at Columbus during its first years, then moving to Cincinnati, this school was opened in the mid–1830s only to disappear by the end of the 1840s. It may also have been called the Physiopathic College of Ohio.

Medical Department of Cincinnati College. This summer medical school was open in the late 1830s. It was alleopathic and it merged with the Medical College of Ohio in 1846.

Cincinnati College of Medicine and Surgery. An eclectic institution, it was open during the 1850s.

College of Medicine and Surgery. An institution by this name was located in Cincinnati and was organized in 1851.

Eclectic Medical College of Cincinnati. This school began long before it secured a charter. An eclectic institution, it was open in the late 1840s and merged with the Eclectic Medical Institute of Cincinnati in the late 1850s.

Reformed Medical College/Medical Department of Worthington College Eclectic Medical Institute of Cincinnati. This complex of schools seems to have begun as a Thomsonian institution at Worthington in the early 1830s and was the first chartered sectarian medical school in the

United States. Transfer was made to Cincinnati and the Eclectic Medical Institute in the early 1840s. The school seems to have survived to the Civil War.

Medical College of Ohio. A regular medical school, it began in the 1810s. It received significant state aid and would absorb Miami Medical College. It was located at Cincinnati.

Medical Institute of Cincinnati. This was an alleopathic school which was open from the late 1840s until the eve of the war.

Miami Medical College/Miami Medical College at Cincinnati. This school opened in the 1830s, closed, and was reborn twice.

Ohio College of Dental Surgery. Located at Cincinnati, this school began in the late 1840s.

Physio Medical College. This school was chartered in 1830 and is known to have been in operation in 1859–60 and during the 1880s.

University of Medicine and Surgery. This school was located at Cleveland and was in operation for some time before the war. Nothing but a name reference was found for the school and its tabulation as in operation during the 1850s rests, frankly, on historical intuition.

Western College of Homeopathic Medicine/Cleveland College of Homeopathy. This school was in operation by the early 1850s.

Western Reserve Medical Department/Cleveland Medical College. This was a regular school opened in the mid–1840s.

Willoughby Medical School/Starling Medical College. In operation in Willoughby in the early 1830s, the school moved to Columbus to become Starling in 1847. It was an alleopathic school.

Worthington Medical College. Chartered in 1833, this eclectic school became, in 1845, the Eclectic Medical Institute of Cincinnati.

PENNSYLVANIA.

(Like Ohio, this state's sectarian schools were mercurial, used confusing names, and are still difficult to segregate from each other)

Allentown Academy/North American Academy of Homoeopathic Healing Arts. This school was open for a few years in the mid–1840s.

American Medical College of Pennsylvania/Eclectic Medical College of Pennsylvania, Philadelphia/Eclectic Medical College of Philadelphia. Really two schools, this instituton began in the early 1850s to fail within a few years. It then merged with another school (that cannot be traced) to become the American Medical College in the late 1850s.

Female Medical College/Women's Medical College of Pennsylvania. An alleopathic institution for females, a revolutionary concept in its time, the school was located in Philadelphia during the 1850s.

Franklin Medical College. Located at Philadelphia, this regular school lasted for about three years during the mid–1840s.

Hahnemann Medical College/Washington Medical College of

Philadelphia. This school has a cloudy history before 1860. It may have been open during the 1840s and it may have continued into the 1850s.

Homeopathic Medical College of Pennsylvania. This Philadelphia school opened in the late 1840s.

Jefferson College Medical Department. Located at Philadelphia and opened in the mid–1820s, this regular practice school became one of the largest and most renowned medical schools of the era.

Pennsylvania College Medical Department. Opened in the late 1830s, this school survived until 1861. It was located in Philadelphia and was an alleopathic institution.

University of Pennsylvania Medical Department. Open throughout the era, this Colonial institution drew students from around the country.

Pennsylvania Medical University/Pennsylvania Medical College of Philadelphia/Ladies Institute of Pennsylvania Medical University. An eclectic school which also taught women, it opened in the early 1850s.

Philadelphia Dental College. This school was open during the early 1850s.

Philadelphia College of Medicine. This alleopathic school lasted until the late 1850s when it merged with the Pennsylvania College Medical Department.

Philadelphia College of Medicine and Surgery. Located at Philadelphia, this regular school was chartered in 1857. It is not certain that it opened before the Civil War.

Philadelphia Surgical Institute. Located at Philadelphia, this alleopathic school lasted for a few years in the late 1840s.

Philadelphia College of Pharmacy. Founded in the late 1820s, this small institution lasted until at least the Civil War.

Philadelphia Medical Institute. This school seems to have been open from 1822 to at least 1837. It did not have the power to grant degrees.

Philadelphia School of Anatomy. This regular practice school, which opened in the late 1830s, may never have received any type of charter.

Therapeutic Institute of Philadelphia. Open for a number of years in the 1830s, this seems to have been one of the state's first botanic schools.

RHODE ISLAND.

Brown University Medical School. This was an alleopathic school which was opened in the early 1820s. It was discontinued about 1840. The school was located at Providence.

SOUTH CAROLINA.

Medical College of Charleston/Medical College of South Carolina. A regular school which was founded in 1842 with municipal aid, it disappeared in the early 1840s and merged with the Medical College of the State of South Carolina.

Medical College of the State of South Carolina. Located at Charleston and the recipient of state economic aid, this alleopathic school was opened in the early 1830s.

Southern School of Practical Medicine. This was a regular practice institution at Charleston which may not have been able to open its doors. It was founded in the mid–1830s and disappeared before the end of the decade.

TENNESSEE.

Botanic Medical College of Memphis/Eclectic Medical Institute of Memphis. Founded in the late 1840s, this botanico–eclectic school seems to have survived the antebellum years.

East Tennessee University Medical Department. Located at Knoxville and founded in the mid–1850s, this was an alleopathic school.

Memphis Institute. An irregular practice school which was opened in the late 1840s, it failed within a few years.

Memphis Medical College. The regular practice this school taught did not protect it from several suspensions after its opening in the late 1840s.

University of Nashville Medical Department. Founded in 1850–51, this became one of the largest antebellum schools. It was alleopathic.

Shelby Medical College. Begun in the late 1850s, its Nashville location did not buffer it from failure in 1862.

VERMONT.

Castleton Medical College/Vermont Academy of Medicine. Originally having some connection with Middlebury College, this alleopathic school was founded in the late 1810s and was extinct by 1861.

Medical Society/University of Vermont. Opened in the mid–1820s, the school suspended operations from 1836 to 1853. It taught regular medicine and was located at Burlington.

Vermont Medical College/Woodstock Medical. Located at Woodstock and begun in the late 1820s, this regular practice school closed in the mid–1850s.

VIRGINIA.

Hampden–Sidney Medical Department/Virginia Medical College. Located at Richmond and opened in the late 1830s, this regular practice school received substantial economic support from both the city and the state in its early years. It ended its connection with the college in the mid–1850s.

Randolph–Macon Medical Department. Located at Worsham and the result of the evolution of the Mettauer Institute, this alleopathic school began in the late 1840s and died by 1855.

Richmond Association for Medical Instruction. This alleopathic school opened in the early 1860s.

Scientific and Eclectic Medical Institute of Virginia. Located at Richmond for one year, then at Petersburg, this eclectic school survived for only a few years after its opening in the mid–1840s.

University of Virginia Medical School. Located at Charlottesville and gaining appreciable aid from the state, this regular institution opened in the mid–1830s.

Winchester Medical College/College of Physicians of the Valley of Virginia. A regular practice institution at Winchester, the school received some state aid. It was opened in the late 1820s, went through several suspensions and recoveries only to be burned by Federal troops because its students had dissected the body of John Brown's brother.

Law Schools in Operation 1800–1860, By States

(This list is probably incomplete because there is evidence that legal instruction was given within many liberal arts colleges. However, much of that was probably preparatory.)

ALABAMA.

University of Alabama Law School. This attempt at professional training at Tuscalusa seems to have started in the 1840s and lasted to the early 1850s.

CONNECTICUT.

Litchfield Law School. This famous early attempt to formalize legal training was begun in 1798, reached its enrollment peak in the 1810s with 43 students then continued with low enrollments until the mid–1830s.

GEORGIA.

Law School. This Augusta proprietary school seems to have opened and closed in 1836–37. But it did have at least twenty students.

INDIANA.

Butler University/North West Christian University Law School. This college had an associated law school and graduates from it by 1858. Between 1858 and 1861 it had at least eighteen graduates.

Indiana Asbury (DePau) Law School. Located in Greencastle, this school may have begun as early as 1853 and it is known to have survived to the Civil War.

Indiana State University Law School. Located at Bloomington and formally opened in 1840, it probably did not have students until 1844. It prospered during the era.

KENTUCKY.

University of Louisville Law School. This school opened in 1847.

Transylvania Law School. Planned before the nineteenth century and receiving aid from the city of Lexington at various times, this famous school survived temporary closures and fires and managed to continue until the Civil War.

Western Military Institute Law School. Planned in the early 1850s, this Dannon Springs school may not have opened until just before the war.

LOUISIANA.

University of Louisiana Law School. Located in New Orleans and formally organized in 1848, this school appears to have begun operation before 1850 and may well have survived to the Civil War.

MARYLAND.

(A law school was open in Baltimore during the early 1830s and had twenty–two students. No other information about the school was found.)

MASSACHUSETTS.

Harvard University Law School. Becoming as expensive as the undergraduate college by the 1840s, this school began with more modest demands in 1816 and was formally established in 1818. Facing declining enrollments in the 1830s, it rebounded and by the 1850s, despite its high cost and full two–year course, had over one hundred forty student.

MICHIGAN.

University of Michigan Law School. The school opened in 1859–60 with a great national advertising campaign.

MINNESOTA.

Hamline College Law Department. Located at Red Wing, the school seems to have been in operation by the mid–1850s.

MISSISSIPPI.

University of Mississippi Law School. Located at Oxford and organized in 1854, this school may not have begun continuous operation until 1855.

NEW JERSEY.

College of New Jersey Law School. Begun in the 1840s, this school attracted few students until the late 1850s. It was in Princeton.

NEW YORK.

University of Albany Law School. Opened in 1851–52, this remnant of the great plans for a research oriented university grew rapidly and had over one hundred twenty students by the coming of the war.

Columbia College Law School. Located in New York City and opened in the late 1850s, this school had over sixty students in 1860.

Hamilton College Law School. Again, denominational "colleges" had ties to professional schools. In this case, however, the substantial donation it received to start a law school in the 1830s was not used until 1853–54.

New York University Law School. Begun in 1837–38, this school survived temporary closures in the late 1850s and continued into the postbellum era.

State and National Law School. Located in Poughkeepsie and planned in the 1840s, the school probably did not begin formal instruction until the early 1850s.

NORTH CAROLINA.

Law School, Mocksville. This school opened in 1841–42 and survived about one year.

Law School, Raleigh. This school opened in the early 1840s. There are some indications that it continued operation for some years but no enrollment information was available for the 1850s.

University of North Carolina Law School. Begun in 1849 in Chapel Hill with relatively low charges to students, this school was not able to enroll more than thirty students per term up to the Civil War.

OHIO.

Law School, Cincinnati. This school opened in the early 1830s with three faculty members but its enrollment level was low, twenty–five men, just before the Civil War.

PENNSYLVANIA.

Dickinson College Law School. Located at Carlisle and begun in the late 1830s, this school struggled along with less than twenty students until it was closed in the early 1850s.

LaFayette College Law School. Its Easton location probably kept its enrollments low from its beginnings in the late 1840s through to the Civil War.

Marshall College Law School. This school may have been founded in 1837. It is known that it was open with less than ten students per term in the 1840s just before it failed. It was in Mercersburg.

University of Pennsylvania, Law Department. This department began in 1850, charged a high fee and demanded two years of attendance. It grew quite rapidly to over seventy–five students by the late 1850s.

SOUTH CAROLINA.

Law School, Charleston. This institution probably began in 1831. It had approximately thirty students when it was closed in 1834.

TENNESSEE.

Cumberland University Law School. Located at Lebanon and in operation by 1849, this became one of the largest law schools in the country. By the late 1850s it had over one hundred ninety students.

University of Nashville Law School. This innovative school, which began in the early 1850s, had a three–year course with perhaps a forty week term.

TEXAS.

Baylor University Law School. This school opened in 1851 and had at least thirty–three students by 1859–60.

VIRGINIA.

Law School, Fredericksburg. This school began in the 1830s and closed about 1840.

University of Virginia Law School. Located in Charlottesville and founded in 1825 , this school had approximately one hundred twenty students in 1860.

William and Mary College Law School. Formal instruction in law may have begun as early as the mid–1800s, but 1825 seems to be the year of the founding of the permanent school. The school attracted few students and had less than thirty–five enrolled in 1859–60.

Law School, Stauton. A law school was opened in this town in the 1830s.

Theological Schools in Operation, 1800–1860, By States

ALABAMA.

Howard College Theological Department. This was opened in Marion in the early 1850s.

CONNECTICUT.

Theological Institute of Connecticut. Located at East Windsor, this school was founded in the mid–1830s and lasted to at least the Civil War.

Yale College Theological Department. Founded in 1822 at New Haven, this school began with a three–year term. For as yet unexplained reasons, the enrollments diminished from close to one hundred fifty–five in the 1830s to approximately twenty in 1859–60.

GEORGIA.

Mercer College Theological Department. Located at Penfield, this department seems to have been founded in 1833 and to have survived the era with a small number of students.

ILLINOIS.

Alton Theological Seminary. This Baptist seminary in Upper Alton was founded in 1835, then merged with Shurtleff College.

Garrett Bible Institute. Established in 1854 and located at Evanston, this school was associated with the Methodists.

Shurtleff College Theological Department. This department was open from the mid to late 1840s. It was unable to attract significant numbers of students.

INDIANA.

Hanover Seminary/New Albany Theological School/Indiana Theological Seminary. (1857, Chicago, Illinois). Begun in the early 1830s, this school struggled along with some ten to fifteen students.

IOWA.

German Presbyterian Theological School of the Northwest. This seems to have been regarded as a private school until the Civil War and it may not have been a true theological seminary. It was located in Dubuque.

KENTUCKY.

Danville Theological Seminary. Opening in 1853, this famous school attracted increasing numbers of students.

Western Baptist Theological Seminary–Institute. In Georgetown, then Covington, this school began in 1840, survived a fire, and lasted through the period. It may have offered a scientific course within the seminary.

MAINE.

Bangor Theological Seminary. In Hampden, 1816–19, then Bangor, this prosperous school continued through to the Civil War with approximately forty students per term.

MASSACHUSETTS.

Andover Theological Seminary. Founded before the nineteenth century, this rich seminary ended the period with about forty–five students. Although it had high admission standards, it charged no tuition and provided generous support to needy students.

Harvard Theological School/Theological School, Cambridge. Founded in 1816 and in operation by at least 1824, the school had less than twenty–five students per term in the 1850s. It offered instruction in the German language, reflecting its growing concern for modern theological scholarship.

Massachusetts Episcopal Seminary. Begun in Cambridge in the early 1830s, the school failed and merged with the Harvard Seminary.

Theological Seminary–Institution. This seminary in Newton began in the mid–1820s and continued to the Civil War with approximately thirty–three students per term.

MICHIGAN.

Kalamazoo Theological Seminary. This tuition–free seminary was founded in 1849–50 and ended the era with perhaps ten students per term.

NEW HAMPSHIRE.

Academic and Theological Institute. (New Hampton then Fairfax, Vermont) This may have been an all–purpose institution and seems to have prepared few men directly for the Baptist ministry. It was open by the late 1820s, moved to Vermont in the 1850s, and had about thirty ministry–bound students in 1860.

Gilmanton Theological Seminary. Founded in 1833, this school continued on to the Civil War with few students.

Methodist General Biblical Institution. Although many very early founding dates were given for this school at Concord, it seems to have begun continuous operation in the 1850s and enrolled approximately thirty–five students per year.

NEW JERSEY.

Burlington Theological Department. This seminary began with the college in 1848.

Rutgers Theological Seminary. Located in New Brunswick and known to be in operation as a separate department by the early 1810s, this school ended the period with an enrollment of fifty students.

Theological Seminary of the Presbyterian Church, United States. With low tuitions (free in many cases) as well as subsidies to many students, this became one of the largest seminaries in the country. It had over one hundred fifty students per term at its Princeton campus in the 1850s. It began as a separate school in the early 1810s.

NEW YORK.

Theological Institution of the Episcopal Church. Located at New York City and organized in 1817–18, the seminary opened for students in the early 1820s. Its free–tuition policy attracted sixty students in 1859–60.

Hamilton Literary and Theological Institution. Begun in 1819–20, this school ended the period with perhaps thirty students.

Hartwick Seminary. Opened in 1819, this school hobbled along with little funding and less than ten students a year.

St. Lawrence University Theological Department/Canton Theological Seminary. This seminary began in 1858. It was a Universalist institution.

Hobart Theological Seminary. The dates of the formal opening of this school are unclear but it is known that some ten students were enrolled in the early 1850s.

Rochester Theological Seminary. Offering free tuition and other costs, this department was able to enroll close to forty men it is tenth year, 1859–60.

St. Joseph's Theological Seminary. Located at Fordham, this seminary, one of the few Catholic schools regarded as a true seminary by contemporaries, lasted for only a few years after its founding in 1846.

Theological Seminary Associate Reformed Church. Located at Newburgh, the school seems to have opened in 1836 and to have survived to the Civil War when it had approximately twelve students.

Theological Seminary of Auburn. Begun in 1821, this school prospered in its early years. But in 1859–60 it had twenty students.

Union Theological Seminary. Founded at New York City in 1836, this very wealthy school ended the period with over one hundred students.

OHIO.

Theological Seminary Associate Reformed Church. Located at Oxford until it moved to Monmouth, Illinois in the late 1850s, this remained a poor and perhaps poorly attended seminary.

Ohio Wesleyan Bible Department. This department seems to have begun in the late 1840s and survived to the war. It was located in Delaware, Ohio.

Capital University Theological Department/German Evangelical Lutheran Seminary. Moving to Columbia from an unknown location in 1831, this seminary had very few students by the coming of the war.

Fairmont Theological Institution. Located in Cincinnati and in operation by 1853, this school had fifteen students in 1860.

Granville Theological Department. This Baptist school was founded in 1832. In 1854 it had only eight students.

Heidelberg College Theological Department. This seminary began in 1850–51 and ended the era with less than ten students.

Kenyon Theological Department. Begun in 1826, it had twenty-one students in 1859–60.

Lane Seminary. Opened in 1829 in Cincinnati, this school suffered an enrollment decline from perhaps sixty-five in the mid-1840s to thirty-five students in 1860–61.

Oberlin College Theological Department. Open in 1833, this seminary also faced enrollment declines after the early 1840s. The number of students went from sixty-five to twenty-one.

Western Reserve Theological Department. Located at Hudson and opening in the early 1830s, this department closed in 1852.

Wittenberg Theological. Located at Springfield and open to students in the mid-1840s, this school never enrolled more than ten students.

PENNSYLVANIA.

Bucknell Theological Department. Opened in 1850–51 at Lewisburg, this department enrolled less than ten students during the decade.

Cannonsberg Theological Department. Although begun in 1794, this school remained poor and enrolled perhaps thirty students by the coming of the war. It migrated from Pennsylvania to Xenia, Ohio.

German Reformed Theological Institution. Moving from Carlisle to Mercersburg after it had begun in York in 1825, this school enrolled about twenty students per year throughout its antbellum history.

Marshall College Theological Department. Located at Mercerburg and opened in the early 1850s, this school enrolled less than twenty students.

Theological Seminary at Pittsburgh. With manual labor included in its program during its first years, this school's history from the mid-1820s was marked by enrollments of approximately thirty students.

Western Theological Seminary at Allegheny. Beginning in the late 1820s, this seminary prospered and was well endowed by the 1850s. It grew from having twenty to one hundred fifty students per term.

Western Theological Seminary at Meadville. Founded in 1844, this institution declined from thirty to twenty students a semester during the 1850s.

Seminary of the Lutheran Church. Located at Gettysburg and begun in 1825, this school had perhaps twenty-five students in 1859–60.

Theological Seminary, Reformed Presbyterian. Located at Philadelphia, this school opened in 1854 with thirteen students.

SOUTH CAROLINA.

Furman Theological. This institution was open by the mid-1830s and, as with many other seminaries, it faced enrollment declines during the 1850s as enrollments dropped from ten to five students a term.

Lexington Theological. Open in the late 1830s, this school survived to the war but with few students.

Southern Theological Seminary. Open in the late 1820s in Columbia, this school doubled its enrollments to over forty in 1859–60.

TENNESSEE.

Cumberland University Theological Department. This department may have opened in the mid–1850s at Lebanon.

Southwest Theological Seminary. Begun in the early 1820s, this school failed in the late 1840s and merged with Maryville College.

VIRGINIA.

Episcopal Theological School of Virginia. Open in the late 1820s in Fairfax County, this school maintained enrollments of between thirty–five and fifty students.

Union Theological Seminary. Located at Hampden–Sidney and opened in 1824, this school's enrollments reached thirty–six in 1859–60.

Virginia Baptist Seminary. Founded in 1832 at Richmond, this school grew to over sixty students in 1854.

List of Normal Schools in Operation
Before the Civil War, By States

(This list is incomplete because so many private colleges maintained teachers' courses during the antebellum period and some schools may have been the equivalent of the private normal schools of the postbellum era. This list is confined to government–supported schools and programs and a few private courses which were repeatedly cited as normal schools by contemporaries.)

CONNNECTICUT.

New Britain Normal School. Founded 1849.

ILLINOIS.

Chicago Normal, 1856.

Illinois State Normal. This school was located at Bloomington but the exact date of its opening could not be determined.

INDIANA.

Indiana University Teachers'. This institution was open in the 1850s.

MASSACHUSETTS.

Bridgewater. Founded 1840.

Framingham. Founded 1836.

Girl's, Boston. Founded 1852.

Salem. Founded 1854.

Westfield. Founded 1830.

MICHIGAN.

Ypsilanti. Founded 1852.

MISSOURI.

St. Louis City Normal School. Founded 1857.

NEW JERSEY.

Farnum Preparatory–Normal School. This school was open in the 1850s.

State Normal, 1856.

NEW YORK.

Albany Normal. Founded 1844.

Oswego Normal. Founded 1861.

PENNSYLVANIA.

Girl's Philadelphia. Founded 1841.

Millersville Normal. Founded 1859.

Edenboro Normal. Founded 1861(?).

RHODE ISLAND.

Bristol Normal.

OHIO.
Kenyon College Teachers Course.
Miami University Teachers Course.
Muskingum College Teachers Course.
Oberlin Teachers Program.

List of Women's Colleges in Operation
Before the Civil War

(This list contains the names of institutions which appear to have been regarded as offering a level of instruction close to that at men's colleges. The list should be regarded as tentative and incomplete because although there are already several major works on early women's education, it will take a massive study to compile complete lists of the different types of women's institutions during the era. A major investigation is needed to differentiate women's colleges from the other types of schools among the five hundred claimed to exist by the 1860 Census.)

ALABAMA.

Masonic University. Located at Selma, this school was chartered in 1843 and opened in 1847.

GEORGIA.

Wesleyan Female College. Located at Macon, this school seems to have opened in 1851.

ILLINOIS.

Knox Female College. This institution began in the 1840s.

MICHIGAN.

Albion College. This school was open in the 1840s and 1850s.

Hillsdale. This school was open as a "college" in the 1850s.

Kalamazoo. This was also open in the 1850s.

MISSOURI.

Centenary. This female college was another 1850s creation.

Christian University. Again, it began in the 1850s as females received more and more benefits from the new economic era.

Mount Pleasant. This was another 1850s institution.

OHIO.

Heidelberg Female Department. This was opened in the 1850s.

Oberlin College. Female instruction began in the 1830s and became equal to that offered to males.

Otterbein Female. This school opened as a "college" in the 1850s.

WISCONSIN.

Lawrence University Female Department. This school also began in the 1850s.

Milwaukee Female. The 1850s also generated this school.

List of Military Schools and Technical Schools and Departments in Operation Before the Civil War

Amherst College Science Department. Founded 1852–53.

Centre College Science Department, Danville, Kentucky. Founded 1853.

The Citadel, South Carolina.

Columbian College Science Department, Washington, D.C. Founded 1855.

Cumberland University Engineering Department, Lebanon, Tennessee.

Dartmouth College, Chandler Scientific School. Founded 1851–3.

Delaware College Science Department. Founded 1852.

Farmer's College, Ohio. Founded in 1848, some scientific and practical instruction seems to have been offered by this reformist institution.

Farmers High School (Pennsylvania State).

Georgia Military Institute.

Hamilton College, New York, Engineering–Science Department. This department seems to have been open from 1843 to the early 1850s.

Hanover College, Indiana, Science Department.

Harvard College (Lawrence Scientific School).

Iberia College, Ohio. This school had a farmers course and a rudimentary practical technology program.

Iowa State Agricultural and Mechanical Arts College. Founded 1859.

Lawrence University Engineering Department. Founded in 1858.

Maryland Agricultural College. Some questions remain as to how much science and agriculture this school taught before the Civil War.

University of Michigan Chemistry and Agricultural Departments.

Michigan Agricultural College.

Michigan College of Mining and Technology, Houghton. Founded in 1855, this school was impossible to trace in the antebellum period. It is not certain that it functioned before the Civil War.

New York Central College.

New York University Chemistry and Civil Engineering Departments.

Norwich University, Vermont.

Polytechnic College, Philadelphia, Pennsylvania. This school needs intensive historical investigation.

Rensselaer Institute, Troy, New York.

Shurtleff College Science Department.

U.S. Military Academy.

U.S. Naval Academy.

Western Military Institute, Kentucky.

APPENDIX B

NonCollegiate Institutions

(This list contains the names and very brief notes on institutions which one or more sources mentioned as operating colleges in the period 1800–1860. The evidence gathered in this study indicated that these schools were not male or coeducational colleges, according to contemporary standards.)

(To the immediate right of the name of each of the institutions are either two capital letters or astericks. Y in the first position indicates that the institution was listed as operating in 1869–70 while the second letter indicates whether or not it was listed in major compendia during the years 1900–1907. Astericks indicate that a search was not applicable. A question mark signifies that some question remained as to whether the college in question should be considered as having been correctly identified. In most cases it was found that the "college" was either an academy or a girls' school before the Civil War.)

Adrain, Michigan.YY A Methodist academy.

Albany, New York. NN This projected science school never opened.

Albany, Oregon. NY No trace was found of this twentieth century school.

Albion, Michigan. YY Chartered in 1843, it was a female "college".

Albany Manual Labor College, Athen County, Ohio. NN No trace was found of this school. The reference may have been to an established institution.

Albright, Pennsylvania. NY This German Evangelical female school did not conduct college work until 1907.

Alcorn, Rodney, Mississippi. NN No trace was found of this school.

Almira, Illinois. NN This Baptist institution may have opened in 1857 .but it was a female school.

Allegheny College, West Virginia. NN This Baptist academy opened in 1860 and closed in 1861.

American School of Mines. NN Chartered in 1858, it never opened.

Amity College, Iowa. YY Its college charter was probably issued in the 1870s and the 1855 charter was not used for college work.

Ammasa College, Texas. NN Founded in 1850, there is no evidence of college work.

Andalusia College, Pennsylvania. YN Episcopal and chartered in 1860, it did not open until 1870.
Andrew College, Cuthbert, Georgia. NN Southern Methodist and founded in 1854, this was a female "college".
Arkansas College, Fayette, Arkansas. NN This institution was founded well before the Civil War and was burned by Confederate forces in 1862. Although it had a large student population and claimed a few graduates it was not categorized as a college because of much evidence, including the state reports on education in the census of 1860.
Arkansas College, Batesville, Arkansas. NY This Presbyterian college was not in operation until 1872–73.
Arcadia College, Arcadia, Missouri. NN With a claim to an 1843 beginning, this Southern Methodist school probably survived as an academy.
Arkansas Synodical College, Arkdelphia, Arkansas. NN Cited as open before the war and chartered in 1860, this school was found to have operated at the preparatory level.
Asbury College, Baltimore, Maryland. NN This fascinating Methodist enterprise existed in Baltimore between 1816 and, it appears, the late 1820s. It would have been classified as a college except that it was found to have a junior class consisting of 12 year olds.
Auburn, New York. NN Founded in 1826, this was a female school.
Augustana, Richland, Illinois. YY Started at Paxton by Evangelical Lutherans in 1860, it may have begun some college work in the 1870s.
Augustana, Rock Island, Illinois. NY This may have been Augustana, above.
Austin, Effingham, Illinois. NY No trace was found during the antebellum era.
Avery, Pennsylvania. NN This school was chartered in 1849 but no indication of college work was found. It died in 1873.
Augusta, Atlanta, Georgia. NN No trace was found of this school.

Baker, Baldwin City, Kansas. YY This Methodist school opened in 1857 and was chartered in 1858, but it was found to be an academy.
Baltimore City College, Baltimore, Maryland. NY This institution was chartered in 1839 but did not come into full operation until the 1850s. It was known as Central High School and its graduates were much younger than 18 years old.
Bates, Lewiston, Maine. YY Chartered in 1862–63, Bates did not operate as a college before the war.
Beaver, Pennsylvania. NN This was a female school during the era and had many denominational sponsors and founding dates.
Beaver Dam, Wisconsin. ** See Wayland University.

Bellefontaine, Ohio. NN An institution with this name was chartered before 1860, but no trace was found.
Benzonia, Michigan. NN This Congregational school appears to have received its charter in the 1890s.
Berea, Kentucky. YY. This famous and innovate school was an academy before the Civil War. It received a charter in 1865. The school was linked to frontier Presbyterianism. This institution deserves a complete history because of its alternative policies and approaches in the nineteenth and twentieth centuries.
Bessie–Tift, Tennessee. NN This female college was known as Forsythe Collegiate Institute before the war. It was Baptist and opened in 1847.
Bethel, Cuthbert, Georgia. NN This was a female school.
Bethel, Kansas. NN No trace was found of this school.
Bethel, Oregon. NN This Disciples school, chartered in 1856, appears to have been an academy and to have failed in 1860.
Bethel, Tennessee. NY In 1907 this school claimed a founding date of 1850, but no trace was found. It was a Cumberland Presbyterian institution.
Bethany, Kansas. *N This school did not attain college status until 1881.
Bethany, Oregon. NN The reference to this school may have been a misprint for Bethel.
Beverly, Ohio. NN Chartered before 1861 and open in the mid–1840s, this Cumberland Presbyterian school was probably an academy.
Blackburn, Carlinsville, Illinois. NY Presbyterian and chartered in 1861, this was a theological training school before the war.
Bloomington, Tennessee. NN The reference to this school may have contained a misprint. The reference was probably to Indiana because no trace was found for such a Tennessee school.
Bluemont Central, Kansas. NN Chartered in 1858 and motivated by a desire to found a farmers and teachers college, the school was ended by the chaos of Bleeding Kansas. However, it has been claimed as a precursor of Kansas State.
Blue Mountain, Mississippi. NN This was a female school.
Bordentown, New Jersey. YN No trace was found of this female school in the 1850s or 1860s.
Boromeo, Pikesville, Maryland. Y* This Catholic Diocesan school, chartered in 1860, seems to have been a prep school.
Bowdon Collegiate Institute, Atlanta, Georgia. YY Although chartered in 1857 Bowdon did not begin to call itself a college until the 1870s.
Boonville, Missouri. NN Listed as Cumberland Presbyterian and chartered in 1853, it could not be traced.
Boston College, Boston, Massachusetts. YY This Catholic Jesuit college was chartered in 1863 but did not begin full operations until the 1870s.

Brooklyn Polytechnic, New York. YN This technical training school, which was chartered in 1855, seems not to have been considered as a "college". It appears to have had a fascinating history and deserves historical attention.
Brockway College, Ripon, Wisconsin. NN Open in 1853–54, this school must have been an academy.
Brockport College, New York. NN Chartered in 1830, it was never organized.
Brookville College, Indiana. YN The claims to an 1849 beginning for this Methodist school were never substantiated.
Buchanon, Troy, Missouri. NN No trace was found of this institution.
Buffalo, University of New York. NN No indication was found of it ever being in operation.
Burritt, Spencer, Tennessee. NY Although chartered in 1848 and open during the 1850s, there is no evidence of this Christian school operating as a college.
University of Chicago, Chicago, Illinois. YY Although planned in 1859, this famous school did not begin before the Civil War.
University of California, Berkeley, California. YY Before the Civil War it was a preparatory school and was denominationally sponsored.
Campbell, Missouri. NN Chartered in 1846–47, it appears to have never operated as a college.
Cambridge, Ohio. NN Although an institution with this name was chartered before 1860, no trace was found of such a college.
Camden Point College, Missouri. NN This military and female academy was chartered in 1856–57 by the Disciples.
Cane Hill, Arkansas. NN With Cumberland Presbyterian support and open from 1835 to the Civil War, this institution focused upon preparation for the ministry. Although some college level work may have been done by its students, it might not have had a charter. The suspicion that it was not regarded as a college was supported by the 1860 census.
Canton College, Illinois. NN No trace was found of this 1863 chartered school.
Canton Seminary, Missouri. ** See Christian University.
Carthage College, Illinois. YN This Lutheran school did not begin until the 1870s.
Carthage, Wisconsin. NN No trace was found of such a college.
Carson–Newman, Jefferson City, Tennessee. NY Chartered in 1851 as Mossy Creek Academy, this Southern Baptist school did not offer college level work until after the Civil War.
Catawba, North Carolina. NY This German Reformed school was not regarded as a college before the war.

Carleton, Farmington, Missouri. NY The claim of an 1854 beginning was not substantiated.
Cayuga College, New York. NN The proposed charter for this school was refused and it never opened.
Chapill, Texas. NN Founded in 1849, this Presbyterian school seems to have been for females and preparatory education.
Cherokee College, Casville, Georgia. YN The Baptists' claim of an 1855 opening was not substantiated.
Centerville, Indiana. NN No trace was found of such a college.
Chapel Hill(s), Missouri. NN This Cumberland Presbyterian school was chartered in 1848–49 and was open by at least 1852. However, it was not a college during the period.
Chapel Hill College, Dangerfield, Texas. NN Founded in 1850 and known to have been open in 1853, this appears to have been an academy.
Charles College, Virginia. NN Founded in 1839 and in operation in the mid–1840s, this Methodist school, which may not have been in Virginia, could not be traced as a college.
Chowan, North Carolina. NY This was a Baptist female college.
Christian University, Waco, Texas. NY(?) Founded in 1853 by Methodists, this school might have been what was called Waco University before the Civil War. There was no evidence of antebellum college work.
Christian University, Canton, Missouri. NY(?) This Christian school claimed an 1853 opening and an 1856 charter, but this study and A.F. West's work found it to be an academy.
Christian College, Canton, Missouri. NY This was a Christian female school.
Christian Brothers, St. Louis, Missouri. YY Although founded in 1851 and chartered in 1859, it was not a college during the era.
Christian Brothers College–University, St. Louis, Missouri. YN This 1857 school was operating at the academy level before the war.
Cecil, Elizabethtown, Kentucky. NN This lay Catholic school was founded in 1860 and chartered in 1867. It appears to have operated as an academy.
Central University, Kentucky. NY This school probably did not open as a college until 1874.
Central College, Fayette, Missouri. NY This may have been a reorganized version of the other school at Fayette.
Central Normal, Danville, Indiana. NN This Episcopal preparatory and normal school opened in 1839. It appears to be a fine example of what later became the trend towards parochial normal schools.
Central High School, Philadelphia, Pennsylvania. NN This school was

chartered with, it appears, the power to grant degrees in 1839, but it never claimed to be a college.

Central College, Ohio. NN This untraceable school was chartered at Blendon before 1860.

Central Pennsylvania College, Pennsylvania. NN Founded in 1855, it never appeared on college lists.

Central University, Tennessee. YN Although chartered before the war, only its medical school, Shelby, came into operation. It had Methodist support.

Cleveland University, Ohio. NN Founded in 1852 and chartered before the Civil War, this school left no evidence of college level work.

Clark College, Missouri. No trace of this 1856–57 chartered school was found.

Clark College, Iowa. ** See Mt. St. Joseph's.

Classical Manual Labor College, Covington, Georgia. NN Founded in 1835, this Methodist school was open in the mid–1840s but was not regarded as a college.

Clinton, Missouri. NY(?) In 1902 it was classified as a female school. No other trace was found.

Clinton College, New York. NN Chartered in 1849, it was never organized.

Clinton, Tennessee. NN This seems to have been a short–lived academy which opened in the early 1850s.

Columbus University, Pennsylvania. NN Chartered in 1858, this Presbyterian school died in 1870. See, Kittaning College.

College Hill College, York, Pennsylvania. NN In 1860 this school was listed as a Methodist academy and it did not have a college charter.

College Temple, Newnan, Georgia. NN This was a female school of the 1850s.

Collegiate Institute of Learning of the Southwest, Missouri. NN No trace of this Cumberland Presbyterian school, supposedly founded in 1855, was encountered.

College of St. Andrew, Van Buren, Arkansas. NN This was an academy which was founded in 1850 and which is known to have been open in 1851.

Collegiate Institute, Ohio. NN Chartered as a college before 1860, it may never have opened as such.

Colorado College, Columbus, Texas. YN Although the Lutherans claimed it began in 1857, other sources stated that it was not chartered and that it did not operate as a college.

Cokesbury College, Baltimore, Maryland. NN This Methodist school was open between 1784 and 1796.

College of Rapides, North Carolina. NN Founded in 1819, it was an academy.
Cokesbury Manual Labor School, South Carolina. NN Founded in 1839, this school left no trace of college work.
Columbia Institute, Tennesse. NN This was an Epsicopal female school that opened in the late 1840s.
Coe College–Cedar Rapids Collegiate Institute, Iowa. NN This was a Presbyterian supported academy.
Columbus Institute, Columbus Missisippi. NN No evidence of pre–war college level work was found.
Columbia College, Eugene City, Oregon. NN Cumberland Presbyterian and opened in 1855–56 with a charter, this school closed in 1860 because of a fire. It appears that it never quite began college work.
Concordia, Fort Wayne, Indiana. YY This German Lutheran school was chartered in 1839. It was primarily a German language theological preparatory school.
Concordia, St. Louis, Missouri. NN Although the New York state Cenus of the 1850s called it a college, it was a theological school.
Concordia, Milwaukee, Wisconsin. YN This was a female college.
Concordia, New York. NN This school could not be traced.
Concord, Statesville, North Carolina. NN No evidence was found indicating that the Presbyterians operated this school as a college.
Concordia, Conover, North Carolina. NN No trace of this institution was found.
Corvallis College, Oregon. NN This nondenominational school was chartered in 1857–58 and died in 1860. It probably never operated as a college.
Cox, College Park, Georgia. NN This school was in operation in 1842 but no other trace was found.
Culver–Stockton, Missouri. ** See, Christian University.
Davenport, Griswald, Iowa. YN Opened in 1859, this Episcopalian school was an academy.
Davenport, Lenoir, North Carolina. YN This was an 1857 academy.
Dayton University–St. Mary's Institute, Ohio. NN Catholic and open in 1850, this school was not regarded as a college before the war.
Danville College, Indiana. NN A school with this name was in operation in 1858–59 but was probably an academy.
Defiance, Ohio. NY In 1902 the Christians claimed an 1850 founding date, but no trace was found of this school before the Civil War.
DeKalb (Institute), Red River County, Texas. NN This school received a charter and state aid in 1838 but there is no evidence that it opened or that it operated as a college.

Des Moines, Iowa. NY Although it had advocates who claimed that it was founded in 1850, this school did not receive a charter until 1865 and there is no indication that it was an antebellum college.
Des Peres (Institute), Missouri. NN Aided by the Cumberland Presbyterians and perhaps receiving a full charter in 1855, it seems to have been an academy.
Davenport Manual Labor, Iowa. NN Chartered in 1838, this school was never organized as a college.
De Vaux, Suspension Bridge, New York. YN The claim that this Episcopalian school began in 1857 was not substantiated.
Drury, Springfield, Missouri. NY This Congregational school did not become a college until 1873.
Drake–Des Moines, Iowa. NY This institution, sponsored by the Christians, had a tangled history and did not operate as a college before the war.
Dubuque–Waverly–Wartburg, Iowa. N(?)* This complex of institutions began as a normal school and as a German Lutheran theological seminary.

Eastern Texas University, St. Augustine, Texas. NN Open in the 1840s and 1850s, this nondenominational school failed, then became a Masonic "college". See, also, St. Augustine University.
East Alabama Male College, Auburn, Albama. NN This academy is known to have been open between 1856 and 1861.
East Florida Seminary, Ocala, Florida. NY This early 1850s school, despite state and local support, remained an academy and normal school to at least the 1870s.
East Tennessee Memorial–Grant Memorial, Athens, Tennessee. YY This Methodist school probably did not begin college work until 1866.
Eaton College, Ohio. NN No trace of this school was found.
Edinburg, Ohio. NN Its 1854–55 charter did not lead to its opening.
Elden, Missouri. NN Although chartered as a college before 1860, no evidence of the organization of a college was found.
Eleutherian, Lancaster, Indiana. NN This was a very radical school because it opened as coeducational and as racially integrated in 1849. However, its program and Baptist support did not lead to college work.
Elmira–Auburn, New York. YY This was a female school which later became famous.
Emminence, Kentucky. NN This institution started as a high school in 1855 and lasted into the 1870s as such.
Episcopal Theological Seminary and Classical School, Raleigh, North Carolina. NN This school was founded in 1832 and died in 1834.
Ewing, Knoxville, Illinois. NY This 1900s Baptist school was founded in 1867.

Ewing, Texas. NN This appears to have been an 1852 Presbyterian academy.

Fairmont College, Ohio. NN This was a preparatory school.

Floral Hill, Missouri. NN Although chartered in 1859–60 it appears to have confined itself to being an academy.

Florida State College. NY Its claim to an 1857 founding date is not justified. See, East Florida Seminary.

Flushing College, New York. NN This proposed college was refused a charter in 1845.

Fort Meigs University, Ohio. NN Its pre–Civil War charter did not lead to the establishment of a college.

Fort Wayne, Indiana. YY In 1846 this was a Methodist female school. It opened a male department in 1855 but seems to have remained a prep school.

Fort Wayne, Indiana. N* This projected German Luthern school never opened.

Franklin Collegiate Institute, Louisiana. YN There was no evidence to substantiate the claim that this school began as a college.

Franklin Literary and Medical, Missouri. NN Although chartered in 1848–49, the liberal arts school never seems to have opened.

Franciscan College and Convent, Allegheny, New York. NN No trace of this school was found.

Franklin College, Baltimore County, Maryland. NN This proposed school, chartered in 1834, never opened.

Frederick College, Maryland. NY Although dating from 1799, chartered as a college in 1830 and listed as a college by the 1850 census, it seems to have been regarded as a high school.

Gale College, Illinois. NN The reference to this school was probably a misprint.

Gale College, Wisconsin. YY This Methodist institution was chartered in 1854 but did not even obtain buildings until 1866.

Galveston Univerisity, Texas. NN This school opened in 1840 and was chartered in 1841. There is no evidence of college work.

Gardiner, Maine. NN No trace was found of this school.

German College of Columbus, Ohio. NN This might be another name for or be institutionally related to Baldwin–Wallace College. It was chartered before 1860, but no trace of it was found.

German College, Mt. Pleasant, Iowa. NN No institution under this name was identified, but the title might be one of the common names for Iowa Wesleyan.

German Evangelical, Warren, Missouri. NN Chartered in 1854–55, it was a normal school, at most.

Gethsemeni, Kentucky. NN This Trappist school was never chartered and there is no evidence of college work.

Giles, Tennessee. NN Although open in the 1850s, it was not regarded as a college.

Glendale, Ohio. YN In 1870 this female school claimed it was founded in 1854.

Girard, Pennsylvania. YY This nondenominational school in Philadelphia operated as an academy during the period.

Glenwood (Collegiate Institute) New Jersey. YN No trace of this school was found.

Godfrey–Monticello, Illinois. NN The only evidence on this school was that it was a female school in 1836.

Gonzales, Texas. NN Its 1860–61 charter did not lead to the opening of a college.

Goshen, Missouri. NN No trace of this college, which was chartered in 1860–61, was found.

Guilford, North Carolina. YY This 1833 Friends school operated as an academy before the war.

Grand River–Carthage, Trenton, Missouri. N(?)N Chartered in 1850–51 and known to have been in operation in 1854–55, this Christian school operated as an academy.

Greenfield, Missouri. NN This Cumberland Presbyterian school, chartered in 1852–53 probably was an academy.

Greensboro, Alabama. ** See, Southern University.

Greensboro, North Carolina. YN Founded in 1832, this was a Methodist female school.

Gustavus–Adolphus College, Minnesota. YN This Luthern school was founded in 1826 at St. Peter. It did not operate as a college.

Haverfordwest College. NN Only one reference to this school was noted and no trace of such a school was found.

Hamilton, Kentucky. NN No trace was found of such a college.

Hannable(?), Missouri. NN Chartered in 1856–57 and linked to the Methodists, it was a female school.

Henry College. NN This school without a known location was never found.

Hanover, Ohio. NN This may have been a reference to the Illinois College.

Hope, Michigan. NY This school was not chartered until 1865 and had its first graduate in 1869.

Hartford Collegiate Institute, Kansas. YN This was an 1860 Methodist school which conducted academy work.

Hedding, Iowa. NN Chartered in 1853 and open in 1854, this seems to have been a prep school.

Hedding, Illinois. NY No trace of such an antebellum school at Abingdon was found.

Hillsboro, Illinois. NN No trace was found of such a school.
Highland University, Kansas. YY Old School Presbyterian and chartered in 1857–58, the school was a grammar school during the period.
Highland University, Missouri. NN No such institution was located.
Holston College. NN This school was never mentioned in the Methodist Alamanac although the reference to the school claimed they sponsored it.
Hollins College, Virginia. NN It did not operate at the college level.
Howard College, Kokomo, Indiana. NN This Disciples school was an academy.
Howard, Missouri. NN This was an 1859 Methodist female school.
Humboldt, Iowa. NN This school began after the Civil War.
Huntingdon College, Mississippi. NN No trace was found of this school.

Indianola Male–Female Seminary, Iowa. NN This was a Methodist prep school which opened in 1860 and closed in 1861.
Ingham, New York. NN Open in 1852 and chartered in 1857, it did not offer college level work and was a female school.
Irving, Tennessee. NN There was no indication that this school was regarded as a college.
Irving College, Carroll County, Maryland. NN Chartered in 1858 and closing in 1880, it never functioned as a college.
Irving, Pennsylvania. NN This was a chartered female college of the 1850s.
Iowa Lutheran College, Albion, Iowa. Y* No trace of antebellum college work was found.
Iowa City College, Iowa City. NN This was a Methodist academy which opened and closed in the 1840s.
Ithica College, New York. ** This proposed school was refused a charter in 1822.
Illinois (Female), Jacksonville, Illinois. NN No evidence of college work was encountered.
Immaculate Conception, New Orleans, Lousiana. YY Begun in the 1840s, this school was probably called a college by the census but much other evidence indicated that it was not regarded as a college .
Immaculate Conception, Iberville, Louisiana. NN No evidence of college work was found for this 1850s Catholic school.
Immaculate Conception, Galveston, Texas. NN This was also an 1850s school which left no traces.
Iowa State Agricultural College, Iowa. YY Although chartered in 1858 this state school did not begin until after the Civil War.

Jefferson City University, Missouri. YN This Methodist school did not operate as a college before the war.
Judson College, Marion, Alabama. NN This was a Baptist female school.

Judson, Ohio. NN Although chartered, no indication of college work being conducted was encountered.

Keatchie College, DeSoto, Lousisiana. NN This was an 1856 female school.

Kentucky College–University, Harrodsburg, Kentucky. YY No substantiating evidence was found for the Christian claim that this school was a college.

Kentucky Wesleyan, Millersville, Kentucky. YN The 1860 opening date for this school did not mean that it was regarded as a college.

Kingston College, New York. NN This projected school was refused a charter in the 1779–1811 period.

Lawrence University, Kansas. NY This school was open for a few months before the war but it was closed because of the chaos in Kansas.

Lafayette University, Ohio. NN No evidence that this school's pre 1860 charter led to the opening of a college was found.

Laforgeville, New York. NN This Catholic school opened without a charter in 1838 and closed in 1839.

LaGrange, La Grange, Missouri. NY This Baptist school was chartered in 1858 but there was no evidence that it opened as a college.

LaGrange, Pennsylvania. NN No trace of this school was found.

Lake Forest–Lind, Illinois. NY Seemingly founded in 1857, the weight of the evidence points to college work beginning in the 1870s.

Lake Erie, Plainsville, Ohio. NN No trace of such a college was found.

Laurel Hill, Pennsylvania. NN This Catholic school failed within a year of its opening in 1835.

LaSalle, Pennsylvania. NY Opened in 1862 and chartered in 1863, this Catholic school gave its first degree in 1869.

Lawrence, Tennessee. NN This was an 1850s academy.

Lebanon, Illinois. ** See, McKendree.

Lebanon, Tennessee. ** See, Cumberland University.

Lebanon Valley College, Pennsylvania. YY This United Brethren college did not begin until the mid–1860s and had its first graduate in 1870.

Lenox–Bowen Collegiate Institute. NY Founded in 1856 and chartered in 1859, this school's leaders conducted precollege work before the Civil War.

Lehigh, Pennsylvania. YY The evidence indicates that this nonsectarian school did not organize until 1866.

Leander Clark College, Toledo, Ohio. YN There was no evidence substantiating the claim of an 1856 founding date for this school.

Lewis, Chicago, Illinois. NN No trace of such a college was found.

Lewisburg, D. C. NN No trace of such a school was encountered. The reference may have contained a misprint.

Lewisburg, Pennsylvania. YN The later claim by the Baptists that this school did college work before the war seems unfounded.
Lincoln University–Ashman Institute. YY This Presbyterian school for blacks began in 1854 but was a prep school in the antebellum period.
Linfield, Oregon, ** See, McMinnville College in the active college list.
Lindenwood, Missouri. YN Beginning in the 1820s with aid from the Cumberland Presbyterians, this female school was chartered in 1852–53.
Loras–St. Joseph's–Dubuque College. YN No trace of antebellum college work was found for this Catholic school which was founded in 1839.
Logan College, Ohio. NN No trace of this school seems to remain.
Loretta–St. Charles, Pennsylvania. YN This Catholic prep school began in 1849 and was chartered in 1858.
Louisville, Kentucky. NY(?) This institution had a very intricate history after the Civil War and had only a law school in operation before the conflict. Although it was later called a state college, it seems to have been tied to the Baptists.
Louisiana State University, Baton Rouge, Louisiana. YY The claim to antebellum college work by the later administrations of this school do not seem justified. This college's history and the relation between the state and its higher educational system should be the subject of deep historical investigation.
Loyola, Chicago, Illinois. NN No trace of such a school was found.
Loyola, New Orleans, Louisiana. NN This school was not operating at the college level before the war.
Luther, Decorah, Iowa. NY This Lutheran school may have been founded in 1861 but probably did not operate as a college. Another Luther college was reported in Wisconsin and may have been the same school.
Lutherville, Maryland. NN This female school was founded in 1853.
Lycoming, Pennsylvania. This Methodist school began in 1812 but did not become a college until 1948.
Maars Hill, North Carolina. NN This was an 1856 Baptist female school.
Madison, Indiana. NN No trace of such a college was found.
Mekemic, Batesville, Arkansas. NN This was an academy chartered in 1853.
Maine Wesleyan, Maine. NN This Methodist female school began in the 1820s and was chartered in 1853.
University of Maine. NN No trace of such a college was encountered.
Maimodides College, Pennsylvania. NN This Jewish school was chartered in 1849, but did not begin anything approaching college level work until the mid–1860s.

Manhattan College, New York. YY This Christian Brothers school was chartered in 1863.
Marion, Indiana. NN This school could not be traced.
Marion, New York. NN No trace of such a male or coeducational college could be found.
Marion College, Alabama. NN(?) Founded in 1842, no trace of an operating college by this name could be found. However, this might have been a school connected with Howard College.
Marshall University, Texas. NN Chartered in 1856 and receiving nominal state aid, this school opened in 1862, but not at the college level.
Marshall College, Griffin, Georgia. NN This academy seems to have opened in 1857.
Marquette, Milwaukee, Wisconsin. YY This Jesuit school was founded in 1857 and was chartered in 1864 but it seems that it operated at the preparatory level before the war.
Maryland College–Bel Aire Academy, Maryland. NN This school was granted a charter in 1828 but never organized for college work.
Marymount, New York. NN No trace of such a college was found.
Martin Luther, Buffalo, New York. YN This Lutheran school seems to have been established in either 1853 or 1859 but it did not have a college charter and it left no evidence of pre–war college work.
Maryhurst College, Oswego, Oregon. NN This was an 1859 Catholic female school.
Masonic University, Selma, Alabama. NN This female school was open in 1853 and was chartered in 1847.
Masonic, Kentucky. NN No trace of such a school was encountered.
Matagorda University, Texas. NN This joint venture of local and Episcopal interests never opened despite its 1845–46 charter. See, St. Charles, Texas.
McGraw College, New York. NN No trace of such an institution was found but the reference might have been to People's College, New York.
McDonough Institute, Maryland. NN This secondary school seems to have started in 1877.
McMinnville–Linfield, Oregon. NY Begun in 1857 and chartered in 1859, this Baptist school may have done some college work before the war but most evidence indicated that it was recognized as an academy.
McMurray, Springfield, Illinois. NN This was a female school.
McKenzie, Texas. NN Located near Clarksville, this school started in the 1840s and lasted until the war broke out. It had a large student population and claimed 67 "graduates" between 1845 and 1861. However, the overwhelming weight of the evidence indicates that it was a secondary school.

McMicken University, Cincinnati, Ohio. NN This school started in 1859 but no trace of college work was found.
Milsaps College, Jackson, Mississippi. YY In the twentieth century this school claimed to have been founded in both 1862 and 1892. No trace of pre–war college work was found.
Mills College–Benicia Seminary, California. YY This was a secondary school and female college.
Milton College–Dulac Academy, Wisconsin. YY Founded in 1844, this Seventh Day Baptist school did not offer college work until the late 1860s. In the 1900s it became a college–prep school.
Milton College–Columbia College, Oregon. NN This projected Methodist institution never began operation.
Missionary Institute, Selin's Grove, Pennsylvania. YN This Lutheran school for the training of ministers was probably founded in 1858.
Mission Dolores, San Jose, California. NN This Jesuit school did not receive a charter and it had the character of a seminary.
Mission House, Wisconsin. NN This Baptist school was chartered in 1859, but there was no evidence of college work.
Milwaukee–Downer. NN See, Milwaukee Female College.
Montville, Oregon. NN This Congregational school received a charter in 1857. Some college work may have been conducted before the war but there is no record of any graduates.
Mossy Creek Male and Female, Arkansas. NN Chartered in 1852, this was an academy.
Mossy Creek Baptist College, Knoxville, Tennessee. NN This preparatory school may have begun in 1856.
Moravian College, Pennsylvania. Y(?)Y This school began in the 1700s, but did not receive a college charter until 1863. It appears that during the antebellum period it was a prep and theological school.
Mt. Carroll (Seminary) Illinois. YN Founded in 1851, this was a normal school for females.
Mt. Holyoke, Massachusetts. YN Founded in the 1830s, this was a female school.
Mt. Holyoke, Oxford, Ohio. ** See, Ohio Female College.
Mt. Enon, Georgia. NN This Baptist school was chartered in 1806 and was dead by 1810. It appears never to have been regarded as a college.
Mt. Hope, Michigan. ** An old academy, it obtained a charter in 1833 but never organized the college.
Mt. Morris, Illinois. NN No trace of this school was found.
Mt. Pleasant, Pennsylvania. This United Brethren school was chartered in 1851 and died in 1858 without any graduates. The same year, it moved to Ohio to follow its denomination's members.

Mt. Pleasant, Iowa. ** See Iowa Wesleyan University.
Mt. Pleasant, North Carolina. ** See North Carolina College.
Mt. Pleasant Union College, Iowa. NN This school was chartered in 1861 only to die because of the war. It did not engage in college work.
Mt. St. Mary's, Cincinnati, Ohio. YN This Diocesan school claimed to have begun in 1851 or 1856. It is very doubtful that it competed in the college market before the war.
Mt. St. Joseph's, Dubuque, Iowa. ** See, Clark College.
Mt. St. Joseph's, Ohio. NN No trace of such a school was found.
Mt. St. Vincent, Ohio. NN No evidence of the existence of such a college was found.
Mt. Vernon Wesleyan Seminary, Iowa. ** See, Cornell College.
Mt. Washington, Maryland. NN This seems to have been a female school which was open between 1856 and 1861.
Mt. Washington, Ohio. NN This institution was chartered before 1861 but no trace of college work could be found.
Muhlenberg, Ohio. NN This Lutheran school did not become a college until 1867.
Muhlenberg, Pennsylvania. YY This was the Lutheran Allentown Seminary. It received a charter in 1867.

Nachadoches College–University, Texas. NN This school was chartered in 1843 or 1845 and opened in 1853. No evidence of college work was found.
New York Literary Institute, New York. ** This Catholic school may have begun in 1809. It failed in 1821.
Newberry, South Carolina. YY This well endowed Lutheran school was chartered in 1858 and probably opened in the next year. But its first graduating class was in 1869.
New Concord, Ohio. ** See, Muskingum College.
New Orleans Classical and Commercial, Louisiana. NN No trace of such a college was found.
New Orleans (Normal). NN Chartered in 1858, the school did not operate at the college, or even the normal school level, before the war.
College of New Orleans, Louisiana. NN This Catholic school did not have a charter and failed by 1825.
Newton University, Baltimore, Maryland. NN This very ambitious effort to fill the educational void in Baltimore began with a charter in 1845 and ended in failure in 1859. Some graduates are recorded but because graduation age was 18 or below and because it was never listed as a college by usual sources, it was decided to categorize it as an academy.
New York Free Academy–City College of New York, New York. Y(?)Y(?) This was one of the most interesting and flexible schools in the nation. The only reason it was not included in the active college list was

that its charter dated from 1866 and its name rarely appeared in college lists after its mid–1850s opening.
Newton, Ohio. N* This Disciples school was chartered before the war but seems not to have opened.
Niagra University, New York. NY(?) This Catholic school had some claim to an 1856 opening and an 1863 charter. However, it was known as the Seminary of Our Lady of Angels and was a Lazzarist school before the war.
New York State Agricultural College, New York. ** This school was not open before the war.
North Carolina College, Mt. Pleasant, North Carolina. YY(?) This Evangelical Lutheran school, chartered in 1859, seems to have operated as an academy before the Civil War.
North Western Christian University. ** See, Butler College and note this school had law graduates before the war.
Northern Illinois University, Fulton, Illinois. Y(?)N This school may have opened in 1861 but may not have had a charter until 1865.
Northwestern College, Napiersville, Illinois. YY The early history of this Evangelical Luthern school is cloudy. It may have begun in 1856 or 1861 but did not engage in college work.
Norwegian Luther College, Decorah, Iowa. This school may have been founded in 1861, but no evidence of college work was found.
North Western University, Sioux City, Iowa. NN No trace of such a school was encountered.
North Western University, Watertown, Wisconsin. YY It appears that this Lutheran school did not begin until 1864.
North Mississippi College, Mississippi. NN This Old School Presbyterian school was chartered in 1840. It remained a prep school.
New Hampton Institute, Fairfax, Vermont. NN In 1869 this Baptist school claimed a founding date of 1825, but no evidence of college work was found.

Olin College, Iredell County, North Carolina. NY No evidence of pre–war college work was found for this 1853 school.
Olivet College, Michigan. NY This Presbyterian–Congregational female school started in 1844 and was chartered in 1855.
Oskaloosa College, Iowa. NY This Christian school seems to have been chartered in 1858 and was opened in 1862.

Oregon College, Oregon City, Oregon. YN This Baptist school, which opened in the 1860s, was not a college during the antebellum period.
Oxford, North Carolina. NN This was a female school.
Oxford, Ohio. YY This was a Presbyterian female school.
Oxford University, Mississippi. ** No trace of such a school was found but this may have been another name for the University of Mississippi.

Pacific Methodist College, Santa Rosa, California. NN This school was founded in 1861 and died by 1900.
Pacific Methodist, Vacaville, California. NY This school was founded in 1851 and, like the other schools in this list, seems to have used the term "college" to indicate a more formal curicula than an academy.
Packer Collegiate Institute, New York. NN This was an 1840s female school.
Parkville Union, Missouri. NY This Cumberland Presbyterian school was chartered in 1855–56 but did not operate at the college level until the 1870s.
People's College, New York. NN This school was chartered in 1826 but was never organized.
People's College, Havanna, New York. NN This interesting attempt at technical education did not begin work until 1864 and its history illustrates the lack of effective demand for such schooling during the period.
University of Northern Pennsylvania. NN This Methodist school was chartered in 1848 and died in 1856. No graduates were recorded.
Pennington Seminary, New Jersey. NN Although "graduates" were noted as early as 1842, this seems to have been a prep school.
Philosophical and Classical Seminary of Charleston, South Carolina. NN This school was open by 1822 but there is no evidence that it competed for college students.
Pleasant Ridge Male and Female, Missouri. NN No trace of college work was found for this school.
Pennsylvania Central High School. NN This school gave its first AB in 1850, but it was regarded as a secondary school.
Providence College, New Athens, Ohio. N? Its 1860 charter may not have led to a founding before the turn of the century.
Paydras College, Point Coupe, Lousiana. NN This was an unchartered Catholic school founded in 1854.
Pea Ridge Masonic College, Pea Ridge, Arkansas. Y* This school was founded in 1853 but was not regarded as a college before the war.
Phi Kappa Sigma, Monticello, Arkansas. NN This school, open in 1859, was regarded as an academy.
Polytechnic and Commerical College, Cincinnati, Ohio. NN This lay Catholic school was founded in 1854 but was not chartered.
Protestant University of the United States, Ohio. NN Although a charter was issued before the Civil War, no trace of such a school was found.

Quachita College, Camden, Arkansas. NN This was an academy open in 1857.
Quachita College, Tulip, Arkansas. NN This may have been the same school as the above. No positive traces of such a college were found.
Queens College, Charlotte, North Carolina. NN Founded in 1857, this was a female school.

Quincy College, Illinois. NN Founded about 1853, this Methodist school seems to have been an academy.

Racine, Ohio. NN No trace of such a school was encountered.

Ravenscroft, Tennessee. NN Although open in the 1850s, this school was not a college.

Richmond College, New York. NN Its 1838 charter did not lead to the organization of a school.

Richmond College, Missouri. NN This Cumberland Presbyterian academy–prep school was chartered and opened in the mid–1850s.

Richmond College, Richmond, Ohio. YY This nonsectarian school was chartered in 1835 but it was not a college until the postbellum period.

Ripley College, Ohio. NN This proposed school was chartered before the war but there is no evidence of college operation.

Ripon, Wisconsin. Y(?)Y This nondenominational school opened in the early 1850s and received a charter in 1863 but confined itself to academy work before the war.

Rittenhouse College, Philadelphia, Pennsylvania. NN This school was chartered in 1837 but never opened.

Rittenhouse College, Bedford County, Pennsylvania. NN Chartered in 1850, this school never opened.

Rockford, Illinois. NN No trace of such a college was found.

Rock Hill, Ellicott City, Maryland. NY This Catholic school of the 1850s operated at the preparatory level until the 1890s.

Rock Springs, Illinois. NN No trace of such a college was found but this may have been the academy that was turned into Shurtleff College.

Roger Williams University, Tennessee. NN An institution with this name was chartered in 1863 but no evidence of its opening was found.

Rutherford College, North Carolina. NY(?) This school was chartered in 1853 but no trace of college work was found. A college–prep school with the same name existed in 1907.

Sacred Heart, Buffalo, New York. NN This 1848 Catholic school did not operate as a college.

Sacred Heart, Rochester, New York. NN This 1848 Diocesan school did not operate as a college.

Sacred Heart, Grand Cocteau, Louisiana. NN This 1821 female school was difficult to trace.

Sacred Heart, New York, New York. NN No trace of this school was encountered.

San Ynez, California. NN Founded in 1850 and known to be open in the 1850s, no indications were given that this was regarded as a college.

Salem, North Carolina. NN This was the famous Winston–Salem female academy.

Searcy (Polytechnic) NN Chartered in 1859, this school was an example of the early A–and–M movement in the South.

Seton–Hall, South Orange, New Jersey. YY This Diocesan school was founded in 1856 and chartered in 1861. It did not operate as a college until the 1870s.
Scio College, Scio, Ohio. NY Founded in 1852, this Methodist affiliate did not engage in college work before the war.
Seminary West of the Suwanee River, Florida. ** See, West Florida.
Sensinew Mound College, Brant County, Wisconsin. NN This Catholic school was chartered in 1846 and is known to have been open in 1859.
Silliman, Clinton, Lousiana. NN This was an female academy.
Simpson, Indianola, Indiana. YN This school seems to have begun some college work in 1867.
Sonoma College, California. NN This school may have opened in 1858.
Stephens College, Missouri. NN This Baptist school probably ended the period as Columbia Female Academy.
Stuart (Seminary) Texas. ** This was an 1850s female school.
Soulesbury College, Batesville, Arkansas. NN This was an academy which opened in 1850.
Soule University–Chappell Hill, Texas. NN This was an 1850s female school.
Soule, Tennessee. NN This female school opened in 1856.
Susquehana University. YY This was a Lutheran female school until the 1890s.
Stockwell Collegiate Institute, Indiana. Y?. This Methodist school perhaps began in 1855.
State Normal, Winona, Minnesota. NN This school was founded in 1858–59 and may not have even operated as a normal school.
Sublimity College, Sublimity, Oregon. YN Its United Brethren sponsors later claimed an 1858 beginning for this school.
St. Agnes, Memphis, Tennesse. NN This was a female school.
St. Aloysis, Louisville, Kentucky. NN This was a Jesuit school which opened in 1848 and which was chartered in 1851.
St. Andrews, Fort Smith, Arkansas. NN This Diocesan school was founded in the late 1840s and lasted until the late 1850s.
St. Augustine Univerisity–St. Augustine Masonic Institute, Texas. NN This school was chartered in 1837 and passed through the hands of several sponsors before it failed and merged with the University of East Texas. There was a strong temptation to list this school as a college but there was no evidence of graduates and the school did not appear on college lists.
St. Boneventure, Allegheny, New York. NY The chartering dates for this institution ranged from 1856 through 1875.
St. Benedicts, Atchison, Kansas. YY Founded in 1858, this Catholic school did not receive a charter until 1868 and may not have even opened before the war.

St. Charles, Grand Cocteau, Louisiana. YN This Jesuit school began in 1837 and was chartered in 1852. Despite the longevity of this school it was decided not to list it as an active college because none of its graduates were found in the biographical search and because it was not mentioned in the vast majority of college lists.
St. Charles, Missouri. NN Perhaps the Methodists help sustain this school which was open in 1848–49.
St. Charles Boromeo, Pennsylvania. NN This school began in 1835 but did not receive a charter until 1928. Furthermore, it was a theological school.
St. Charles, Ellicott City, Maryland. NN Founded in the 1830s and chartered in 1848, this Catholic school, despite a few references to it as a college, was classified as a preparatory level school. The age of its "graduates" also helped decide its classification.
St. Dominics, Sinsinawa, Wisconsin. NN This Dominican school was chartered in 1848 but may have opened in 1846.
St. Elizabeth, New Jersey. NN This was a female school open in 1859.
St. Francis, Brooklyn, New York. NY This Franciscan school appears to have opened in 1859 and to have had its charter granted in 1868.
St. Francis Solanus, Chicago, Illinois. NN This school was founded in 1860.
St. Francis, Loretta, Pennsylvania. YN This Franciscan school had opening dates cited as 1845 through 1850 and charter dates from 1847 through 1858.
St. Francis, Wisconsin. NN This school may have opened in 1846.
St. Francis Xavier, New York. NY This Jesuit school was founded in 1847 and claimed some graduates by 1859. Its charter date of 1861 and its lack of citations in college lists led to its inclusion in this list.
St. Francis Xavier, Chicago, Illinois. NN Founded in 1846, this was a female school.
St. Gabriels, Vincennes, Indiana. NN No trace of this school was found.
St. Geneveive, Missouri. NN This was a Catholic female school which is known to have been open in the 1850s.
St. Ignatius, Chicago, Illinois. ?Y The pre–war school operated as a typical Catholic "college".
St. Francis Solanus College, Quincy, Illinois. ?Y This Franciscan school was founded in 1860 and was chartered in 1873.
St. James, Vancouver, Washington. NY No trace of this school, which may have been open in 1852, could be found.
St. John's, Collegeville, Massachusetts. NN No trace of this school was found.
St. John's, Little Rock, Arkansas. NY This Masonic school began in the late 1850s and was a normal and military school, at most.
St. John's, Brooklyn, New York. YN This school may have received a

charter in 1846, but A. F. West claimed that it did not become a college before 1870.

St. John's Literary Institute, Frederick, Maryland. NN This Catholic school was founded in 1829 and failed in 1853. No evidence was found indicating that it competed in the college market.

St. John's University, Collegeville, Minnesota. NY This Benedictine school was chartered in 1857.

St. John's, Cleveland, Ohio. NY This Diocesan school was opened in 1845 but did not receive a charter.

St. Joseph's, Louisiana. ** See, Spring Hill.

St. Joseph's, Teutopolis, Illinois. NY This Franciscan school was founded in 1862 and chartered in 1881.

St. Joseph's, Philadelphia, Pennsylvania. NY(?) This Jesuit school seems to have begun in the early 1850s and to have received some sort of charter in 1852. It died in 1864 to be revived later in the century.

St. Joseph's, Troy, New York. NN No trace of this school was found.

St. Joseph's, Buffalo, New York. YN This Christian Brothers school was active between 1849 and 1855. Another one seems to have been founded in 1861.

St. Joseph's, Maryland. NN No trace of this school was encountered.

St. Joseph's, Williamette, Oregon. NN This Diocesan school began in 1843 and was chartered in 1852.

St. Joseph's, Iowa. NN No trace of this school was found.

St. Josephs's, Natchiteochas, Mississippi. NN This school was founded in 1856 without a charter.

St. Joseph's, St. Paul, Minnesota. NN No trace of this school was found.

St. Joseph's, Somerset, Ohio. NY(?) One reference claimed this Diocesan school opened in 1850 and was chartered in 1858. A. F. West claimed it was chartered in 1872.

St. Joseph's, Rhinecliff, New York. NN No trace of this Diocesan school was found.

St. Joseph's, St. Joseph's, Missouri. This school began in 1865.

St. Joseph's, Susquehana, Pennsylvania. NN This Diocesan school began without a charter in 1852.

St. Mary's, Columbia, South Carolina. ** This school was founded in 1851 and chartered in 1857.

St. Mary's, Natchez, Mississippi. This Brothers of Sacred Heart school opened in 1852 without a charter.

St. Mary's, San Antonio, Texas. This Brothers of Mary school began in 1853 without a charter.

St. Mary's, San Francisco, California. This Diocesan school opened in 1863 and was chartered in 1872.

St. Mary's, Kansas. NY This Jesuit school seems to have been founded in 1848, but it did not operate as a college until 1868–69. Even then, it did not appear on national college lists.

City University of St. Louis, Missouri. NN This Cumberland Presbyterian school was founded in 1855. No trace of college work was found.

University of St. Mary's, Chicago, Illinois. NN This Catholic school was chartered and opened in 1844. It failed in 1866.

St. Mary's, North East, Pennsylvania. NN No trace of this school was encountered.

St. Mary's, Grand Rapids, Michigan. NN This Episocopal school was chartered in 1839–40 without the power to grant degrees. It failed in the 1850's.

St. Mary's, Notre Dame, Indiana. NN It is unclear whether the reference to this school was meant to be "Notre Dame".

St. Mary's, Dayton, Ohio. NN This Brothers Mary school opened in 1850 and was chartered in 1854. Some relationship to Dayton University may have existed.

St. Mary's Hall, New Jersey. NN This Episopalian school was in operation in the 1830s and perhaps beyond.

St. Mary's, Charleston, South Carolina. NN This Diocesan school began in 1850 and was chartered in 1853.

St. Mat(?)y's, Kentucky. This reference was probably to St. Mary's above.

St. Mark's, Grand Rapids, Michigan. NN Although it received a charter in 1839, no trace of this school was found.

St. Mary's, North Carolina. ?Y This Catholic school began in the 1870s.

St. Mary's, Oakland, California. NY Although claims were made that this school began in 1863, no trace of antebellum work by the school was found.

St. Mary's University, Galveston, Texas. YY This Catholic school was chartered in 1854.

St. Mary's of the Lake, Chicago, Illinois. NN This Diocesan school was founded in 1845 and is known to have been open in 1853.

St. Meinrad College, Indiana. YN This Benedictine "seminary" seems to have begun in 1854 and to have been chartered in 1857 or 1860.

St. Michaels, Santa Fe, New Mexico. NN A Christian Brothers school, it opened in 1859 without a charter.

St. Paul's, Minnesota. NY(?) The only information on this institution was the mention of a Methodist school in 1907.

St. Paul's College, College Point, New York. NN Episcopal, it opened in 1835 and was chartered in 1838. It died within a few years.

St. Paul's, Palmyra, Missouri. One source claimed that this Episcopal school was chartered in 1844 while another claimed that it received state

sanction in 1852–53. It is known that the school was open between 1841 and 1851. It failed within a few years.
St. Peter's, Chillocothe, Ohio. NN This Diocesan institution was founded in 1855 without a charter.
St. Peter's, Troy, New York. NN This Catholic school began in 1858 without a charter.
St. Peter's, Milwaukee, Wisconsin. This Diocesan institution opened in 1852 without a charter.
St. Stephens, Annandale, New York. YY This Episcopalian school was chartered in 1860 but no evidence of antebellum college work was found.
St. Stanaslaus, Bay St. Louis, Missouri. YN This Brothers of Sacred Heart school began in 1854 and was chartered in 1870.
St. Stanaslaus Preparatory College, White Sulphur, Kentucky. NN This Diocesan school was founded in 1856 without a charter.
St. Vincents, Beatty, Pennsylvania. NY This Catholic school may have opened in the mid–1840s but it did not receive a full college charter until the 1870s.
St. Vincents, Wheeling, West Virginia. NN Catholic and founded about 1850, it failed by 1859.
St. Vincents, Richmond, Virgina. NN No trace of this school was found.
St. Vincents, Ohio. NN No trace of such a college was found.
St. Vincents, Latrobe, Pennsylvania. NN This Benedictine school, begun in 1846, did not receive a charter until 1870.
St. Xavier (Institute), Louisville, Kentucky. YN This school began in 1864 and was chartered in 1872.

Tabor, Iowa. YN Founded by ultra–reform Congregationalists in the mid–1850s, this institution operated as an academy and normal school. It did not receive a full college charter until 1909.
Territorial University, Vincennes, Indiana. NN This state school was open between 1810 and 1825, but no evidence of college work was encountered.
Trenton, Missouri. NN This school was chartered in 1852–53.
Thiel, Pennsylvania. NY This Lutheran school was not begun until 1866.
Tennessee State (Female) YY This Methodist institution began in 1856.
Trinity College, Waxahachi, Texas. NY Cumberland Presbyterian, founded in 1856, this school did not operate as a college until 1869–70.

Union Christian College, Meron, Indiana. YY Founded in 1859, this was a preparatory level school in the antebellum period.
University of the South–Sewanee. Y(?)Y This Episcopal supported school was started in 1860 but did not begin college work until the end of the Civil War.
University of Utah. NN This Mormon school did not begin higher level instruction until the late 1860s.

Union Seminary, New Berlin, Pennsylvania. Y(?)N Opened in 1856 as a normal preparatory school which trained up to the "junior year" of college, this Evangelical Lutheran school closed because of the Civil War. It was later revived as a college.
Union College, Ohio. NN Although this school was chartered in 1860, no trace of it was found.
University College, San Francisco, California. NY(?) Founded by Presbyterians in 1859, the only trace of the school was a reference to a Catholic college of the same name in the 1870s. Its connection to the Univeristy of California's history is unknown.
Valipariso, Indiana. NN No trace of such a school was found.
Van Rennselar (Academy) Missouri. NN Chartered in 1853, this school operated at the academy level.
Wayland University, Wisconsin. NN This Baptist school opened as an academy in 1855. In 1876 it taught only to the junior level.
Washington, Richmond County, New York. NN Chartered in 1839, this school never opened.
Washington, Louisiana. NY(?) The reference to this school may really have been to a school founded in 1858 at Washington County, Franklin Collegiate Institute.
Washington University, St. Louis, Missouri. YY Founded in the mid–1850s, this school did not perform college work until the postbellum period.
University of Washington, Washington. NY There is no evidence to support the claim of college work in the 1860s or a true founding date of 1862.
Walamut University, Oregon ** See, Williamette.
Webster, Missouri. NN Chartered in 1852–53, this school did not operate as a college before the war.
Wesley Manual Labor School, Georgia. ** See, Emory.
West Tennessee, Tennessee. Y(?)Y(?) This was not a college in the antebellum period.
Western College, Oxford, Ohio. ** This may have been another name for Oberlin.
Western Mount Holyoke, Oxford, Ohio.** This was probably another name for Oxford Female.
Wesleyan, Macon Georgia. YY This was a Methodist female school which began in 1838.
Wesleyan, Kentucky. NN This Presbyterian (?) school was chartered in 1863 but did not open before the Civil War.
Wesleyan University, St. Augustine, Texas. See, St. Augustine.
Wesleyan, West Virginia. NN No trace was found of such a college.
Western Maryland, Maryland. YN This Methodist affiliated school was organized in 1858 but it probably did not open before the war.

Western University of New York, Buffalo, New York. ** Although chartered in 1832, this school was never organized.
Westfield College, Illinois. NY This United Brethren school, associated with the denomination at least during the twentieth century, may have begun in 1861, but not as a college.
West Union (Institute) Oregon. NN This Baptist school was chartered in 1850 but it never opened.
Westminister College, Buffalo, New York. ** Although chartered in 1851, it never opened.
West Florida (Seminary) Tallahasse, Florida. NY(?) This state school was chartered and open in 1856–57 but operated as a grammar school.
Western University of Iowa, Muscatine, Iowa. NN This was a United Brethern grammar school during the period.
Whitman, Walla Walla, Washington. N(?)Y(?) Several founding dates were given for this Congregational institution, ranging from 1852 to 1866. It appears that the school did not operate as a college.
Wesley, Delware. NN This was a female school.
Westmoreland, Pennsylvania. NN This German Reformed school was chartered in 1862 and had its first "graduate" in 1864. It died in 1872.
Western University (np) NN. Planned in 1861, this unlocatable school seems never to have opened.
Wilberforce, Xenia, Ohio. YY This African Methodist school was chartered in 1863 and was open for some years before then. It was the leading black "college" of its time.
Wilmington, Delaware. NN Chartered in 1803, this school never opened.
William Penn College, Pennsylvania(?) Although chartered in 1848 no trace of such a school could be found.
Wirt, Tennessee. NN This school was open in the 1850s, but not as a college.
Worthington, Ohio. NN This school began as a Episcopalian attempt at higher education on the frontier in the late 1810s, but it never achieved college status and was abandoned in a very few years. Its charter was later used for a medical school.
Willoughby, Willoughby, Ohio. NY Seemingly a different institution from the one in the active college file, this school began in 1852 as an academy.
Wittenberg Manual Labor College, Iowa. (?)Y This Free Presbyterian school was founded in 1855.
Yadkin College, North Carolina. N* Open near Lexington as a high school between 1859 and 1861, a charter was finally attained on the eve of the Civil War. However, this Methodist Protestant aided school did not operate as a college.

Index